THE UNITED NATIONS AND THE QUESTION OF PALESTINE

Contrary to conventional wisdom, there has been a continuing though vacillating gulf between the requirements of international law and the United Nations (UN) on the question of Palestine. This book explores the UN's management of the longest-running problem on its agenda, critically assessing tensions between the Organization's position and international law. What forms has the UN's failure to respect international law taken, and with what implications? The author critically interrogates the received wisdom regarding the UN's fealty to the international rule of law, in favour of what is described as an international rule *by* law. This book demonstrates that through the actions of the UN, Palestine and its people have been committed to a state of what the author calls 'international legal subalternity', according to which the promise of justice through international law is repeatedly proffered under a cloak of political legitimacy furnished by the international community, but its realization is interminably withheld.

Ardi Imseis is Assistant Professor, Faculty of Law, Queen's University. Previously, he was Legal Counsel and Senior Policy Advisor, United Nations Relief and Works Agency for Palestine Refugees in the Near East (UNRWA, 2002–2014), Editor-in-Chief of the *Palestine Yearbook of International Law* (2008–2019), and Human Rights Fellow, Columbia Law School (2001–2002). Imseis has provided testimony before the UN Security Council, Human Rights Council, and Committee on Economic, Social and Cultural Rights, among other international fora. His scholarship has appeared widely, including in the *American Journal of International Law*, *European Journal of International Law*, *Harvard International Law Journal*, and *Oxford Journal of Legal Studies*.

The United Nations and the Question of Palestine

RULE BY LAW AND THE STRUCTURE OF INTERNATIONAL LEGAL SUBALTERNITY

ARDI IMSEIS

Shaftesbury Road, Cambridge CB2 8EA, United Kingdom

One Liberty Plaza, 20th Floor, New York, NY 10006, USA

477 Williamstown Road, Port Melbourne, VIC 3207, Australia

314–321, 3rd Floor, Plot 3, Splendor Forum, Jasola District Centre, New Delhi – 110025, India

103 Penang Road, #05–06/07, Visioncrest Commercial, Singapore 238467

Cambridge University Press is part of Cambridge University Press & Assessment, a department of the University of Cambridge.

We share the University's mission to contribute to society through the pursuit of education, learning and research at the highest international levels of excellence.

www.cambridge.org
Information on this title: www.cambridge.org/9781009074957

DOI: 10.1017/9781009076272

© Ardi Imseis 2023

This publication is in copyright. Subject to statutory exception and to the provisions of relevant collective licensing agreements, no reproduction of any part may take place without the written permission of Cambridge University Press & Assessment.

First published 2023
First paperback edition 2025

A catalogue record for this publication is available from the British Library

ISBN 978-1-316-51389-7 Hardback
ISBN 978-1-009-07495-7 Paperback

Additional resources for this publication at www.cambridge.org/imseis

Cambridge University Press & Assessment has no responsibility for the persistence or accuracy of URLs for external or third-party internet websites referred to in this publication and does not guarantee that any content on such websites is, or will remain, accurate or appropriate.

*For my father Michel
and my children, Kinan, Yasmin and Laila.
That justice may one day be realized.*

Contents

List of Maps	*page* ix
Foreword	xi
Preface	xv
Acknowledgements	xix
Table of Cases	xxiii
Table of Treaties and International Instruments	xxvii
List of Abbreviations	xxxi

1 Introduction   1
1 Subalternity in the International System   3
2 The Counter-Hegemonic Potential of International Law and Institutions   8
3 International Legal Subalternity as a Long-Range Condition   11
4 TWAIL and the Question of Palestine   16
5 A Word on the Nature of the UN   18
6 Overview   21

2 The Interwar Period   26
1 Introduction   26
2 The Institutionalization of the International Rule by Law   26
3 The Origins of Palestine's International Legal Subalternity   29
4 Conclusion   50

3 1947: The UN Plan of Partition for Palestine   52
1 Introduction   52
2 The UN as the Guardian of International Law   53
3 Resolution 181(II) and the International Rule by Law   55
4 UNSCOP and the General Assembly Debates   76
5 The Nakba and UNSCOP's Cognitive Dissonance   100
6 Conclusion   107

vii

viii   *Contents*

4   1948 and After: The UN and the Palestinian Refugees   110
   1   Introduction   110
   2   The UN, Refugees, and International Law   112
   3   Palestinian Refugees and the International Rule by Law   121
   4   Conclusion   170

**5   1967 and After: The UN and the Occupied Palestinian
       Territory**   172
   1   Introduction   172
   2   Decolonization, Third World Sovereignty, and the UN   174
   3   Palestine as an Embodiment of Third World Quasi-Sovereignty   176
   4   The Illegality of Israel's Continued Presence in the OPT   187
   5   Conclusion   214

6   2011 and After: Membership of Palestine in the UN   217
   1   Introduction   217
   2   UN Membership and the Principle of Universality   218
   3   UN Practice on Membership Criteria   223
   4   UN Membership of Palestine and the International
       Rule by Law   228
   5   Non-member Observer State Status for Palestine   249
   6   Conclusion   252

7   Conclusion   255

     Postscript   264

Index   269

Maps

I Pre-war Turkish administrative districts comprised in Syria and Palestine showing the boundaries of mandated Palestine and the Hejaz railway   *page* 36

II Map illustrating territorial negotiations between H. M. G. and King Hussein   37

III The Sykes–Picot arrangement of 1916 in regard to Syria and Palestine. Map to illustrate the agreement of 1916 in regard to Asia Minor, Mesopotamia, and so on   39

IV Palestine, plan of partition with economic union proposed by the Ad Hoc Committee on the Palestinian Question, Map No. 103.1(b), United Nations, February 1956   61

V Palestine, distribution of population by sub-districts with percentages of Jews and Arabs (Estimated at 1946), Map No. 93, United Nations, November 1947   62

VI Palestine, land ownership by sub-districts (1945), Map No. 94(b), United Nations, August 1950   64

VII Territories occupied by Israel since June 1967, Map No. 3243 Rev.4, United Nations, June 1997   178

Foreword

Readers are forewarned. This is a fine study that follows the customary rules of scholarship in presenting the history of a geopolitical situation from a legal perspective with fulsome and fair examination of authority and argument. But at the same time, it is a distressing tale of international duplicity in the interpretation of the Charter of the United Nations in order to advance the interests and welfare of one people at the expense of another. In the best traditions and language of legal scholarship, Ardi Imseis tells the story of Palestine's 100 years on the agenda of the organized international community, acting through the League of Nations and the UN.

The theme that runs like a thread through Imseis's study is the notion of 'legal subalternity' according to which 'the promise of justice through international law is repeatedly proffered under a cloak of political legitimacy furnished by the international community, but its realization is interminably withheld'. He chooses four situations that have confronted the UN to illustrate this thesis: the partition of Palestine in 1947; the response to the refugee crisis following the Nakba of 1948–1949; the failure to bring Israel's occupation of Palestine that began in 1967 to an end; and the refusal in 2011 to admit Palestine to UN membership.

In all these situations, the UN has been guided by political expediency and not the international rule of law. It has consistently interpreted international law to favour Israel and in the process showed little regard for issues of self-determination, human rights, and elementary principles of natural justice. General Assembly Resolution 181(II) partitioning the Mandate territory into a Jewish State and an Arab State was adopted in violation of the principle of self-determination proclaimed in the Charter of the United Nations and showed no regard for considerations of fairness in allocating more territory to the minority Jewish community than the Arab majority. Attempts to create a distinctive institutional and normative regime for Palestinian refugees in the

xi

aftermath of the ethnic cleansing of Palestine in the Nakba failed to seriously address the return of Palestinians to their homes or secure their protection. So committed was the UN to upholding the newly declared State of Israel that it failed to play its trump card to achieve the return of the Palestinian refugees by refusing to make Israel's admission to membership of the UN conditional upon allowing the return of the refugees. The UN has not seriously attempted to bring the occupation of Palestine to an end. Instead of addressing the illegality of the occupation, it has insisted on negotiations between Israel and Palestine as the means to end the occupation – a course not followed in other situations of illegal occupation. Documenting the violations of international humanitarian law and international human rights law has been offered as a political placebo to placate the Palestinians but no meaningful effort has been made to end the occupation. The refusal to admit the State of Palestine to UN membership in 2011 ran counter to both precedent and the goal of universal membership asserted in other cases. In addition, it displayed a narrow interpretation of the UN's admission procedures and standards.

The UN is the sum of its parts. Decisions of the UN on Palestine have been imposed by the West, often by devious means involving political promises, the careful selection of membership of decision-making committees or referring decisions to European members of the Secretariat sympathetic to the West's cause. Here the United States has played a leadership ably abetted by the United Kingdom. These decisions have consistently been motivated by a determination to advance the interests of Israel. Resolution 181 (II) on partition was guided by the wish to find a home for Jews in a State of their own even if this meant ignoring the interests of Palestinians comprising over 60 per cent of the population. The failure to allow the return of Palestinian refugees was driven by the wish to cement the newly established Jewish State even though it was premised on massive ethnic cleansing. The unwillingness to confront the prolonged occupation and to admit the State of Palestine to UN membership are/were influenced by the wish not to antagonize Israel, now viewed as a bastion of democracy in a hostile region supported by active pro-Israeli lobbies in Western capitals. A good example of the West's *modus operandi* in promoting its influence is afforded by the manner in which senior UN bureaucrats, nationals of Western States, compelled Secretary-General Kofi Annan to withdraw his comment that Israel's occupation of Palestine was 'illegal'.

Imseis describes decisions of the above kind as guided by rule *by* law and not rule *of* law. They are probably more accurately viewed as evidence of the West's recently propounded commitment to a 'rules based international order' which in essence is the West's version of international law that allows

Foreword xiii

it to treat certain States, such as Israel, as exempt from universal international law and the law of the Charter.

Imseis shows that many of the interpretations of international law preferred by the West have come to haunt the UN. This is illustrated by the decision to resolve the 'Palestine Question' in 1947 by partition of the Mandate of Palestine into two States instead of granting independence to Palestine, as had occurred with other mandate territories in the region, or placing it under UN trusteeship. Partition, now portrayed as the 'two-State solution' remains the West's only solution to the 'Palestine problem' despite the mounting evidence presented by Israel's *de facto* annexation of large parts of the West Bank that have made a single-state solution more feasible.

Many of the West's interpretations of international law that have favoured Israel at the expense of the Palestinians are rooted in the West's wish to find a solution to the 'Jewish Question' arising from the Holocaust and the understandable guilt flowing from the West's failure to protect Jews from the savagery of the Nazi regime. This has resulted in a determination to create and promote a Jewish State in the Mandate territory of Palestine in the course of which the right of self-determination of the Palestinian people has been denied. In 1961, the English historian, Arnold Toynbee, was compelled to remind the West that '[i]t was not the Palestinian Arabs who committed genocide against the European Jews. It was the Germans. The Germans murdered the Jews: the Palestinian Arabs have been made to pay for what the Germans did.'[1] This admonition fell on deaf ears in the capitals of the West.

The West has manipulated or ignored international law in favour of Israel in the political organs of the UN, and in the Secretariat and Office of Legal Affairs. Despite this, the State of Palestine has increasingly turned to International law for its salvation. It has laid a complaint of international criminality before the International Criminal Court, instituted an inter-State dispute before an *ad hoc* Conciliation Commission of the UN Committee on the Elimination of Racial Discrimination and initiated a request for an advisory opinion from the International Court of Justice (ICJ) on the question of the legality of Israel's prolonged occupation of Palestine. Whether international law will prevail in the judicial organs of the world remains to be seen.

It is surprising that the issue of the UN's manipulation of international law on the Palestine question has not before been the subject of a critical scholarly study. A possible explanation for this omission is an understandable desire on the part of international lawyers to protect their discipline. Imseis

---

[1] 'Two Aspects of the Palestine Question' in Toynbee, A., ed., *Importance of the Arab World* (London: National Publications House Press, 1962) at 57.

has therefore done a service to international law by embarking on the present study. It is both timely and necessary. Imseis's book may conceal the pain of the Palestinian people over their treatment by the UN in the language of law and scholarship, but it does not conceal the harm done to international law by the double standards employed by the West in its handling of the Palestine question. As Imseis writes in conclusion: 'it is difficult to deny that Palestine remains *the* litmus test for the credibility of international law and the international system as a whole'.

John Dugard
The Hague, Netherlands

Preface

Writing in 1987, Brian Urquhart, former UN Undersecretary-General for Special Political Affairs, lamented that '[t]he Palestine problem has haunted the development of the United Nations ever since 1948', and that the UN's involvement in the question of Palestine 'has twisted the organization's image and fragmented its reputation and prestige as no other issue has'.[1]

This assessment was given by Urquhart in his account of the 1948 assassination of Count Folke Bernadotte, then UN Mediator for Palestine. Bernadotte was murdered while on mission in Jerusalem providing good offices in the midst of the first Arab–Israeli war. He was killed by Zionist irregulars only one day after issuing his Progress Report in which he affirmed the right of hundreds of thousands of Palestinian Arab refugees to return to their homes and property from which they had been expelled in what became the State of Israel.[2] Bernadotte's assassination, and how it was subsequently treated at the UN, aroused no small measure of consternation in Urquhart. Although there 'was never much doubt as to who had killed him', he bemoaned, the 'conspiracy of silence' at the UN following the assassination left him cold, especially because 'in all the subsequent indignation about terrorism he [i.e. Bernadotte] was rarely mentioned'.[3]

Although Bernadotte's mission was not the beginning of the UN's engagement with the question of Palestine – that task would belong to the 1947 General Assembly – both his report and resultant killing set in motion a series of events that would indelibly mark both Palestine and the UN in legal terms, as if newborn siblings conjoined at the hip.

---

[1] Urquhart, B. A *Life in Peace and War* (Harper & Row, 1987) at 114.
[2] Progress Report of the United Nations Mediator on Palestine, A/648, 16 September 1948, at 14. See also Chapter 4.
[3] Urquhart, *supra* note 1 at 114.

xv

xvi   *Preface*

For Palestine, Bernadotte's recommendations resulted in General Assembly resolution 194(III) of 11 December 1948 which, *inter alia*, affirmed the right of the refugees to return and to compensation, and created the United Nations Conciliation Commission for Palestine (UNCCP) ostensibly to help realize that goal.[4] As covered in Chapter 4, the UNCCP would ultimately fail in this task, leaving generations of Palestinian refugees in a lurch, dependent on other UN bodies for humanitarian aid and assistance while remaining intent, to this very day, on the promise of the UN's affirmation of their international legal rights.

For the UN, Bernadotte's assassination resulted in an advisory opinion of the ICJ that would immediately become required reading for international lawyers for generations to come. The 1949 *Reparation for Injuries Suffered in the Service of the United Nations* advisory opinion established the UN's capacity to bring international claims against states for reparation for damages caused to both the Organization and to persons in its service.[5] As an opinion of the principle judicial organ of the UN, this gave the *Reparations* case a unique constitutional character, affirming the Organization's international legal personality which remains a fixed feature in international life.

One curious element of the *Reparations* case, however, is that nowhere in the opinion is any account given by the Court of the facts that actually gave rise to it. Bernadotte, his assailants, Palestine – nothing appears to suggest that these people or that place ever figured into the case. The ICJ thus rendered its opinion as though emerging from a complete vacuum. Technically, it is of course possible (oftentimes even preferable) to give advisory opinions in the abstract, as they are sometimes sought to answer broad legal questions. Nevertheless, there is an allegorical point in Palestine's absence from the opinion.

On the one hand, but for the question of Palestine which, as we shall see, the UN had a central role in creating, the Court's affirmation of the UN's international legal personality would never have arisen at that pivotal time. In a sense, then, the UN owes its international legal standing to Palestine. On the other hand, by keeping Palestine out of the story, *Reparations* can be read as reflecting the Organization's desire to hide its own demons when it comes to the role it has played in failing to uphold and apply international law in Palestine's case. With Palestine hidden from view, the Organization has thus been able to carry on as the self-proclaimed guarantor of the international rule

---

[4] A/RES/194(III), 11 December 1948.
[5] *Reparations for Injuries Suffered in the Service of the United Nations*, Advisory Opinion, 11 April 1949, ICJ Reports 1949, at 174 ['Reparations'].

Preface   xvii

of law without regard to the plight of Palestine or its people, who have yet to benefit fully from law's promise.

Some seventy-five years on, Palestine looms large in the life of the UN. This book is a modest attempt to chart that story, with a view to better understand the Organization and the unique and important role it can play in ensuring that justice is done in accordance with a truly universal international law, responsive to the needs of those many in our world would rather wish away.

Acknowledgements

This book finds its origins in questions encountered long-before the decision to pursue them academically was taken. Early intellectual influences that triggered my ongoing commitment to contemporary Palestine studies include the pivotal works of Ibrahim Abu Lughod, Sami Hadawi, Walid Khalidi, Rashid Khalidi, Nur Masalha, Ilan Pappe, and Edward Said. International law influences include the seminal writings of Michael Akehurst, Ian Brownlie, Antonio Cassese, James Crawford, John Dugard, Richard Falk, Gerhard von Glahn, Thomas Mallison, Sally V. Mallison, and John Quigley.

Between 2002 and 2014, I served in various capacities with UNRWA, first in Gaza City and then in East Jerusalem, with occasional duty taking me to Jordan, Lebanon, and Syria. Among other things, it was in service of the Palestine refugees that my appreciation for both the limits and possibilities of international law took shape; a sensibility developed during this time thorough exposure to the works of various critical international legal scholars, including Martti Koskenniemi and Antony Anghie, along with the rest of the Third World Approaches to International Law network of scholars.

More concretely, this book emanates from doctoral study undertaken at Fitzwilliam College, Cambridge, between 2014 and 2018, following my time with UNRWA. Gratitude is owed to my supervisor at the Lauterpacht Centre for International Law, Marc Weller, who provided just the right measure of advice and critique to help bring the project to fruition, as well as to Glen Rangwala in the Department of Politics and International Studies, and Nicky Padfield, Master, Fitzwilliam College. Most of the research presented here, with the exception of that which forms the basis of Chapter 4, was completed and largely written up in that period, although the ideas pursued predate it considerably. But for interruptions occasioned by my appointment to the UN commission of inquiry on Yemen in 2019, followed by the global pandemic, this book would have appeared much earlier. Alas, somethings remain outside of our control.

xx   *Acknowledgements*

The list of people to whom thanks are owed is longer than I can recount. To begin with, I am particularly indebted to Professors Dugard and Falk, who were my examiners on the *viva* and have since become cherished colleagues. Beyond the conferral of the doctorate itself, knowing that the project that formed the basis of this book met the exacting standards of those towering mentors was achievement enough. Their detailed comments helped sharpen the book in ways that I hope I have managed to capture.

Many people read and heavily commented on drafts, while others provided guidance and assistance on points large and small. Others provided feedback in discussion, all of which helped hone my thinking as the book evolved. Still others provided essential friendship and camaraderie along the way. In some or all of these respects, thanks are due to Salman Abu Sitta, Karen Abu Zayd, Feda Abdelhady, Ihsan Adel, Susan Akram, Francesca Albanese, M. Muhannad Ayyash, Reem Bahdi, Kaitlin Ball, Jason Beckett, Orna Ben Naftali, Catherine Bevilacqua, George Bisharat, Michelle Burgis-Kasthala, Christine Cervenak, John N. Clarke, Stephanie Diepeveen, Catriona Drew, Noura Erekat, Aeyal Gross, David Hughes, Anne Irfan, Anis Kassim, Victor Kattan, Elinor Lipman, Michael Lynk, Mazen Masri, Usha Natarajan, Sarah Nouwen, Alice Panepinto, Dena Qaddumi, John Quigley, Surabhi Ranganathan, John Reynolds, Yaël Ronen, Michal Saliternik, Nahed Samour, William Schabas, Iain Scobbie, Nimer Sultany, Victoria Stewart-Jolley, Virginia Tilley, Lex Takkenberg, Mandy Turner, and the blind reviewers.

Gratitude must also be extended to the countless individuals who provided invaluable feedback in talks, workshops, and conferences at Cambridge and beyond, including the American University in Cairo, the American University of Paris, the Australian National University, Birzeit University, the University of California, Los Angeles, the University of Cork, the University of Manchester, Queen's University Belfast, and the School of Oriental and African Studies.

Thanks are also due to the staff at the Squire Law Library, Cambridge, who warmly hosted me for close to three years and offered willing assistance when requested, in particular Leslie Dingle, Kay Naylor, and David Wills. The staff at the UN Library at the Palais des Nations, Geneva, in particular Adriano Gonçalves and Amanda Howland, were key in helping locate obscure sources. Back in Canada, special thanks must be extended to Graeme Campbell, Alexandra Cooper, Daniella Cruz, Amy Kaufmann, Alyssa Lunney, Courtney Matthews, Doug Ottney, and Nathalie Soini at Queen's University, and Catherine McGoveran at the University of Ottawa.

Last, but not least, my greatest debt of gratitude is owed to my family, in particular my father and first mentor, Michel, my partner, Rema, and our children, Kinan, Yasmin, and Laila. But for their collective patience and

Acknowledgements xxi

support between Jerusalem, Cairo, Geneva, Cambridge, and Ottawa, none of this would have been possible.

Parts of this book have been previously published, in different form, as: 'Negotiating the Illegal: On the United Nations and the Illegal Occupation of Palestine, 1967–2020' (2020) 31:3 *European Journal of International Law* 1055; 'The United Nations Partition of Palestine Revisited: On the Origins of Palestine's International Legal Subalternity' (2021) 57 *Stanford Journal of International Law* 1; and 'On Membership of the United Nations and the State of Palestine: A Critical Account' (2021) 34:4 *Leiden Journal of International Law* 855.

Table of Cases

INTERNATIONAL

Permanent Court of International Justice

Case Concerning the Factory at Chorzow (Claim for Indemnity)
(Jurisdiction), 26 July 1927, PCIJ, Ser. A, No. 9, p. 21   *page* 119, 136
Case Concerning the Factory at Chorzow (Claim for Indemnity) (Merits),
13 September 1928, PCIJ, Ser. A, No. 17, p. 47   119, 136
Phosphates in Morocco (Preliminary Objections),
14 June 1938, PCIJ, Aer. A/B/, No. 74   119

International Court of Justice

Admissibility of Hearings of Petitioners by the Committee on South-West Africa,
Advisory Opinion, 1 June 1956, ICJ Reports 1956, p. 23   213
Application of the Convention on the Prevention and Punishment of the
Crime of Genocide (Bosnia and Herzegovina v. Serbia and Montenegro),
26 February 2007, ICJ Reports 2007, p. 43   119, 188
Case Concerning Armed Activities on the Territory of the Congo
(Democratic Republic of the Congo v. Uganda), 19 December 2005,
ICJ Reports 2005, p. 168   120, 196, 209
Case Concerning East Timor (Portugal v. Australia), 30 June 1995,
ICJ Reports 1995, p. 90   194
Competence of the General Assembly for the Admission of a State to
the United Nations, Advisory Opinion, ICJ Reports 1950, p. 4   220
Conditions of Admission of a State to Membership in the United Nations
(Article 4 of the UN Charter), Advisory Opinion, ICJ Reports
1948, p. 57   220, 221, 233
International Status of South-West Africa, Advisory Opinion, 11 July 1950,
ICJ Reports 1950, p. 128   69, 190
Legal Consequences for States of the Continued Presence of South
Africa in Namibia (South-West Africa) Notwithstanding Security
Council Resolution 276 (1970), Advisory Opinion, 21 June 1971,
ICJ Reports 1971, p. 16   43–44, 56, 58, 196, 213–214

xxiv   *Table of Cases*

Legal Consequences of the Construction of a Wall in
  the Occupied Palestinian Territory, Advisory
  Opinion, 9 July 2004, ICJ Reports 2004   120, 182, 192, 195, 199–201, 203, 211, 212, 229
Legal Consequences of the Separation of the Chagos
  Archipelago from Mauritius in 1965, Advisory
  Opinion, 25 February 2019, ICJ Reports 2019, p. 95   120, 188, 212
Legality of the Threat or Use of Nuclear Weapons, Advisory
  Opinion, 8 July 1996, ICJ Reports 1996, p. 226   73, 75, 214
Military and Paramilitary Activities in and Against Nicaragua
  (Nicaragua v. US) (Merits), 27 June 1986, ICJ Reports 1986, p. 14   72–73
North Sea Continental Shelf, Judgment, ICJ Reports 1969, p. 3   224
Reparations for Injuries Suffered in the Service of the United
  Nations, Advisory Opinion, 11 April 1949, ICJ Reports 1949, p. 174   xvi
Voting Procedure on Questions Relating to Reports and Petitions
  Concerning the Territory of South-West Africa, Advisory Opinion,
  7 June 1955, ICJ Reports 1955, p. 67   213

International Military Tribunal

Trial of the Major War Criminals before the International Military Tribunal,
  Nuremberg, vol. XXII, IMT Secretariat, 1948   117

Court of Justice of the European Union

Bolbol v. Bevándorlási és Állampolgársági Hivatal, C-31/09, Court
  of Justice of the European Union, 17 June 2010   167

Arbitral Awards

Island of Palmas (Netherlands v. US) (1928) 2 Reports of
  International Arbitral Awards 829   42, 131, 132, 135

DOMESTIC

Germany

Bundesverwaltungsgericht, Urteil vom 4.6.1991- Bverwg 1 C 42.88   166

Israel

George Rafael Tamarin v. State of Israel, (1970) 26 PD I 197   130, 203
Ornan v. Ministry of the Interior, (2013) CA 8573/08   130

United Kingdom of Great Britain and Northern Ireland

Amer Mohammed El-Ali v. The Secretary of State for the Home Department
  and *Daraz v. The Secretary of State for the Home Department*,
  United Kingdom Court of Appeal, 26 July 2002, [2002] EWCA Civ. 1103   167
Capel's Case (1581), Jenk. Cent. 250   42

Table of Treaties and International Instruments

African Charter on Human and Peoples' Rights, 27 June 1981,
  1520 UNTS 217   *page* 117
Agreement for the Prosecution and Punishment of the Major War Criminals
  of the European Axis, 8 August 1945, 82 UNTS 280   117
British Mandate for Palestine, 24 July 1922 (1922) LNOJ 1007   45, 46
Charter of the United Nations, 24 October 1945, 59
  Stat. 1031, TS 993, 3 Bevans 1153   1, 7, 53-55, 57, 58, 67, 142, 217, 257
Compact of Free Association, United States-Federated States
  of Micronesia-Marshall Islands, U.S. Congress, §311(a), 99 Stat. 1770   225
Convention against Torture and Other Cruel, Inhumane or
  Degrading Treatment or Punishment, 10 December 1984, UNTS 112   250
Convention on the Elimination of All Forms of Discrimination against
  Women, 18 December 1979, 1249 UNTS 13   250
Convention on the Prevention and Punishment of the Crime of Genocide,
  9 December 1948, 78 UNTS 277   250
Convention on the Rights and Duties of States, Montevideo,
  26 December 1933, 165 LNTS 19   202, 223, 235
Convention on the Rights of the Child, 20 November 1989, 1577 UNTS 3   250
Convention Relating to the Status of Refugees, 28 July 1951,
  189 UNTS 137   15, 112–114, 116, 123, 165, 166
Convention Relating to the Status of Stateless Persons, 28 September
  1954, 360 UNTS 117   112
Convention Respecting the Laws and Customs of War on Land,
  18 October 1907, 36 Stat. 2277, 1 Bevans 631   193, 194
Convention to Suppress the Slave Trade and Slavery, 25 September 1926,
  60 LNTS 253, Reg. No. 1414   10
Covenant of the League of Nations, 28 June 1919, 112 BFSP 13   27, 28, 53, 54
Declaration of Principles on Interim Self-Governing Arrangements,
  Israel-Palestine Liberation Organization, Art. V, 13 September
  1993, 32 ILM 1525   233, 241
Declaration on Principles of International Law concerning Friendly
  Relations and Co-operation among States in accordance with the
  Charter of the United Nations, UN Doc. A/RES/2625(XXV),
  24 October 1970   54, 174, 175, 195

xxvii

xxviii   *Table of Treaties and International Instruments*

*Declaration on the Granting of Independence to Colonial Countries
and Peoples*, UN Doc. A/RES/1514(XV), 14 December 1960   174
*Draft Articles on Responsibility of States for Internationally
Wrongful Acts*, Report of the International Law
Commission on the Work of its Fifty-Third Session
(23 April–1 June and 2 July–10 August 2001), Yearbook
of the International Law Commission, 2001, II(2),
A/CN.4/SER.A/2001/Add.1 (Part 2)   119, 120, 237, 188, 189, 195
Egypt-Israel, General Armistice Agreement, Rhodes, 23 February 1949,
UN Doc. S/1264/Corr.1   123, 226
French Mandate for Syria and The Lebanon, 24 July 1922 (1922) LNOJ 1013   45
*Geneva Convention for the Amelioration of the Condition of the Wounded
and Sick in Armed Forces in the Field*, 12 August 1949, 75 UNTS 31   250
*Geneva Convention for the Amelioration of the Condition of the Wounded,
Sick and Shipwrecked Members of Armed Forces at Sea*, 12 August 1949,
75 UNTS 85   250
*Geneva Convention Relative to the Protection of Civilian
Persons in Time of War*, 12 August 1949, 6 UST 3516, 75
UNTS 287   117, 118, 180, 193, 194, 197, 250
Geneva Convention Relative to the Treatment of Prisoners of War, 12 August
1949, 75 UNTS 135   250
Hashemite Jordan Kingdom – Israel, General Armistice Agreement,
Rhodes, 3 April 1949, UN Doc. S/1302/Rev.1   123
*Interim Agreement on the West Bank and Gaza Strip, Israel-Palestine
Liberation Organization*, 28 September 1995, 36 ILM 551   198, 241
*International Convention on the Elimination of all forms of Racial
Discrimination*, 7 March 1966, 660 UNTS 195   117, 203–206, 250
*International Convention on the Suppression and Punishment
of the Crime of Apartheid*, 30 November 1973, 1015 UNTS 243   206, 250
International Covenant on Civil and Political Rights, 16 December
1966, 999 UNTS 171   56, 116, 135, 136, 250
International Covenant on Economic, Social and Cultural Rights,
16 December 1966, 993 UNTS 3   56, 250
Israel-Syria, General Armistice Agreement, Hill 232, 20 July 1949,
UN Doc. S/1353   123, 226
Lebanon-Israel, General Armistice Agreement, Ras Naqura, 23 March 1949,
UN Doc. S/1296   226
New York Declaration for Refugees and Migrants, UN Doc. A/RES/71/1,
3 October 2016   15
*Protocol Additional to the Geneva Conventions of 12 August 1949
Relating to the Protection of Victims of International Armed Conflicts*,
12 December 1977, 1125 UNTS 3   117, 118, 194
*Protocol Additional to the Geneva Conventions of 12 August 1949, and
Relating to the Protection of Victims of Non-International Armed Conflicts*,
8 June 1977, 1125 UNTS 609   118
Protocol Relating to the Status of Refugees, 31 January 1967, 606 UNTS 267   112, 113

Table of Treaties and International Instruments   xxix

Rome Statute of the International Criminal Court, 17 July 1998, 2187
UNTS 3   118, 182, 197, 206, 250, 251
Statute of the International Court of Justice, 59 Stat. 1055, TS No. 993
at 25, 3 Bevans 1179   7, 54, 72
Statute of the Office of the United Nations High Commissioner for Refugees,
attached as annex to UN Doc. A/RES/428(V), 14 December 1950   113, 166
Treaty Establishing the Relations of France with the Principality of Monaco,
17 July 1918, 981 UNTS 359   225
Treaty of Peace with Turkey signed at Lausanne, 24 July 1923, 28 LNTS 11   131
United Nations Declaration on the Rights of Indigenous Peoples,
UN Doc. A/RES/61/295, 13 September 2007   10, 15
Universal Declaration of Human Rights, A/RES/217A(III), UNGAOR,
3rd Sess., Supp. No. 13, UN Doc. A/810 (1948) 71   116, 135, 152, 169, 177
Vienna Convention on the Law of Treaties, 23 May 1969, 1155 UNTS 331   250

Abbreviations

A/	United Nations General Assembly Document Symbol
Bevans	Treaties and Other International Agreements of the United States of America, 1775–1949
BFSP	British and Foreign State Papers
CERI	Consolidated Eligibility Registration Instructions (UNRWA)
E/	United Nations Economic and Social Council Document Symbol
ESM	Economic Survey Mission
HRC	United Nations Human Rights Council
ICJ	International Court of Justice
ICL	International Criminal Law
ICTR	International Criminal Tribunal for Rwanda
ICTY	International Criminal Tribunal for the Former Yugoslavia
IDP(s)	Internally Displaced Person(s)
IHL	International Humanitarian Law
IHRL	International Human Rights Law
ILC	International Law Commission
ILM	International Legal Materials
IMT	International Military Tribunal
IRL	International Refugee Law
JNF	Jewish National Fund
LNOJ	League of Nations Official Journal
LNTS	League of Nations Treaty Series
NAM	Non-Aligned Movement
OCHA	United Nations Office for the Coordination of Humanitarian Affairs
OHCHR	Office of the United Nations High Commissioner for Human Rights

OPT	Occupied Palestinian Territory
PA	Palestinian Authority
PCIJ	Permanent Court of International Justice
PLO	Palestine Liberation Organization
PMC	Permanent Mandates Commission
S/	United Nations Security Council Document Symbol
ST/	United Nations Secretariat Document Symbol
Stat.	United States Statues at Large
TS	Treaty Series
TWAIL	Third World Approaches to International Law
UN	United Nations
UNCCP	United Nations Conciliation Commission for Palestine
UNCEIRPP	United Nations Committee on the Exercise of the Inalienable Rights of the Palestinian People
UNDRIP	United Nations Declaration on the Rights of Indigenous People
UNESCO	United Nations Educational, Scientific and Cultural Organization
UNHCR	United Nations High Commissioner for Refugees
UNPC	United Nations Palestine Commission
UNROD	United Nations Register of Damage Caused by the Construction of the Wall in the Occupied Palestinian Territory
UNRPR	United Nations Relief for Palestine Refugees
UNRWA	United Nations Relief and Works Agency for Palestine Refugees in the Near East
UNSCOP	United Nations Special Committee on Palestine
UNTS	United Nations Treaty Series
US	United States
USSR	Union of Soviet Socialist Republics
WWI	World War I
WWII	World War II

1

Introduction

Owing to its unparalleled representative scope, what the United Nations (UN) says and does globally is widely perceived to be accompanied by an unequalled moral and political legitimacy linked to its status as the principal guardian of the international legal order. In his 12 January 2023 address to the General Assembly, Secretary-General Antonio Guterres affirmed what many of his predecessors had before him: that the 'primacy of the rule of law' is 'foundational to the United Nations' and 'essential to the maintenance of international peace and security'.[1] A lofty proposition, indeed. But what happens when the acts or omissions of the UN do not accord with international law but are rather the result of political expediency, great power politics, or bureaucratic inertia? In such circumstances, what is to be made of the UN's solemn obligation to maintain international peace and security 'in conformity with the principles of justice and international law'?[2] What impact does this have on the UN's legitimacy, particularly from the standpoint of the global south, where most UN operations and the majority of the world's population are located? As part of the growing critique of the UN, there is a general consensus that its value in the twenty-first century will increasingly rest upon its ability to maintain and encourage full respect for international law in the discharge of its functions, thereby enhancing the legitimacy of its actions.[3] While the UN has successfully done this in some spheres, serious doubt remains as to whether its handling of the question of Palestine has been one of them.

---

[1] Guterres, A. 'Secretary-General's Remarks to the Security Council on the Promotion and Strengthening of the Rule of Law in the Maintenance of International Peace and Security: The Rule of Law among Nations,' 12 January 2023, at: www.un.org/sg/en/content/sg/speeches/2023-01-12/secretary-generals-remarks-the-security-council-the-promotion-and-strengthening-of-the-rule-of-law-the-maintenance-of-international-peace-and-security-the-rule-of-law.

[2] *Charter of the United Nations*, TS 993, 24 October 1945, art. 1(1) ['UN Charter'].

[3] Thakur, R. 'Law, Legitimacy and United Nations' (2010) 11 *Mel. J. Int'l L.* 1 at 4.

Since its founding in 1945, no other geopolitical conflict has occupied as much time within the UN system as the question of Palestine.[4] As one of the longest-running disputes on the UN's agenda, now in its eighth decade, the conventional wisdom holds that the UN's position on Palestine offers the only normative basis of a just and lasting peace between Israelis and Palestinians grounded in international law. Contrary to this position, this book argues that there has been a continuing though vacillating gulf between the requirements of international law and the position of the UN on the question of Palestine, which has inevitably helped frustrate rather than facilitate the search for a just and lasting peace. To this end, this book examines several areas in which the UN has assumed a leading role in the question of Palestine since 1947. It critically explores the tensions that exist between the positions adopted by the Organization on the one hand and various requirements of international law on the other. If the UN has failed to respect the normative framework of international law in its management of the question of Palestine, what forms has this taken? How long have they persisted? What are the implications, not only for the Palestinian people – whose contemporary leadership has long resorted to the UN as *the* forum within which its international legal entitlements must be pressed – but also for the Organization itself? By addressing these questions, this book aims to critically interrogate the received wisdom regarding the UN's fealty to the international rule of law. It demonstrates that through the actions of the Organization, Palestine and its people have been committed to a condition that I shall call 'international legal subalternity', the defining feature of which is that the promise of justice through international law is repeatedly proffered under a cloak of political legitimacy furnished by the international community, but its realization is interminably withheld.

The choice of Palestine as the focus of this book is valuable for at least two reasons. First, owing to its prolonged nature, the question of Palestine offers a window into the role of international law in UN action over virtually the entirety of the Organization's existence. Temporally, this window covers the major paradigmatic shifts and political divides in the international system that have marked the UN's evolution from its very origins, that is late-empire/ post-colonial, East/West, North/South. Second, it is striking that despite the copious international legal literature that exists on the Palestine problem on the one hand and the very rich experience of the UN in dealing with its many aspects on the other, there has yet to be written an independent and critical study that attempts to bring these two strands together in any meaningful

---

[4] For example, the work of the Committee on the Exercise of the Inalienable Rights of the Palestinian People, especially the Division for Palestinian Rights.

1 Subalternity in the International System

way. To be sure, no sustained scholarly volume on the UN and the question of Palestine exists, as such. The closest one comes to any general treatment of the subject is found in a series of UN and Arab League public information pamphlets, a few monographs that cover aspects of the Palestine problem within the UN but are not focused on the UN as such, and several edited volumes that offer a glimpse of the UN's coverage of the question of Palestine through the narrow prism of partially reproduced UN documents.[5]

While this book cannot reasonably cover every facet of the UN's handling of the question of Palestine, by critically examining key moments of the Organization's engagement with it over time through the prism of international law, an attempt will be made to provide a picture that has yet to be offered. While previous doctrinal legal analyses of some of these moments have been undertaken extensively, and others have not, this book adds to the literature by collectively interpreting the key moments through a subaltern approach which draws and builds upon on the critical international legal theory associated with the Third World Approaches to International Law (TWAIL) school of thought.

1 SUBALTERNITY IN THE INTERNATIONAL SYSTEM

A useful point of departure is to make two separate but related observations about the nature of the international system, each of which is rooted in a subaltern perspective. Before setting them out, however, we must first ask who or what is the 'subaltern'? The origins of the term can be traced to Antonio Gramsci, who understood it to mean that which is in a positional opposite to a 'dominant', 'elite', or hegemonic position of power.[6] To Gramsci, it was the interaction between dominant and subaltern communities that formed the essence of human history.[7] Today, subaltern studies scholars use the term

---

[5] See The Question of Palestine and the United Nations (UN, 2008); The United Nations and the Palestine Question (Arab League); Nuseibeh, H.Z. Palestine and the United Nations (Quartet, 1981); Tomeh, G.J. The Palestine Case in the United Nations; Forsythe, D. United Nations Peacemaking: The Conciliation Commission for Palestine (Johns Hopkins, 1972); Hawley, D.C. The United Nations and the Palestinians (Exposition, 1975); Hadawi, S., ed. The Palestine Problem Before the United Nations (IPS, 1966); Hadawi, S., ed. United Nations Resolutions on Palestine, 1947–1966 (IPS, 1966); Quigley, J. The International Diplomacy of Israel's Founders (Cambridge, 2016); The United Nations and the Question of Palestine: A Documented History (Wolf, 2009); Allen, L. A History of False Hope (Stanford, 2021). The Nuseibeh monograph is conspicuous in that, despite its title, it offers very little examination of the UN's position on Palestine.

[6] Said, E.W. 'Foreword' in Guha, R. & Spivak, G.C. Selected Subaltern Studies (Oxford, 1988) at v–vi.

[7] Hoare, Q. & Smith, G.N., eds. Selections from the Prison Notebooks of Antonio Gramsci (Lawrence and Wishart, 1996) at 52–55. See also id., p. vi.

4   *Introduction*

broadly, to connote all those subordinated in global society, whether according to 'traditional' categories such as race, class, gender and religion, or more recently acknowledged categories such as age, sexual orientation, physical ability, etc.[8] Viewed in the positivist context of modern international law and institutions, where the state is the principal actor on the system, individuals, non-self-governing peoples, and, in many respects, developing states, are among those that constitute the subaltern. This includes Palestine and the Palestinian people.

The first observation concerns a point that may seem self-evident, given the subject matter of this book, but one that cannot be taken for granted owing to prevailing skewed and at times anti-Palestinian sentiment in some mainstream circles, particularly in the West:[9] any study devoted to examining Palestine, including before the UN, requires us to take the place and its people *seriously*. One might balk at this proposition, given the inordinate amount of time the UN has devoted to the question of Palestine over the decades. It may also seem inconsistent with the oft-recited mantra (regularly, though not exclusively, expressed within UN circles) that good faith engagement requires 'balance' and 'neutrality' between competing claims in Palestine.[10] But that would miss the point. By taking Palestine seriously, I refer to the imperative that the lived reality of the Palestinian people over the course of its modern history from the late nineteenth century onward – colonized, dispossessed, forcibly exiled, occupied, and discriminated against – must remain at the forefront of any study of it; not as an object to be ignored, casually dismissed, or represented for, but as a subject with a sustained history, presence, and agency of its own. This was well demonstrated by Edward Said, who urged us to view the matter of Palestinian subalternity as an 'issue involving representation', in order to counter the 'blocking operation by which the Palestinian cannot be heard from (or represent himself) directly on the world stage'.[11] The result has been to misrepresent or efface, figuratively and literally, the lived reality of Palestine and its people in order for power to justify its engagement with Palestine, whether for geostrategic purposes (as in the case of Great Britain and the

---

[8] Guha & Spivak, *supra* note 6. Morris, R., ed., *Can the Subaltern Speak?* (Columbia, 2010).

[9] Edward Said lamented that the 'common discourse of enlightened American liberal democracy' on Palestine was characterized by 'the complete hegemonic coalescence between the liberal Western view of things and the Zionist-Israeli view'. Said, E.W. *The Question of Palestine* (Routledge, 1980) at 37. *See generally*, Chomsky, N. *The Fateful Triangle* (South End, 1999); Said, E.W. & Hitchens, C. *Blaming the Victims* (Verso, 2001).

[10] For a critique of this 'trap of false-symmetry', *see* Sharoni, S. *Gender and the Israeli-Palestinian Conflict* (Syracuse, 1995) at 5.

[11] Said, *supra* note 9 at 39.

1 Subalternity in the International System

United States (US)) or in order to transform it into a settler-colonial state (as in the case of political Zionism and, eventually, Israel).[12] By taking Palestine seriously, it is therefore vital to adopt an approach that critically interrogates how and at what points in Palestine's modern history its position in the international system was superseded and compromised in *legal* terms. This will allow for a better understanding of the UN's engagement with it beyond the realm of the political, humanitarian, and developmental spheres. The character of contemporary Palestine as a place of unfulfilled promise whose people continue to be denied their internationally sanctioned legal rights, yet stubbornly refuse to submit themselves to such fate, is a useful window through which international legal subalternity can be explained and understood. Therefore, while this book necessarily takes account of competing hegemonic claims and interests in Palestine, its recourse to a subaltern view of things allows for greater insight, rejecting the common tendency of power to disregard the lived reality of the indigenous people of that land.

The second observation concerns the nature of international law, not only as a series of rules upon which the international state system is based in the classical positivist sense but also as a legal narrative organically connected to the European imperial setting in which it was constituted and then replicated, to varying degrees, in the international institutions created in the first half of the twentieth century.[13] Critically understanding this pedigree and evolution of modern international law will allow us to shed light on the role of international law in the actions of the UN in Palestine, most particularly in the defining period immediately following World War II (WWII). Central to the argument is the work of the TWAIL network of scholars.[14] In particular, Antony Anghie has focused on the imperial and colonial origins of international law 'to show how these origins create a set of structures that continually repeat

---

[12] Herzl, T. *The Jewish State* (Sylvie d'Avigdor trans., Dover, 1998) (1896).

[13] Imseis, A. 'Introduction' (2009) XV *Pal. YIL* 1. *See also* Anghie, A. *Imperialism, Sovereignty and the Making of International Law* (Cambridge, 2005).

[14] *See* Anghie, *id*; Anghie, A, Chimni, B.S., Mickelson, K. & Okafor, O., eds., *The Third World and International Legal Order* (Brill, 2003); Chimni, B.S. 'A Just World Under Law: A View from the South' (2007) 22 *Am. U. ILR.* 199; Fakhri, M. 'Law as the Interplay of Ideas, Institutions, and Interests: Using Polyani (and Foucault) to Ask TWAIL Questions' (2008) 10:4 *Int'l. CLR* 455; Gathii, J.T. 'Alternative and Critical: The Contribution of Research and Scholarship on Developing Countries to International Legal Theory' (2000) 41 *Harv. ILJ* 263; Gathii, J.T. 'Neoliberalism, Colonialism and International Governance: Decentering the International Law of Governmental Legitimacy' (2000) 98:8 *Mich. L. R.* 1996; Mutua, M. 'What Is TWAIL?' (2000) 94 *ASIL Proc.* 31; Okafor, O. 'Critical Third World Approaches to International Law (TWAIL): Theory, Methodology or Both?' (2010) 10 *Int'l. CLR* 371; Rajagopal, B. 'From Resistance to Renewal: The Third World, Social Movements and the Expansion of International Institutions' (2000) 41:2 *Harv. IL J* 529.

6   *Introduction*

themselves at various stages in the history of international law'.[15] According
to him, 'colonialism was central to the constitution of international law' in
that many of its 'basic doctrines' going back to the sixteenth century 'were
forged out of' Europe's 'attempt to create a legal system that could account
for relations between the European and non-European worlds in the colonial
confrontation'.[16] The fundamental point, according to Anghie, is that international law 'did not *precede* and thereby effortlessly resolve' European/non-
European relations; rather, international law was created by imperial Europe
in its encounter with its colonial Other.[17] Examples of this hegemonic/subal-
tern binary, and the process by which the former reconceptualized or created
new law to regulate the latter, abound in the annals of public international
law and institutions.[18] One of the goals of this book is to demonstrate how this
process – what I shall call rule *by* law – has played itself out at key stages of the
UN's engagement with the question of Palestine.

What makes this rule by law process intriguing is that it has unfolded at a
time when the organizing principle of the post-WWII international community has ostensibly been based upon an international rule *of* law framework,
the defining feature of which requires universal application of international
law without regard to the power or station of the actors in question. As a central pillar of modern liberal political order, the rule of law posits that 'people
in positions of authority should exercise that power within a constraining
framework of well-established public norms' to which they are also accountable.[19] By contrast, the rule by law framework is characterized by the exercise of power 'in an arbitrary, *ad hoc*, or purely discretionary manner' on the
basis of the 'preferences or ideology' of those in charge.[20] In this sense, law
becomes a tool to further the interests of power under the guise of legality,
while encouraging and relying upon double-standards in its application. As
noted by Brian Tamanaha, on the municipal plane '[r]ule by law carries scant
connotation of legal *limitations* on government, which is the *sine qua non* of

---

[15] Anghie, *supra* note 13 at 3.
[16] *Id.*
[17] *Id.*, at 15.
[18] For instance, it was common for European colonial powers to grant a form of quasi-sovereign
authority over non-European peoples to private European agents, settlers and commercial
companies to better serve their imperial interests abroad. Anghie, *supra* note 13 at 68–69.
Likewise, the dissociation of Latin America from Europe expressed in the 1823 Monroe
Doctrine, unilaterally proclaimed by the US against European intervention in the Western
hemisphere, served as the legal basis for numerous military interventions by the US in Latin
America. Rossi, C. *Whiggish International Law* (Brill, 2019).
[19] 'The Rule of Law,' *Stanford Encyclopedia of Philosophy*, 22 June 2016, at: https://plato
.stanford.edu/entries/rule-of-law/.
[20] *Id.*

1 Subalternity in the International System

the rule of law tradition'.[21] Transposing this to the international plane, the rule by law is manifested in the cynical use, abuse, or selective application of international legal norms by hegemonic actors under a claim of democratic rights–based liberalism, but with the effect of perpetuating inequity between them and their subaltern opposites. It is this form of rule by law upon which this book's central claims rest.

Structurally, there appears to be three crosscutting themes that animate subalternity in the international legal system. To the extent that these themes overlap with one another, they inform the episodes examined in these pages. First, is the theme of the Eurocentricity of the modern international legal order as rooted in Europe's imperial and colonial past. In this respect, an important problematic for TWAIL theorists is the notion of *la mission civilisatrice*; the idea that 'justified colonialism as a means of redeeming the backward, aberrant, violent, oppressed, underdeveloped people of the non-European world by incorporating them into the universal civilization of Europe'.[22] In juridical terms, this manifested itself in the social-Darwinistic standard of 'civilization', the prime legal determinant for membership and standing in the international system in the imperial age.[23] Although reaching its zenith in the second half of the nineteenth century, use of this standard persisted through the turn of the twentieth century, featuring prominently in the League of Nations mandate system. Second is the theme of the circumscribed nature of Third World sovereignty and international legal personality in the post-decolonization era. The end of WWII ushered in a New World order in which classic forms of European empire ostensibly gave way to more liberal principles set out in the UN Charter. This included the principles of sovereign equality of states, suppression of acts of aggression, equal rights, and self-determination of peoples.[24] Yet for all the promise of the UN, following decolonization a continued tension between the old imperial rule by law structure and these new liberal rule of law ideals remained.[25] Third is the theme of neo-imperial power and the role it has played in perpetuating the contingency and marginalization of global subaltern classes. In the post-WWII era, the victorious allied powers have sometimes used international law to further their

---

[21] Tamanaha, B. *On the Rule of Law* (Cambridge, 2004) at 92.

[22] Anghie, *supra* note 13 at 3.

[23] Wheaton, H. *Elements of International Law*, 8th ed. (Little, Brown & Co., 1866) at 17–18; Oppenheim, L. *International Law*, Vol. 1, McNair 4th ed. (Longmans, 1928) at 36–37; *and* Koskenniemi, M. *The Gentle Civilizer of Nations* (Cambridge, 2008) at 127.

[24] UN Charter, *supra* note 2, art. 1.

[25] The composition and procedural rules of the Security Council and the codification of 'general principles of law recognized by civilized nations' as a source of international law in the ICJ Statute are two examples; UN Charter, *supra* note 2, ch. V; *Statute of the International Court of Justice*, art. 38(1), 33 UNTS 933.

own national interests at the expense of the international rule of law. In this respect, and particularly since the end of the Cold War, the US has played the most significant role under cover of a purported commitment to a progressive, democratic, and rights-based international order.

The above cross-cutting themes span the history of modern international law and institutions, including as embodied in the UN from 1945 to the present. Here, Anghie's analysis of a basic paradox in the evolution of international law and institutions is instructive in helping us understand the hegemonic/subaltern binary in the system itself. A critical reading of the history of international law and institutions reveals that the mechanisms, doctrines, and technologies created as a means of achieving a liberal rights-based global order have at times shown themselves to be the very tools through which that order has been frustrated or undermined to the detriment of subaltern classes. This is 'inherently problematic', Anghie argues, 'because it is sometimes precisely the international system and institutions that exacerbate, if not create, the problem they ostensibly seek to resolve'.[26]

This book attempts to show that perhaps more than any single geopolitical issue the UN's engagement with the question of Palestine stands out as an obvious example of the phenomenon described above. As will be demonstrated, through the acts of some of its principal and subsidiary organs over the course of more than seven decades, the UN has presided over both the unmaking of Palestine (i.e. its attempted partition, military conquest, depopulation and political effacement between 1947 and 1949) and its qualified re-emergence, at least in truncated, fragmented, and subjugated form (i.e. in the occupied Palestinian territory (OPT) post-1967). Throughout this prolonged episode, the failure of the UN to abide by the full range of prevailing international legal norms in its management of the question of Palestine has been demonstrative of a larger failure by the Organization to take Palestine and its people seriously. This has ultimately resulted in the Organization perpetually conceiving of them and their putative membership in the system as subordinate and contingent, thereby reifying, maintaining, and perpetuating their legal subalternity over time.

2 THE COUNTER-HEGEMONIC POTENTIAL OF INTERNATIONAL LAW AND INSTITUTIONS

In recent decades, TWAIL scholarship has become an important part of the critical discourse on modern international law and institutions. Nevertheless, its proponents have for the most part resisted succumbing to a nihilistic view

---

[26] Anghie, *supra* note 13 at 192.

2 The Counter-Hegemonic Potential of International Law and Institutions 9

of the discipline. Foremost among them, Balakrishnan Rajagopal has argued that there remains a counter-hegemonic potential that the Third World can bring through its use of international law and institutions.[27] Thus, while the state-centric nature of international law is what reinforces the inequity inherent in its evolution, lending international law a quality of being nothing more than 'a mask for power relationships' and a tool for the maintenance of the established international order,[28] leading TWAIL thinkers have taken a more accommodating view. Many recognize that in the interdependent UN Charter era, where a multiplicity of actors increasingly engages with one another in infinite ways, international law has come to represent something potentially more than a politics of domination by other means. For subaltern groups, negotiating the state-centric international order has sometimes entailed using the very legal principles that underpin it to challenge that order on its own terms. The great paradox, therefore, is that beyond its utility in the evolution and maintenance of a hegemonic international order, in so far as international law now claims and has the potential to serve as an authentically universal standard for all peoples, it contains what Dianne Otto calls the 'seeds of resistance' for those that remain unable to fully benefit from its promise.[29] Put another way, despite its inequitable origins, elements of which clearly linger on in the contemporary period, international law remains an important means by which to measure, in legal terms, the acts of subjects of the international system.

This critical duality of international law is a theme running throughout this book. All law inherently possesses a duality of this sort. On the one hand, law is the product of the exercise of political power by subjects who wish to impose on society some form of normative order consistent with their interests and worldview. On the other hand, once created, law acts as the embodiment of such normative order under a claim that it stands apart from the very political power and interests of the subjects that created it and whom it now binds. Throughout this process, law operates as both an expression of the values and interests of political authority, and as a check and balance on that very same authority. In the context of international law, Martti Koskenniemi identified this tension as giving rise to law as both an apology for power and a harbinger of a utopia.[30] Always in discord with one another, never definitively cancelling

---

[27] Rajagopal, B. 'Locating the Third World in Cultural Geography' (1998) *Third World Leg. Stud.* 1 at 3.

[28] Brunnée, J. & Toope, S.J. *Legitimacy and Legality in International Law* (Cambridge, 2010) at 3.

[29] Otto, D. 'Subalternity and International Law: The Problems of Global Community and the Incommensurability of Difference' 5:3 *Soc. & Leg. Stud.* 337 at 343.

[30] Koskenniemi, M. *From Apology to Utopia* (Cambridge, 2005).

10   *Introduction*

each other out, the law as apology/utopia dialectic has become a fixed feature of how we understand the international system. This is particularly so when viewed from the vantage point of weaker nations and peoples.

For example, from ancient times, slavery was considered a natural element of the Roman *jus gentium*. It was the very legality of the holding of property in other humans that allowed the trans-Atlantic slave trade to flourish as the economic backbone of the settler colonies of the so-called New World. As Great Britain's engagement with the slave trade became unprofitable and post-Enlightenment philanthropic and populist sentiment emerged in some (but by no means all) quarters eschewing the practice as uncivilized, there emerged sufficient moral resolve to end it through gradual changes in the law based on both naturalist and positivist schools of legal thought. This was embodied in British abolitionist positions at the Congress of Vienna in 1815, American abolitionism following the American Civil War in 1865, and the eventual universal proscription of slavery in a series of international instruments concluded in the late nineteenth and early twentieth centuries, culminating in the *Slavery Convention* of 1926.[31]

A more contemporary example concerns the status of indigenous peoples in international law. While decolonization in the 1960s 'promoted the emancipation of colonial territories' modelled along a distinctly Westphalian standard according to which independence was granted the new territorial states under the principle of *uti possidetis*, it 'simultaneously promoted the assimilation of members of culturally distinctive indigenous groups into the dominant political and social orders that engulfed them'.[32] In response, a rights-based international movement emerged in the 1970s arguing for increased recognition of the human and people's rights of indigenous groups. Led by a host of nongovernmental indigenous people's organizations and independent experts, and facilitated by the UN, this effort has made some incremental gains in the realm of *lex ferenda*. Thus, the 2007 UN Declaration on the Rights of Indigenous Peoples (UNDRIP) affirms that indigenous peoples 'are equal to all other peoples' and therefore enjoy the right to 'self-determination', a recognition that has allowed for the expansion of self-government in a number of states.[33] This evolution in the rights of indigenous peoples would not have

---

[31] *Convention to Suppress the Slave Trade and Slavery*, 25 September 1926, 60 LNTS. 253, Reg. No. 1414. Allain, J. *Slavery in International Law* (Martinus Nijhoff, 2013) at 59–60, 64ff; Drescher, S. 'From Consensus to Consensus: Slavery in International Law' in Allain, J. ed., *The Legal Understanding of Slavery* (Oxford, 2012) at 316–355.

[32] Anaya, J. *Indigenous Peoples in International Law*, 2nd ed. (Oxford, 2004) at 55.

[33] *United Nations Declaration on the Rights of Indigenous Peoples*, A/RES/61/295, 13 September 2007, at preamble, arts. 2, 3 ['UNDRIP'].

been possible but for the active reliance on evolving concepts of prevailing human rights law by indigenous rights activists themselves.

These two examples demonstrate international law's duality as both a tool for the maintenance of a hegemonic order and one in which those subaltern classes who are overlooked or ill-served by such order may challenge it on its own terms. In both, criticism of prevailing law by and for subaltern groups was rooted in a critical application of that law against evolving social mores and sensibilities. This in turn produced fresh claims of fairness, ultimately resulting in some form of progressive development of the law.

3 INTERNATIONAL LEGAL SUBALTERNITY AS A LONG-RANGE CONDITION

Does the counter-hegemonic potential of international law and institutions mean that the inequity for legal subalterns at their root can be eliminated? Despite its decentralized, heterogeneous and polycentric nature,[34] TWAIL literature broadly seems to suggest so. According to Anghie and Bupinder Chimni, Third World jurists of the decolonization period to whom the TWAIL moniker has been affixed *post hoc* (TWAIL I) – for example Georges Abi-Saab, Francisco Garcia-Amador, R. P. Anand, Mohammed Bedjaoui, and Taslim Elias – tempered their critique of classical European international law and institutions by adopting a 'non-rejectionist stance'.[35] According to this position, 'the contents of international law could be transformed to take into account the needs and aspirations' of the colonized and newly independent Third World states.[36] This transformation was to be achieved primarily through the UN, and key doctrines of modern international law were to be employed in levelling the playing field between Europe and its former colonies. Foremost of these were the principles of sovereign equality of states and non-intervention.[37]

From the mid-1990s, contemporary TWAIL theorists (TWAIL II) – for example James Gathii, Obiora Okafor, Makau wa Matua, Rajagopal, Otto, Anghie, Chimni, etc. – have critiqued this view. At issue has been TWAIL I's apparent deference to the Third World post-colonial state as a site in which modern international law and institutions have been employed not

---

[34] Gathii, J.T. 'TWAIL: A Brief History of Its Origins, Its Decentralized Network, and a Tentative Bibliography' (2011) 3:1 *Trade L. & Dev.* 26 at 34.
[35] Anghie, A. & Chimni, B.S. 'Third World Approaches to International Law and Individual Responsibility in Internal Conflicts' (2003) 2 *Chin. JIL* 77 at 81.
[36] *Id.*
[37] *Id.*

to emancipate Third World peoples from the yolk of European colonialism, but to entrench authoritarian and corrupt native elite rule over them. TWAIL II writers have taken issue with their predecessors' failure to see beyond the sovereignty of the Third World state as an emancipatory end in itself, rather than regard it as a tool through which Third World citizens would realize true freedom and equality. TWAIL II writers have accordingly offered deeper theoretical critiques of international law and institutions, focusing on their colonial and imperial origins, to demonstrate a continuing structural bias in the international legal system far more difficult to dislodge than was previously understood.[38]

Yet, despite their more critical approach, TWAIL II scholars appear to take the view that the prospect of dislodging international law's structural bias against subaltern classes remains possible. Thus, to the views of Otto and Rajagopal regarding the counter-hegemonic potential of international law and institutions, Matua has added that TWAIL 'present[s] an alternative normative legal edifice for international governance' distinct from the contemporary international legal system.[39] Likewise, through its 'empowering radical epistemology that liberates international law' from its 'colonial and elitist shackles', Richard Falk argues that TWAIL 'validates the transformative and liberationist potential of international law'.[40] Adopting a Marxist approach, Chimni argues that despite international law's 'imperialist' pedigree, 'the idea of international rule of law continues to make sense' for what he calls the Transnational Oppressed Class, which must rely on various 'foundational principles of international law (e.g. the principle of non-use of force)' to overcome its subaltern status.[41] For him, 'legal nihilism is not the appropriate counter. What is called for is a creative and imaginative use of existing international laws and institutions to further the interests of the "wretched of the earth".'[42] Finally, David Fidler argues that along with its critique of 'the use of international law for creating and perpetuating Western hegemony', TWAIL's *raison d'etre* is necessarily to 'construct the bases for a post-hegemonic global order'.[43]

---

[38] *Id.*, 82–86; Imseis, *supra* note 13 at 2–3.

[39] Matua, *supra* note 14.

[40] Falk, R. 'Foreword: Third World Approaches to International Law (TWAIL) Special Issue' (2016) 37:11 *TWQ* 1943 at 1944.

[41] Chimni, B.S. 'Prolegomena to a Class Approach to International Law' (2010) 21:1 *EJIL* 57 at 75–76.

[42] Chimni, B.S. 'An Outline of a Marxist Course on Public International Law' in Marks, S. ed. *International Law on the Left* (Cambridge, 2008) at 90–91.

[43] Fidler, D.P. 'Revolt against or from within the West? TWAIL, the Developing World and the Future Direction of International Law' (2003) 2 *Chin. JIL* 29 at 31.

3 International Legal Subalternity as a Long-Range Condition

It is unclear whether this optimistic, liberationist view of international law and institutions is fully warranted, leading to the possibility that TWAIL literature may suffer from a blind spot of sorts. This arises through what appears to be a failure to account for international law and institutions as social phenomena, which by their nature are in constant flux and evolution. Because international law, institutions and society are ever changing, it follows that the law-making/challenging process described above can theoretically never end so long as humanity continues to exist and organize itself internationally with reference to any form of rule of law: *ubi societas ibi jus*. That is to say, there is no legal threshold beyond which all subaltern groups will achieve the full range of international legal personality and rights, thereby putting an end to legal subalternity once and for all. As law is challenged by the subaltern, and changes are thereby introduced to law over time, the interests served by that law produce either partially assuaged or wholly new subaltern classes who in turn challenge prevailing law. In many ways, therefore, the international rule by law operates within a cycle between hegemonic and subaltern actors that, it would appear, cannot be broken.

An implied acknowledgement of this is found in Gathii's observation that 'a central component of TWAIL is to challenge the hegemony of the dominant narratives of international law … by teasing out encounters of difference along many axes – race, class, gender, sex, ethnicity, economics, trade etc'.[44] For him, this teasing 'create[s] fruitful tensions or new conceptual spaces for richer, subtler and more nuanced renditions of international law'.[45] Far from eradicating these axes of human interaction, however, critical examination of international law and institutions reveals how such axes are reaffirmed, restructured, or regenerated in similar or new forms. This ultimately allows for fresh intellectual terrain to develop, allowing for a more fulsome understanding of the inequity inherent in the discipline. In this sense, international legal subalternity emerges as a distinct category within the international legal and institutional framework, and one that, subject to the maintenance of an international society based upon some form of legal order, must exist in perpetuity.

Two points should be made at this stage. First, it is notable that TWAIL scholarship has yet to clearly identify such a distinct category for the subaltern half of what I have called the hegemonic/subaltern binary. To be sure, the notion of hegemony in international law and organization has been well traversed in both mainstream and critical international legal literature. It connotes the existence of a hyper-concentration of power in one or a few

---

[44] Gathii, 'TWAIL: A Brief History,' *supra* note 34 at 37.
[45] *Id.*, 40.

14   *Introduction*

states, rendering them capable of arbitrarily ignoring, enforcing or reshaping legal norms through an unapologetic and implacable will to do so.[46] Yet, only a small minority of TWAIL scholars have used the term 'subaltern' in relation to the various classes of groups they have found subjected to the hegemonic effect of the international legal and institutional order.[47] Even then, these authors have curiously failed to find the predicament and features shared by those classes pronounced enough to warrant an acknowledgement that they have given rise to a common condition that must be appropriately diagnosed and named.[48] The closest one comes to what I have identified as international legal subalternity is found in the sociological writings of Boaventura de Sousa Santos and César Rodríguez-Garavito.[49] They posit a sociolegal idea they term 'subaltern cosmopolitan legality'. The aim of this idea is to 'challenge our sociological and legal imagination and belie the fatalistic ideology that "there is no alternative" to neoliberal institutions'.[50] The authors make clear that their notion is not descriptive (i.e. of a class or group sharing a common condition), but rather prescriptive (i.e. of an idea and approach to be employed metaphysically). In addition, they affirm that it is not focused on the international legal and institutional order as much as it is on law in the transnational and domestic perspective *vis á vis* the forces of 'hegemonic, neoliberal globalization'. It therefore seems clear that subaltern cosmopolitan legality is not synonymous with international legal subalternity.[51]

Second, the permanency of international legal subalternity as a condition should not be taken to suggest that it is immutable and fixed on one or more specific groups. The permanency of this condition rests not in the fact that given subaltern groups cannot utilize the potential of international law and institutions to challenge and, at some point, break free from their subservient circumstances. Rather, it is to suggest that even as such groups register

---

[46] Vagts, D. 'Hegemonic International Law' (2001) 95 *AJIL* 843; Alvarez, J. 'Hegemonic International Law Revisited' (2003) 97 *AJIL* 873; Gathii, J.T. 'International Law and Eurocentricity' (1998) 9 *EJIL* 184.

[47] *See, e.g.*, Otto, *supra* note 29; Rajagopal, 'From Resistance to Renewal,' *supra* note 14; Chimni, 'Prolegomena,' *supra* note 41.

[48] In discussing international law's 'Others', Marks, *supra* note 42 at 16, indicates that scholars have used a number of terms including 'subaltern classes', 'subordinate groups' and 'oppressed classes', or otherwise imply the existence of such groups, in reference to 'those seeking emancipatory change'.

[49] De Sousa Santos, B. & Rodríguez-Garavito, C.A. 'Law, Politics, and the Subaltern in Counter-Hegemonic Globalization' in De Sousa Santos, B. & Rodríguez-Garavito, C.A. eds., *Law and Globalization from Below* (Cambridge, 2005).

[50] *Id.*, 1.

[51] *Id.*, 11.

3 International Legal Subalternity as a Long-Range Condition   15

success in pushing back from time to time, the overall condition of legal subalternity as a structural component of the international system cannot fundamentally be eradicated. Organically, as international law and organizations are challenged and new law is made within and by that structure, the condition of legal subalternity may morph in respect of one or more subaltern groups, or otherwise shift from one or more of them to other, likely new, subaltern groups as part of the law-making/challenging cycle.

Returning to our earlier examples, it is notable that despite the abolition of slavery in international law in the late nineteenth and early twentieth centuries, the racism embedded within the domestic legal structures of former slave-holding states (the paragon being the US) that enabled and sustained slavery in the first place was morphed but not eradicated. For formerly enslaved persons, this structural racism remained basically untouched from an international legal standpoint, given the collective operation of doctrines of non-intervention, the standard of civilization and state-centrism that placed them beyond international legal scrutiny.[52] Likewise, although indigenous peoples are said to enjoy a right of self-determination under the 2007 UNDRIP, this purported right remains limited for two reasons. First, it is curtailed through an express provision of UNDRIP that constricts the exercise of that self-determination to the realm of internal or local affairs within the territorial sphere of existing sovereign and independent states.[53] Second, it is limited by the doctrinal prescription that deprives declarations like UNDRIP of any binding legal force as a matter of positive international law.

The above are examples where the subalternity of the underclass has essentially remained in place under international law, despite some measure of change introduced within that law. Examples where wholly new categories of subaltern classes have been created through changes in international law include the emergence of internally displaced persons (IDPs) and economic migrants, both of which evolved as recognized groups in need of protection *only after* international law had recognized a preceding subaltern group – refugees – as a distinct subject of persons with legally binding rights in relation to states.[54] In a sense, the crystallization of refugee rights under international

---

[52] Alexander, M. *The New Jim Crow: Mass Incarceration in the Age of Colorblindness* (The New Press, 2010).

[53] UNDRIP, *supra* note 33, preamble, arts. 3, 4, 46.

[54] Contrast the *Convention Relating to the Status of Refugees*, 28 July 1951, 189 UNTS 137, a binding international treaty codifying customary international legal obligations on states, with the 1998 *Guiding Principles on Internal Displacement*, E/CN.4/1998/53/Add.2 and the *New York Declaration for Refugees and Migrants*, A/RES/71/1, 3 October 2016, both of which represent non-binding soft law at most in so far as they deal with IDPs and migrants, respectively.

16   *Introduction*

law opened up space for the emergence, in legal terms, of IDPs and migrants, to whom a greater measure of the burden of subalternity has shifted.

What each of these examples illustrates is that whatever value exists in the counter-hegemonic use of international law and institutions, the limits of that value are to be found in the unbroken cyclical discourse between those in power and those on its periphery at the root of the international legal order. This book will attempt to show that the UN's management of the question of Palestine is a good example of this cycle and the subaltern condition it has produced on the international legal plane. Over time, the international law and order created or affirmed by the UN on the question of Palestine has both propelled and compelled the Palestinian leadership to adjust its position in order to assert the rights of its people, often times in a curtailed measure. This has only resulted in the Organization shifting the legal goalposts in a manner that has frustrated those purported rights in some fashion or another while simultaneously holding itself out as the guarantor of those very rights.

4 TWAIL AND THE QUESTION OF PALESTINE

Given the raft of potential issues at play, it is surprising that TWAIL literature on the question of Palestine has only appeared over the past fifteen years. The 2009 volume of *The Palestine Yearbook of International Law* (of which I was then editor-in-chief) was perhaps the first to delve into the area, but it was perforce too cursory a treatment given its thematic journal format.[55] More recently, Noura Erakat has offered a sustained critical assessment of how law has been employed to advance Israeli interests in the struggle over Palestine. Touching on some of the broad themes in this book, she convincingly shows 'how the law's ability to oppress is evidence not of its failure but rather of the fact that it can be strategically deployed' for harmful ends.[56] All in all, while this critical literature dealing with Palestine has broken important ground, at least three shortcomings stand out which this book attempts to fill to some degree.

First, to the extent it critiques the field of international law, as such, as being complicit in the unmaking of Palestine, some of the literature misses the mark by neglecting to account for the catalytic role of hegemonic actors in the equation. As a metaphysical phenomenon, international law is not self-executing. That function is left to the states that create it, almost always in concert with one another. In the context of the question of Palestine, the key

---

[55] Imseis, *supra* note 13.
[56] Erakat, N. *Justice for Some* (Stanford, 2019) at xii.

4 TWAIL and the Question of Palestine

international legal institutional protagonists have been the League of Nations and the UN, the latter to a much greater extent than the former. It is therefore striking to find that the current TWAIL literature on Palestine tends to highlight the complicity of international law almost as an actor *suo motu*, over the actions and omissions of those actually responsible for creating and giving it effect. Thus, in her otherwise insightful analysis of Palestinian 'quasi-sovereignty', Laura Ribeiro repeatedly indicts 'international law', as such, for simultaneously having 'colonized' and 'liberated' in Palestine while paying insufficient attention to the acts and omissions of the international actors that made it so.[57]

Second, the TWAIL literature has largely tended to focus on two areas of analysis – namely, criticism of international law as manifested through the League of Nations Mandate for Palestine and the subsequent application and operation of international humanitarian and criminal law in the OPT.[58] This work has been vital in helping us critically understand how international law has been used in these moments to push the Palestinian people to the periphery of the international system. Yet one result of its relatively narrow focus has been to neglect the important role of the UN as not merely a forum within which much of this has taken place, but also as an actor responsible for this outcome in a variety of other areas from 1947 to the present.[59]

Third, although an increasing volume of TWAIL literature on Palestine has engaged in important sociolegal analyses of how international law is articulated by its protagonists in 'narratives' and 'discursive techniques', it tends to neglect how law is created and employed by international institutions for unjust ends. Michelle Burgis has been the most prominent voice in this respect and her ethnographic work on the narratives of statehood as

---

[57] Ribeiro, L. 'International Law, Sovereignty and the Last Colonial Encounter: Palestine and the New Technologies of Quasi-Sovereignty' (2009) Vol. XIII *Pal.YIL* 67 at 87. *See also* Burgis, M. 'Discourse of Distinction? Palestinians, International Law, and the Promise of Humanitarianism' (2009) Vol. XIII *Pal.YIL* 42.

[58] Ribeiro, *id.*; Burgis, 'Discourse of Distinction,' *id.*; Burgis, M. 'Discourses of Division: Law, Politics and the ICJ Advisory Opinion on the Legal Consequences of the Construction of a Wall in the Occupied Palestinian Territory' (2008) 7:1 *Chin. JIL* 33; Sayed, H. 'The Fictions of the Illegal Occupation in the West Bank and Gaza' (2014) 16 *Oregon. RIL.* 79; Reynolds, J. & Xavier, S. "The Dark Corners of the World': TWAIL and International Criminal Justice' (2016) 14 *Int'l. Crim. Just.* 959.

[59] Although writers such as John Strawson and Victor Kattan have examined some of these moments, the Mandate in particular, they do not identify as TWAIL scholars nor utilize the critical methods typically associated with TWAIL scholarship but have instead favoured positivist doctrinal methodologies. *See* Strawson, J. 'British (and International) Legal Foundations for the Israeli Wall: International Law and Multi-Colonialism' (2004–05) Vol. XIII *Pal. YIL* 1; and Kattan, V. *From Coexistence to Conquest* (Pluto, 2009).

18   *Introduction*

employed by Palestinian legal practitioners in the field, although powerful and novel, is a good example of this.[60]

By utilizing a TWAIL sensibility to assessing how the UN has managed the question of Palestine over key periods of its engagement with the issue, this book hopes to both build upon and add to the important body of scholarship currently evolving in this area.

5 A WORD ON THE NATURE OF THE UN

In keeping with this book's exhortation to take Palestine seriously and to critically understand how international law has been employed to opposite effect, it is vital that we take brief critical account of the nature of the UN as the site where both of these phenomena uniquely intersect. The UN is today 'the only truly global institution of a general purpose which approximates universality'.[61] From an original membership of fifty-one states in 1945, the body currently boasts 193 Member States, with two non-Member Observer States, one of which is the State of Palestine.[62] The Organization is comprised of six principal organs, each with its own powers and mandates: the General Assembly, Security Council, International Court of Justice, Economic and Social Council, Trusteeship Council, and Secretariat. In addition, there are a host of other bodies subsidiary to one or another of the principal organs, each mandated to perform specific functions on behalf of the Organization.

Because the constituent members of each of the principal organs and the subsidiary bodies are either made up of representatives of Member States, UN personnel, or a combination of both, and because each of these organs or bodies is empowered to perform widely divergent functions, the nature and extent to which they operate independently of state interest and power differ. This gives rise to questions as to whether the UN can be spoken of in homogenous terms, as is often done, or if it is more appropriate to address it in heterogeneous ones. Put another way, is the UN independent or merely the sum of its parts? And how does that help us understand the hegemonic-subaltern relations inherent in the work of the Organization?

Simon Chesterman has noted that there are 'divergent views as to whether the UN should be a forum for intergovernmental cooperation or

---

[60] Burgis-Kasthala, M. 'Over-Stating Palestine's UN Membership Bid? An Ethnographic Study on the Narratives of Statehood' (2014) 25:3 *EJIL* 677. *See also*, Burgis, M. 'Discourses of Division,' *supra* note 58; and Burgis, M. 'The Promise of Solid Ground: Arab Territorial Disputes and the Discourse of International Law' (2008) 10 *Int'l. Comm. LR* 73.

[61] Thakur, *supra* note 3 at 4.

[62] The other is the Holy See.

5 A Word on the Nature of the UN

an independent actor that can lead on issues of global import'.[63] Within both international law and international relations literature these views find expression in the debate between what Veijo Heiskanen identifies as the realist (or reductionist) and idealist (or institutionalist) schools of thought.[64]

For realists, 'international organizations have no independent role or function in international affairs, but are simply extensions of instruments of state power'.[65] As such, international organizations are merely the handmaidens of the states that create and use them to do in concert that which would be more difficult to do unilaterally. Within this statist framework, the only political will of consequence is that which resides within and among states, with international organizations merely serving as *fora* where international laws are collectively dictated in the Gramscian sense, not independently created.[66] 'Consequently, in the realists' view, an excessive focus on formal international organizations and their internal structure is mistaken, as it diverts attention from the real subject matter of international relations: the relationships among states and governments.'[67]

For idealists, the situation is radically different. Although they acknowledge the role of states in their creation, they hold that 'international organizations play a role in international affairs that is somewhat independent of states and governments'.[68] They point to various technical legal and political functions exercised by international organizations – such as the capacity to sue and be sued, or the political independence of officials of the organizations in exercising their functions – as evidence of the fact that these organizations possess an autonomy that separates them from the states responsible for their creation and financial upkeep. As a result, idealists are of the view that 'international organizations have to be understood as players that not only have to be taken into account, but also have to be made accountable'.[69]

Despite the juxtaposition of these two schools of thought, however, what the literature does not appear to contemplate is that the UN actually embodies a mix of *both*. An implicit explanation of this is offered by Jan Klabbers

---

[63] Chesterman, S. 'Reforming the United Nations: Legitimacy, Effectiveness and Power After Iraq' (2006) 10 *Sing. YIL* 59 at 61.

[64] Heiskanen, V. 'Introduction' in Coicaud, J. & Heiskanen, V. *The Legitimacy of International Organizations* (UN University, 2001) at 5. *See also* Klabbers, J. 'The Changing Image of International Organization' in Coicaud & Heiskanen, *id.* at 224–225.

[65] Heiskanen, V. 'Introduction' in Coicaud & Heiskanen, *id.* at 5.

[66] '[L]egality is determined by the interests of the class which holds power in any society'; Gramsci, A. *Pre-prison Writings* (Cambridge, 1994) at 230.

[67] Heiskanen, V. 'Introduction' in Coicaud & Heiskanen, *supra* note 64 at 5.

[68] *Id.*

[69] Klabbers, *in* Coicaud & Heiskanen, *supra* note 64 at 225.

who, in discussing the relationship between international organizations and their members, emphasizes that it is more than merely symbiotic in so far as the two 'tend, eventually, to fade into each other so as to become indistinguishable'.[70] This derives from the fact that '[w]hatever volonté distincte international organizations may possess, it derives, eventually, from a volonté not their own; and however much states may wish to control organizations, their very creation involves a loss of control'.[71]

Support for this double-sided nature of the UN system is found in the highly varied memberships, powers and functions of the UN's principal organs, the terms of which are set out in the UN Charter itself and therefore legislated within the corpus of international law. For example, the General Assembly and Security Council embody, to varying degrees, intergovernmental cooperation under chapters IV and V of the UN Charter. Likewise, the Secretariat, and by extension the Secretary-General and the staff, are bound to exercise their functions in an independent manner under article 100. However, even the most cursory examination of UN practice reveals the hegemonic/subaltern binary as a common thread that winds its way throughout the Organization in these respects. Thus, as the plenary of all 193 Member States, the intergovernmental representativeness of the General Assembly lends it a political legitimacy that no other organ enjoys, but owing to the generally non-binding character of its resolutions relegates it to a secondary status *vis á vis* the Security Council. Likewise, the fifteen-member Security Council is solely empowered to render decisions that legally bind all other Member States in relation to threats to international peace and security, despite the lack of political legitimacy such decisions can sometimes be perceived as having owing to the Security Council's limited membership and its dominance by the five hegemonic permanent veto-wielding powers. Finally, although the Secretary-General and the staff must not seek or receive instructions from any governments, and Member States undertake not to influence them in the discharge of their functions, the long-standing practice of allocating senior UN posts to the various hegemonic global powers calls these legal requirements into question.

The divide between hegemons and subalterns is therefore manifest in much of the work of the UN. In deference to this, the book takes critical account of the nuanced and multifaceted nature of the Organization and the varying roles, functions, and powers of its constituent parts. At the same time, it assesses the UN against the single standard of international law whereby it is,

[70] *Id.*, 227.
[71] *Id.*

at once, neither the 'captive of its own interests' as an independent actor and 'more than the sum of its parts' as an intergovernmental forum.[72] By juxtaposing certain rule by law practices and features of the UN against its ostensible rule of law organizing principle, it is hoped that new critical understandings of how the Organization has managed long-term conflict in line with international law and justice can be developed using Palestine as the most apt case study.

6 OVERVIEW

Organized along an axis that juxtaposes the international rule of law with the international rule by law, this volume argues that the gulf between international law and UN action in its management of the key moments of the question of Palestine forms part of an arc of history that runs, to varying degrees, from 1947 to the present. Examined through a subaltern lens, this arc of history demonstrates that far from being a consistent standard-bearer of international law when it comes to Palestine, the UN has demonstrated a less than principled approach to it. At times the UN has adopted positions that overtly run contrary to prevailing international law; at others it has sidestepped the full range of international law's stipulations for what appear to be reasons of political expediency. Despite claims to the contrary, the result has been to commit Palestine and its people to a seemingly perpetual state of legal subordination in the international system, where the promise of justice and international law is repeatedly proffered under a cloak of political legitimacy furnished by the international community, but its realization is interminably withheld. This has underscored the international rule by law that lays at the heart of much of the work of the UN and the paradoxical nature of the Organization as the occasional author of the global problems it is mandated to resolve in accordance with principles of justice and international law.

Building on this introduction, Chapter 2 offers a short historical survey of the origins of Palestine's subaltern condition. Rather than within the UN system itself, these origins are located in British secret treaty-making and diplomacy between 1915 and 1947, particularly as institutionalized within the League of Nations system. While the literature on the history of Palestine in this period tends to focus on political themes, this chapter examines this period through the cross-cutting theme of the Eurocentricity of international law and organization then prevailing. It is set against the backdrop of the

---

[72] Charlesworth, H. & Coicaud, J., eds. *Fault Lines of International Legitimacy* (Cambridge, 2010) at 80.

global paradigm shift then occurring in the international system, from one based on the norms and values of the late-imperial age grounded in an international rule by law, to one based on those of an emerging liberal Western rights-based discourse ostensibly based on an international rule of law. The main systemic issue that emerges for Palestine at this time is its contingent and subaltern status in the international legal order, a status that was eventually placed before the UN in 1947.

Chapter 3 covers how the UN managed this inheritance through an examination of UN General Assembly resolution 181(II) of 29 November 1947 recommending the partition of Palestine. It undertakes an international legal analysis of resolution 181(II) with specific reference to the work of the United Nations Special Committee on Palestine whose report to the General Assembly in September 1947 formed the basis of the resolution. Contrary to the traditional international legal historiography, this chapter posits that the resolution was neither procedurally *ultra vires* the General Assembly, as argued by some pro-Palestinian legal scholars, nor were its terms substantively consistent with prevailing international law as regards self-determination of peoples, as argued by some pro-Israeli legal scholars. Set against the larger context of the international legal status of Palestine from WWI to the end of the British Mandate, this chapter argues that resolution 181(II) was, in a sense, the opening act in the reification of Palestine's legal subalternity within the newly minted UN system. It demonstrates that the resolution was an embodiment, in legal terms, of the lingering tension between the rule by law of late-European empire and the ostensible rule of law of the post-WWII era. More concretely, it shows that the resolution also helped hasten the dissolution of Palestine and the dispersal of its people, followed by a long series of successive questionable legal moments in UN decision-making thereafter.

Chapter 4 turns to the immediate consequences of the 1948 war for one such moment, namely the UN's response to the Palestinian refugee problem. Set against the international law governing refugee status, it critically examines the distinctive institutional and normative regime created by the UN for the Palestinian refugees in the form of two subsidiary organs of the General Assembly – the United Nations Conciliation Commission for Palestine and the United Nations Relief and Works Agency for Palestine Refugees in the Near East. It then juxtaposes that regime against the international institutional and normative regime applicable to all other refugees in the world, as administered by the United Nations High Commissioner for Refugees. The received wisdom holds the special regime for Palestinian refugees out as demonstrative of the UN's unique responsibility for their plight, given it resulted from a war that was, in part, induced by the General Assembly's own disregard for the international rule of law embodied in resolution 181(II). Yet a critical examination of the UN record on the early history, mandate, and regulatory framework underpinning this regime reveals that it was never intended to give effect to Palestinian refugee rights as established under prevailing international law, including as affirmed by the UN itself. The resulting 'protection gap' that has consequently emerged for Palestinian refugees, marked by uneven and confused state practice concerning their plight as well as ongoing gender discrimination against them by the UN, is demonstrative of the Organization's role in the maintenance of Palestinian legal subalternity on the international plane.

Chapter 5 examines the issue of the UN's position on the legal status of Israel's prolonged occupation of the OPT. Under international law, occupation of enemy territory is meant to be temporary and occupying powers may not claim sovereignty over such territory. Despite this, since 1967 Israel has systematically altered the status of the OPT with the aim of annexing it, *de facto* or *de jure*. During this time, while the UN has focused on documenting the legality of a range of individual violations of international law by the occupying power, scant attention has been paid by the Organization to the legality of the occupation regime as a whole. Emphasis has instead been placed on encouraging the parties to bring the occupation to an end through continued, though widely discredited and grossly unbalanced, bilateral negotiations. This chapter asks by what rationale can it be said that Israel's prolonged occupation of the OPT remains either legal or legitimate in the absence of good faith on its part in negotiating the occupation's end? What accounts for the UN's failure to definitively identify the occupation as illegal as such in line with its rule of law organizing principle, and how can its end reasonably be made contingent on negotiations between occupier and occupied? This chapter is set against the re-emergence and relative gains made by the Palestinian people within the UN during the decolonization period resulting, *inter alia*, in the UN's explicit acknowledgement of its 'permanent responsibility' for the question of Palestine until it 'is resolved in all its aspects in accordance with international law',[73] including an express recognition of the *erga omnes* right of the Palestinian people to self-determination in the OPT. The conventional wisdom presents this shift as emblematic of the UN's commitment to upholding the international rule of law in Palestine following the ostensible empowerment of the Third World through decolonization. In contrast, this chapter argues that the UN's failure to take a more principled position on the very legality of Israel's half-century 'temporary'

---

[73] A/RES/70/15, 24 November 2015.

occupation of the self-determination unit of the Palestinian people is demonstrative of the maintenance of Palestine's legal subalternity in the UN system, under a different guise.

Moving to the present day, Chapter 6 examines the issue of Palestine's admission to the UN as a Member State. Following the Palestine Liberation Organization's (PLO) historic acceptance of resolution 181(II) in 1988, and the commencement of over two decades of state-building undertaken as a consequence of the Madrid and Oslo peace processes, Palestine made considerable legal advances on the road to being universally recognized as a state, the *sine qua non* for UN membership. By 2011, this included Palestine's recognition by over 130 other states, and membership in several international intergovernmental entities. Set against this backdrop, this chapter critically examines Palestine's unsuccessful bid for membership in the UN between September and November 2011. It undertakes an international law assessment of the report of the UN Committee on the Admission of New Members, which concluded under the certainty of a US veto that it could not unanimously recommend Palestine's membership in the UN to the Security Council after having examined whether Palestine satisfied the criteria for membership as set out in article 4(1) of the UN Charter. Propelled by this unsuccessful bid, Palestine turned to the General Assembly which upgraded its status to that of a non-Member Observer State on 29 November 2012. While the legal consequences of this upgrade have been considerable, including allowing the State of Palestine to accede to a host of international treaties and multilateral organizations, its juxtaposition against the refusal of the Committee on the Admission of New Members to recommend membership to the Security Council in accordance with the international rule of law is demonstrative, yet again, of the international rule by law principle at work. Over seventy-five years after the UN's initial foray into the question of Palestine, this chapter demonstrates that while the Organization has allowed for a gradual and qualified recognition of some Palestinian legal subjectivity and rights, under the influence of the neo-imperial power of one permanent member of the Security Council, it continues to fail to provide the full range of legal and political foundations upon which those rights may actually be realized, thereby continuing to disenfranchise Palestine and its people.

Chapter 7 concludes this book by summarizing its principal findings and situating them in the larger context of the questions posed at the outset. It will show that, rather than the international rule of law ordering principle, it is the international rule by law principle that finds sustained illustration in the UN's management of the question of Palestine. This phenomenon is rooted in the clash between hegemonic and subaltern interests that produce and reproduce situations in which the promise of international law is repeatedly presented as the basis of international legitimacy and peaceful coexistence among a citizenry of formally equal nation-states, but which relegates non-self-governing peoples and other subaltern societies to partial and qualified access in the system.[74] The result is the presence of international legal subalternity as a long-range condition, a fixed feature of the international order with wider relevance for a variety of other subaltern actors and regions.

[74] Otto, *supra* note 29 at 337–338, 351.

2

The Interwar Period

1 INTRODUCTION

Although this book focuses on how the United Nations (UN) has helped maintain Palestine's contingent status on the international legal plane, it does not claim that this condition originated within the UN itself. No phenomenon arises in a vacuum. This chapter offers a short historical survey of the origins of Palestine's international legal subalternity, setting the stage for the issues explored in subsequent chapters. It does this through a critical reading of the nature of international law and organization during the interwar period with specific reference to Palestine's treatment thereunder. It shows that despite important political shifts in the international order at this time, epitomized by the formation of the League of Nations and the Wilsonian anti-imperial ideals that ostensibly fueled it, the ordering legal principle of the international community remained thematically rooted in the Eurocentricity of international law and organization through which imperial Europe continued to produce and rely upon law to rule over its colonial subjects. It was through the operation of the rule by law principle that Palestine and its people were wholly disenfranchised under the international legal order then prevailing, with effects that have lasted to the present day.

2 THE INSTITUTIONALIZATION OF THE INTERNATIONAL RULE BY LAW

Between 1914 and 1945, considerable developments in the international legal order took place. These changes were marked by a tension resulting from the global paradigmatic shift from the age of late empire to the post-World War II (WWII) ascendancy of 'enlightened' liberal values. The classical imperial age of the sixteenth to nineteenth centuries was one in which it was regarded as legitimate for international law to have been utilized as a tool by European

26

2 The Institutionalization of the International Rule by Law

imperial powers to manage their interaction with the non-Europeans whose lands and resources they coveted. But international law in the late-imperial age of the early twentieth century took a slightly different form. This difference lay in the *institutionalization* of the international legal order through the creation of the League of Nations.

Following World War I (WWI), the League was formed at the behest of US President Woodrow Wilson under an effective plea for the introduction of a modicum of international rule of law, where predictability in international relations would be based on a more universal application of norms between actors on the system. In his Fourteen Points of January 1918, he declared 'the day of conquest and aggrandizement' of the imperial powers over, denounced the practice of secret treaties and diplomacy as a principal cause of the war, and called for the establishment of a 'general association of nations' in order to establish 'guarantees of political independence and territorial integrity to great and small states alike'.[1] Accordingly, the Covenant of the League imposed hitherto unrecognized limits on the use of force (while not outlawing it altogether). It also required all international treaties concluded by its members to be registered and published.[2]

With the creation of the League, for the first time in history a measure of institutional multilateralism challenged European great power rivalry and freedom of action as the organizing framework of the international community. This was in measure only because key international powers remained outside the League for much or all of its twenty-six-year existence, with Germany only admitted in 1926 (dropping out in 1933), Turkey in 1932, the Soviet Union in 1934 (expelled in 1939), and the United States never joining despite Wilson's pivotal role. Needless to say, the vast majority of the millions of Europe's colonial subjects were not members of the League.[3] The League was essentially a college of imperial Europe and was therefore predisposed to a continuation of imperial rule by law. This was most evident in its international mandate system.

The mandate system was a means adopted by the victorious allied powers to divide and administer the former German and Ottoman colonial possessions *post-bellum*. Although this system was influenced by Wilson's principles of non-annexation and self-determination,[4] its architect, South African Field

---

[1] Woodrow Wilson's Fourteen Points, 8 January 1918, at: http://avalon.law.yale.edu/20th_century/wilson14.asp.

[2] *Covenant of the League of Nations*, 28 June 1919, 112 BFSP 13, arts. 10–13, 18 ['League of Nations Covenant'].

[3] Although the most populous colony, India, did have separate membership of the League, it was represented by its colonial power, Britain, rather than by a popularly elected government.

[4] Wright, Q. *Mandates under the League of Nations* (Greenwood, 1968) at 24–25.

28 *The Interwar Period*

Marshall and racial segregation advocate, Jan Christiaan Smuts,[5] incorporated the imperial standard of civilization into it.[6] Thus, Article 22 of the League of Nations Covenant resolved that 'the well-being and development' of the former possessions of the Central Powers, 'which are inhabited by peoples not yet able to stand by themselves under the strenuous conditions of the modern world', formed 'a sacred trust of civilization'. To that end, 'the tutelage of such peoples should be entrusted to advanced nations', namely the victorious imperial powers. Article 22 further resolved that the communities formerly belonging to the Ottoman Empire (designated 'class A' mandates), including Palestine, had 'reached a stage of development where their existence as independent nations can be provisionally recognized subject to the rendering of administrative advice and assistance by a Mandatory until such time as they are able to stand alone'. It accordingly affirmed that '[t]he wishes of these communities must be a principal consideration in the selection of the Mandatory'.[7]

The mandate system was an embodiment of Europe's unwillingness to cede its imperial interests in any fundamental way, high-sounding Wilsonian rhetoric notwithstanding.[8] In a recent history of the mandate system, Susan Pedersen tends to adopt this view, but nevertheless argues that the system had a redeeming feature. To her, though 'League oversight could not force the mandatory powers to govern mandated territories differently' than their more conventional colonies, 'it obliged them to *say* they were governing them differently'.[9] Obligatory reporting to the Permanent Mandates Commission (PMC) introduced a 'level of international diplomacy, publicity, and "talk" that' had the unintended consequence of checking imperial power, at least at the discursive level. The mandates system was therefore a vehicle for what Pedersen calls 'internationalization', that is 'the process by which certain political issues and functions are displaced from the national or imperial, and into the international, realm'.[10]

The occurrence of internationalization through the League is hard to dispute, given the complete dearth of centralized organization for the conduct of international relations out of which it emerged. But Pedersen overstates its overall impact in helping to bring about a global order based upon universal application of an international rule of law. Despite the League's ostensibly

---

[5] Wilson, M. & Thompson, L. eds. *The Oxford History of South Africa*, vol. II 1870–1966 (Oxford, 1978) at 340–343.

[6] Wright, *supra* note 4 at 32; Anghie, A. *Imperialism, Sovereignty and the Making of International Law* (Cambridge, 2005) at 119.

[7] League of Nations Covenant, *supra* note 2, art. 22.

[8] Anghie, *supra* note 6 at 115–195.

[9] Pedersen, S. *The Guardians* (Oxford, 2015) at 4.

[10] *Id.*, at 4–5.

revolutionary principles aimed at non-annexation and self-determination of colonial territories, a subaltern reading suggests something equally if not more plausible: that League machinery effectively institutionalized an international rule by law, through which imperial rule over the globe continued under a discursive cloak of internationalism. In short, the more things changed, the more they remained the same.

This is evident in the actual terms of Article 22 of the League of Nations Covenant based as it was on the racist imperial standard of civilization. Although its drafters believed themselves altruistic in their accommodation of Europe's colonial peoples, the continued paternalism and contempt expressed by them remained normative and was therefore hardly in need of disguise. The choice of language used in Article 22 was thus a perfect embodiment of Rudyard Kipling's Whiteman's Burden, though set in legal terms: the non-Europeans were not yet 'able to stand on their own', not capable of confronting 'the strenuous conditions of the modern world', and therefore requiring of the 'tutelage' of 'advanced nations' under a 'sacred trust of civilization'. This legal provision was clearly rooted in the imperial values that had shaped the face of international law to that point.

Moreover, it is evident in the way the sacred trust of civilization was actually discharged under the League's supervision by 'advanced' mandatory powers. Far from facilitating independence of former colonies of the Central powers, the legal framework introduced by the League codified continued empire in international law. Mandatory powers were enabled to comfortably administer their sacred trust in line with their own imperial interests, though mandatory subjects struggled to break free, materially and normatively. This accentuated the legal subalternity that colonized peoples the world over had been relegated to in bilateral engagement with individual imperial powers in the preceding 300 years. For the first time in history, the contingent status of the colonies was formalized at the global level through the legal framework underpinning the League. The emergence of an international rule by law during the interwar years, with its consequent production of international legal subalternity, was the novel and inevitable result. The impact of this is readily apparent when examining the status of Palestine at this time.

3 THE ORIGINS OF PALESTINE'S INTERNATIONAL LEGAL SUBALTERNITY

In locating the origins of Palestine's international legal subalternity in the interwar years, of particular importance is the role of British imperial secret treaty-making and diplomacy at the time, and the international legal

30 *The Interwar Period*

codification through the League of Nations of its patronage of European Jewish nationalism in the form of the Zionist movement. In broad terms, the relevant milestones are fivefold: (1) the 1915–1916 Hussein–McMahon correspondence; (2) the 1916 Sykes–Picot Agreement; (3) the 1917 Balfour Declaration; (4) the 1920 Covenant of the League of Nations; and (5) the 1922–1947 mandate for Palestine.

Historians of the modern Middle East will readily identify these events for the pivotal impact they had on the geopolitical evolution of the region in the contemporary period. Yet, for the most part, the literature tends to examine them more from political perspectives than from the standpoint of international law. Although few in number, those studies that have addressed these milestones through the lens of international law tend to do so from a strictly positivist standpoint. The result is to merely highlight rights and wrongs as measured against prevailing legal norms without appropriately interrogating the imperial legal framework upon which they were based.[11] Insufficient or no critique is offered of the underlying object and purpose of the agreements and laws being examined, as the legitimacy of the interests that animate them is assumed or simply ignored. As a result, historiographically, this segment of the literature on Palestine largely fails to identify relevant *themes* that emerge through these events from a critical international law perspective. Foremost of these is the evolution of Palestine's international legal subalternity as a product of the Eurocentricity of the international legal order. In particular, critical examination of these events reveals how legal text and agreement were utilized by imperial power, including as exercised by the newly established League of Nations, to obfuscate, marginalize, or otherwise efface Palestinian Arab legal subjectivity under prevailing international law.

3.1 *Zionism, Colonialism, and the Civilizing Mission as a Legal Technology in Palestine*

Because of the increasing desire of non-self-governing peoples to assume an equal place within the international order in the late nineteenth and early twentieth centuries, the legal standard of civilization required that European modes of public administration and political organization be emulated by them. This resulted in the spread and adoption of European forms of nationalism and the nation-state. In respect of Palestine, two distinct nationalisms

---

[11] *See e.g.*, Grief, H. *The Legal Foundation and Borders of Israel under International Law* (Mazo, 2010); Kattan, V. *From Coexistence to Conquest* (Pluto, 2009); Mazzawi, M. *Palestine and the Law* (Garnet, 1997); and Stone, J. *Israel and Palestine* (Johns Hopkins, 1981).

3 The Origins of Palestine's International Legal Subalternity   31

arose at roughly the same time in this period, one indigenous, the other European. With respect to the former, it was among the educated urban classes that Arab nationalism first emerged among Palestinians in the last quarter of the nineteenth century. Spurred on by a growing independent Arabic language press, greater exposure to European intellectual and political thought, and a palpable decline in *Pax Ottomana*, increased calls for pan-Arab independence from what came to be regarded as foreign and imperial rule from Istanbul gained currency.[12] These calls soon gave way to the development of a distinctly Palestinian national identity in the years just prior to the outbreak of WWI.[13] In so far as indigenous Palestinian Arab nationalism developed within an Ottoman and Islamic context, it was not the product of racialized social hierarchies then prevalent in European legal and political thought. In contrast, the Zionist movement was a direct result of a politics of those hierarchies and their projection globally through European empire and legal discourse.[14]

Zionism's adherents argued that the enduring attempts of European Jews to coexist and assimilate with their Gentile counterparts were futile and required urgent redress. As Jews were the European continent's perennial subaltern underclass, anti-Semitism was 'the archetypal Western prejudice'[15] and was therefore the driving force behind the so-called 'Jewish question', according to which the place of the Jew in nineteenth-century Europe was openly impugned in the public sphere.[16] In answer to this question, Theodor Herzl posited the establishment of an independent Jewish national existence outside of Europe. Although a similar call had been made by Leo Pinsker in 1882,[17] Herzl's 1896 monograph, *Der Judenstaat*, galvanized the movement.[18]

In so far as it fashioned itself in accordance with then-prevailing European notions of ethnic or tribal nationalism[19] and successfully aligned itself with

---

[12] Khalidi, R. *Palestinian Identity* (Columbia, 1997) at 64–65.

[13] *Id.*, at 149–151.

[14] Taylor, A.R. 'Vision and Intent in Zionist Thought' in Abu-Lughod, I. ed., *Transformation of Palestine* (Northwestern, 1987) at 14 ff.

[15] Beit-Hallahmi, B. *Original Sins* (Olive Branch, 1993) at 9.

[16] Herzl, T. *The Jewish State* (Sylvie d'Avigdor trans., Dover, 1998) (1896) at 85–97. *See also* Kattan, *supra* note 11 at 9–10.

[17] Pinsker's *Auto-Emancipation*, reprinted in Pinsker, L. *Road to Freedom* (Scopus, 1975) at 74.

[18] Herzl, *supra* note 16.

[19] According to German Jewish philosopher Hannah Arendt, 'tribal nationalism [was] the driving force behind continental imperialism' of the period, giving rise to the pan-Slavic and pan-Germanic nationalisms that would eventually morph into reactionary and totalitarian regimes in the twentieth century. Arendt, H. *The Origins of Totalitarianism* (Harcourt, 1966) at 227. Of note, was Arendt's observation that '[Theodor] Herzl thought in terms of nationalism from German sources'. Arendt, H. *The Jewish Writings* (Kohn, J. & Feldman, R. eds., Schocken, 2007) at 382.

The Interwar Period

European colonial and imperial ideals, methods and power, the Zionist movement situated itself within the paradigm of late-European empire then colliding with emerging liberal rights-based values. In short, it was a product of its time. Because the political *zeitgeist* of imperial Europe exalted colonialism and because the Zionists lacked any territorial base in which to give effect to their programme in Europe, the colonial nature of Zionism and its role in *la mission civilisatrice* were openly propagated by its leaders. Thus, Pinsker wrote that 'the auto-emancipation of the Jewish people as a nation' would be realized through 'the foundation of a colonial community belonging to the Jews, which is some day to become our inalienable home, our fatherland'.[20] Likewise, Herzl spoke of Zionism as a 'colonial idea'[21] and presented Zionist settlement of Palestine as 'form[ing] a portion of the rampart of Europe against Asia, an outpost of civilization against barbarism'.[22] In addressing the fourth Zionist Congress in 1900, Herzl said it was in 'the interest of the civilized nations and of civilization in general that a cultural station be established on the shortest road to Asia. Palestine is this station and we Jews are the bearers of culture who are ready to give our property and our lives to bring about its creation'.[23] Between the establishment of the first Zionist colony in 1882 and 1914, the Jewish population in Palestine is estimated to have accounted for approximately 60,000, or 7.6 per cent of the total population, of whom two-thirds were European settlers.[24] Altogether, they owned no more than 2 per cent of the land.[25]

Zionism's structural reliance on European colonialism and imperialism is of particular relevance to understanding the evolution of Palestine's legal subalternity in this period. It would be incorrect to understand the movement's asseverations to colonialism and European civilization in strictly political and socio-cultural terms, as most treatment of this period tends to do. At the time these ideas were articulated, they were also key components of the content and structure of public international law, as it was then composed. The expansion of European empire, undertaken as of right by colonial and self-styled 'civilized' powers, was not only legal at the time, but its legality was a derivative of the very colonial and civilizational attributes of the European imperialists themselves. Thus, writing in 1866, Henry Wheaton opined that '[t]he public law, with slight exceptions, has always been, and still is, limited to the civilized

---

[20] Pinsker, *Auto-Emancipation, supra* note 17 at 104.

[21] Schleifer, A. *The Fall of Jerusalem* (Monthly Review, 1972) at 23.

[22] Herzl, *supra* note 16 at 96.

[23] *The Congress Addresses of Theodor Herzl*, trans. Nellie Straus (Federation of American Zionists, 1917) at 24.

[24] Strawson, J. *Partitioning Palestine* (Pluto, 2010) at 26–27.

[25] *Id.*, at 27.

3 The Origins of Palestine's International Legal Subalternity   33

and Christian people of Europe or to those of European origin'.[26] Likewise, in 1894 John Westlake explained that '[i]nternational law has to treat natives as uncivilized' as '[i]t regulates, for the mutual benefit of the civilized states, the claims which they make to sovereignty over' colonial territory 'and leaves the treatment of the natives to the conscience of the state to which sovereignty is awarded'.[27] To pursue and present its goals in those terms was therefore a conscious and strategic choice by Zionism's founders to furnish their movement with a measure of *legal* legitimacy among its European adherents and benefactors beyond any historical, cultural, or political imperative.

It was in this context that the first Zionist Congress in 1897 affirmed that '[t]he aim of Zionism is to create for the Jewish people a home in Palestine *secured by public law*'.[28] In the interwar period, this strategy would be directed at obtaining international legal recognition of the Jewish people as a nation, establishing a legal nexus between that people and Palestine, and obtaining international legal recognition for the Zionist Organization (founded at the 1897 Congress) as the official representative of the Jewish people.[29] Would that it were simply a matter of exclusive concern for the legal rights of the Jewish people alone, the question of Palestine would never have arisen. The point is that, although Zionism presented itself to its hopeful recruits as an emancipatory movement *vis-à-vis* European anti-Semitism, in so far as it sought to give effect to that emancipation by adopting and utilizing, *inter alia*, late nineteenth-century legal technologies and discourses of civilizing and colonizing an already inhabited non-European land through the patronage of a European imperial power, it helped set the cornerstone for Palestine's international legal subalternity. Key to the endeavour was the use to which that imperial power, Great Britain, made of secret treaties and the League of Nations in laying the foundation of the international rule by law in Palestine.

3.2 1915–1916 Hussein–McMahon Correspondence

The first historical moment relevant to the evolution of Palestine's legal subalternity is the Hussein–McMahon correspondence. In seeking to consolidate its position against the Central Powers during WWI, Britain enlisted

---

[26] Wheaton, H. *Elements of International Law*, 8th ed. (Little, Brown & Co., 1866) at 17–18. *See also*: Walker, T.A. *A History of the Law of Nations, Vol. I* (Cambridge, 1899) at 138, 331; Oppenheim, L. *International Law, Vol. 1*, McNair 4th ed. (Longmans, 1928) at 36–37.

[27] Westlake, J. *Chapters on the Principles of International Law* (Cambridge, 1894) at 143, *as quoted in* Koskenniemi, M. *The Gentle Civilizer of Nations* (Cambridge, 2008) at 127.

[28] Kattan, *supra* note 11 at 21 [emphasis added].

[29] Strawson, *supra* note 24 at 15–16.

34 *The Interwar Period*

Arab support against the Ottoman Empire. This came in the form of an exchange of letters between Hussein ibn Ali, the Hashemite Sherif of Mecca and a leader of the Arab nationalist movement, and Sir Henry McMahon, the British High Commissioner in Cairo.[30] In exchange for Arab military support against the Ottomans, Hussein demanded that the British recognize post-war Arab independence in the Middle East, comprised of the whole of the Arabian Peninsula (with the exception of Aden), Syria and what would later become Lebanon, Palestine, Iraq, and Transjordan. Following a number of detailed exchanges, McMahon made the following representation to Hussein in a letter dated 24 October 1915:

> The two districts of Mersina and Alexandretta and portions of Syria lying to the west of the districts of Damascus, Homs, Hama and Aleppo cannot be said to be purely Arab, and should be excluded from the limits demanded. With the above modification, and without prejudice to our existing treaties with Arab chiefs, we accept those limits. As for those regions lying within those frontiers wherein Great Britain is free to act without detriment to the interests of her ally, France, I am empowered in the name of the Government of Great Britain to give the following assurances and make the following reply to your letter: (I) Subject to the above modifications, Great Britain is prepared to recognize and support the independence of the Arabs in all the regions within the limits demanded by the Sharif of Mecca....[31]

Acting in reliance upon this assurance, the Arabs provided the requested military support and were successful in assisting the Allies in ousting the Ottomans from their lands.

At the end of the war, however, a dispute arose. It was not about whether the correspondence created binding treaty obligations under international law, for the British had established a practice throughout the nineteenth century of entering into binding treaty relations with rulers of the Arabian gulf through similar exchanges of letters, despite the fact that these rulers did not exercise dominion over the areas in question.[32] The dispute was

---

[30] *See* Pappe, I. A *History of Modern Palestine*, 2nd ed. (Cambridge, 2006) at 64–65 *and* Kattan, *supra* note 11 at 39–40, 98–107.

[31] Hussein–McMahon Correspondence, *as quoted in* Ingrams, D. *Palestine Papers, 1917–1922* (John Murray Publishers Ltd.) at 2.

[32] Although it is thought that in the nineteenth and early twentieth centuries treaties could only be entered into between states, there were exceptions to this rule as demonstrated by numerous treaties concluded between the British government and Arab sheikhs in 1820, 1835, 1853, 1861, 1868, and after. According to Kattan, '[n]ot once did Britain claim that these agreements were not binding between them because the Sheikhs did not have the capacity to enter into binding obligations with Britain'. *See* Kattan, *supra* note 11 at 98, 103–104.

3 The Origins of Palestine's International Legal Subalternity   35

rather about whether Palestine was excluded from the region within which
the British agreed to recognize and support Arab independence. Although
much of the literature treats this as a disagreement of equal merit, the available evidence suggests that the Arabs were victims of deliberate obfuscation
from Whitehall and were correct in their understanding that post-war Arab
independence included Palestine.[33] To be sure, the districts of Mersina
and Alexandretta were both Turkish, whereas those portions of Syria lying
to the west of the four Ottoman districts (or *sanjaks*) of Damascus, Homs,
Hama and Aleppo were, as a matter of geographical fact and Ottoman
administration, comprised of what is today Lebanon and the north-western
Mediterranean coast of Syria (Map I). Furthermore, this latter portion of
the Levant was known by the great powers, foremost Britain, to have been
of strategic interest to France, going back at least to 1860 when Napoleon III
intervened to protect the large Maronite Catholic population from sectarian
persecution. Thus, both of the areas excluded were regarded by the British
as not being 'purely Arab'. In contrast, the population of Palestine, which
lay *south-southwest* of the districts of Damascus, Homs, Hama, and Aleppo
was known to have been virtually exclusively populated by Arabs (i.e. over
95 per cent).[34]

These were the views expressed in private by British government officials
following the issuance of the correspondence. On 5 December 1918 Lord
Curzon, then Foreign Secretary, stated in a meeting with Arthur Balfour,
former Prime Minister and a fellow Cabinet member, that 'Palestine was
included in the areas as to which Great Britain pledged itself' under the
correspondence to 'be Arab and independent in the future'.[35] This was
reflected in a map 'illustrating the territorial negotiations' concluded in
the correspondence prepared by the Foreign Office in that year (Map II).
Likewise, a memorandum of the Political Intelligence Department of the
Foreign Office prepared for the British delegation to the 1919 Versailles
peace conference provided that 'with regard to Palestine, His Majesty's
Government are committed by Sir H. McMahon's letter to the Sherif on 24
October 1915, to its inclusion in the boundaries of Arab independence'.[36]

---

[33] *Id.*, at 98. *See also* Smith, C.D. *Palestine and the Arab-Israeli Conflict* (New York: St. Marten's
  Press, 1992) at 42–47; and Pappe, I. *The Making of the Arab-Israeli Conflict 1947–1951* (London:
  I.B. Taurus, 2006) at 5.
[34] Kattan, *supra* note 11 at 107.
[35] Ingrams, *supra* note 31 at 48.
[36] *Memorandum on British Commitments to King Hussein*, Political Intelligence Department,
  Foreign Office, Special 3, FO 608/92, Peace Conference, British Delegation 1919, *as quoted
  in* Kattan *supra* note 11 at 109.

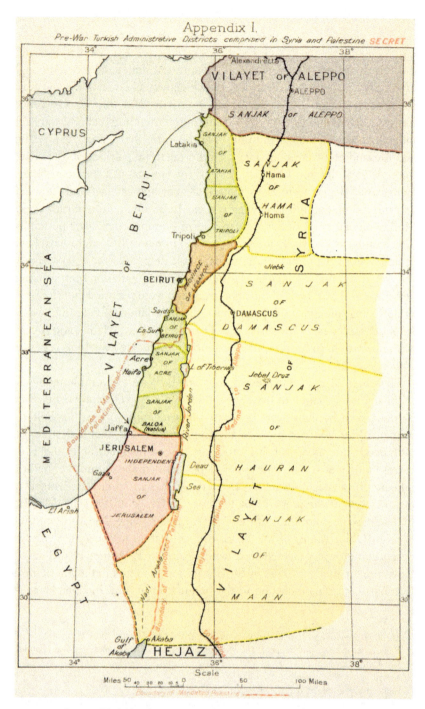

MAP 1 *Pre-war Turkish administrative districts comprised in Syria and Palestine showing the boundaries of mandated Palestine and the Hejaz railway.*

3 *The Origins of Palestine's International Legal Subalternity*

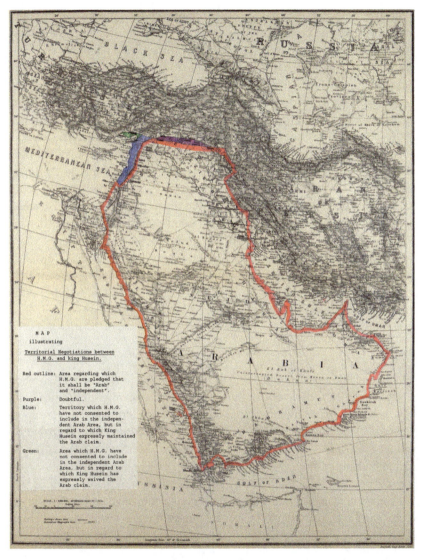

MAP II *Map illustrating territorial negotiations between H. M. G. and King Hussein.*

Notwithstanding these private positions, a 1922 White Paper prepared under Winston Churchill, then Colonial Secretary, indicated that the exclusion of 'territories lying to the west of the district of Damascus' had 'always been regarded by His Majesty's Government as covering the vilayet of Beirut and the independent Sanjak of Jerusalem', thereby excluding 'the whole of Palestine' from the area envisioned for Arab independence. Scarcely two

38   *The Interwar Period*

years later, however, that same British Colonial Office repudiated this position in yet another confidential memorandum to Cabinet dated 12 February 1924 which provided that '[t]he natural meaning of the phrase "west of the district of Damascus", has to be strained in order to cover an area lying considerably to the south as well as to the west of Damascus city'.[37] Finally, in 1939, when the British government disclosed the text of the correspondence to the public for the first time – some twenty-three years after it was initially entered into – this position was reiterated by Sir Michael McDonnell, Chief Justice of Palestine (1927–1937), whose legal opinion was sought on the matter by the government.[38] In his view, 'the grammatical and ordinary sense of the words used in the correspondence' were so clear as to not admit of any controversy at all.[39] The reason that the purported controversy arose, of course, was because the British had been double-dealing on Palestine with third parties, the full details of which were as yet unknown to the Arabs (see below). In this context, the importance of the Hussein–McMahon correspondence stands out as the first international legal agreement that, through its manifestly bad faith interpretation by the British, set in motion the operation of the international rule by law in Palestine.

3.3 *1916 Sykes–Picot Agreement*

On 16 May 1916, seven months after the conclusion of the Hussein–McMahon correspondence, Britain entered into another secret treaty with France (with the assent of Tsarist Russia) that contradicted the terms of the correspondence.[40] Under the Sykes–Picot agreement, so named after its principal negotiators,[41] the Anglo-French Entente agreed, *inter alia*, that upon the fall of the Ottoman Empire in WWI they would be 'prepared to recognize and protect an independent Arab State or a Confederation of Arab States ... under the suzerainty of an Arab chief' in areas now comprising large portions of Jordan, Lebanon, Iraq, and Syria. Yet they also agreed to retain the right 'to establish such direct or indirect administration or control as they desire and as they may

---

[37] *Palestine: Memorandum by Middle East Department, Colonial Office*, para. 5, C.P. 21 (24), 12 February 1924, Secret, CAB/24/165 *as quoted in* Quigley, J. *The Statehood of Palestine* (Cambridge, 2010) at 12.

[38] Kattan, *supra* note 11 at 107–108.

[39] *Id.*, at 108.

[40] Cocks, S.F. *The Secret Treaties and Understandings* (Union of Democratic Control, 1918) at 43–48. On secret treaties in general, *see* Grosek, E. *The Secret Treaties of History* (William S. Hein, 2007).

[41] Sir Mark Sykes (1879–1919) and François Georges-Picot (1870–1951).

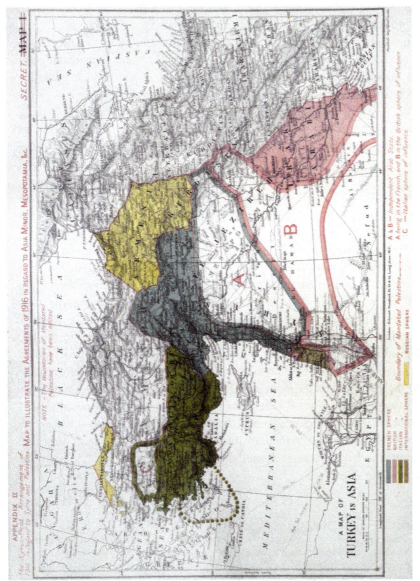

MAP III *The Sykes–Picot arrangement of 1916 in regard to Syria and Palestine. Map to illustrate the agreement of 1916 in regard to Asia Minor, Mesopotamia, and so on.*

think fit to arrange with the Arab State or confederation of Arab States'. As for Palestine, the Entente agreed that 'there shall be established an international administration, the form of which is to be decided upon after consultation with Russia, and subsequently in consultation with the other Allies, and the representatives of the Shereef of Mecca' (Map III).[42]

It would appear, therefore, that the pledge made by the British in the Hussein–McMahon correspondence as to post-war Arab independence in the Middle East had been violated. Nowhere in the correspondence was any reference made to a qualified independence under an arrangement in the nature of a suzerainty, as provided for in the Sykes–Picot agreement. Nor was it suggested that Palestine would be denied Arab independence in favour of being handed over to some form of international administration. In short, this was a classic case of late European imperial power dictating terms, and in a manner that had international legal effect without the input or knowledge of the non-European population primarily affected. As one of the many secret treaties between the great powers, the Sykes–Picot agreement carried weight under prevailing international law.[43] Its terms were drafted with the intention of setting legally opposable rights and duties as between its immediate parties, as well as in respect of those colonial subjects and territories governed by it. Again, the fact that the treaty was kept secret from these colonial subjects did not vitiate its normative force under prevailing international law. In this respect, like its predecessor in the Hussein–McMahon correspondence, the Sykes–Picot agreement was a manifestation of a rule by law that undermined the international legal position of the indigenous people of Palestine, as elsewhere in the non-European world. It was not until the Bolsheviks disclosed the existence of the secret treaties on 23 November 1917 as evidence of the 'world-wide plans of annexation' of the imperial powers that the Palestinian Arab leadership became aware of the Sykes–Picot agreement.[44] Unbeknownst to them matters would only get worse, as in that same month the British made yet another undertaking regarding Palestine, this time to the Zionists.

---

[42] Kattan, *supra* note 11 at 40–41.

[43] Cocks, *supra* note 40 at 43–48. As to the conflict between Sykes–Picot and the Hussein–McMahon correspondence, it is not clear as to whether the latter would have taken legal precedence over the former, the former being a treaty later in time and between two imperial and 'civilized' states, the latter earlier in time and between a European imperial state and the representative of a non-self-governing non-European people. This says nothing, of course, of the more important thematic issue these two agreements reveal regarding how law was used by the British to effectively rule in the Middle East.

[44] Cocks, *supra* note 40 at 11.

3.4 1917 Balfour Declaration

On 2 November 1917, the British Cabinet issued a public declaration in the form of a letter from British Foreign Secretary Arthur Balfour to Lord Lionel Walter Rothschild, a prominent Zionist, indicating, in relevant part, that:

> His Majesty's Government view with favour the establishment in Palestine of a national home for the Jewish people, and will use their best endeavours to facilitate the achievement of this object, it being clearly understood that nothing shall be done which may prejudice the civil and religious rights of existing non-Jewish communities in Palestine, or the rights and political status enjoyed by Jews in any other country.[45]

The Balfour Declaration was the result of lengthy negotiations between the British government and members of the Zionist Organization led by Chaim Weizmann and Nahum Sokolow.[46] For the Zionists, securing support from the British was both natural and vital; natural, because of the imperial and colonial legal technologies they adopted to further the movement, vital because the British were poised to take control of Palestine following WWI.[47] For the British, offering support to the Zionists represented an attempt to shore up pressing geostrategic interests, primarily ensuring greater Russian and American support in the waning war effort. Encouraged by Weizmann and others, the British believed that support for Zionism would garner the purported influence of Russian and American Jewry to pressure Petrograd and Washington to further commit to the war.[48] In addition, the Declaration was motivated by Britain's goal of resolving Europe's vexing Jewish question, as well as by the Christian Zionist fervor of some members of government, including then Prime Minister David Lloyd George, Mark Sykes, and Balfour himself.[49]

From a subaltern perspective, the Balfour Declaration stands out for three reasons. First, harkening back to Said's critique of hegemonic representations of the Palestinian people, although the Declaration concerned the political and legal future of Palestine, its drafters failed to refer to the indigenous Palestinian Arab population by name, choosing instead to designate

---

[45] Smith, *supra* note 33 at 54. The Balfour Declaration appeared in *The Times*, 9 Nov. 1917.
[46] Mallison, T. & S. *The Palestine Problem in International Law and World Order* (Longman, 1986) at 24.
[47] Kattan, *supra* note 11 at 26.
[48] Pappe, A *History*, *supra* note 30 at 67–68. *See also* Quigley, J. *The International Diplomacy of Israel's Founders* (Cambridge, 2016) at 14–16. This has led some authors to suggest that British support for Zionism was tainted with anti-Semitic stereotypes, including the mythical 'clandestine power' of the Jews. *See* Segev, T. *One Palestine Complete* (Metropolitan, 2000) at 5.
[49] Smith, *supra* note 33 at 55.

42 *The Interwar Period*

them dismissively as the 'existing non-Jewish communities'. By adopting this frame of reference in relation to a place whose population was then 92 per cent Palestinian Arab, the Declaration effectively erased Palestinian Arab existence from the record.[50] Second, although the Declaration contained an important safeguard 'that nothing shall be done which may prejudice the civil and religious rights' of the Palestinian majority, its failure to safeguard their *political* rights underscored British intent to prioritize those of the Jewish people in Palestine, despite earlier British pledges of support for Arab independence. Third, at the time the Declaration was issued, neither the British nor the Zionists actually had physical possession or legal title to Palestine. Yet, in promising Palestine to the Zionists without so much as consulting the Palestinian population, British decision-making seems to have been informed primarily by European imperial fiat, with its negative assumptions regarding the contingency of non-European legal rights. Although prevailing international law included a general principle that one could not give what one did not possess (*nemo dat quod non habet*), it is doubtful that this principle applied to the property of colonial peoples at the time.[51] Perhaps one mitigating factor was that in supporting the Jewish national home project in Palestine, the British were running up against the then-emerging right of self-determination, according to which the legitimacy of post-war rule was understood as deriving from the consent of the governed. The extent to which London was contemptuous of this emerging norm was made clear, however, when it formally incorporated the Balfour Declaration into the terms of the League of Nations mandate for Palestine, an act subsequently endorsed by the Council of the League of Nations (see below). This constituted the most vital element of the rule by law paradigm then shaping Palestine's legal subalternity in the interwar period.

[50] One is here reminded of Said's observation that language is 'a highly organized and encoded system which employs many devices' to express 'not "truth" but representations,' which are ultimately informed by the 'culture, institutions, and political ambience of the representer'. Said, E.W. *Orientalism* (Vintage, 1979) at 21, 272.

[51] Deriving from Roman law and established in English law since at least the sixteenth century (*Capel's Case* (1581), Jenk. Cent. 250), the *nemo dat* principle was recognized under international law as applying to states at the time the Balfour Declaration was issued. *See* the *Island of Palmas* case, where the principle was applied by the Permanent Court of Arbitration to oust a claim by the United States to an island that it asserted had been ceded to it by Spain in 1898, as against a competing claim to the island by the Netherlands. In finding that Spain never actually held proper title over the territory in question when it purported to transfer it to the US, Arbitrator Huber found that 'Spain could not transfer more rights than she herself possessed.' *Island of Palmas (Netherlands v. US)* (1928) 2 Reports of International Arbitral Awards 829 at 842. *See also* Crawford, J. *Brownlie's Principles of Public International Law*, 8th ed. (Oxford, 2012) at 213.

3 The Origins of Palestine's International Legal Subalternity

3.5 1920 Covenant of the League of Nations

The sacred trust of civilization codified in Article 22 of the League of Nations Covenant provided for a three-tier system of territorial administration based on the relative 'advancement' of the territory in question: the more advanced 'class A' mandates were those formerly belonging to the Ottoman empire, namely Iraq, Lebanon, Palestine, and Syria; the middle 'class B' mandates were those formerly under German control in Central Africa; whereas the least advanced 'class C' mandates were made up of South-West Africa and certain Pacific island territories. 'The essential purpose of the system', according to Anghie, 'was to protect the interests of backward people, to promote their welfare and development and to guide them toward self-government and, in certain cases, independence'.[52] In view of the abject servitude that would have been ordained under classical nineteenth-century international law upon conquest of these territories, the mere contemplation of such new forms of self-government represented a watershed. Yet they were in many ways a continuation of the imperial order, including by contemporaneous standards. Thus, writing about the workings of the PMC in 1928, Arnold McNair indicated that the mandate system 'in the course of time would create new and higher standards of colonial administration than have prevailed in the past in certain parts of the world'.[53] Likewise, the League made no secret of the fact that the PMC was itself staffed by experts in colonial administration who were mandated to bring that expertise to bear in reporting on how the mandates were to be discharged.

The Article 22 sacred trust of civilization was premised on the idea that colonial peoples in class A mandates enjoyed a right to political independence based on the principle of the consent of the governed and majority rule. This is why the Article also provided that the wishes of those peoples were to be 'a principal consideration' in the League's selection of a mandatory power. Subject to the discharge by a mandatory power of its sacred trust, such territories were to eventually enjoy full self-determination and independence. To be sure, self-determination was not yet part of the corpus of positive international law. That development would have to await the promulgation of the 1945 UN Charter and subsequent practice.[54] Nevertheless, as noted by the International Court of Justice in its 1971 *Namibia* advisory opinion, there is 'little doubt that

---

[52] Anghie, *supra* note 6 at 120.
[53] Oppenheim, *supra* note 26 at 206.
[54] Cassese, A. *Self-Determination of Peoples* (Cambridge, 1995) at 27 & 43.

44   *The Interwar Period*

the ultimate objective of the sacred trust was the self-determination and independence of the peoples concerned'.[55]

As it happens, the people concerned in Palestine – namely its overwhelming indigenous majority – made it clear that they preferred the United States to be selected as the mandatory power in line with Article 22 of the Covenant. This followed the findings of the King-Crane Commission, an American committee created at President Wilson's request to assess the postwar wishes of the inhabitants of Syria, including Palestine. In August 1919, the Commission – which admitted that it began its 'study of Zionism with minds predisposed in its favour' – recommended, *inter alia*, the 'serious modification of the extreme Zionist program for Palestine of unlimited immigration of Jews, looking finally to making Palestine distinctly a Jewish State'.[56] It noted the that '"a national home for the Jewish people" is not equivalent to making Palestine into a Jewish State; nor can the erection of such a Jewish State be accomplished without the gravest trespass upon the "civil and religious rights of existing non-Jewish communities in Palestine"'.[57] Indeed, the commissioners made a point of noting that '[n]o British officer' they consulted 'believed that the Zionist program could be carried out except by force of arms'.[58] In light of the Wilsonian principle that post-WWI territorial settlements needed to be based upon the 'free acceptance of that settlement by the people immediately concerned and not upon the basis of the material interest or advantage of any other nation or people which may desire a different settlement for the sake of its own exterior influence or mastery', the Commission observed that the wishes of Palestine's population, 90 per cent of whom were 'emphatically against' the Zionist programme, had to prevail.[59]

This conclusion of the King-Crane Commission was particularly important for its exaltation of the principle of democratic and majority rule at a time when the hegemonic prerogatives of late-European empire, though on the wane, were still prevalent and given force in international legal instruments. Because of the US commitment to these principles and the sheer fact of an approximately 90 per cent majority Arab population, the Zionists were adamantly against the US from becoming the mandatory and in favour

---

[55] *Legal Consequences for States of the Continued Presence of South Africa in Namibia (South-West Africa) Notwithstanding Security Council Resolution 276 (1970)*, Advisory Opinion, 21 June 1971, ICJ Reports 1971, 16, at para. 53.

[56] King-Crane Commission Report, 28 August 1919, I. The Report Upon Syria, III. Recommendations, Zionism, at: www.hri.org/docs/king-crane/syria-recomm.html.

[57] *Id.*

[58] *Id.*

[59] *Id.*

3 The Origins of Palestine's International Legal Subalternity 45

of the British doing so. In the event, despite the findings of the King-Crane Commission, the British were appointed by the League as mandatory against the express wishes of the indigenous population paving the way for further crystallization of Palestine's international legal subalternity.[60]

3.6 1922–1947 Mandate for Palestine

Despite the use of the standard of civilization to codify the contingency of subaltern communities in the League of Nations Covenant, the mandate system did eventually facilitate the emergence of several sovereign independent states based on majority rule and the consent of the governed. This included Lebanon, Iraq, Jordan, and Syria.[61] In Palestine, however, the mandate system singularly had the result of undermining – in legal terms – indigenous independence and majority rule, ostensibly the very object and purpose of the system itself.

This was particularly evident in the text of the mandate for Palestine, which was negotiated between the Zionist Organization and the British in 1920, again without the participation of the Palestinian Arabs. Unsurprisingly, its terms were openly committed to the Zionist programme at the expense of the indigenous population. Following its adoption by the Supreme Council of the Principal Allied Powers at San Remo on 25 April 1920,[62] and then by the Council of the League of Nations on 24 July 2022,[63] the Balfour Declaration was expressly incorporated into the preamble of the mandate for Palestine indicating that 'recognition has thereby been given to the historical connection to the Jewish people with Palestine and to the grounds for reconstituting their national home in that country'.[64] To this end, the mandatory was to be furnished with 'full powers of legislation and of administration',[65] without needing to come to agreement with the indigenous authorities or take into account their rights, interests, and wishes as was provided for in other mandates, for instance the French Mandate for Syria and Lebanon.[66] Instead, the Palestine mandate provided that the 'Mandatory shall be responsible for

---

[60] Quigley, *supra* note 48 at 24–25.

[61] Anghie, *supra* note 6 at 190–191.

[62] Grief, *supra* note 11 at 18.

[63] Akram, S. 'Palestinian Nationality and 'Jewish' Nationality: From the Lausanne Treaty to Today' in Farsakh, L. ed., *Rethinking Statehood in Palestine* (University of California Press, 2021) at 195.

[64] *British Mandate for Palestine*, 24 July 1922 (1922) League of Nations Official Journal 1007, preamble ['British Mandate for Palestine'].

[65] *Id.*, art. 1.

[66] *French Mandate for Syria and The Lebanon*, 24 July 1922 (1922) League of Nations Official Journal 1013, art. 1.

placing the country under such political, administrative, and economic conditions as will secure the establishment of the Jewish national home'.[67] To secure this, it indicated that 'an appropriate Jewish Agency shall be recognized as a public body for the purpose of advising and co-operating with the Administration of Palestine in such economic, social and other matters as may affect the establishment of the Jewish national home' and named the Zionist Organization as that body.[68] Finally, the mandate provided that the Administration of Palestine 'shall facilitate Jewish immigration' and 'shall encourage, in co-operation with the Jewish Agency ... close settlement by Jews on the land'.[69] In contrast, nowhere in all of its 2,757 words does the term 'Arab' appear, preferring instead the jaundiced 'existing non-Jewish communities' (one reference) or 'other sections of the population' (one reference).[70] Likewise, the word 'Palestinian' appears only once, though in relation to the Mandatory's obligation to 'facilitate the acquisition of Palestinian citizenship by Jews who take up their permanent residence in Palestine'.[71]

Having been adopted by the Council of the League of Nations, the rights, duties, and obligations enshrined within the mandate were of a qualitatively different international legal character than those previously enshrined in the bilateral and secret treaties described above. Although authors have debated the international legal character of those arrangements extensively,[72] there is little question that with one stroke of the pen the mandate for Palestine provided the Zionists with something that had hitherto eluded them, namely recognition of: (1) the Jewish people; (2) its historical connection with the land of Palestine; and (3) its political representative in the form of the Zionist Organization. In this way, the mandate not only fulfilled the key strategic goal of the first Zionist Congress of 1897 'to create for the Jewish people a home in Palestine secured by public law',[73] but it also helped mitigate the subalternity of European Jewry *vis á vis* their own imperial benefactors.

All of this was done when the approximately 90 per cent Palestinian Arab majority population made no secret of its opposition to foreign control of their country, including through Zionist colonization, and their expectation that

---

[67] British Mandate for Palestine, *supra* note 64, art. 2.

[68] *Id.*, art. 4.

[69] *Id.*, art. 6.

[70] *Id.*, preamble & art. 6.

[71] *Id.*, art. 7.

[72] *See, e.g.*, Mallison, *supra* note 46 at 18–78; Cattan, H. *The Palestine Question* (Saqi, 2000) at 10–16; Kattan, *supra* note 11 at 58–59, 98–116; Strawson, *supra* note 24 at 36–37; Quigley, *supra* note 48 at 10–15.

[73] Kattan, *supra* note 11 at 21.

3 The Origins of Palestine's International Legal Subalternity   47

Arab independence would be realized as per British wartime pledges and Article 22 of the League of Nations Covenant.[74] Notwithstanding the clear contradiction between these pledges, the terms of Article 22 and the terms of the mandate for Palestine, the latter was made to prevail through sheer force of British arms and the suppression of indigenous forms of political representation and governance. As noted by Rashid Khalidi, '[i]t could not have been otherwise, since no indigenous majority would have voluntarily ceded its country to a settler minority'.[75] In this light, the mandate for Palestine thematically stands out as yet another example of the misrepresentation and effacement of the lived reality of Palestine and its people, this time embedded in an international legal instrument that openly violated the principles of self-determination, rule by consent, and the democratic idea of majority rule. It was for these reasons that the British House of Lords symbolically voted to reject the terms of the mandate for Palestine on 21 June 1922 in a non-binding motion.[76] Tellingly, it was also something not lost on those responsible for imposing this international rule by law on Palestine. In a memorandum written to Prime Minister Lloyd George on 19 February 1919, Balfour himself admitted that:

> [t]he weak point in our position, of course, is that in the case of Palestine we deliberately and rightly decline to accept the principle of self-determination. If the present inhabitants were consulted they would unquestionably give an anti-Jewish verdict. Our justification for our policy is that we regard Palestine as being absolutely exceptional.[77]

In a subsequent memorandum to Lord Curzon dated 11 August 1919, Balfour noted that:

> [t]he contradiction between the letter of the Covenant and the policy of the Allies is even more flagrant in the case of the 'independent nation' of Palestine than in the 'independent nation' of Syria. For in Palestine we do not propose even to go through the form of consulting the wishes of the present inhabitants of the country.... The four great powers are committed to Zionism and Zionism, be it right or wrong, good or bad, is rooted in age-long tradition, in present needs, in future hopes, of far profounder import than the desire and prejudices of the 700,000 Arabs who now inhabit that ancient land.[78]

It is precisely this disregard for Palestine's indigenous people that enabled Britain to legislate Palestine's legal subalternity into international law through

[74] *Id.*, at 43–44.
[75] Khalidi, R. *The Iron Cage* (Beacon, 2007) at 40.
[76] *Id.*, at 75. *See also* Cattan, *supra* note 72 at 16.
[77] Kattan, *supra* note 11 at 121.
[78] *Id.*, at 123.

48   *The Interwar Period*

the mandate. Positivist international legal historiography of Israel/Palestine uncritically employs this moment as its starting point, unwitting testament to the hegemonic use of international law in suppressing the presence, history, and agency of Palestine's indigenous population. By virtue of the mandate, Palestinians are said to have possessed no more than a right to be a 'protected minority' with 'only civil and religious rights' within a Jewish State.[79] Some even argue that it was the Jewish people who were designated the ultimate 'national beneficiary' of the sacred trust of Article 22, despite comprising only approximately 10 per cent of the population.[80] In this regard, the mandate privileged, in legal terms, the political rights of a people, the vast majority of whom had never set foot in the country over that of the country's indigenous inhabitants. The effect was 'that an almost indeterminate number of dispersed people had a legal presence in mandate Palestine before they had a physical one'.[81] At the same time, the indigenous population of the country had, at best, a rarified legal presence as an unrecognized group with no national or political rights whatsoever. As noted in 1925 by Leopoldo Palacios, the Spanish member of the PMC, with the passage of the mandate 'Zionism had the law entirely in its favour'.[82] Viewed through a subaltern lens, this was the epitome of the international rule by law.

Over the course of the mandate's twenty-five-year duration, the British facilitated the establishment of the Jewish national home in Palestine in furtherance of the international rule by law inherent its provisions. All the while, the indigenous Palestinians refused to recognize the mandate's legitimacy, arguing before both the Council of the League and the PMC that it violated the terms of Britain's wartime pledges and its sacred trust under Article 22 of the League of Nations Covenant.[83] The new international law introduced through the mandate could not be legitimate, they said, as it did not emerge from the will of the people. If self-determination in Palestine was envisioned in Wilson's new post-imperial order, that right must surely have resided with the indigenous majority. These arguments ultimately proved in vain as late European empire prevailed over Wilsonian principles.

---

[79] Dinstein, Y. 'The International Legal Dimensions of the Arab-Israeli conflict' in Kellermann, A. et al., eds., *Israel Among the Nations* (Kluwer, 1998) at 140. *See also*, Grief, *supra* note 11 at 18–44; and Strawson, *supra* note 24 at 2.

[80] Grief, *supra* note 11 at 35, argues that '[t]he dual or joint application of the Balfour Declaration with Article 22 conclusively meant that Palestine was reserved for the Jewish People as a whole, not merely for the approximate 60,000 Jews living in Palestine at the end of the Great War'.

[81] Wheatley, N. 'Mandatory Interpretation: Legal Hermeneutics and the New International Order in Arab and Jewish Petitions to the League of Nations' (2015) 227 *Past and Present* 205 at 215.

[82] *Id.*, at 216.

[83] *Id.*, at 216–217, 220–225.

3 The Origins of Palestine's International Legal Subalternity   49

During this time, a Jewish *imperium in imperio* was formed under the tutelage of Britain. As noted by Tom Segev, between 1922 and 1948, the British facilitated the growth of the Jewish population of Palestine more than tenfold and promoted independent Zionist land purchase, agricultural development, and the establishment of industries and banks. Hundreds of new colonial settlements were established, including a number of towns. An independent Jewish labour organization, school system, and military were developed. This was in addition to the development of in-country Zionist political leadership and institutions, all of which were actively invited to coordinate and work within the British Administration to further develop the Jewish national home.[84] Indeed, Zionists held the highest posts in the Administration, beginning with Herbert Samuel, the first High Commissioner.[85]

Importantly, the colonial nature of the whole project remained a matter of public record. A particularly poignant articulation of this appears in July 1947, just months before the end of the twenty-five-year mandate. Addressing the UN Special Committee on Palestine, Chaim Weizmann, a founder of the Jewish Agency, gave evidence on the ostensible difficulties presented to Zionist colonization during the mandate period, considering the principles underpinning the League:

> Other peoples have colonized great countries, rich countries. They found when they entered there backward populations.... In olden times, such backward countries were built up by charter companies. All of you will remember the East Indian Charter Company. But charter companies were hard to fashion in 1918, the first quarter of the twentieth century. The Wilsonian conception of the world certainly would not have allowed a charter company. Therefore, we had to create a substitute. This substitute was the Jewish Agency which had the function of a charter company, which had the function of a body which would conduct the colonization, immigration, improvement of the land, and do all the work which a government usually does, without really being a government. We had all the difficulties of a government and none of its advantages. The Jewish Agency was given a special position in the Mandate. It was not much of a privilege; *it was a great burden* [emphasis added].[86]

[84] Segev, *supra* note 48 at 5.
[85] Smith, *supra* note 33 at 71. *See also* evidence given on 16 June 1947 to UNSCOP by Sir Henry Gurney, Chief Secretary of the Palestine Government, UNSCOP, Verbatim Record of the Sixth Meeting, A/AC.13/SR.6/Rev.1, 23 June 1947.
[86] UNSCOP, Report to the General Assembly, 2nd Sess, Vol. III, Annex A, Oral Evidence Presented at Public Meetings, A/364 Add. 2, at 75–76, 9 September 1947.

50   *The Interwar Period*

In this most candid Kiplingesque account of the Jewish elder statesman, the unique form of imperial administration through the League of Nations mandate system was well represented. Despite his misgivings about having to circumvent the 'Wilsonian conception of the world', there is no gainsaying that the League structures did indeed allow such a workaround. In this sense, the colonizing efforts of two generations of European Jews in Palestine were not only the product of a highly motivated group of people committed to undertaking the hard material tasks involved in settling what Herzl called an 'old-new' land. They were also the product of a specific non-material legal support aimed at their facilitation, namely the administrative and quasi-governmental structures created by imperial Britain through the League of Nations and ratified under an old-new international legal regime in service of the Jewish national home. At bottom, the settler-colonial transformation of Palestine during the mandate period could not have happened but for the operation of the international rule by law as was codified in the British Mandate for Palestine.

Given the variables at play, tumult was inevitable. Arab-Jewish riots rooted in Palestinian Arab frustration with the structural violence of ongoing Zionist colonization in 1920, '21, '29, and '36 erupted. This was followed by the Great Arab Revolt of 1936–1939, violently suppressed by the British resulting in the killing, wounding, imprisonment, or exile of over 10 per cent of the Palestinian Arab male population and the decimation of the Palestinian political elite heading into WWII. By the end of the war, as news emerged of the horrors of the Holocaust in Europe, tensions between the British and armed reactionary Zionists who demanded an immediate end to the mandate and unrestricted Jewish immigration emerged. To this were added increased acts of inter-communal violence that compounded the situation. Against the exhaustion of the war and the quickening retreat of the Empire globally, Britain chose to hand the matter over to the newly formed UN.[87]

4 CONCLUSION

From the above, it is possible to locate the origins of Palestine's legal subalternity in British secret treaty-making and diplomacy between 1915 and 1947, with particular emphasis on the League of Nations mandate period. This condition was a product of a rule by law that not only remained the

---

[87] UNSCOP, Report to the General Assembly, 2nd Sess, Vol. II, Annex I, A/364 Add. 1, supplement 11, at 1, 9 September 1947.

4 Conclusion

ordering principle of the world at a time when European imperial powers were ostensibly on the decline, but was actually institutionalized and internationalized in the conventional law of the League of Nations by those selfsame powers. By legally privileging the Zionist movement's Jewish national home project over the previously assured political rights of the majority Arab population, Palestine's legal subalternity became embedded in the interwar international legal order through the terms of the British Mandate. The result was that Palestine's indigenous Arab population had become disenfranchised through the operation of prevailing Eurocentric international law.

As this book proceeds from a view of the international order as one rooted in imperial Europe's employment of international law to regulate its encounter with the colonial world, one can better understand the international rule by law nature that characterized Palestine's ordeal in the interwar period. Indeed, the international rule by law was both a description of what was happening to the Palestinian people at the time, but also a prognostication of what was to come. Although the 1945 establishment of the UN has been presented as a break from the European imperial past through the emergence of a truly universal international rule of law, its management of the question of Palestine as inherited from the British demonstrates that it was heavily influenced by the old order from the start. As will be seen, this manifested itself through the reification of Palestine's legal subalternity within the UN, beginning with General Assembly resolution 181(II).

3

1947: The UN Plan of Partition for Palestine

1 INTRODUCTION

This chapter focuses on United Nations (UN) General Assembly resolution 181(II) of 29 November 1947, through which the partition of mandate Palestine into a Jewish State and an Arab State was recommended. The main claim is that the resolution was more an expression of a continued international rule by law inherited from the interwar period than an espousal of the Charter-based international rule of law. As such, it helped reify Palestine's international legal subalternity in the newly formed UN system. To this end, it undertakes a legal analysis of resolution 181(II) with specific reference to the verbatim and summary records of the United Nations Special Committee on Palestine (UNSCOP) whose September 1947 report to the General Assembly formed the basis of both the resolution's text and its underlying rationale. Contrary to the traditional international legal historiography, this chapter posits that the resolution was neither procedurally *ultra vires* the General Assembly, nor was it substantively consistent with prevailing international law as regards the self-determination of peoples. Rather than being governed by the objective application of international law, the resolution was driven by distinctly European political goals and condescending attitudes that privileged European interests over the prevailing requirements of international law. The result was to legislate into UN law the two-state framework as the legal cornerstone of the Organization's position on Palestine against the wishes of the country's indigenous Palestinian majority. For them, resolution 181(II) was the opening act of disenfranchisement and contingency in the UN that continues to the present day.

The remainder of this chapter is divided into four parts. It begins by briefly setting out the UN's role as the ostensible standard-bearer of the international rule of law in the post-World War II (WWII) era. It then juxtaposes this against

52

2 *The UN as the Guardian of International Law*   53

the UN as a site of continued rule by law, demonstrated through an analysis of the terms of resolution 181(II). An examination of the UNSCOP records and report then follows to uncover the factors that went into the production of the rule by law legislated in resolution 181(II). It then closes with discussion of the practical consequences of the resolution through a subaltern Palestinian lens.

2 THE UN AS THE GUARDIAN OF INTERNATIONAL LAW

Following WWII, the founders of the UN drew many lessons from the failures of the League of Nations. Among the most important was the need to ensure the universality of the new organization. This manifested itself in two significant and related ways, both ultimately facilitating the emergence of the UN as the apparent guardian of the international rule of law in the contemporary period.

First was the introduction of the principle of universality in the UN's *membership*. Both the League and the UN were founded by victorious great/ imperial powers following a world war. Both thereby excluded from original membership a majority of the colonized world and the defeated powers. Yet the UN's conditions for acquired membership were made to be far less stringent than the League's. Indeed, with the exception of the period between 1946 and 1955, these conditions have largely been a procedural formality as a matter of practice.[1] With the exception of a handful of cases, including the membership of Palestine (see Chapter 6), this more liberal approach to joining the UN has resulted in the emergence of the Organization as the most globalized intergovernmental and multilateral institution ever.

Second, building on its universality of membership, the UN's commitment to develop and adhere to *international law* assumed a greater import than ever existed with the League. Although the League of Nations Covenant provided that 'the firm establishment of the understandings of international law' was to be a means through which international peace and security would be achieved, its drafters buried this lofty aspiration in its preamble.[2] In contrast, the maintenance of international peace and security 'in conformity' with international law was codified as an explicit purpose of the UN in its Charter.[3] Accordingly, the commitment of the UN to international

---

[1] Simma, B. ed. *The Charter of the United Nations: A Commentary*, 2nd ed., Vol. II (Oxford, 2002) at 180.

[2] *Covenant of the League of Nations*, 28 June 1919, 112 BFSP 13, preamble ['League of Nations Covenant'].

[3] *Charter of the United Nations*, 24 October 1945, TS 993, art. 1(1) ['UN Charter'].

54   *1947: The UN Plan of Partition for Palestine*

law and its progressive development was, on its face, more apparent. This is demonstrated by various other operative provisions of the UN Charter and related practice.

For example, the regime governing the use of force is far more restrictive under the UN Charter than it was under the League of Nations Covenant, with the Charter imposing a general prohibition on its 'threat or use' with two relatively specific exceptions, whereas the Covenant imposed unclear general limits on war without any comparable proscription of it.[4] Likewise, the principle of the sovereign equality of states finds express recognition in both the Charter and relevant binding resolutions of its political organs, whereas the Covenant was wholly silent on the issue.[5] Moreover, the Charter regime governing conflicts of law is far more restrictive than it was under the Covenant, with the Charter assuming quasi-constitutional status in the international sphere.[6] Finally, the role of the UN in the affirmation and development of customary international law through its principal organs is unprecedented. For instance, the resolutions of the now 193-member strong General Assembly can offer unique evidence of state practice and *opinio juris*.[7] Likewise, through the International Law Commission, the General Assembly facilitates 'the progressive development of international law and its codification'.[8] This, of course, is in addition to the authority of the Security Council to issue legally binding decisions on Members in accordance with the Charter[9] and the mandate of the International Court of Justice (ICJ) to exercise compulsory and advisory jurisdiction on legal questions put before it.[10]

In a very real sense, therefore, the UN can lay rightful claim to being the guardian of the primacy of the international rule of law in the post-WWII order in ways that its predecessor never was. Yet when examined from a subaltern perspective, is it possible to arrive at a different conclusion? Might there be a continuity in the maintenance of the international rule by law as an organizing principle from the interwar through the post-war years, now

---

[4] UN Charter, *id.*, arts. 2(4), 39–51; League of Nations Covenant, *supra* note 2, arts. 10–16.

[5] UN Charter, *id.*, art. 2(1); Declaration on Principles of International Law concerning Friendly Relations and Co-operation among States in accordance with the Charter of the United Nations, A/RES/2625(XXV), 24 October 1970; League of Nations Covenant, *supra* note 2, arts. 3, 4.

[6] UN Charter *supra* note 3, art. 103; League of Nations Covenant, *supra* note 2, art. 20. *See also* Simma, *supra* note 1 at 2110–2113.

[7] Higgins, R. *The Development of International Law Through the Political Organs of the United Nations* (Oxford, 1963) at 1–10.

[8] UN Charter, *supra* note 3, art. 13(1)(a).

[9] *Id.*, art. 25.

[10] *Statute of the International Court of Justice*, 33 UNTS 933, 26 June 1945, art. 38(1) ['ICJ Statute'].

3 Resolution 181(II) and the International Rule by Law

manifest in the work of the UN? To the extent that the UN Charter codified inequitable distributions of power as between the permanent five and the rest of the membership of the Organization, for example, this seems self-evident. But has the UN been complicit in the maintenance of the international rule by law in even greater measure than that? And if so, how might its proposed partition of Palestine in 1947, with its resultant reification of Palestinian legal subalternity, help us increase our understanding of this?

3 RESOLUTION 181(II) AND THE INTERNATIONAL RULE BY LAW

3.1 The UN Charter, Self-Determination, and the Role of the UN in the Mandate for Palestine

Legal texts reflect the values of the time in which they are produced.[11] The UN Charter is no different. In line with the Organization's ostensible commitment to international law, this included a commitment to develop friendly relations among nations based on respect for the principle of self-determination of peoples.[12]

During the interwar period, self-determination was not a part of the corpus of international law, but was rather a political principle rooted in Wilsonian precepts for an anti-imperial order.[13] Though not expressly referred to in the League of Nations Covenant, self-determination did, however, inform the sacred trust of civilization underpinning the mandate system.[14] By 1945, self-determination of peoples had developed sufficiently to be expressly included in the UN Charter as both a purpose of the Organization and a principle guiding its action.[15] Nevertheless, owing to the continued influence of the European imperial powers, self-determination remained undefined in the text of the Charter. It wasn't until the decolonization period that Member

---

[11] Strawson, J. *Partitioning Palestine* (Pluto, 2010) at 5.

[12] UN Charter, *supra* note 3, art. 1(2).

[13] One of the four ends for which Wilson asserted the Allies fought World War I (WWI) – namely, that '[t]he settlement of every question, whether of territory, of sovereignty, of economic arrangement or of political relations' should be built 'upon the basis of the free acceptance of that settlement by the people immediately concerned, and not upon the basis of the material interest or advantage of any other nation or people which may desire a different settlement for the sake of its own exterior influence or mastery' – offered a prescient articulation of the self-determination principle in embryonic form at the time. UNSCOP, Report to the General Assembly, 2nd Sess, Vol. II, A/364 Add. 1, supplement 11, 9 September 1947, at 24 ['UNSCOP Report, Vol. II'].

[14] Cassese, A. *Self-Determination of Peoples* (Cambridge, 1995) at 43.

[15] UN Charter, *supra* note 3, arts. 1(2), 55.

56   *1947: The UN Plan of Partition for Palestine*

States were able to arrive at a commonly agreed definition of the right, codified in common Article 1 of the 1966 international human rights covenants.[16] Because of the lack of a clear definition of the content and meaning of self-determination in 1945, a debate exists as to whether a *de jure* right to self-determination of peoples *per se* had emerged by that time or if it only emerged with the commencement of decolonization a decade later.[17] Irrespective of where one stands in this debate, however, there is little doubt that by 1947 – the year the General Assembly recommended the partition of Palestine – the general content of self-determination of peoples was sufficiently established under international law *as regards class A mandated territories*. On this basis, the principle required the immediate, or at the very least, promptly realized, political independence of such territories based on the precepts of consent of the governed and majority rule. This follows from the fact that the political independence of class A mandates was provisionally recognized as far back as 1920 by the League of Nations, subject only to the rendering of administrative advice and assistance by the Mandatory under a 'sacred trust' until such time as these nations were 'able to stand alone' (*see* Chapter 2). According to the ICJ, the ultimate objective of this sacred trust was the self-determination and independence of the peoples concerned.[18] As a matter of state practice, by 1947, all class A mandates, except Palestine, had achieved full independence (Iraq, 1932; Lebanon, 1943; Syria, 1945; Transjordan, 1946). Finally, and as will be explored below, in 1947, UNSCOP itself unanimously determined that because 'the peoples of Palestine are sufficiently advanced to govern themselves independently', political 'independence shall be granted in Palestine at the earliest practicable date'.[19]

---

[16] *International Covenant on Civil and Political Rights*, 16 December 1966, 999 UNTS 171, art. 1; *International Covenant on Economic, Social and Cultural Rights*, 16 December 1966, 993 UNTS 3, art. 1.

[17] For the argument that self-determination did not exist as a legal principle in 1945, *see* Hannum, H. *Autonomy, Sovereignty and Self-Determination* (Pennsylvania, 1990) at 33; and Weller, M. & Metzger, B. *Settling Self-Determination Disputes* (Martinus Nijhoff, 2008) at 44. For the position that it did, *see* Simma, *supra* note 1 at 49; and Cassese, *supra* note 14 at 43.

[18] *Legal Consequences for States of the Continued Presence of South Africa in Namibia (South-West Africa) Notwithstanding Security Council Resolution 276 (1970)*, Advisory Opinion, 21 June 1971, ICJ Reports 1971, 19, at para. 53 ['Namibia'].

[19] UNSCOP, Report to the General Assembly, 2nd Sess, Vol I, A/364, supplement 11 at 43, 3 September 1947 ['UNSCOP Report, Vol. I']. Although UNSCOP's use of the plural (*i.e.* 'peoples') may be read as suggesting that both the Jewish and Arab people of Palestine possessed the legal right to independence in separate states, it should be recalled that a minority of UNSCOP also recommended the establishment of a unitary federal state as a means through which Palestine's 'peoples' could exercise self-determination. *See* text accompanying *infra* notes 164–167.

3 *Resolution 181(II) and the International Rule by Law* 57

If self-determination of peoples required the political independence of Palestine as a class A mandate based on the principles of consent of the governed and majority rule, the question arises: what actions were required of the UN in respect of this independence under prevailing international law in 1947? Answering this matters because it sets the parameters of what the international rule of law prescribed at the time, allowing us to test whether the terms of resolution 181(II) were consistent with it and, if not, why that resolution amounted to a continuation of the international rule by law. In short, a review of the text of both the League of Nations Covenant and the UN Charter, as well as relevant state practice, suggests that prevailing international law admitted of only two possibilities for Palestine in 1947: (1) immediate independence in accordance with the freely expressed wishes of Palestine's inhabitants, whatever its eventual constitutional structure; or (2) temporary delay of independence through conversion into a UN trusteeship under the Charter.[20]

As to immediate independence, it will be recalled that, dismissive of Palestinian Arab rights though it was, the terms of the mandate for Palestine only required the establishment in Palestine of a Jewish national home, *not* a Jewish State. According to a 1939 White Paper, the UK itself acknowledged that the Jewish national home had been established in Palestine by that time. This would suggest that it had discharged its obligation under the terms of the mandate *vis-à-vis* the Zionists and could proceed with granting the country full independence in accordance with Article 22 of the League of Nations Covenant. The problem was that the minority Zionists insisted on transforming all of Palestine into a Jewish State against the wishes of the indigenous Palestinian majority who had long argued for a unitary, democratic, and non-denominational state. This is, in part, what lead the British to conclude that the mandate was unworkable and should be handed over to the UN. In a very practical sense, the issue before the UN was how to deal with the impediment that Palestinian demography placed in the way of the establishment of what the Zionists intended to be a Jewish State.

Short of immediate independence in a unitary democratic state, the only other option was conversion of Palestine into a UN trusteeship. Under Chapter XII of the Charter, the International Trusteeship System was established for the administration and supervision, *inter alia*, of mandated territories that had yet to achieve independence.[21] Under Article 76, one of the basic objectives of the trusteeship system was 'to promote' the 'progressive development toward self-government or independence as may be appropriate

---

[20] Quigley, J. *The Statehood of Palestine* (Cambridge, 2010) at 88.
[21] UN Charter, *supra* note 3, art. 77(1)(a).

58   *1947: The UN Plan of Partition for Palestine*

to the particular circumstances of each territory and its peoples *and the freely expressed wishes of the peoples concerned'*.[22] As between self-government and independence, Palestine's status as a class A mandate rendered the former nugatory and latter obligatory. Indeed, as a matter of state practice, it was only class B and C mandates – neither of which enjoyed a provisionally recognized right of independence under the League of Nations Covenant – that were transformed into trust territories under the Charter.[23] Neither was the fact that the League of Nations was now defunct a bar to the requirement and inevitability of independence. On the contrary, the final resolution of the League of Nations of 18 April 1946 recognized 'that, on the termination of the League's existence, its functions with respect to the mandated territories will come to an end, but note[ed] that chapters XI, XII and XIII of the Charter of the United Nations embody principles corresponding to those declared in Article 22 of the Covenant of the League'.[24] It further noted 'the expressed intentions of the Members of the League now administering territories under mandate to continue to administer them for the well-being and development of the peoples concerned in accordance with the obligations contained in the respective Mandates, until other arrangements have been agreed between the United Nations and the respective mandatory Powers'.[25]

According to Hersch Lauterpacht, this was understood as having the effect of maintaining 'the general principles and the regime of the Mandatory system', pending conclusion of new arrangements under the UN Charter.[26] As subsequently affirmed by the ICJ in *Namibia*, '[t]o the question whether the continuance of a mandate was inseparably linked with the existence of the League, the answer must be that an institution established for the fulfilment of a sacred trust cannot be presumed to lapse before the achievement of its purpose'.[27] As a matter of positive UN law, this was ensured by the safeguarding clause in Article 80 of the Charter. That provided, in relevant part, that 'nothing shall be construed in or of itself to alter in any manner the rights whatsoever of any states or any peoples or the terms of existing international instruments to which Members of the United Nations may respectively be parties'.[28] This meant that

---

[22]   *Id.*, art. 76(b) [emphasis added].
[23]   Simma, *supra* note 1 at 1104–1105.
[24]   *Resolutions Adopted on the Reports of the First Committee, Mandates*, 18 April 1946 (1946) League of Nations Official Journal, Spec. Supp. 194 at 278.
[25]   *Id.*, at 279.
[26]   Lauterpacht, E. ed. *International Law: Being the Collected Papers of Hersch Lauterpacht*, Vol. 3, *The Law of Peace, Parts II-IV* (Cambridge, 1977) at 509.
[27]   *Namibia*, *supra* note 18 at para. 55.
[28]   UN Charter, *supra* note 3, art. 80(1).

3 *Resolution 181(II) and the International Rule by Law* 59

Article 22 of the League of Nations Covenant along with the terms of the mandate remained in effect. As noted by the ICJ in *Namibia*, a 'striking feature' of Article 80 of the Charter was 'the stipulation in favour of the preservation of the rights of "any peoples", thus clearly including the inhabitants of the mandated territories *and, in particular, their indigenous populations*'.[29] Thus, with the Jewish national home having been established in 1939, the only international legal requirement that remained unfulfilled was the realization of the political independence of the territory of Palestine in accordance with the wishes of its majority indigenous population.

In sum, the Charter regime included a commitment to the principle of 'consent of the governed' that underpinned Wilson's world-vision. On the one hand, if self-determination of peoples was sufficiently established in 1947 to justify application to the Palestinian people, the country would have to follow the other class A mandates by having its independence recognized and being admitted to membership in the UN if it so wished. On the other hand, if self-determination of peoples lacked sufficient legal force under the Charter to give immediate effect to Palestinian independence, that problem was alleviated by the fact that eventual realization of independence was already established under a sacred trust that survived the League through the trusteeship system. In either case, as a matter of prevailing international law, the freely expressed wishes of the peoples concerned were to be determinative.

Given that Palestine's indigenous population was both in the majority and adamantly against partition, political independence invariably meant the establishment of the country as a unitary democratic state, the Jewish national home having already been established. As will be demonstrated, all of this ran up against prevailing European political winds. This included the imperative presented by a predominately Western and European bloc of states for the need to find a durable solution to Europe's vexing Jewish question, epitomized at the time by the plight of Jewish displaced persons in post-war Europe and revelations of the horrors of the Holocaust. By recommending partition, UN General Assembly resolution 181(II) introduced a rupture in the purportedly new international legal order and challenged the primacy of the international rule of law as affirmed in its own Charter. As will be demonstrated, this rupture reified Palestine's legal subalternity in the UN system. By going beyond the terms of what prevailing international law required by recommending the establishment of a Jewish State through partition of the country, the international legal and political goalposts fundamentally shifted for the indigenous subaltern majority, with effects that last to this day.

---

[29] *Namibia, supra* note 18 at para. 59 [emphasis added].

3.2 Resolution 181(II): Its Terms

On 3 September 1947, UNSCOP submitted its report to the General Assembly, in which the majority of the special committee favoured a plan of partition with economic union, whereas the minority favoured a unitary federal state plan.[30] The UNSCOP report was debated in the General Assembly between 25 September and 29 November 1947, first by an ad hoc committee of all members of the General Assembly ('ad hoc committee'), which set up two sub-committees to study a slightly adjusted majority plan and a unitary state plan respectively, and then in full plenary session. This resulted in the passage of General Assembly resolution 181(II) on 29 November 1947 by a vote of 33 to 13, with 10 abstentions.[31]

Resolution 181(II) provided for the partition of Palestine into an Arab State and a Jewish State in economic union, with the city of Jerusalem and its environs established as a *corpus separatum* to be administered by the UN Trusteeship Council (see Map IV). Under the plan, both states were required to adopt democratic constitutions, establish government on the basis of universal suffrage, and guarantee to all persons equality before the law. Aside from the act of partition itself, the extent to which the resolution reified Palestinian legal subalternity is best illustrated in the specific details of the plan as regards the related issues of both the territorial boundaries and the demographic composition of each of the proposed states.

As to territorial boundaries, under the plan, the Jewish State was allotted approximately 57 per cent of the total area of Palestine,[32] despite the Jewish population comprising only 33 per cent of the country (see Maps IV & V).[33] In addition, according to British records relied upon by the ad hoc committee, the Jewish population possessed registered ownership of only 5.6 per cent of Palestine[34] and was eclipsed by the Arabs in land ownership

---

[30] The majority was Canada, Czechoslovakia, Guatemala, the Netherlands, Peru, Sweden, and Uruguay. The minority was India, Iran, and Yugoslavia. UNSCOP Report, Vol. I, *supra* note 19 at 47–64. Australia abstained from voting on the respective plans. *See* UNSCOP Report, Vol. II, *supra* note 13 at 23.

[31] A/RES/181(II), 29 November 1947 ['A/RES/181(II)'].

[32] Kattan, V. *From Coexistence to Conquest* (Pluto, 2009) at 152.

[33] The total population of Palestine was 1,846,000 of which 1,203,000 were Arabs and 608,000 were Jews. *See* UNSCOP Report, Vol. I, *supra* note 19 at 11.

[34] In 1945, of the 26,323,023 million dunam landmass of Palestine, the Jews owned only 1,491,699 million dunams to the Arab's 12,574,774 dunams (48 per cent), the remainder being publicly owned land. Ad Hoc Committee on the Palestinian Question, Summary Records of Meetings 25 September – 25 November 1947, UN GAOR, 2nd Sess, Annex 25, Report of Sub-Committee 2, A/AC.14/32 and Add.1 at 292–293 & Appendix VI ['UN Ad Hoc Committee, Report of Sub-Committee 2'].

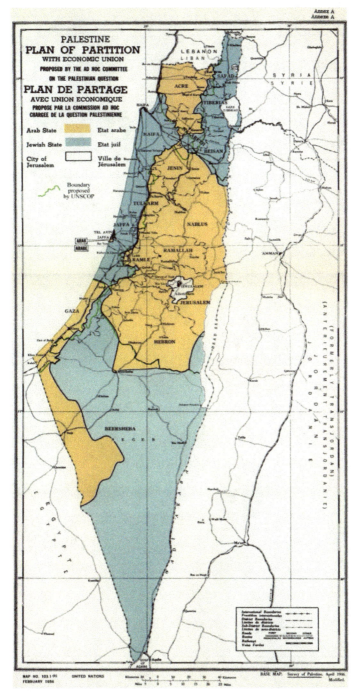

MAP IV *Palestine, plan of partition with economic union proposed by the Ad Hoc Committee on the Palestinian Question, Map No. 103.1(b), United Nations, February 1956.*

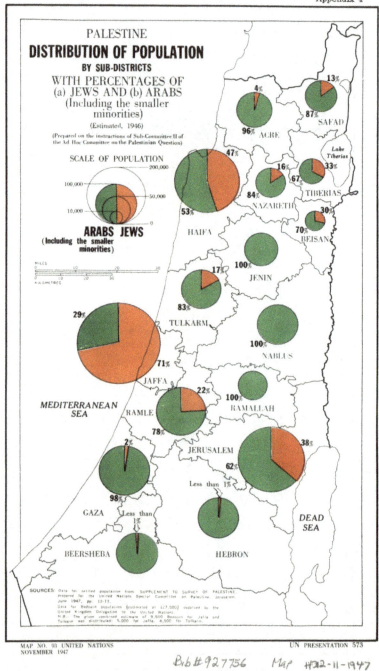

MAP V *Palestine, distribution of population by sub-districts with percentages of Jews and Arabs (Estimated at 1946), Map No. 93, United Nations, November 1947.*

3 *Resolution 181(II) and the International Rule by Law* 63

in each of Palestine's 16 sub-districts (see Map VI).[35] Moreover, the quality of the land granted to the proposed Jewish State was highly skewed in its favour. UNSCOP reported that under its majority plan '[t]he Jews will have the more economically developed part of the country embracing practically the whole of the citrus-producing area'[36] – Palestine's staple export crop – even though approximately half of the citrus-bearing land was owned by the Arabs.[37] In addition, according to updated British records submitted to the ad hoc committee's two sub-committees, 'of the irrigated, cultivable areas' of the country, '84 percent would be in the Jewish State and 16 per cent would be in the Arab State'.[38]

As to demographic composition, the UNSCOP report indicated that although the proposed Arab State would include a clear majority of approximately 725,000 Arabs to 10,000 Jews, the proposed Jewish State would include approximately 498,000 Jews to 407,000 Arabs. Curiously, UNSCOP acknowledged that '[i]n addition, there will be in the Jewish State about 90,000 Bedouins', providing virtual parity in the ethnic composition of the proposed Jewish State, with 498,000 Jews to 497,000 Arabs.[39] This was further compounded by the findings of sub-committee 2 of the ad hoc committee, which reported to the General Assembly that UNSCOP's estimated figures required correction in light of updated information furnished to it by the British. That information indicated that there would be 105,000 Bedouin in the Jewish State, not 90,000. As noted by the sub-committee, this meant that 'the proposed Jewish State will contain a total population of 1,080,800, consisting of 509,780 Arabs and 499,020 Jews. *In other words, at the outset, the Arabs will have a majority in the proposed Jewish State'.*[40]

Although the Zionists coveted the whole of Palestine, the Jewish Agency leadership pragmatically, if grudgingly, accepted Resolution 181(II).[41] Although they were of the view that the Jewish national home promised in the mandate was equivalent to a Jewish State, they well understood that such

---

[35] In eight of Palestine's 16 sub-districts, Jewish land ownership did not exceed 5 per cent and in no case did it exceed 39 per cent. *Id.*

[36] Citrus was the principal export of Palestine at the time. UNSCOP Report, Vol. I, *supra* note 19 at 48.

[37] UN Ad Hoc Committee, Report of Sub-Committee 2, *supra* note 34 at 293 & Appendix VI.

[38] Statement of Sir Mohammed Zafrullah Khan (Pakistan), UN GAOR, 2nd Sess., 126th Plen. Mtg. at 1374, A/PV.126, 28 November 1947.

[39] UNSCOP report, Vol. I, *supra* note 19 at 54.

[40] UN Ad Hoc Committee, Report of Sub-Committee 2, *supra* note 34 at 291 [emphasis added].

[41] Ad Hoc Committee on the Palestinian Question, Summary Records of Meetings 25 September – 25 November 1947, UN GAOR, 2nd Sess, 4th Mtg. at 16–17, 2 October 1947.

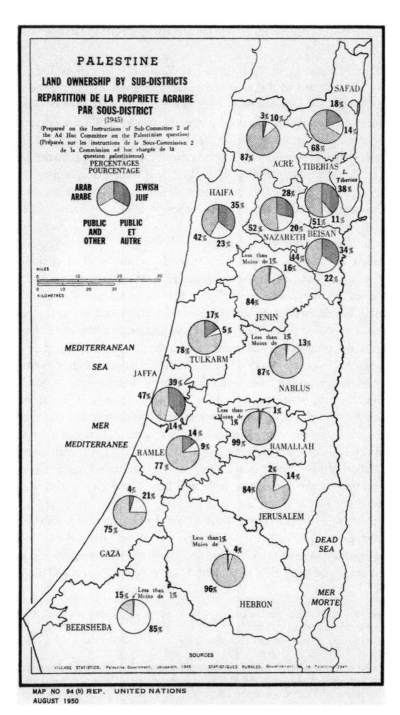

MAP VI *Palestine, land ownership by sub-districts (1945), Map No. 94(b), United Nations, August 1950.*

3 *Resolution 181(II) and the International Rule by Law* 65

a claim could not be maintained under prevailing international law. In this way, UN recognition of the Jewish State in resolution 181(II) represented a fundamental shifting of the goalposts. Based on its own terms, it is impossible to escape the conclusion that the partition plan privileged European colonial interests over those of Palestine's indigenous people and, as such, was an embodiment of the Eurocentricity of the international system that was allegedly a thing of the past. For this reason, the Arabs took a more principled position in line with prevailing international law, rejecting partition outright.[42] This rejection has been presented in some of the literature as indicative of political intransigence,[43] and even hostility towards the Jews as Jews.[44] Yet an examination of the terms of the resolution as above offers an explanation rooted in what is reasonably characterized as a rejection of the hegemonic dictates imposed on the Arabs of Palestine by the General Assembly and the legal subalternity it wrought for them within the UN system. Far from an opportunity to establish their right to political independence and self-determination in their homeland in line with the international rule of law, resolution 181(II) represented an abuse of UN legal authority to undermine indigenous rights in Palestine in favour of European interest, and was therefore an embodiment of the international rule by law.

3.3 *Resolution 181(II): Assessment under International Law*

The international legality of resolution 181(II) has long been a matter of debate. Among the key protagonists, Israel relies on the resolution as one of the legal bases of its juridical right to exist. The declaration of its establishment of 14 May 1948 provides that the 'recognition by the United Nations of the right of the Jewish people to establish their state' contained in resolution 181(II) 'is irrevocable' and that the state was established 'on the strength' of this resolution.[45] For its part, the Palestine Liberation Organization (PLO) regarded resolution 181(II) as illegal until 1988, when it accepted it as a condition for entering into diplomatic talks in accordance with a two-state settlement.[46] The international legality of resolution 181(II) has also been well

---

[42] Ad Hoc Committee on the Palestinian Question, Summary Records of Meetings 25 September – 25 November 1947, UN GAOR, 2nd Sess, 3rd Mtg. at 11, 29 September 1947.

[43] Strawson, *supra* note 11 at 101–102.

[44] Grief, H. *The Legal Foundation and Borders of Israel Under International Law* (Mazo, 2010) at 166–167.

[45] *Declaration of the Establishment of the State of Israel*, 14 May 1948, at: www.knesset.gov.il/ docs/eng/megilat_eng.htm ['Declaration of Establishment of Israel'].

[46] *See infra* text accompanying note 84 and Chapter 5.

66   1947: The UN Plan of Partition for Palestine

traversed in the literature. Positions adopted by pro-Israel legal scholars regard the resolution as illegal for violating a purported right of the Zionists to the whole of Palestine.[47] Others consider it 'conditionally legal' on the basis that it would have bound both Israel and the Arab States if the latter had accepted it.[48] On the other hand, some pro-Palestinian legal scholars regard the resolution as illegal for being wholly *ultra vires* the General Assembly[49] or in violation of the UN Charter and self-determination of peoples.[50] Still others regard it as legal based on acceptance of it by an overwhelming majority of states within the General Assembly, both at the time of its passage and subsequently through sponsorship of the two-state framework.[51]

Despite this difference of opinion on the international legality of resolution 181(II), one common thread running throughout is the tendency to collapse the separate issues of the General Assembly's procedural powers with its substantive powers, thus giving rise to some confusion. The diplomatic record reveals that this was an issue for some delegations in the debate over the terms of the resolution.[52] One example, drawn from the secondary literature, is found in the following view of James Crawford:

> It is doubtful if the UN has a capacity to convey title, in part because it cannot assume the role of territorial sovereign: in spite of the principle of implied powers, the UN is not a state and the General Assembly only has a power of

---

[47] Grief, *supra* note 44 at 156–157.

[48] Stone, J. *Israel and Palestine* (Johns Hopkins, 1981) at 62.

[49] Cattan, H. *The Palestine Question* (Saqi, 2000) at 38.

[50] *Id.*, at 39. *See also* Crawford, J. *Brownlie's Principles of Public International Law*, 8th ed. (Oxford, 2012) at 246.

[51] Mallison, T. & S. *The Palestine Problem in International Law and World Order* (Longman, 1986) at 171–173.

[52] *See* Statement of Semen K. Tsarapkin (USSR), Ad Hoc Committee on the Palestinian Question, Summary Records of Meetings 25 September – 25 November 1947, UN GAOR, 2nd Sess, 30th Mtg. at 184, 24 November 1947 ('Such doubts [*i.e.* about the legal competence of the GA to deal with the Palestinian problem] as were being expressed in the Ad Hoc Committee were completely unjustified, because Article 10 of the Charter gave the General Assembly the right and the duty to discuss the Palestinian question. It was in complete accordance with the provisions of Article 10 that the special session had been called, the Special Committee established and the Palestinian question considered by the General Assembly. *Any* recommendations which the Assembly made would have sound juridical foundations' [emphasis added]). *But see*, in response, statement of Sir Zafrullah Khan (Pakistan), Ad Hoc Committee on the Palestinian Question, Summary Records of Meetings 25 September – 25 November 1947, UN GAOR, 2nd Sess, 30th Mtg. at 189, 24 November 1947 ('Article 10 of the Charter certainly authorized the General Assembly to consider the question of Palestine and to make recommendations, but the solution which the General Assembly proposed must be within the scope of the Charter').

3 Resolution 181(II) and the International Rule by Law 67

recommendation. On this basis it can be argued that GA Resolution 181(II) of 29 November 1947, approving a partition plan for Palestine, was if not *ultra vires* at any rate not binding on member states.[53]

It is apparent that the legal capacity of the General Assembly to convey title is a matter of substantive power, whereas its legal capacity to make recommendations to member states is a matter of procedural power. Questioning the authority of the General Assembly to impose a territorial partition in Palestine, however accurate, cannot be fully justified by referencing the limits of its power to bind member states procedurally. The better approach to assess the overall legality of resolution 181(II) would seem to call for a two-pronged test that severs the procedural and substantive authority of the General Assembly, as follows: (1) does the General Assembly have the procedural power to issue recommendations under the Charter? (2) If so, what are the substantive limitations on the General Assembly in the exercise of that power, if any?

As to the first prong, under Article 10 of the Charter the General Assembly 'may make recommendations to the Members of the United Nations or to the Security Council or to both…'.[54] Based on the ordinary meaning of these terms, the General Assembly is thus vested with the procedural competence to issue recommendations to members of the UN and/or to the Security Council. As to the second prong, are there any substantive limits on the General Assembly in exercising this procedural authority? The answer is yes. Article 10 provides, in relevant part, that the General Assembly may make recommendations, as above, but only on 'any questions or any matters within the scope of the present Charter or relating to the powers and functions of any organs provided for in the present Charter…'.[55]

An argument can therefore be advanced that it is incorrect to assert that resolution 181(II) was *ultra vires* the General Assembly insofar as the resolution is understood to have *imposed* a political solution for 'the future government of Palestine' on the people of Palestine.[56] Nothing in the text of the resolution suggests that the General Assembly went beyond its limited powers of making a recommendation. To be sure, the resolution's terms expressly provide that the General Assembly '[r]ecommends to the United Kingdom, as

---

[53] Crawford, *supra* note 50 at 246.
[54] UN Charter, *supra* note 3, art. 10.
[55] *Id.*, art. 10.
[56] Although resolution 181(II) is entitled 'Future government of Palestine', and the partition plan was presented as a recommendation in respect of same, the terms of reference of UNSCOP whose majority report served as the basis of the partition plan were not as narrow, but examined 'all questions and issues relevant to the problem of Palestine' See A/RES/181(II), *supra* note 31, and Section 4.1 of this chapter.

68   *1947: The UN Plan of Partition for Palestine*

the mandatory Power for Palestine, and to all other Members of the United Nations the adoption and implementation' of a certain course of action relevant to the future government of Palestine. At the time it was issued, therefore, the resolution constituted nothing more than a recommendation that was, as a matter of procedure, properly made by the General Assembly and which, as a rule, would not normally be binding under international law.[57]

At the same time, however, in exercising its procedural power to make a recommendation on the future government of Palestine, the General Assembly was bound, in substantive terms, by the scope of the Charter, including its provisions relating to the powers and functions of any organs provided for in it. This must have been delimited by what we might call for our purposes 'the sacred trust principles' deriving from the continuation of the mandate regime following the demise of the League of Nations – *viz.* self-determination of peoples in the context of class A mandates, Article 22 of the League of Nations Covenant, the mandate for Palestine, and Chapter XII of the Charter concerning the International Trusteeship System. As noted above, given the satisfaction of the establishment of the Jewish national home under the terms of the mandate, and the fact that the indigenous majority of the population of the country was against partition, this meant that the substantive scope of the General Assembly's power to make any recommendation on Palestine must have been limited to either one of two results: immediate independence of the country or delayed independence through transformation of the country into a UN trusteeship. In either case, partition would not be legal without the freely expressed consent of the governed.

Various arguments have been proffered that differ from this conclusion. One of the earliest was advanced by Hersch Lauterpacht who, in October 1947, was asked by the Jewish Agency to advise 'on the best legal grounds for refuting the suggestion that the General Assembly has no legal competence to partition Palestine'.[58] He opined that because Great Britain exercised effective 'sovereignty over Palestine' and it had requested the UN 'to pronounce a finding upon the question of Palestine and its political future in all its aspects', the General Assembly was within its power to recommend partition.[59] Likewise, he affirmed that the General Assembly possessed 'unrestricted powers ... to

---

[57] Kattan, *supra* note 32 at 155. Jessup, P. *The Birth of Nations* (Columbia, 1974) at 264 ('I do not believe that the most ardent advocates of the binding legal effect of such resolutions' as resolution 181(II) 'would attribute legislative force to the partition resolution. Like most General Assembly resolutions, it was merely a recommendation'). *But see* text accompanying *supra* notes 7, and *infra* notes 76–81.

[58] Lauterpacht, *supra* note 26 at 508.

[59] *Id.*

3 Resolution 181(II) and the International Rule by Law   69

recommend the solution of the problem of Palestine'.[60] These views suffer from a number of defects. First, the British request of the UN was not directed towards the broad end of 'the question of Palestine and its political future in all its aspects' but rather only towards the much more limited end of 'the future government of Palestine'.[61] As discussed below, this implies that the territorial unity of the country would remain intact, save where the freely expressed wishes of the population determined otherwise. Second, it is clear from the terms of Article 10 of the Charter – which Lauterpacht curiously failed to cite in his advice – that the procedural power of the General Assembly to make recommendations to members of the UN and/or the Security Council is not unrestricted. To the contrary, it is expressly limited by the scope of the Charter, which includes the sacred trust principles and the continuing mandates regime. In view of the object and purpose of these principles and regime, the heart of which was the need to make inquiry of and respect the freely expressed wishes of the inhabitants of mandated territories, there would not seem to be any substantive scope for the General Assembly to suggest partition in exercising its procedural power of recommendation under Article 10 of the Charter. After all, partition had been consistently rejected by the great majority of the people of Palestine.

Another, more recent example of a differing view is a detailed opinion advanced by Victor Kattan, who rightly points out that resolution 181(II) was merely a recommendation.[62] But in assessing the resolution's legality, he seems to have maintained the general tendency to collapse the procedural and substantive powers of the General Assembly, as noted above. He states that there is 'no basis in the UN Charter or in international law to argue that the General Assembly does not have the power to recommend to states that they adopt a plan partitioning a particular territory over which it has a special responsibility'.[63] For support, he relies on the 1950 advisory opinion of the ICJ in *South-West Africa*, where the court unanimously concluded that 'competence to determine and modify the international status of [the mandated territory of] South-West Africa rests with the Union of South Africa [as mandatory power] acting with the consent of the United Nations'.[64] On this basis, he concludes that 'the UN General Assembly, acting with the consent of the mandatory, can modify the status of a mandated territory and that, in so doing, it is competent

---

[60] *Id.*

[61] A/RES/181(II), *supra* note 31, preamble. *See also* UNSCOP Report, Vol. II, *supra* note 13 at 1.

[62] Kattan, *supra* note 32 at 155.

[63] *Id.*, at 154.

[64] *International Status of South-West Africa*, Advisory Opinion, 11 July 1950, ICJ Reports 1950, p. 128, at 143 ['South-West Africa'].

to decide on claims of self-determination put forward by communities living in the territory'.[65] Similar to the problems encountered with Lauterpacht, this seems questionable for one key reason. Nowhere in *South-West Africa* did the ICJ indicate that the authority of the UN to modify the status of a mandated territory with the consent of the mandatory power was *substantively unlimited*. Indeed, the Court made it clear that South Africa remained the mandatory power in South-West Africa,[66] that it was bound by the terms of Article 22 of the League of Nations Covenant,[67] that the General Assembly was 'legally qualified to exercise the functions previously exercised by the League of Nations',[68] and that the provisions of Chapter XII of the Charter applied to the territory of South-West Africa 'in a sense that they provide a means by which the territory may be brought under the trusteeship system'.[69] Thus, as previously noted, the scope of the General Assembly's authority to make recommendations under Article 10 in respect of mandated territories must necessarily have been circumscribed by the sacred trust principles. These, in turn, were rooted in the principle of the consent of the governed.

In both abovementioned opinions, missing is the fundamental importance of assessing the legality of resolution 181(II) through the prism of the primacy of the consent of the governed, a crucial frame of reference if subaltern interests are to be given their due. This primacy arises from the substantive limits on the exercise of the procedural right of the General Assembly to make recommendations under Article 10 of the Charter. By the very terms of that article, these limits are in turn defined by the scope of the Charter, which, because of the continuation of the principles and regime of the mandate system, necessarily includes the sacred trust principles embodied in Article 22 of the League of Nations Covenant and self-determination of peoples living within class A mandated territories. In the end, therefore, resolution 181(II) was illegal under international law, not because it purported to impose a decision that went beyond its powers of recommendation, but because its substantive content – namely, partition against the will of the indigenous majority of Palestine – was *ipso facto* in violation of the Charter and the international rule of law.

Admittedly, the legality of resolution 181(II) is a complex issue. It was for that reason that in October 1947, Egypt, Iraq, and Syria proposed that

---

[65] Kattan, *supra* note 32 at 154.
[66] *South-West Africa*, *supra* note 64 at 143.
[67] *Id*.
[68] *Id*., at 137.
[69] *Id*., at 144.

3 *Resolution 181(II) and the International Rule by Law* 71

an advisory opinion be sought from the ICJ on, *inter alia*, the competence of the General Assembly to recommend the partition of Palestine without the consent of its people.[70] This effort was narrowly defeated in the ad hoc committee of the General Assembly,[71] giving rise to concern among some that the international rule of law was being sacrificed for other ends.[72] The Colombian delegate opined that '[t]he legal competence of the General Assembly to set up two independent States in Palestine, without regard to the principle of self-determination' and without 'the consent of the inhabitants of Palestine', has 'not been established to our satisfaction'.[73] The Iraqi delegate stated that 'if the General Assembly were to adopt this [partition] plan' without the benefit of first going to the ICJ, 'the legality of the matter would still be seriously questioned'.[74] Finally, the Cuban delegate noted that refusal to have resort to the ICJ 'was a mistake', not least because it 'may well give the impression that the Assembly is avoiding solutions which conform to the law'.[75]

At its heart then, the problem with resolution 181(II) was that it recommended a purported solution to the question of Palestine on terms that manifestly ran counter to prevailing international law. If the General Assembly's goal of establishing a Jewish State in Palestine was viewed by it as a politically legitimate end, that end was arrived at the expense of the international rule of law as it existed at the time and the rights of the indigenous people of Palestine thereunder. How could partition be legal if the only possibility envisioned under the UN Charter was independence of the country, either immediately as with other Class A mandates, or at some point in the

---

[70] Ad Hoc Committee on the Palestinian Question, Summary Records of Meetings 25 September – 25 November 1947, UN GAOR, 2nd Sess., Annexes 15, 16, 17, at 239–241.

[71] As Iraq, Egypt, and Syria put more than one question forward, these were amalgamated in a combined proposal that was defeated in two votes, as follows: 25 to 18, with 11 abstentions; 21 to 20, with 13 abstentions. Ad Hoc Committee on the Palestinian Question, Summary Records of Meetings 25 September – 25 November 1947, UN GAOR, 2nd Sess, 32nd Mtg. at 203, A/AC.14/SR.203, 24 November 1947.

[72] *See, e.g.*, Potter, P.B. 'The Palestine Problem Before the United Nations' (1948) 42:4 *AJIL* 859 at 860 (stating contemporaneously that failure to put the question of UN jurisdiction over the Palestine question to the ICJ 'tends to confirm the avoidance of international law in dealing with international problems manifested only too often in the history of Great Power behavior in the United Nations').

[73] Statement of Alfonso Lopez (Colombia), UN GAOR, 2nd Sess., 127th Plen. Mtg. at 1397, A/PV.127, 28 November 1947.

[74] Statement of Mohamed Fadhil Jamali (Iraq), UN GAOR 2nd Sess., 126th Plen. Mtg. at 1390, A/PV.126, 28 November 1947.

[75] Statement of Ernesto Dihigo (Cuba), UN GAOR, 2nd Sess., 126th Plen. Mtg. at 1384, A/PV.126, 28 November 1947.

immediate future following temporary administration as a UN Trusteeship? What of the principle of self-determination of such mandated territories, rooted in the precepts of consent of the governed and majority rule? Even if the Jewish people possessed an internationally recognized right to a Jewish *national home* in Palestine by virtue of the mandate, how did that legally justify the General Assembly's recommendation to establish a Jewish *State* in Palestine? At any rate, how would the 'Jewishness' of that state be secured, if the ratio of Arabs to Jews in it was virtually on par or the Jews were a minority in it from the start, and the plan required it to adopt a democratic constitution guaranteeing universal suffrage and equality before the law? As will be seen, following these lines of inquiry will assist us in better understanding the rule by law essence of resolution 181(II) and why it reified Palestine's international legal subalternity.

3.4 Resolution 181(II) as an Embodiment of the International Rule by Law

There seem to be two ways through which the rule by law nature of resolution 181(II) can be understood. The first is through the lens of positivist international law doctrine or hard law. The second is through the prism of discursive international norms or soft law.

Doctrinally, the assertion that resolution 181(II) was declarative of law and therefore amounted to a form of rule by law may seem surprising. This is because the resolution was merely a recommendation of the General Assembly and therefore not normally binding under international law. Although this may have been true of the resolution when it was passed in 1947, an argument can be made that over time, through its express and implied acceptance by states and other subjects of the international community – most importantly, the Israeli and Palestinian protagonists with whom it is concerned – it has come to have binding legal force if not *in toto*, then in respect of its embodiment of the principle of the territorial division of mandate Palestine.

It is a general principle that law may arise from a long and consistent practice: *ex factis oritur jus*.[76] The formation of customary international law is understood as requiring 'evidence of a general practice accepted as law'.[77] This practice may be global or regional/local in nature.[78] Accordingly, as noted by the ICJ in *Nicaragua*, settled practice accompanied by *opinio juris*

---

[76] Shany, Y. 'Legal Entitlements, Changing Circumstances and Intertemporality: A Comment on the Creation of Israel and the Status of Palestine' (2016) 49:3 *Isr. L.Rev.* 391 at 392.
[77] ICJ Statute, *supra* note 10, art. 38(1)(b).
[78] Crawford, *supra* note 50 at 29.

3 *Resolution 181(II) and the International Rule by Law*   73

sive necessitatis – the subjective belief that the practice engaged in is required as matter of law – qualifies as binding customary international law.[79] Here, the universality of the UN is of direct relevance. As noted by Rosalyn Higgins, the practice of the UN's political organs – the General Assembly in particular – can provide a 'rich source of evidence' of customary international law as the '[c]ollective acts of states, repeated by and acquiesced in by sufficient numbers with sufficient frequency, eventually attain the status of law'.[80] This has been affirmed by the ICJ in its Advisory Opinion on the *Legality of the Threat or Use of Nuclear Weapons*, where it opined that General Assembly resolutions 'can provide evidence important for establishing the existence of a rule or the emergence of an *opinio juris*'.[81]

It is admittedly difficult to argue that the terms of resolution 181(II) would *in toto* qualify as customary international law on these bases. Support for this conclusion rests in the fact that key specific terms of the resolution – including the proposed territorial delimitations of the envisioned Jewish and Arab states, the proposed economic union, guarantees intended for the protection of civil and political rights of minorities, and the envisioned means of the resolution's enforcement – were never in fact followed by the concerned states and had been overtaken by events on the ground during the 1948 war. Thus, as noted by Crawford, 'both the Security Council and Britain refused to enforce the partition plan' and the functions of the UN Palestine Commission (UNPC) – established in resolution 181(II) to administer the transfer of power from Britain to the two proposed states during a transitional period – were subsequently terminated by the General Assembly in resolution 186(S-2) of 14 May 1948 during the course of the war.[82]

Nevertheless, in the intervening seventy-six years since the passage of resolution 181(II), a good case can be made that there has emerged enough state practice, including by both the State of Israel and the State of Palestine, but also within the UN system, suggestive of the legally binding character of the resolution's fundamental object and purpose: namely, the principle of a peaceful resolution of the dispute over mandate Palestine *through its territorial division into two states*. As noted, the declaration of the establishment of Israel provides that 'recognition by the United Nations of the right of the Jewish people to establish their state' contained in resolution 181(II) 'is irrevocable' and that the

---

[79] *Military and Paramilitary Activities in and against Nicaragua (Nicaragua v. US)* (Merits), 27 June 1986, ICJ Reports 1986, p. 14, at para. 207 ['Nicaragua'].

[80] Higgins, *supra* note 7 at 2, 5.

[81] *Legality of the Threat or Use of Nuclear Weapons*, Advisory Opinion, 8 July 1996, ICJ Reports 1996, p. 226, at para. 70 ['Nuclear Weapons'].

[82] Crawford, J. *The Creation of States in International Law*, 2nd ed. (Oxford, 2006) at 432.

74   *1947: The UN Plan of Partition for Palestine*

state was established 'on the strength' of the resolution.[83] Likewise, since 1988, the PLO has recognized resolution 181(II) as one of the bases upon which the State of Palestine's establishment rests, albeit within the smaller territorial confines of the occupied Palestinian territory (OPT).[84] As for the attitude of the rest of the international community, the best evidence that a custom exists in this regard comes in the form of the numerous resolutions of the General Assembly over the years, usually adopted by a large or overwhelming majority, in which resolution 181(II) is recalled or affirmed.[85] For example, resolution 48/158D of 20 December 1993 passed following the commencement of the Oslo process and adopted by a vote of 92 to 5, with 51 abstentions, reaffirmed a number of principles 'for the achievement of a final settlement and comprehensive peace' including '[g]uaranteeing arrangements for peace and security of all States in the region, including those named in resolution 181(II) of 29 November 1947, within secure and internationally recognized boundaries'.[86] Likewise, in relation to the Madrid Peace Conference, the same principle was affirmed by the General Assembly in its resolutions 44/42 of 6 December 1989 (151 to 3, with 1 abstention), 45/68 of 6 December 1990 (144 to 2, with 0 abstentions), and resolution 46/75 of 11 December 1991 (104 to 2, with 43 abstentions).[87] In line with these resolutions, widespread state practice as reflected in bilateral and multilateral treaty, diplomatic, economic, and political relations affirms that historical Palestine is today legally recognized by the vast majority of the international community as being shared by two distinct self-determination units, Israel and Palestine (*see* Chapters 5 & 6). Thus, it is possible to argue that beyond its specific terms and mechanics, which were rendered moot by the 1948 war and subsequent events, the legal effect of the two-state principle that underpinned resolution 181(II) has arguably taken on a binding character through its treatment by states within the UN system. This has given the resolution its rule by law quality, which has, in turn, reified Palestine's legal subalternity within the UN.

---

[83] Declaration of Establishment of Israel, *supra* note 45.

[84] Letter dated 16 November 1988 from the Deputy Permanent Observer of the Palestine Liberation Organization to the United Nations Addressed to the Secretary-General, A/43/827, 18 November 1988. *See also Enhancement of Palestine's Status at the UN*, Negotiations Support Unit, Palestine Liberation Organization, 26 November 2012, at: www.nad-plo.org/etemplate.php?id=357.

[85] *See, e.g.*, A/RES/77/22, 30 November 2022 (101-17-53); A/RES/74/10, 3 December 2019 (92-13-61); A/RES/71/25, 30 November 2016 (149-7-8); A/RES/71/23, 30 November 2016 (153-7-7); A/RES/70/15, 24 November 2015 (155-7-7); A/RES/66/18, 26 January 2012 (164-7-5); A/RES/52/250, 13 July 1998 (124-4-10); A/RES/43/177, 15 December 1988 (104-2-36).

[86] A/RES/48/158D, 20 December 1993.

[87] A/RES/44/42, 6 December 1989; A/RES/45/68, 6 December 1990; A/RES/46/75, 11 December 1991.

3 Resolution 181(II) and the International Rule by Law 75

Even if the two-state paradigm that underpins resolution 181(II) is not regarded as binding international law doctrinally, might it still possess a discursive/normative force that informs its rule by law character? In *Nuclear Weapons*, the ICJ noted that 'General Assembly resolutions, even if they are not binding, may sometimes have normative value'.[88] Based on the historical record subsequent to the passage of resolution 181(II), there is little question that the resolution produced a discursive/normative imagery that structured the way the UN has come to understand the conflict over Palestine and how it should be peacefully resolved in accordance with other relevant bodies of international law. As will be fleshed out in Chapters 5 and 6, this includes the law on self-determination of peoples as crystalized in the post-decolonization era, the law prohibiting acquisition of territory through the threat or use of force, and the law governing belligerent occupation. In so far as these bodies of law have been applied within and by the UN system to affirm the rights and obligations of the protagonists in the question of Palestine, the *only* confines within which they have legitimately been allowed to do so – those of the two-state paradigm – were set forth in principle in resolution 181(II). Thus, from a discursive/normative standpoint, resolution 181(II) provided what has become the fundamental architecture of the UN's seventy-six-year engagement with the question of Palestine: the two-state framework.[89] This has also bolstered the resolution's rule by law quality, with its resulting reification of Palestine's legal subalternity within the Organization.

In light of the above, when viewed from a subaltern perspective, resolution 181(II) stands out as the first example of the rule by law in operation in the UN's work on the question of Palestine. As noted, the PLO would later be compelled to accept the legitimacy of the resolution as a price to be paid in return for a modicum of Palestine's international legal rights being recognized and hopefully realized (see Chapter 5). Yet, from the standpoint of the PLO's constituents, the introduction of the two-state paradigm through resolution 181(II) represented a signal disaster at the time it was passed. At bottom, it was the clash between the interest of the hegemonic and European-dominated General Assembly in the juridical establishment of a Jewish State in Palestine, and the obstacle to doing so in the form of the very presence of a majority indigenous Muslim and Christian Arab population who persistently objected to it, that forms the essence of the rule by law character of the resolution and the subsequent reification of Palestine's legal subalternity inherent in its terms. In order to better understand the nature and genus of this problem,

---

[88] *Nuclear Weapons*, *supra* note 81, para. 70.
[89] Falk, R. *Palestine's Horizon* (Pluto, 2017) at 4.

76   *1947: The UN Plan of Partition for Palestine*

it is useful for us to look deeper into the diplomatic record with a subaltern sensibility. To this end, we must give particular critical focus to the terms of UNSCOP's report, the verbatim and summary records on which it was based, and the debates that subsequently took place in the ad hoc and plenary sessions of the General Assembly between 25 September and 29 November 1947.

4 UNSCOP AND THE GENERAL ASSEMBLY DEBATES

UNSCOP was created by the General Assembly on 15 May 1947.[90] It held sixteen public and thirty-six private meetings with a variety of stakeholders in Lake Success, Jerusalem, Beirut, and Geneva between June and August 1947.[91] In addition, it visited a range of Jewish displaced persons camps in Germany and Austria.[92] As noted, UNSCOP proposed two plans for the future government of Palestine: a majority plan proposing partition with economic union and a minority plan proposing a unitary federal state. It also unanimously adopted twelve recommendations, including that the mandate 'shall be terminated' and 'independence shall be granted in Palestine at the earliest practicable date', and that the new state or states to be formed in Palestine shall be constitutional democracies guaranteeing 'full equality of all citizens with regard to political, civil and religious matters'.[93]

An examination of UNSCOP records reveals at least three factors that demonstrate a continuation of the international rule by law in its work. They were rooted in UNSCOP's disregard for prevailing international law throughout the course of its deliberations, which was carried through to the General Assembly debates following the submission of its report on 3 September 1947, ultimately resulting in the passage of resolution 181(II). These factors were: (1) an apparent bias in UNSCOP's composition and terms of reference directing it away from recommending immediate independence for Palestine upon the dissolution of the mandate, as per the normal course for class 'A' mandates under international law; (2) an unwillingness to sufficiently engage Palestinian Arab opinion in its deliberations; and (3) a contempt for democratic governance and the empirical reality of the indigenous Arab population in Palestine as the main problem to be overcome. As each of these is addressed below, the Eurocentricity of international law and institutions as a structural component of international legal subalternity will be readily apparent.

[90] UNSCOP Report, Vol. I, *supra* note 19 at 3.
[91] *Id.*
[92] *Id.*, at 8.
[93] *Id.*, at 42–43, 45.

4 UNSCOP and the General Assembly Debates

4.1 Bias in UNSCOP's Composition and Terms of Reference

In 1947, the General Assembly was composed of only fifty-five member states, forty of whom were either European or settler-colonial offshoots of Europe. The other sixteen consisted of newly independent Asian, African, and Middle Eastern states, the majority of those regions remaining under some form of European imperial control at the time. Notwithstanding this 5:2 ratio, of the eleven members of UNSCOP, nine were drawn from the European and settler-colonial group (Australia, Canada, Czechoslovakia, Guatemala, Netherlands, Peru, Sweden, Uruguay, and Yugoslavia), whereas only two (India and Iran) were drawn from the non-European group. No Arab state was named to UNSCOP and only one member (Iran) was drawn from the Middle East. It is apparent, therefore, that UNSCOP's membership empirically reflected a continuation of the 'civilized' Eurocentricity of international law and institutions that had hitherto been a marked feature of the international system. As noted by John Quigley, UNSCOP was 'friendly territory for the Jewish Agency from the cultural standpoint'.[94] Set against the calamitous backdrop of WWII, the evidence further suggests this bias was also political, as a key feature of the work of UNSCOP was the desire of some of its members (and other states in the General Assembly) to find a solution to Europe's long-standing Jewish question. This was to be done through the juridical transformation and recognition of the Jewish national home into a Jewish State in Palestine, something that could only happen at the expense of the international rule of law and the rights of the Palestinian Arabs thereunder. Despite one writer having rejected this claim as mere 'myth',[95] such a position seems warranted on a close reading of the diplomatic record.

The record suggests that these ends were enabled initially through UNSCOP's unduly broad terms of reference. When the United Kingdom

---

[94] Quigley, J. *The International Diplomacy of Israel's Founders* (Cambridge, 2016) at 51.

[95] *See* Strawson, *supra* note 11 at 5, ('[S]ome myths that have achieved the status of facts can be disposed of. The partition resolution [*i.e.* GA resolution 181(II)] is a case in point. The creation of Jewish State in 1948 is now commonly regarded as a form of international compensation to the Jews for the Holocaust. It is regularly claimed that guilt, in particular "Western guilt", led the international community to foist the Jews onto the innocent Palestinians, thus provoking the conflict. However, through a systematic reading of contemporary UN debates and the partition proposal contained in the report of the United Nations Special Committee on Palestine (UNSCOP) no such intention can be found. The Holocaust is rarely mentioned. There are certainly no expressions of guilt. Indeed the UNSCOP report in a sideways reference to the Holocaust explicitly says that its recommendations for partition are not intended as a solution to the "Jewish problem". In reading the debates in particular I was struck by the callous manner in which the Holocaust was either ignored or sometimes referred to.... It is thus a myth that the source of the problem was a legal decision to hand over part of Palestine to the Jews at the expense of the Palestinians.')

78   *1947: The UN Plan of Partition for Palestine*

referred the matter of Palestine to the UN on 2 April 1947, it asked the General Assembly 'to make recommendations under Article 10 of the Charter, concerning the future government of Palestine'. To this end, the UK requested the General Assembly to constitute and instruct a special committee to help it consider this question.[96] Thus, the envisioned special committee was asked to work within the relatively narrow confines of advising on Palestine's *future government* within the scope of the Charter. It was not asked to entertain dismemberment of the territory in favour of a European settler minority colonizing it against the will of the indigenous non-European majority. This was consistent with Palestine's status as a single administrative unit under international law whose independence had been provisionally recognized in 1920 and whose legal fate under the Charter was either to have its independence immediately recognized or be converted into a UN trust territory until such time as independence was recognized in accordance with the freely expressed wishes of its inhabitants.

The First Committee of the General Assembly was tasked with composing UNSCOP's terms of reference. During its deliberations, the scope of the terms originally referred by Britain was considerably broadened in a manner that directed the matter away from Palestine's independence. This allowed for consideration of a number of factors more amenable to Zionist and associated post-war European goals of establishing a Jewish State. To begin with, Chile, Guatemala, and Uruguay succeeded in gaining approval for expanding the political scope of UNSCOP's investigation by replacing reference to it having to report on 'the future government of Palestine' to the more opaque 'question of Palestine'.[97] This was justified by the Guatemalan and Uruguayan representatives – both of whom were members of UNSCOP – ostensibly as a measure to ensure against 'directing', 'limiting', and 'restricting' the committee's task.[98] The British representative realized that this skewed his government's original intention in referring the matter to the General Assembly. He accordingly requested the removal of any reference to 'the request of the Government of the United Kingdom' in the terms of reference.[99] Furthermore, despite objections from Lebanon and Syria, the Guatemalan representative succeeded with assistance from Australia and South Africa to gain support for an expansion of the geographical scope of

---

[96] UNSCOP Report, Vol. II, *supra* note 13 at 1.

[97] UN GAOR, 1st Spec. Sess., Vol. III, 55th Mtg. at 276–278, 12 May 1947.

[98] *Id.*, at 278.

[99] *Id.*, at 278–279. Notwithstanding, the preamble of A/RES/181(II), *supra* note 31, references 'the request of the mandatory Power to constitute and instruct a special committee to prepare for the consideration of the question of the future government of Palestine'.

4 UNSCOP and the General Assembly Debates 79

UNSCOP's investigation. This scope was enlarged from merely 'Palestine' to 'Palestine *and wherever it may deem useful*'.[100] As stated by the Guatemalan representative, this was done with the specific purpose of empowering the committee to 'obtain official knowledge of the wishes of the Jews in the European camps' regarding their possible future settlement in Palestine.[101] Finally, various attempts to ensure UNSCOP's terms of reference included 'a proposal on the question of establishing without delay the independent democratic State of Palestine' were repeatedly defeated by the Western European and settler-colonial bloc of states.[102] In the end, UNSCOP's final terms of reference were set out in General Assembly resolution 106 (S-1) of 15 May 1947, mandating it to prepare 'a report on the question of Palestine' and granting it 'the widest powers to ascertain and record facts and to investigate all questions and issues relevant to the problem of Palestine'. To that end, UNSCOP was empowered to 'conduct investigations in Palestine and wherever it may deem useful', and to 'receive and examine evidence' from 'the mandatory Power, from representatives of the population of Palestine, from Governments and from such organizations and individuals as it may deem necessary'.[103] No reference was made to Palestine's independence, the UN Charter, or the League of Nations Covenant.

Given UNSCOP's wide mandate, Arab fears that Palestinian independence in line with the freely expressed wishes of its inhabitants, immediate or delayed, was being sacrificed for the broader political goals of partitioning the country were not taken seriously by the General Assembly. Indeed, the Dominican and Brazilian representatives each attempted to allay such concerns by suggesting that failure to mention independence in the terms of reference, for instance, would not necessarily exclude independence from being considered.[104] These efforts were in vain. As pointed out by the Lebanese delegate – and as would later be testified to UNSCOP by Jewish Agency Chairman, David Ben Gurion[105] – the Zionists had been open in their opposition 'to the independence of Palestine until the Jews form a majority there. [...] Consequently this apparent shyness of the term "independence for Palestine" on the part of many, when considered in conjunction with

---

[100] *Id.*, at 283–287 [emphasis added].

[101] *Id.*, at 283.

[102] *See, e.g.,* UN GAOR, 1st Spec. Sess., Vol. III, 56th Mtg. at 308–310, 13 May 1947.

[103] A/RES/106 (S-1), 15 May 1947.

[104] UN GAOR, 1st Spec. Sess, Vol. I, 79th Plen. Mtg. at 168, 180, 15 May 1947.

[105] UNSCOP, Report to the General Assembly, 2nd Sess, Vol. III, Annex A, Oral Evidence Presented at Public Meetings, A/364 Add. 2, at 49–50, 9 September 1947 ['UNSCOP Report, Vol. III'].

80   *1947: The UN Plan of Partition for Palestine*

the declared and avowed intentions of the Jewish Agency, is exceedingly disquieting. [...] The word "independence" already exists in the Covenant of the League of Nations, on which the mandate was based, and therefore, obviously, it is not the act of using an already used term which prejudges the issue, but precisely the act of omitting to use a term which was already in use thirty years ago."[106] Similar concerns were repeatedly expressed by each of the Egyptian,[107] Iraqi,[108] and Syrian[109] delegations, to no avail. The Lebanese delegate summed it up succinctly before the General Assembly on 13 May 1947:

> The ground of this concern is the fact that not only has any mention of independence for Palestine been severely suppressed from the terms of reference, but also, the basis on which this extraordinary session of the General Assembly was convened in the first place has finally shifted, in the course of the last two weeks from preparing to advise the United Kingdom Government

---

[106] UN GAOR, 1st Spec. Sess., Vol. III, 55th Mtg. at 288–289, 12 May 1947; *id.*, at 288–289.

[107] *See, e.g.*, UN GAOR, 1st Spec. Sess, Vol. I, 78th Plen. Mtg. at 145, 14 May 1947 ('Whereas by the stroke of a pen, the reference to the independence of Palestine has been in effect removed by the committee failing to confirm the spirit of the request of the British government as embodied in its letter of appeal to the United Nations for a settlement of this problem'; 'the First Committee has exceeded its powers and was not within it rights when it decided to delete the sentence referring to "the future government of Palestine" and replaced it by a vague and broad reference to "the question of Palestine"').

[108] UN GAOR, 1st Spec. Sess, Vol. I, 77th Plen. Mtg. at 125–126, 14 May 1947 ('The First Committee, however, after three days of discussion and after drafting six alternative texts containing the term "independence", has, by a magic move, deleted the word "independence" from the terms of reference. [...] The terms of reference have actually avoided ideas and concepts like freedom, independence, self-determination, democracy, the Charter, unity, harmony, peace and justice. The situation is strange not because these words are not included – and they are conspicuous by their absence – but because of the firmness of the opposition from certain quarters to the inclusion of such words for fear of prejudicing the issue. As if the demand to investigate any people's right to freedom and independence were an indication of partiality!').

[109] UN GAOR, 1st Spec. Sess, Vol. I, 78th Plen. Mtg. at 142, 14 May 1947 ('We have voted against the terms of reference of the special committee because no mention was made in the terms of reference to the word "independence". I am sorry some of the speakers in the [First] Committee avoided the word "independence" as if it were something injurious or as if it were out of order, claiming that it would prejudge the action of the special committee. We said that it would not prejudge action. This is the essential and sole object of the mandate, that it be ended by independence, and by the termination of an unworkable mandate. It is the general principle of all mandates and trusteeships, that the end in view be independence. It is in the Charter and the Covenant of the League of Nations. Should we not then instruct the special committee to direct its studies toward realizing this end, which is the essential end? Would that be prejudging? I cannot see any way in which that would be prejudging. We ask that the provisions of the Covenant of the League of Nations and the provisions of the Charter of the United Nations be the basis for any solution to be found for Palestine, and nothing else').

4 UNSCOP and the General Assembly Debates 81

on the future government of Palestine to preparing for the consideration of the so-called problem of Palestine in general, a phrase which by its very generality may mean anything and which is therefore unacceptable.[110]

And then again on 14 May 1947:

The phrase 'future government of Palestine' has now completely vanished. In its place we have the phrase 'the problem or question of Palestine'. This replacement has taken place without any previous adequate discussion of this problem, without even any proper indication as to what it really is. [...] For instance, it has been taken for granted by many quarters that the problem of the [Jewish] refugees and displaced persons [of WWII] is somehow related to the problem of Palestine. The Jewish Agency affirmed that the two problems were one and the same, and the introduction of the phrase, 'and wherever it may deem useful [in the terms of reference] was expressly intended by those who introduced and supported it to enable the committee to visit displaced persons' camps and thus bring about a connexion, however strained and artificial, between these two problems.[111]

The chief concern of the Arab states, therefore, was that the General Assembly was furnishing UNSCOP with terms of reference that were biased in favour of what its majority European and settler-colonial bloc wished to impose on the natives of Palestine; namely the establishment of a Jewish State in their country and at their expense, in contravention of what prevailing international law required. This seems to have been a reasonable concern to have had at the time. This was demonstrated by the fact that the Danish delegate, in his capacity as Rapporteur of the First Committee, urged members of the committee to consider the 'problem of Palestine' as 'not a purely legal problem'.[112] More to the point, after extensively recounting the devastation of the Holocaust on the Jews of Europe, the Soviet delegate stated:

As we know, the aspirations of a considerable part of the Jewish people are linked with the problem of Palestine and of its future administration. [...] The time has come to help these people, not by word, but by deeds. It is essential to show concern for the urgent needs of a people which has undergone such great suffering as a result of the war brought about by hitlerite Germany. This is a duty of the United Nations. [...] The fact that no western European State has been able to ensure the defence of the elementary rights of the Jewish people, and to safeguard it against

[110] UN GAOR, 1st Spec. Sess., Vol. III, 57th Mtg. at 359, 13 May 1947.
[111] UN GAOR, 1st Spec. Sess, Vol. I, 78th Plen. Mtg. at 155–156, 14 May 1947.
[112] UN GAOR, 1st Spec. Sess, Vol. I, 77th Plen. Mtg. at 125, 14 May 1947.

82   *1947: The UN Plan of Partition for Palestine*

the violence of the fascist executioners, explains the aspirations of the Jews to establish their own State. It would be unjust not to take this into consideration and to deny the right of the Jewish people, to realize this aspiration. It would be unjustifiable to deny this right to the Jewish people, particularly in view of all it has undergone during the Second World War. Consequently, the study of this aspect of the problem and the preparation of relevant proposals must constitute an important task of the special committee.[113]

When UNSCOP issued its report, although it noted that 'any solution for Palestine cannot be considered as a solution of the Jewish problem in general',[114] this didn't mean that Palestine wasn't to feature as a *prominent part* of a solution for the Jewish problem. Thus, when UNSCOP's report was put before the ad hoc committee of the General Assembly just before the adoption of resolution 181(II), similar views as those expressed by the Soviet delegate above were expressed by the Netherlands,[115] Norway,[116] and Poland.[117] The Uruguayan delegate summed things up by stating that the establishment of a Jewish State in Palestine would represent 'a complete plan for a territorial solution of the Jewish problem'.[118]

Thus, the desire to resolve Europe's Jewish question took precedence for key members of the hegemonic European and settler-colonial bloc of states over the requirements of international law including the rights of the subaltern Palestinian Arabs. The concerns of bias of UNSCOP's composition and terms of reference are certainly vindicated by the record. To be sure, concern for the Jewish refugees and of the historic injustice faced by European Jewry

---

[113] *Id.*, at 131–132.

[114] UNSCOP Report, Vol. I, *supra* note 19 at 89.

[115] Ad Hoc Committee on the Palestinian Question, Summary Records of Meetings 25 September – 25 November 1947, UN GAOR, 2nd Sess, 19th Mtg. at 129, 21 October 1947 ('It was abundantly clear that there was a very close link between the solution of the Palestine problem and of the Jewish refugee problem').

[116] Ad Hoc Committee on the Palestinian Question, Summary Records of Meetings 25 September – 25 November 1947, UN GAOR, 2nd Sess, 16th Mtg. at 108, 16 October 1947 ('The delegation of Norway in a spirit of complete impartiality and of equal amity for the two peoples, had finally decided to vote for the majority plan [*i.e.* to partition Palestine into an Arab State and a Jewish State] … because of the wrongs which the Jews had suffered at the hands of mankind.').

[117] Ad Hoc Committee on the Palestinian Question, Summary Records of Meetings 25 September – 25 November 1947, UN GAOR, 2nd Sess, 8th Mtg. at 42, 8 October 1947 ('… the problem of the distressed European Jews [needs to] be dealt with as a matter of extreme urgency. The Polish delegation considered, however, that the problem could and ought to be solved primarily by Jewish immigration into Palestine').

[118] Ad Hoc Committee on the Palestinian Question, Summary Records of Meetings 25 September – 25 November 1947, UN GAOR, 2nd Sess, 6th Mtg. at 31, 6 October 1947.

4 UNSCOP and the General Assembly Debates 83

was shared by a number of the Asian and Middle Eastern States.[119] Indeed, empirically speaking, Palestine itself had done more than its fair share in providing refuge for hundreds of thousands of displaced European Jews,[120] whereas many Western states refused to open their doors in any remotely comparable way.[121] But because these non-European states had nothing to do with the persecution of European Jews, any talk of using the UN to partition Palestine in order to resolve Europe's Jewish question contrary to prevailing international law – a result enabled by the bias inherent in UNSCOP's composition and terms of reference – was proof of a lingering imperialism in the New World order. As the representative of Yemen submitted to the General Assembly: 'If Jews were persecuted in Europe what have the people of Palestine to do with that?'[122]

[119] *See, e.g.*, Ad Hoc Committee on the Palestinian Question, Summary Records of Meetings 25 September – 25 November 1947, UN GAOR, 2nd Sess, 7th Mtg. at 36–37, 7 October 1947, where the Pakistani representative stated that '[t]he outbreak of anti-Semitism in Europe had introduced complications into the Palestinian question. The Pakistan delegation had every sympathy with those sufferings, but considered that the problem was one of humanitarian concern which should not affect the rights of the peoples of Palestine and which should be dealt with as an international problem. With regard to the relief for the persecuted Jews, Palestine had done more than its share in settling more than 500,000 Jews in that country. [...] [The Pakistani delegate] acknowledged the urgency of the matter, but considered that those displaced persons should be absorbed in other States where there was already a prosperous and appreciable Jewish population rather than wait for admission to Palestine'.

[120] *Id. See also* UN GAOR, 2nd Sess., 126th Plen. Mtg. at 1368, A/PV.126, 28 November 1947, where Sir Zafrullah Khan (Pakistan) stated: 'What has Palestine done? What is its contribution toward the solution of the humanitarian question as it affects Jewish refugees and displaced persons? Since the end of the First World War, Palestine has taken over four hundred thousand Jewish immigrants. Since the start of the Jewish persecution in Nazi Germany, Palestine has taken almost three hundred thousand Jewish refugees. This does not include illegal immigrants who could not be counted. One has observed that those who talk of humanitarian principles, and can afford to do most, have done the least at their own expense to alleviate this problem. But they are ready – indeed, they are anxious – to be most generous at the expense of the Arab'.

[121] *See, e.g.*, Ad Hoc Committee on the Palestinian Question, Summary Records of Meetings 25 September – 25 November 1947, UN GAOR, 2nd Sess, 15th Mtg. at 94, 16 October 1947, where the Saudi representative stated that '[t]he intervention of the United States and its support of the Zionists was incomprehensible, especially since it would not open its own doors to the destitute refugees', and Jewish 'suffering should not be used as a weapon for encroaching on the rights of others. If the gates of the world had not been closed to the Jews, they would have been able to find shelter away from Europe'.

[122] Statement of H.R.H. Prince Seif El Islam Abdullah (Yemen), UN GAOR, 2nd Sess., 124th Plen. Mtg. at 1316, A/PV.124, 26 November 1947. *See also*, Ad Hoc Committee on the Palestinian Question, Summary Records of Meetings 25 September – 25 November 1947, UN GAOR, 2nd Sess, 18th Mtg. at 120, 18 October 1947, where a representative of the Arab Higher Committee stated: 'Nations which had initiated or permitted anti-Semitism had no right to ask tiny Arab Palestine to pay by the loss of its rights for the mistakes of others'; *and* UN GAOR, 2nd Sess.,

84   *1947: The UN Plan of Partition for Palestine*

4.2 *UNSCOP's Unwillingness to Sufficiently Engage Palestinian Arab Opinion*

A second factor that informed the rule by law character of resolution 181(II) was UNSCOP's unwillingness to sufficiently engage the opinion of the Palestinian Arab leadership during its deliberations. At first glance, this may appear to be a thin claim given that the Arab Higher Committee for Palestine (AHC) took a specific decision to boycott UNSCOP. That decision, however, was motivated by an understandable and widely known frustration with the British and League of Nations role in violating Palestine's legal position in the interwar period. As the AHC representative to the ad hoc committee explained:

> The Arabs of Palestine could not understand why their right to live in freedom and peace, and to develop their country in accordance with their traditions, should be questioned and constantly submitted to investigation. [...] The rights and patrimony of the Arabs in Palestine had been the subject of no less than eighteen investigations within twenty-five years, and all to no purpose. Such commissions of inquiry had made recommendations that had either reduced the national and legal rights of the Palestine Arabs or glossed over them. The few recommendations favourable to the Arabs had been ignored by the Mandatory Power. It was hardly strange, therefore, that they should have been unwilling to take part in a nineteenth investigation.[123]

Be that as it may, the literature tends to treat the boycott and its negative consequences as an instance of 'exceedingly inept diplomacy'[124] on the part of the Palestinian Arabs. This blaming-the-victim approach apportions any negative consequences wholly, if impliedly, on the subaltern class.[125] It is likely because of this that little attention has been paid to the role UNSCOP may have had in neglecting to engage the understandably skeptical Arab leadership of Palestine. In a Wheatonian sense, UNSCOP's attitude towards

---

126th Plen. Mtg. at 1385, A/PV.126, 28 November 1947, where Ernesto Dihigo (Cuba) stated: 'With regard to the Jewish or non-Jewish refugees now in camps for displaced persons, a problem on which so much emphasis has been laid by those in favour of partition ... it should be solved by good will on the part of all United Nations, each of which should receive a proportion of refugees in accordance with its ability to do so and in the particular conditions in each country. But we do not see why Palestine should be expected to solve the whole problem alone, especially as that country had no hand in determining the circumstances which originally caused the displacement of all these persons'.

[123] Ad Hoc Committee on the Palestinian Question, Summary Records of Meetings 25 September – 25 November 1947, UN GAOR, 2nd Sess, 3rd Mtg. at 6, 29 September 1947.

[124] *See, e.g.*, Smith, C.D. *Palestine and the Arab-Israeli Conflict* (St. Marten's, 1992) at 135.

[125] *See, e.g.*, Strawson, *supra* note 11 at 114; *and* Kattan, *supra* note 32 at 147, 159.

4 UNSCOP and the General Assembly Debates 85

engaging the Palestinian leadership at this time is reminiscent of the denial of international legal standing to the non-European thorough operation of the classical standard of civilization.[126]

It is axiomatic that the work of high-stakes UN diplomacy requires a great deal of flexibility, creativity, tenacity, and patience, all underscored with a belief in the universal vocation of the mandate of the Organization. These traits are the lifeblood of the UN which, in the words of Trygve Lie, first Secretary-General (1946–1952), 'is dedicated to encouraging and facilitating effective cooperation in matters of mutual interest and to the peaceful adjustment of international differences'.[127] It is surprising to find, therefore, that the record reveals a relative indifference, even nonchalance, of UNSCOP towards the boycott of the AHC. UNSCOP cannot reasonably be blamed for the AHC's initial boycott decision. But questions arise in respect of its conspicuous unwillingness, in response, to sufficiently encourage or facilitate the AHC's engagement in what appears to have been an abandonment of the usual tools of diplomacy. This is particularly so, given that at least five members of UNSCOP were leading judges or lawyers in their countries. They would therefore have been well versed in the need to ensure objectivity and fairness in their fact-finding mission, both in real terms and as a matter of public perception.[128]

The neglect of the AHC in this respect began on 5 May 1947, when a plenary session of the General Assembly discussed the question of who its First Committee should hear from when considering UNSCOP's composition and terms of reference. The General Assembly had received requests to be heard from a number of Zionist organizations, foremost of which was the Jewish Agency, which indicated that if the Arab States were afforded the right to address the General Assembly, it should be able to as well.[129] In response, the Syrian representative indicated that the Palestinian Arabs were

---

[126] Wheaton, H. *Elements of International Law*, 8th ed. (Little, Brown & Co., 1866) ('The public law, with slight exceptions, has always been, and still is, limited to the civilized and Christian people of Europe or to those of European origin').

[127] Lie, T. *In the Cause of Peace* (Macmillan, 1954) at 422.

[128] Emil Sandstrom, Chair (Sweden) was Chief Justice of Sweden, Ivan Rand (Canada) was a sitting justice of the Supreme Court of Canada, Sir Abdur Rahman (India) was a judge in India, Nasrollah Entezam (Iran) was trained in law at the Sorbonne, and Jose Brilej (Yugoslavia) was a judge in Yugoslavia. *See also* UNSCOP, Summary Record of the Second Meeting (Private), A/AC.13/PV.2, 2 June 1947, where Brilej stated that the Committee's choice of a chairman must reflect 'the greatest possible measure of impartiality', and Rand stated 'I am quite sure that we need as a Chairman someone who has had considerable experience in judicial administration'.

[129] UN GAOR, 1st Spec. Sess., Vol. III, Annex 2, at 363, Letter dated 22 April 1947 from the Jewish Agency for Palestine, A/C.1/139.

86   *1947: The UN Plan of Partition for Palestine*

represented by the AHC and not by any Arab state.[130] Notwithstanding, the General Assembly passed a resolution resolving that the First Committee shall hear *only* from the Jewish Agency, in addition to passing on to the First Committee, for its own decision, communications the General Assembly had received from other non-governmental organizations who wished to be heard.[131] It was only after several delegations pointed out that the AHC was not explicitly mentioned in the above-noted resolution of the General Assembly that the First Committee took a decision the next day to expressly invite the AHC to participate.[132] Thus, although the AHC was invited to be heard by the First Committee, the afterthought-like manner in which it happened – privileging European voices over non-European ones – set the stage for the attitude UNSCOP itself would later adopt.

UNSCOP's mission lasted from 26 May to 31 August 1947, a total of fourteen weeks. Even before committee members arrived in Palestine on 14 June 1947, the committee adopted a practice of receiving information from the Jewish Agency,[133] as well as providing it with all UNSCOP documentation not classified as secret.[134] At UNSCOP's fifth meeting on 16 June, the committee was informed by cablegram from the Secretary-General that the AHC had decided to boycott it.[135] The summary record of that meeting indicates that upon receiving this news, UNSCOP chairman, Justice Emil Sandstrom of Sweden, confined his response to simply expressing 'the hope that contact might be made at a later date with Arab representatives', without stipulating when, how, or with whom such contact might be made.[136] In the meantime, Sandstrom satisfied himself by delivering a radio broadcast later that afternoon *in English*, ostensibly informing the Palestinian public of UNSCOP's mission, affirming its impartiality and indicating that it 'hopes for the full cooperation in its task from all elements in the population'.[137] The following day, at UNSCOP's seventh meeting, an impassioned appeal was made by Jose Brilej, the Yugoslav representative, that UNSCOP address the AHC directly. Yet, the committee not only voted it down, but also approvingly voted 'to defer further action for the time being' on the point.[138]

[130] UN GAOR, 1st Spec. Sess., Vol. I, 75th Plen. Mtg. at 104, 5 May 1947.
[131] UN GAOR, 1st Spec. Sess., Vol. I, 75th Plen. Mtg. at 114–115, 5 May 1947.
[132] UN GAOR, 1st Spec. Sess., Vol. III, 47th Mtg. at 78, Annex 6 at 367 A/C.1/151, 7 May 1947.
[133] *See, e.g.*, UNSCOP, Summary Record of the Fourth Meeting (Private), A/AC.13/SR.4, 6 June 1947.
[134] UNSCOP, Summary Record of the Seventh Meeting (Private), A/AC.13/SR.7, 17 June 1947.
[135] UNSCOP, Summary Record of the Fifth Meeting (Private), A/AC.13/SR.5, 16 June 1947.
[136] *Id.*
[137] UNSCOP Report, Vol. II, *supra* note 13 at 5.
[138] UNSCOP, Summary Record of the Seventh Meeting (Private), A/AC.13/SR.7, 17 June 1947.

4 UNSCOP and the General Assembly Debates   87

In the meantime, UNSCOP continued its public hearings and investigation. Its itinerary was set based on input invited only from the Jewish Agency and the British mandatory Government of Palestine.[139] It wasn't until UNSCOP's twenty-second and twenty-third meetings on 8 July 1947 – six weeks from the start of its work, three weeks since arriving in Palestine and one and a half weeks before departing Palestine – that UNSCOP took a decision to pen a letter to the AHC in an attempt to convince it to reverse its position on the boycott.[140] But the summary and verbatim records of UNSCOP's private meetings leading up to that point indicate that even that decision hadn't come as self-evident. In its twelfth meeting on 22 June 1947, after extensively discussing a number of communications received from jailed Jewish underground fighters seeking clemency through UNSCOP's intervention with the Government, the Indian representative, Sir Abdur Rahman, expressed astonishment. He could not understand why the committee was entertaining such tangential requests from the Zionist side when it had not even reached out to the AHC on the principal issues it was sent to Palestine to investigate.[141] Likewise, at UNSCOP's eighteenth meeting on 6 July 1947, an attempt by the Yugoslav representative to get the committee to re-open the question of AHC engagement that he raised at the seventh meeting was simply ignored.[142] Finally, at the twentieth meeting on 7 July 1947, although the Uruguayan representative, Enrique Rodriguez Fabregat, expressed disappointment that 'we will not be able to hear any testimony from the Arab side', he failed to take up the Yugoslav representative's repeated initiatives or suggest any other way of constructively dealing with the matter.[143]

In the event, the AHC maintained the boycott for the reasons set out above. Notwithstanding UNSCOP's apparent apathy on the boycott, the hegemonic, Eurocentric character of its approach was revealed subsequently. This was found in the manner in which the AHC was publicly singled out and lambasted in the debates before the ad hoc committee and plenary sessions of the General Assembly following the issuance of UNSCOP's report. This was done by certain members of UNSCOP who, now sitting before the General Assembly as representatives of their individual countries, shed all pretence of impartiality and took positions that clearly contradicted UNSCOP's own documentary record. For instance,

---

[139] UNSCOP Report, Vol. II, *supra* note 13 at 4–5.
[140] *Id.*
[141] UNSCOP, Summary Record of the Eleventh Meeting (Private), A/AC.13/SR.11, 22 June 1947.
[142] UNSCOP, Summary Record of the Eighteenth Meeting (Private), A/AC.13/SR.18, 6 July 1947.
[143] UNSCOP, Summary Record of the Twentieth Meeting (Private), A/AC.13/SR.20, 7 July 1947.

88   *1947: The UN Plan of Partition for Palestine*

the Czech representative, Karel Lisicky, assailed 'the uncompromising stand' of the AHC.[144] When UNSCOP was criticized for failing to bring the parties together, Lisicky curiously asserted that UNSCOP 'had made every effort, in vain, both to secure a modification' of the AHC's 'attitude and to induce local Arab representatives to enter into political discussion of the Arab case'.[145] Even more revealing was the intervention of the Guatemalan representative, Jorge Garcia Granados. His statement to the plenary session of the General Assembly was as revisionist as it was racist and colonial:

> Our Chairman and the Committee as a whole sought many times to bring about a settlement between the Arabs and the Jews. Our efforts were frustrated by the intransigent attitude of the Arab Higher Committee, which would not give a hearing even to Judge Sandstrom, and which ordered all its affiliated organizations to refuse to collaborate with the Committee and to threaten and intimidate all Arabs who seemed to favour conciliation. Nothing daunted, UNSCOP made every possible approach to the Arabs, visiting their towns and villages and taking no notice of the hostile reception. Our representatives never failed to hold out the hand of friendship; but in vain, for no Arab would grasp it. [...] *Years of propaganda have filled the simple hearts of the Arabs with a rancor which makes all efforts at conciliation and the establishment of friendly relations seem useless today.* [...] [T]he creation of a Jewish State is a reparation owed by humanity to an innocent and defenseless people which has suffered humiliation and martyrdom for two thousand years. The Palestine Arabs must know that we who vote in favour of this resolution have no desire to harm their interests, and that *the intransigent attitude of their leaders is the only obstacle* to the attainment of liberty by both peoples and to the forging of ties of brotherhood between them.[146]

In short, whatever one's views on the rationale and efficacy of the AHC's decision to boycott UNSCOP, there is no escaping the fact that the verbatim and summary records of UNSCOP's deliberations, as well as the subsequent General Assembly debates, reveal a level of apathy and indifference in securing a reversal of this position, surprisingly uncharacteristic of the modus operandi of UN diplomacy and investigation. Although testimony

[144] Ad Hoc Committee on the Palestinian Question, Summary Records of Meetings 25 September – 25 November 1947, UN GAOR, 2nd Sess, 5th Mtg. at 19, 3 October 1947.

[145] Ad Hoc Committee on the Palestinian Question, Summary Records of Meetings 25 September – 25 November 1947, UN GAOR, 2nd Sess, 15th Mtg. at 105–106, 16 October 1947.

[146] Statement of Jorge Garcia Granados (Guatemala), UN GAOR, 2nd Sess., 126th Plen. Mtg. at 1380–1381, A/PV.126, 28 November 1947 [emphasis added].

4 UNSCOP and the General Assembly Debates

was eventually provided to UNSCOP by some Arab states towards the end of the mission,[147] the committee knew that these states did not represent the Palestinian Arab position as such. As noted by Quigley, there is little question that '[t]he scant participation on the Arab side left the Jewish Agency with a great advantage'.[148] But to blame the Palestinian Arab leadership alone for this result, as some UNSCOP members subsequently did (and with no small measure of racism, to boot), is unfair if not disingenuous. On the contrary, UNSCOP's unwillingness to actively ensure what was a central aspect of its mandate – that is to obtain direct evidence from *both* principal protagonists in Palestine – stands out as a product of the hegemonic and Eurocentric worldview of the majority of its membership. This ultimately enabled the violation of international law embodied in UNSCOP's plan of partition, which in turn contributed to the rule by law character of resolution 181(II).

4.3 UNSCOP's Contempt for Democratic Government and the Empirical Reality of the Indigenous Arab Population

A third and perhaps most important factor of UNSCOP's work, and which heavily influenced the international rule by law nature of resolution 181(II), was the general contempt held by UNSCOP's majority for democratic government as it applied to the non-European population of the country and, concomitantly, the *empirical reality* of the indigenous Palestinian Arab population. This too is reminiscent of international law's classical disregard for non-European rights and standing and the extent to which similar values continued to prevail in the UN system. An examination of UNSCOP's verbatim and summary records demonstrates that it claimed that its work was directed towards democratic ends through the establishment of two self-determination units in Palestine. Both of these states would be required to commit to democratic principles, including the protection of minorities within their territorial borders. Nevertheless, UNSCOP could only paradoxically arrive at this result by violating the democratic right of the indigenous majority to freely determine the whole of the territory's fate as dictated by prevailing international law on class A mandates. The ostensibly liberal, rights-based order heralded by the UN meant that UNSCOP needed to find a clever way around the

---

[147] At its 23rd meeting on 8 July 1947, UNSCOP took a decision for the first time to invite representatives of the Arab States to give evidence to it. UNSCOP, Summary Record of the Twenty-Third Meeting (Private), A/AC.13/SR.23, 8 July 1947.

[148] Quigley, *supra* note 94 at 67.

90   *1947: The UN Plan of Partition for Palestine*

Palestinian Arab majority as a condition precedent to partition. A review of the diplomatic record demonstrates that among the arguments used to justify the legitimacy of partition, most were fraught with a curiously strained logic, at times accompanied by openly racist views, regarding the indigenous majority population and its right to self-determination. What these views shared was a general failure to take the very presence of the native Palestinian Arabs and their international legal rights seriously, an embodiment of the continued imperial Eurocentricity of the international order at the UN.

On 8 July 1947, the Jewish Agency leadership gave evidence before UNSCOP. It was made apparent that the Zionists regarded the Jewish national home as equivalent to a Jewish State. The Zionists further clarified that such a state, although the right of the Jewish people, could not be established until the Jews were in a demographic majority in Palestine.[149] When pressed on the seeming incongruence of the Zionists' recognition of the principle of self-determination of peoples and their request that its exercise be delayed in the case of Palestine until such time as the Jews were in the majority, David Ben Gurion (who would become Israel's first Prime Minister) offered the following cyclical reasoning, citing a purported 'overriding right' of his constituents:

> There are certain rights of self-determination, and when I say the right of the Jew to come back to his country [i.e. Palestine] and the right of our people to be here as equal partners in the world family, it is an over-riding right which applies to Palestine, and therefore no regime – not only an Arab State, should be created, even no trusteeship, no mandate should be created – which will make that right impossible of realization. This is why we oppose it [i.e. immediate application of self-determination in Palestine] ... [i]t can be safeguarded only if there is independence and the Jews are in the majority.[150]

In its report to the General Assembly, this purported conundrum presented by Palestinian demography was well recognized, but surprisingly unquestioned, by UNSCOP. For instance, in its consideration of the issue of Palestinian self-determination and independence in a unitary democratic state, UNSCOP stated:

> With regard to the principle of self-determination, although international recognition was extended to this principle at the end of the First World War and it was adhered to with regard to the other Arab territories, at the time of the creation of the 'A' Mandates, it was not applied to Palestine, obviously

---

[149] UNSCOP Report, Vol. III, *supra* note 105 at 49–50, 93.

[150] *Id.*, at 93.

4 UNSCOP and the General Assembly Debates 91

because of the intention to make possible the creation of the Jewish National Home there. Actually, it may well be said that the Jewish National Home and the sui generis Mandate for Palestine run counter to that principle.[151]

Instead of taking issue with the *sui generis* nature of the mandate and its presumptive violation of the Charter principle of self-determination of peoples, as the liberal rights-based ethos of the day would require, UNSCOP adopted an approach evocative of the erasure of non-European legal subjectivity of the past. Thus, in considering how to reconcile the development of self-governing institutions under the mandate regime with the demands of the Jewish national movement for a state, UNSCOP noted:

> ... if the country were to be placed under such political conditions as would secure the development of self-governing institutions, these same conditions would in fact destroy the Jewish National Home. [...] Had self-governing institutions been created, the majority in the country, who never willingly accepted Jewish immigration, would in all probability have made its continuance impossible, causing thereby the negation of the Jewish National Home.[152]

This recognition of the inimical nature of the mandate's privileging of the rights of a European settler minority in Palestine over the development of self-governing institutions for the whole of its population in line with the sacred trust owed under the League of Nations Covenant and the principle of self-determination of peoples outlined in the Charter could not have been clearer. As an organ of the UN, duty bound to uphold the international rule of law, one would have expected this to give UNSCOP some pause. Instead, UNSCOP effectively adopted a position that maintained the international rule by law inherent in the mandate's negation of the rights and presence of the Arab majority and the principle of consent of the governed. For instance, although UNSCOP understood the Arab position to be one of establishing a unitary democratic state based on proportional representation[153] – the gold standard of democracy by any measure at the time – it curiously rejected this position as 'extreme' because it would have left the Arabs substantially in control of the country.[154] To be sure, UNSCOP also characterized full Jewish control over Palestine as 'extreme', but that would have been reasonable given the Jewish community's status as a settler minority in the country. In drawing this false

---

[151] UNSCOP Report, Vol. I, *supra* note 19 at 35.

[152] *Id.*, at 31.

[153] UNSCOP, Report to the General Assembly, 2nd Sess, Vol. IV, Annex B, Oral Evidence Presented at Private Meetings, A/364 Add. 3, at 43 ['UNSCOP Report, Vol. IV'].

[154] UNSCOP Report, Vol. I, *supra* note 19 at 42.

92   *1947: The UN Plan of Partition for Palestine*

equivalence between majority indigenous rule and minority European settler rule, UNSCOP was effectively expressing its contempt for democratic government and in a manner consistent with the ostensibly antiquated international legal standard of civilization.

This contempt was maintained in UNSCOP's majority plan of partition. Whereas the Zionists' way around the problem of Palestinian demography was to advocate for delay of the application of the principle of self-determination until they surpassed their number, UNSCOP's method was to advocate for its immediate application, but only through the creation of two racially gerrymandered states via partition. The first step in the process was to provide some legitimacy to the Zionist view that the right to a Jewish national home – which UNSCOP itself noted had already been declared established by the mandatory Power in 1939[155] – was somehow equivalent to a right to a Jewish State. Accordingly, although it acknowledged that the notion of a 'national home' had 'no known legal connotation' under international law and that both the Balfour Declaration and the mandate for Palestine intentionally used 'national home' in place of the less restrictive words 'commonwealth' or 'state', UNSCOP curiously found that none of this 'precluded the eventual creation of a Jewish state' in Palestine.[156] The second step was to highlight the impediment posed in the way of the establishment of such a Jewish State by the fact that the Arabs were in a commanding majority of the population, that they enjoyed a much higher birth rate, and that the Jews therefore required immigration to offset this problem or otherwise accept partition to maintain what little majority they could achieve, if at all. UNSCOP wrote:

> ... a Jewish State would have urgent need of Jewish immigrants in order to affect the present great numerical preponderance of Arabs over Jews in Palestine. The Jewish case frankly recognizes the difficulty involved in creating at the present time a Jewish State in all of Palestine in which Jews would, in fact, be only a minority, or in part of Palestine in which, at best, they would immediately have only a slight preponderance.[157]

Thus, stuck between the 'extreme' demands of the Arabs for a unitary democratic state based on proportional representation and recognition of Zionist independence in all of Palestine in which the Jews would be a minority, UNSCOP's majority chose partition, thereby violating the Charter and disenfranchising the indigenous population.[158]

[155] *Id.*, at 24.
[156] *Id.*, at 31–32.
[157] *Id.*, at 30.
[158] *Id.*, at 47.

4 *UNSCOP and the General Assembly Debates* 93

The reasoning offered in support of this decision highlights UNSCOP's contempt for democratic government if the result of such democracy was to place government in non-European hands. In noting that in the Jewish State envisioned under the majority plan, 'there will be a considerable minority of Arabs' – a 'demerit' of the scheme, in UNSCOP's words – it reasoned that 'such a minority is inevitable in any feasible plan which does not place the whole of Palestine under the present majority of the Arabs'.[159] Further, UNSCOP appears to have remained oblivious to the paradox embedded in its unanimously endorsed recommendation VII, under which it affirmed the importance of 'democratic principles and protection of minorities' in any plan the UN considered:

> In view of the fact that independence is to be granted in Palestine on the recommendation and under the auspices of the United Nations, it is a proper and an important concern of the United Nations that the constitution or other fundamental law as well as the political structure of the new State or States shall be basically democratic, i.e. representative, in character, and that this shall be a prior condition to the grant of independence. In this regard, the constitution or other fundamental law of the new State or States shall include specific guarantees respecting … [f]ull protection for the rights and interests of minorities, including … full equality of all citizens with regard to political, civil and religious matters.[160]

In light of this recommendation, it is reasonable to conclude that UNSCOP's majority held the view that the only way to give effect to the emergence of two democratic states in Palestine was to negate the right of the indigenous majority of the whole of the country to those very same democratic rights *ab initio* and without its consent, in violation of prevailing international law. This says nothing of the fact that the population figures it used for the proposed Jewish State were subsequently determined to be incorrect by the findings of sub-committee 2 of the ad hoc committee, which determined that the Jews would, in fact, be in a minority in the Jewish State.[161] Nor does it account for UNSCOP's own admission that partition would not offer any great benefit to the proposed Arab State, the economic viability of which it openly admitted was 'in doubt' from the start.[162] Indeed, this viability was so concerning

---

[159] *Id.*, at 52.

[160] *Id.*, at 45.

[161] *See* text accompanying *supra* notes 39–40.

[162] UNSCOP Report, Vol. II, *supra* note 13 at 55 ('In the case of the plan for the partition of Palestine recommended in this report, as well as in the case of all previous partition plans which have been suggested, it is the viability of the Arab State that is in doubt'.)

94   *1947: The UN Plan of Partition for Palestine*

that the authors of the majority plan felt compelled to issue an appeal in the UNSCOP report that 'sympathetic consideration should be given' to any claims the Arab state may make to the newly formed Bretton Woods institutions 'in the way of loans for expansion of education, public health and other vital social services of a non-self-supporting nature'.[163] Because no such appeal was felt required for the envisioned Jewish State, it is hard not to conclude this concern for the economic wellbeing of the putative Arab state was feigned in light of the fact that it was UNSCOP itself who was the author of the plan that would render the Arabs vulnerable in the first place.

Importantly, UNSCOP's minority plan attempted to balance the competing interests more consistently with 'democratic principles and protection of minorities' without the heavy hand of Eurocentricity animating it. This was in line with the relevant international law on self-determination of peoples in class A mandates, rooted in the consent of the governed, and the overall international rule of law. It proposed the establishment of an independent unitary federal state of Palestine. This federation would be comprised of an Arab state and Jewish State based on a bicameral parliamentary system, with proportional representation the basis of one chamber and equal representation guaranteed in the other. The constitution of the proposed federal state would provide for a division of powers between the federal and state governments. Key positions in the executive and judicial branches would be constitutionally earmarked for members of both communities, with powers of local self-government in the hands of each state (e.g. education, health, local taxation, administration of justice, etc.). Arabic and Hebrew would be the official languages of the country at both federal and state level, and minority rights would be constitutionally protected.[164] In arriving at this plan, UNSCOP's minority essentially deferred to the presence of Palestine's indigenous majority as the controlling factor, but without sacrificing the Jewish national home.[165] Doubtless because Palestine had nothing to do with Europe's persecution of the Jews, UNSCOP's minority also took a clear stand that separated the Jewish question from the question of Palestine.[166] In a separate note appended to UNSCOP's report, Sir Abdur Rahman, the Indian representative, explained

---

[163] *Id.*, at 48.

[164] *Id.*, at 59–64.

[165] *See* Ad Hoc Committee on the Palestinian Question, Summary Records of Meetings 25 September – 25 November 1947, UN GAOR, 2nd Sess, 29th Mtg. at 178, 22 November 1947, where the Yugoslav representative stated that '[t]he federal State solution was based on a recognition of the national aspirations of the Arabs as well as of the Jews, but it respected the unity and guaranteed the genuine independence of the Palestinian homeland'.

[166] UNSCOP Report, Vol. II, *supra* note 13 at 62.

4 UNSCOP and the General Assembly Debates 95

the approach animating the minority report. His intervention highlighted the continued tension between the values of late empire and those of the post-1945 liberal age now before UNSCOP and the justification of the minority plan in erring towards the latter:

> According to the well-known international principle of self-determination, which is now universally recognized and forms a keystone of the Charter of the United Nations, the affairs of a country must be conducted in accordance with the wishes of the majority of its inhabitants. *In 1947, it is too late to look at the matter from any other angle.* And thus looked at, the claim put forward by the Arabs is unanswerable and must be conceded, although it would be highly desirable – nay, almost impossible – to overlook important minorities, such as Jews in Palestine happen to be at present.[167]

With the minority plan having failed to gather enough support among UNSCOP's membership, the majority plan of partition was the focus of debate in the ad hoc and plenary sessions of the General Assembly between 25 September and 29 November 1947. Unsurprisingly, those debates were also characterized by a strained logic among the largely European and settler-colonial bloc of states that supported partition. This was underscored by their obvious disregard for international law, democratic governance, and the indigenous Arab majority, notwithstanding occasional pretentions to the contrary. The most eye-opening justification offered in support of partition came from none other than the Guatemalan representative, Mr. Garcia Granados, who it will be recalled, was a member of UNSCOP. In response to the argument that Palestine's Arab majority was entitled to have its freely expressed wishes accounted for, let alone deferred to, in any future government of Palestine in accordance with prevailing international law, Garcia Granados demonstrated that the old standard of civilization – animating what he called 'a certain order in the world' – continued to hold sway among some in the new UN system:

> [W]hat characterized a nation was its culture and not the number of inhabitants. In twenty-five years, the Jewish people had left upon Palestine the indelible mark of an outstanding culture, which characterized the country even more than the Arab culture: Palestine was no more Arab than certain Spanish countries of Latin America were Indian. The Jews had come to Palestine on the strength of a promise. They had transformed the deserts, and their model farms compelled admiration not only for their productiveness but also for the democratic character of their social structure. [...] [T]he Jews had made a pleasant and healthy country out of a land in which a *sparse and rachitic population had merely vegetated*. It was *incomprehensible*

---

[167] *Id.*, at 42 [emphasis added].

96   *1947: The UN Plan of Partition for Palestine*

that the Arabs should adduce their numerical superiority as an argument
when it was the Jews who had made the increase in the Arab population possible. [...] Could anyone think of placing that flourishing community under
the domination of another community, even a community of a comparable
standard of development? What would happen if the demands of the Arabs
were yielded to and an independent State of Palestine were created? The
Arab population with its *simple religiousness and rudimentary political sense*
[would harm the Jews]. [...] An *ignorant majority* should not be allowed to
impose its will. [...] There was a *certain order in the world* which helped to
maintain the necessary equilibrium. If the United Nations wished to save
that order it must consolidate it.[168]

Although Garcia Granados seems to have parroted some of what the Jewish
Agency had argued before the General Assembly,[169] not all delegations in
favour of partition expressed their support for the plan in such openly racist terms. Nevertheless, many of them shared the same underlying assumptions rooted in the continued hegemonic/subaltern nature of the international
system. This was expressed in the curious view that if the principle of self-
determination was to be applied to Palestine, the exercise of such a right
by the indigenous majority population had to impliedly be suppressed if it
meant that the minority Jewish settler population would remain a minority.
Predictably, the rhetorical moves employed to advance this position included
exhortations to opt for 'justice' over law and to treat the Jewish national home
as tantamount to a Jewish State. In the end, however, the effect was to subvert
the international rule of law based on the requirement to ensure respect for

---

[168] Ad Hoc Committee on the Palestinian Question, Summary Records of Meetings 25
September – 25 November 1947, UN GAOR, 2nd Sess, 10th Mtg. at 56–58, 10 October 1947
[emphasis added].

[169] *See, e.g.*, Ad Hoc Committee on the Palestinian Question, Summary Records of Meetings
25 September – 25 November 1947, UN GAOR, 2nd Sess, 17th Mtg. at 114, 17 October 1947,
where Moshe Shertok of the Jewish Agency rejected the proposal of a unitary democratic state
because 'it would mean that Palestine would be an Arab state with a Jewish minority at the
mercy of an Arab majority', and that in such a state 'a highly democratic minority would be
forced down to the economic and social level of an Arab majority, whereas under partition the
Arab minority would benefit from contact with the progressive Jewish majority'. *See also* Ad
Hoc Committee on the Palestinian Question, Summary Records of Meetings 25 September –
25 November 1947, UN GAOR, 2nd Sess, 18th Mtg. at 124, 126, 18 October 1947, where former
Jewish Agency Chair Chaim Weizmann opined that '[i]t was not in order to become citizens
of an Arab State that the Jews, on the strength of international promises, had made their home
in Palestine'; and that the 'creation of a Jewish State would be a great event in history and
a practical demonstration of liberal and humanitarian thought. A persecuted people would
achieve recognition of its national sovereignty, desert soil would be redeemed for cultivation,
[and] progressive social ideas would flourish in an area that had fallen behind the modern
standards of life'.

4 UNSCOP and the General Assembly Debates 97

the consent of the governed in class A mandates and to impose an international rule by law on the non-Europeans of Palestine.

Thus, the Polish delegate indicated that although 'a single bi-national state' in Palestine was desirable, 'such a solution would be neither just nor appropriate' if it meant that the Arabs 'would preponderate over a Jewish minority'.[170] Likewise, the Chilean delegate noted that although the Arab case 'was easily understandable and their argument was supported by unequivocal fact', partition seemed the only way 'to safeguard peace and justice' in 'the absence of a solution acceptable to both parties'.[171] Echoing earlier exhortations of other delegates,[172] the Dominican representative urged that 'the Palestine question could not be examined from an exclusively legal standpoint' and that partition 'most nearly accorded with justice' as it 'left to the Arabs a country of their own, while endorsing the concept of the Jewish National Home by establishing a Jewish State in Palestine'.[173] The Soviet delegate argued that partition 'gave both the Arab and the Jewish people an opportunity to organize their national life as they desired' because '[i]t was based on the principles of equality of peoples and the right of self-determination', unlike the unitary state framework which allegedly 'paid no regard to democratic principles'.[174] Likewise, the Canadian delegate noted that the Arab case for a unitary democratic state was 'otherwise unanswerable', but for the fact of the Jewish national home policy embedded in the mandate.[175]

Going through these and other similar statements given by the European and settler-colonial bloc of states in the ad hoc and plenary records of the General Assembly, one is constantly confronted by their failure to take international law, democratic government, and the empirical reality of the Palestinian Arab population seriously. Instead, false equivalence abounds. Partition was presented to the Palestinian Arabs as a promising opportunity that was not to be missed. As it happens, other states – largely members of the Asian and Middle Eastern group – refused this approach and took the native population of Palestine seriously. They attempted to counter this Eurocentric international rule by law narrative with one of their own firmly rooted in prevailing international legal norms.

---

[170] Ad Hoc Committee on the Palestinian Question, Summary Records of Meetings 25 September – 25 November 1947, UN GAOR, 2nd Sess, 8th Mtg. at 43, 8 October 1947.

[171] Ad Hoc Committee on the Palestinian Question, Summary Records of Meetings 25 September – 25 November 1947, UN GAOR, 2nd Sess, 29thth Mtg. at 175, 22 November 1947.

[172] See text accompanying supra note 112.

[173] Ad Hoc Committee on the Palestinian Question, Summary Records of Meetings 25 September – 25 November 1947, UN GAOR, 2nd Sess, 29thth Mtg. at 180, 22 November 1947.

[174] Ad Hoc Committee on the Palestinian Question, Summary Records of Meetings 25 September – 25 November 1947, UN GAOR, 2nd Sess, 30th Mtg. at 184, 24 November 1947.

[175] UN GAOR, 2nd Sess., 124th Plen. Mtg. at 1318, A/PV.124, 26 November 1947.

98   *1947: The UN Plan of Partition for Palestine*

One form of response was to question the logic of partition as an application of the self-determination principle. As noted by the representative of Yemen '[s]ince the population of Palestine was predominately Arab, the only logical and just application of that principle was that Palestine should become an independent Arab State with full protection of the rights of Palestinian Jewish minorities. If it were conceded that the principle of self-determination could justify the grant of discriminatory and preferential privileges to a minority over the will of the majority, or the division of a country against the wishes of the majority, then the world would be overwhelmed with similar problems and chaos would prevail'.[176] This view was shared by the representative of Lebanon.[177] He also queried how proponents of partition, who 'admitted that the Arabs in Palestine were in a majority', could nevertheless propose 'that the Arabs should become a minority and the Jews a majority' and expect that 'that would constitute a peaceful solution'.[178] The Cuban representative considered partition illegal and 'unjust because it involves forcing the will of a minority upon an overwhelming majority, in contravention of one of the cardinal principles of democracy'.[179] Unsurprisingly, the most direct of criticisms of the rule by law logic of partition-as-self-determination came from the representative of the AHC, Mr. Husseini, who pointedly noted: 'After the Arabs had been deprived of self-determination for a quarter of a century in order that a [European settler] minority might be artificially created' through the British mandate, 'what ground was there for asking that that artificial minority should have the right of self-determination' against the will of the majority of the population? In his view, '[i]f that request were granted, it would be a stain on the Charter'.[180]

Another form of response was to question the logic of partition through the lens of double-standards in application of the principle of self-determination. If the European Jewish settler minority possessed a right to self-determination justifying the partition of the country against the will of its majority, would the

---

[176] Ad Hoc Committee on the Palestinian Question, Summary Records of Meetings 25 September – 25 November 1947, UN GAOR, 2nd Sess, 14th Mtg. at 92, 15 October 1947.

[177] Ad Hoc Committee on the Palestinian Question, Summary Records of Meetings 25 September – 25 November 1947, UN GAOR, 2nd Sess, 14th Mtg. at 90, 15 October 1947 ('If the United Nations should sanction the partition of Palestine and flout all the rules of democracy, it would mean that in future the political independence of nations and their territorial integrity would be dependent on the whim of the minorities living in their midst, and it would be an encouragement to separatist tendencies within the Member States of the United Nations').

[178] *Id.*, at 88.

[179] UN GAOR, 2nd Sess., 126th Plen. Mtg. at 1385, A/PV.126, 28 November 1947.

[180] Ad Hoc Committee on the Palestinian Question, Summary Records of Meetings 25 September – 25 November 1947, UN GAOR, 2nd Sess, 18th Mtg. at 122, 18 October 1947.

4 UNSCOP and the General Assembly Debates 99

same principle be applicable to the Palestinian Arabs that would end up in the Jewish State, whether they were almost equal in number or in the majority? This slippery slope argument was expressed by the representatives of each of Lebanon,[181] Pakistan,[182] and Yemen.[183] The issue of moral equivalence and justice was also spoken to. For instance, the Pakistani delegate stated that '[i]f it were considered unjust to place 600,000 Jews in an Arab State, it was equally unjust to place 400,000 Arabs in the Jewish State set up by partition'.[184] Elsewhere, he demurred that partition was based on the assumption that '[t]he Jews are not to live as a minority under the Arabs, but the Arabs are to live as a minority under the Jews. If one of these is not fair then neither is the other'.[185] The record demonstrates that, for the non-European states, the issue always came back to the pre-eminence of the principle of consent of the governed, in line with prevailing international law concerning class A mandates. Thus, the Syrian representative affirmed 'that self-determination could not be achieved in Palestine unless the inhabitants of the country were consulted'.[186] The Pakistani delegate stated that '[i]n effect' the partition 'proposal before the United Nations General Assembly says that we shall decide – not the people of Palestine, with no provision for self-determination, no provision for the consent of the governed – what type of independence Palestine shall have'.[187] Perhaps the Cuban delegate put it best when he stated that '[i]n fact the [partition] plan would mean deciding the fate of a nation without consulting it on the matter'. After indicating his view that partition would violate the

---

[181] UN GAOR, 2nd Sess., 125th Plen. Mtg. at 1342, A/PV.125, 26 November 1947 (Partition, if 'pushed to its logical conclusion, would lead to the following sequence of events: self-determination for the Jewish people, therefore a separate Jewish State. Now there is an Arab minority almost equal to the majority in this separate Jewish State, as you have envisaged it. Will the principle of self-determination … apply to this Arab minority?').

[182] Ad Hoc Committee on the Palestinian Question, Summary Records of Meetings 25 September – 25 November 1947, UN GAOR, 2nd Sess, 31st Mtg. at 192, 24 November 1947 ('If the principle of self-determination were to be applied to the Jews in Palestine, it should be borne in mind that the same principle would be applicable to the 435,000 Arabs who would be in the Jewish State').

[183] Ad Hoc Committee on the Palestinian Question, Summary Records of Meetings 25 September – 25 November 1947, UN GAOR, 2nd Sess, 28th Mtg. at 171, 22 November 1947 ('Moreover a dangerous precedent would be established if a minority were given the right to form a separate State. He asked whether the Arab minority in the Jewish state would be allowed to establish a separate State, and why Palestine could not remain a single State for both Arabs and Jews').

[184] Ad Hoc Committee on the Palestinian Question, Summary Records of Meetings 25 September – 25 November 1947, UN GAOR, 2nd Sess, 30th Mtg. at 188, 24 November 1947.

[185] UN GAOR, 2nd Sess., 126th Plen. Mtg. at 1374, A/PV.126, 28 November 1947.

[186] Ad Hoc Committee on the Palestinian Question, Summary Records of Meetings 25 September – 25 November 1947, UN GAOR, 2nd Sess, 28th Mtg. at 172, 22 November 1947.

[187] UN GAOR, 2nd Sess., 126th Plen. Mtg. at 1370, A/PV.126, 28 November 1947.

100   1947: *The UN Plan of Partition for Palestine*

Charter, he continued in a way that underscored the rule by law essence of what was being contemplated by the General Assembly:

> We [e.g. the UN] have solemnly proclaimed the principle of the self-determination of peoples, but we note with alarm that, when the moment comes to put it into practice, we forget it. This attitude seems to us highly dangerous. The Cuban delegation is firmly convinced that true peace and the international justice about which the great leaders of the Second World War spoke so often cannot be brought into being by setting forth certain fundamental principles in conventions and treaties, and then leaving them there as a dead letter; on the contrary, these ends can be attained only if all of us, great and small, weak and strong, are prepared to put our principles into practice when the occasion arises. Why was the democratic method of consulting all the people of Palestine not applied in this case? Is it because it was feared that the results of such a procedure would be contrary to what it was intended the outcome should be in any case? And, if that was so, where are the democratic principles which we are continuously invoking?[188]

In sum, the contempt displayed by UNSCOP's majority report for democratic governance and international law is what led it to adopt a plan of partition for Palestine in furtherance of the rule by law ordering principle. The majority plan fashioned a proposal whose object and purpose was to circumvent the reality of the indigenous Arab population while paradoxically claiming that doing so conformed with the principle of self-determination as applicable to class A mandates under the Charter. The hegemonic/subaltern binary inherent in the work of UNSCOP was thus exposed, underscored by the geographical and philosophical split between its controlling European majority and its largely non-European minority. Although the former operated according to the values of the Eurocentric late-imperial global order, which privileged European interests over colonial ones, the latter remained consistent with the universal values of the ostensibly new liberal, rights-based global order. The result was a failure to take the indigenous population's rights under the international rule of law seriously, thereby helping to reify their legal subalternity in the new UN system.

5 THE NAKBA AND UNSCOP'S COGNITIVE DISSONANCE

Informed by the clash between hegemonic European and subaltern non-European worldviews and interests evident in the work of UNSCOP and subsequent General Assembly debates, it is clear how resolution 181(II) emerged

---

[188] *Id.*, at 1383.

5 The Nakba and UNSCOP's Cognitive Dissonance

as the lingering product of the interwar rule by law ethic inherited by the UN. But beyond its doctrinal and normative/discursive results under international law, the resolution also had immediate tangible consequences for the subaltern Palestinians.

The practical consequences of resolution 181(II) are sometimes overlooked given that it was, in effect, stillborn. But it was precisely because the resolution's terms were so repugnant to the liberal international legal order ostensibly prevailing and, by extension, the rights of Palestine's Arab population, that it gave impetus for them to resist if need be to block it, their general incapacity to do so notwithstanding.[189] Viewed in the context of the preceding thirty years, during which time Palestine's legal subalternity had taken hold through the operation of the League of Nations, such Palestinian resolve was inevitable. The fact that the resolution was passed by a new international organization that, through its Charter, portrayed itself as embodying an end to empire and heralded self-determination of peoples as a new principle upon which friendly relations between sovereign equals was purportedly to be based, only made matters worse. It is no wonder, therefore, that on 1 December 1947, merely two days after the General Assembly's passage of resolution 181(II), the AHC leadership called a three-day general strike in Palestine. This gave rise to rioting and clashes between Jews and Arabs, ultimately setting off the 1948 war.[190]

The war lasted from December 1947 to July 1949 and was fought in two general phases. The first phase was a non-international armed conflict and lasted for six months. It was waged between the European Zionist armed organizations – Haganah, Irgun, and Lehi – and loose bands of Palestinian Arab irregulars, supported by an Arab volunteer force, the so-called Arab Liberation Army. The protagonists were woefully mismatched, with the better-equipped and trained Zionist forces numbering 50,000, mostly under a central command, against the ill-equipped and disunited Arab forces, who numbered less than 10,000.[191] During this phase, over 300,000 Palestinian Arabs from within the borders of the partition plan's proposed Jewish State were forcibly expelled or took flight.[192] The remainder of the war was fought on an inter-state basis following the intervention in Palestine of five Arab states (Egypt, Iraq, Lebanon, Syria,

---

[189] Kattan, *supra* note 32 at 160.

[190] Morris, B. *1948* (Yale, 2008) at 76–77. Although there had been other low-level hostilities prior to the general strike, including on 29 November 1947 – the day of the partition resolution – Morris indicates that it was not clear whether these were related to the passage of the resolution as such (p. 76). *See also* Khalidi, R. *The Iron Cage* (Beacon, 2007) at 130–131.

[191] Khalidi, *id.*, at 131.

[192] Smith, *supra* note 124 at 143. For more on Palestinian refugee numbers, *see* Chapter 4, s. 3.1.

1947: The UN Plan of Partition for Palestine

and Transjordan) on 15 May 1948, the day Israel proclaimed its statehood upon the departure of the British. During this phase, Israel expanded its territory to control some 78 per cent of mandatory Palestine, well beyond the terms of the partition resolution.[193] Over 400,000 more Palestinian Arabs were expelled or fled during this phase.[194] In response, the General Assembly passed resolution 194(III) on 11 December 1948, calling on Israel to repatriate the refugees 'at the earliest practicable date'.[195] Repatriation was barred, however, by a wartime decision of the Israeli cabinet in June 1948 and by the Zionists' deliberate destruction of between 392 and 418 Palestinian villages whence the majority of refugees hailed.[196] Today, according to the United Nations Relief and Works Agency for Palestine refugees in the Near East (UNRWA) – a subsidiary organ of the General Assembly mandated to provide protection and assistance to those displaced in 1948[197] – the *Palestine* refugees, including their descendants, number approximately 5.7 million registered persons.[198] Together with the much larger category of *Palestinian* refugees, upwards of approximately 12 million,[199] these people remain in forced exile (*see* Chapter 4).

What was the role of UNSCOP in all of this? According to the record, UNSCOP's deliberations were tainted by a cognitive dissonance as to the inevitability of violence befalling Palestine following partition. To be sure, UNSCOP knew the mandate period was characterized by occasional outbreaks of low- to medium-grade violence between Jews, Arabs, and Britons. Indeed, although historians have debated the reasons behind Britain's choice to hand Palestine over to the UN, it is generally accepted that one principal factor to which UNSCOP was very much alive was the armed operations

[193] Hadawi, S. *Palestinian Rights and Losses* (Saqi, 1988) at 81.

[194] The figure is arrived at by subtracting the pre-15 May 1948 figure from the overall approximate total of 700,000 Palestinian refugees produced during the Nakba. *See* Morris, B. 'Revisiting the Palestinian Exodus of 1948' in Rogan, E. & Shlaim, A., eds. *The War for Palestine* (Cambridge, 2001) at 37. For further comment on Palestinian refugee numbers, *see* Chapter 4, s. 3.1.

[195] A/RES/194(III), 11 December 1948.

[196] The figure of 392 is given in Morris, B. *The Birth of the Palestinian Refugee Problem Revisited* (Cambridge, 2004) at xvi–xxii. The figure of 418 is offered in Khalidi, W. *All That Remains* (IPS, 1992) at 585.

[197] A/RES/302(IV), 8 December 1949.

[198] UNRWA *in Figures*: www.unrwa.org/sites/default/files/content/resources/unrwa_in_figures_2021_eng.pdf. The actual number of Palestinian refugees from the 1948 war remains disputed. Arab officials have estimated it to be as high as one million, while Israeli officials have usually cited 520,000. In 1949, the United Nations Relief and Works Agency for Palestine Refugees in the Near East (UNRWA) recorded numbers as high as 960,000. *See* Takkenberg, L. *The Status of Palestinian Refugees in International Law* (Oxford, 1998) at 18–19.

[199] Akram, S. 'Palestinian Nationality and 'Jewish' Nationality: From the Lausanne Treaty to Today' in Farsakh, L. ed. *Rethinking Statehood in Palestine* (University of California Press, 2021) at 194.

5 *The Nakba and UNSCOP's Cognitive Dissonance*

of the Zionist underground militias – Haganah, Irgun, and Lehi – directed against the British in the years following WWII and Whitehall's concern of these operations developing into a full-scale clash.[200]

Thus, the record does not suggest that UNSCOP and the General Assembly were oblivious to the possibility of violence occurring, *per se*. Rather, it suggests an unwillingness to account for the possibility that any recommendation of partition would be followed by violence. Worse from the perspective of the subaltern, it suggests an unwillingness to account for the possibility that such violence would, for the most part, be directed against the unprotected Arab civilian population, and in a manner that would fundamentally alter the demographic and political landscape of the country. Although there was no way UNSCOP and the General Assembly could have foretold the exact contours and scope of the seismic demographic shift that would mark the Palestinian Nakba of 1948 – what is described in the literature as the ethnic cleansing of Palestine[201] – there were certainly signposts available for it to have appreciated that the ultimate success of the Zionists in establishing a Jewish State in any partitioned area of the country would necessarily depend on that state having an unassailable Jewish majority. Given the almost 1:1 ratio of Jew to Arab in the proposed Jewish State projected by UNSCOP itself and UNSCOP's specific knowledge that the Zionists were prepared and able to use force to impose it on Palestine's much weaker Arabs in the absence of British protection, it should have been apparent that the forcible removal of substantial portions of the indigenous Arab population would have been a possible, even likely, result of any UN recommendation to partition the country.

This is something that UNSCOP intimated in its report to the General Assembly. In its appraisal of the 'Jewish case', UNSCOP recounted that '[w]hen the Mandate was approved, all concerned were aware of the existence of an overwhelming Arab majority in Palestine' and that 'the King-Crane report, among others, had warned that the Zionist program could not be carried out *except by force of arms*'.[202] Despite concerted Zionist settlement during the mandate period, by 1947 the Palestinian Arabs were still very much the overwhelming majority of the population and still refusing to acquiesce in the partition of their country. As a result, the overall calculus on the inevitability of violence being needed to give effect to Zionist aims could not have

---

[200] Morris, *supra* note 190 at 38.
[201] Khalidi, R. *The Hundred Years' War on Palestine* (Picador, 2020) at 75–76; Pappe, I. *The Ethnic Cleansing of Palestine* (One World, 2006).
[202] UNSCOP Report, Vol. I, *supra* note 19 at 32 [emphasis added].

104   *1947: The UN Plan of Partition for Palestine*

fundamentally changed. It was for these reasons that UNSCOP unequivocally affirmed that 'the history of the last twenty-five years has established the
fact that not only the creation of a Jewish State but even the continuation of
the building of the Jewish National Home by restricted immigration could be
implemented *only by the use of some considerable force'.*[203]

As to the nature of this 'considerable force', the record indicates that
UNSCOP was aware of Zionist military capability and willingness to employ
it if need be. When asked by UNSCOP on 7 July 1947 as to what the Jewish
leadership would do in the event a UN recommendation to establish a Jewish
State in Palestine was rejected by the Arabs, Ben Gurion replied in no uncer-
tain terms: 'First we will go to them and tell them, here is a decision in our
favour. We are right. We want to sit down with you and settle the question
amicably. *If your answer is no, then we will use force against you'.*[204] After being
questioned by UNSCOP chairman, Justice Sandstrom, as to the relationship
between the Jewish Agency and the Haganah, Ben Gurion stated that the
Haganah had been an organized underground armed Jewish force in Palestine
'for at least the last forty years', that he was formerly a member of it and that it
would be happy to appear before UNSCOP, though in private given its status
as an illegal organization.[205] Subsequently, on 13 July 1947, Sandstrom and two
members of the UNSCOP secretariat met privately with four Haganah leaders, including its chief of staff, Yisrael Galili. At that meeting, the Haganah
expressed full confidence in its ability to manage local and international Arab
force, including the ability to attack naval bases and airfields of neighbouring
Arab states. According to Israeli historian, Elad Ben Dror, this meeting left
Sandstrom with the 'strong impression' that the Haganah, in addition to Etzel
and Lehi, 'would defeat the Arabs in the event of hostilities'.[206] Most vitally,
Sandstrom was convinced that if the UN voted for partition, the Jews could be

---

[203] *Id* [emphasis added]. Neither was this a one-off acknowledgement, as UNSCOP elsewhere
noted the inevitability of force being required to ensure Zionist aims if delayed independence
pending the achievement of a Jewish majority was envisioned. It also assailed the 'recurrent
acts of violence, until very recently confined almost exclusively to underground Jewish organizations', and indicated that such violence would render any decision arrived at by the UN
difficult to implement. *See id.,* at 46.

[204] UNSCOP Report, Vol. III, *supra* note 105 at 56 [emphasis added]. *See also* UNSCOP Report,
Vol. IV, *supra* note 153 at 37, where Judge Sandstrom stated to the Lebanese delegate who
was testifying before UNSCOP on 23 July 1947 in Beirut, '[y]ou know as well as we do that
certain disorders in Palestine now are caused by Jews and that the Jews have considerable
underground forces, such as Haganah, and so on. Do you not think it would be necessary to
have a rather strong police force to maintain order in that case?'

[205] *Id.,* at 68.

[206] Ben Dror, E. 'The United Nation Plan to Establish an Armed Jewish Force to Implement the
Partition Plan (United Nations Resolution 181)' (2013) 24 *Diplomacy & Statecraft* 559 at 562.

5 The Nakba and UNSCOP's Cognitive Dissonance

relied upon to implement and impose it on the Arabs in the Jewish State.[207] In an indication of the Eurocentric orientation of UNSCOP's majority, it would appear that far from assessing the threat posed by the Zionist militias to the non-European indigenous population, Sandstrom was more concerned with whether the European settlers could impose themselves militarily.

Of course, the Zionists were not alone in issuing expressions of bellicosity. The verbatim and summary records of the UNSCOP hearings, as well as of the ad hoc and plenary debates of the General Assembly, demonstrate that the Arabs reserved their right to use force to protect against the dismemberment of Palestine.[208] Despite these statements, however, the record suggests that UNSCOP understood that the Arabs were not capable of mounting any effective armed force in this regard and were, in any event, no match for the Zionists who were better armed and organized. This was made amply clear in the testimony given to UNSCOP by Sir Henry Gurney, Chief Secretary of the Palestine Government, on 19 July 1947. According to him, the British were well aware that the Zionists were better armed and organized, they knew that 'no Arab armed organization' existed in the country and they were going out of their way to prevent the establishment of such a force.[209]

The most crucial development in the record appears to have been the United Kingdom's decision that it would refuse to enforce any UN recommendation on Palestine not agreed between the Jews and Arabs. Absent such agreement, the British would withdraw their troops and administration by 1 August 1948.[210] In a sign that the values underpinning the liberal rights-based order might prevail in the eleventh hour, this decision drew heavy criticism, including from members of the European and settler-colonial bloc of states. The Czech delegate indicated that this had 'radically changed the background of the deliberations', as the General Assembly would now 'have to find the means of implementing' any solution it arrived at.[211]

---

[207] *Id.*

[208] *See, e.g.*, Ad Hoc Committee on the Palestinian Question, Summary Records of Meetings 25 September – 25 November 1947, UN GAOR, 2nd Sess, 15th Mtg. at 102, 16 October 1947, where the Iraqi delegate, Fadhil Jamali, stated 'The political consequences of partition would be that the Arabs would never acquiesce, but would fight for their rights even at the risk of civil war'.

[209] UNSCOP Report, Vol. IV, *supra* note 153 at 27.

[210] Ad Hoc Committee on the Palestinian Question, Summary Records of Meetings 25 September – 25 November 1947, UN GAOR, 2nd Sess, 2nd Mtg. at 3–4, 26 September 1947, and 25th Mtg. at 153, 20 November 1947. *See also* UN GAOR 2nd Sess., 124th Mtg. at 1323–1324, A/PV.124, 26 November 1947.

[211] Ad Hoc Committee on the Palestinian Question, Summary Records of Meetings 25 September – 25 November 1947, UN GAOR, 2nd Sess, 8th Mtg. at 45, 8 October 1947.

The American delegate derided the British for imposing 'an impossible condition' of Jewish-Arab agreement and therefore placing 'upon the United Nations a very heavy moral responsibility'.[212] This was echoed by the Soviet representative, who accused the British of 'burying' the General Assembly's recommendation before even making it.[213] Similar rebukes were issued by the Canadian,[214] New Zealand,[215] and Swedish delegates, the latter of whom presciently noted that unless 'a reasonable and realistic solution could be found' to the power vacuum the British would leave behind, 'the possibility that had to be faced was a civil war between the two nascent states in Palestine, a situation which would gravely threaten peace and security in that part of the world'.[216] Despite this apparent concern, however, in the end, each of these states curiously voted *in favour* of partition rather than abstain from or reject it. The cognitive dissonance involved in this respect was, once again, demonstrative of the general disregard for non-Europeans held within an Organization that remained fundamentally Eurocentric in its outlook. This was exhibited, for example, by the Swedish delegate who informed the General Assembly that although his 'Government regrets to note that the method of enforcement' of the partition plan 'does not appear to satisfy [the] essential condition' of being 'practical' and 'efficient', Sweden would vote in favour of resolution 181(II) 'since the efforts of the Assembly have not resulted in anything more perfect than the plan of partition'.[217]

Resolution 181(II) provided for the establishment of the UNPC which, as noted, was mandated to administer the transfer of power from Britain to the two proposed states during a transitional period to last until 1 October 1948. Under this scheme, the UNPC would, *inter alia*, exercise political and military control over the 'armed militia' of each state with a view to maintaining public order. None of these plans came to fruition, however, given the predictable British refusal to allow the UNCP to enter Palestine until May 1948 (merely two weeks before its advanced departure date of 15 May) and, more generally, the Arab rejection of the partition plan – both of which factors were well known to the General Assembly while deliberating partition.[218] Thus, attempts

---

[212] UN GAOR 2nd Sess., 124th Plen. Mtg. at 1326–1327, A/PV.124, 26 November 1947.

[213] UN GAOR 2nd Sess., 125th Plen. Mtg. at 1362–1363, A/PV.125, 26 November 1947.

[214] Ad Hoc Committee on the Palestinian Question, Summary Records of Meetings 25 September – 25 November 1947, UN GAOR, 2nd Sess, 29th Mtg. at 176, 22 November 1947.

[215] UN GAOR 2nd Sess., 125th Plen. Mtg. at 1357, A/PV.125, 26 November 1947.

[216] Ad Hoc Committee on the Palestinian Question, Summary Records of Meetings 25 September – 25 November 1947, UN GAOR, 2nd Sess, 9th Mtg. at 49, 9 October 1947.

[217] UN GAOR 2nd Sess., 124th Plen. Mtg. at 1312, A/PV.124, 26 November 1947.

[218] Grief, *supra* note 44 at 154; Quigley, *supra* note 94 at 79.

6 *Conclusion* 107

to create some form of UN-mandated force that would fill the vacuum left by
the British were stymied from the start. This left a power imbalance in place in
the country between the Zionists and the Palestinian Arabs.

Thus, the record does not establish an awareness of UNSCOP or the
General Assembly of the specific animus and plans Zionist forces had to
expel the Palestinian Arabs from territories they would control in 1948; that
would emerge later with the chronicling of the 1948 war by Palestinian historians in the 1950s and 1960s,[219] and largely corroborated by Israel's 'new
historians' in the 1980's.[220] What it does establish, however, is the clear
understanding UNSCOP had or ought to have had regarding the relative
military capabilities of both sides, and the political imperatives underpinning their respective goals. For the stronger and better organized European
Zionists, these goals were animated by a singular fifty-year effort to establish
a Jewish State in a place in which, by all accounts, they were a decided
demographic minority. It was well understood by the UN that for any Jewish
State to materialize, the demographic balance had to be altered, including
by force, if the opportunity arose. When one considers that the UN knew
partition was anathema to the indigenous population and that enforcement
of partition was futile without British cooperation which was not forthcoming, the writing on the wall was clear for all to see. In this way, the illegality
and rule by law character inherent in the terms of resolution 181(II) helped
further the conditions that, in real terms, led to the consummation of what
the Palestinian Arabs had feared most.

6 CONCLUSION

This chapter has argued that international legal subalternity derives its content, in part, from the structural Eurocentricity of international law and organization. To demonstrate this, it has undertaken a critical international legal
analysis of the UN plan of partition of November 1947 and examined the
effective *travaux preparatoires* of that plan as found in the UNSCOP records
and report and animated in the General Assembly debates that followed.
In 1945, the newly formed UN had a unique opportunity to prove its worth
as an embodiment of a new liberal rights-based global order centred on

---

[219] Arif al-Arif, *The Nakba* (reprinted, IPS, 2013); Zurayq, C. *The Meaning of the Disaster*
(R. Bayley Winder trans. (Khayat, 1956). Khalidi, W. *From Haven to Conquest* (1971). For later
work by Walid Khalidi, *see All That Remains, supra* note 196, and 'Plan Dalet: Master Plan for
the Conquest of Palestine' (1988) 18 *J. Pal. Stud.* 4.

[220] Pappe, *Ethnic Cleansing, supra* note 201; Masalha, N. *Expulsion of the Palestinians* (IPS,
1992); Masalha, N. *A Land without a People* (Faber & Faber, 1997); Morris, *supra* note 196.

108   *1947: The UN Plan of Partition for Palestine*

the international rule of law following WWII. Instead, through the General Assembly's promulgation of resolution 181(II), the UN demonstrated that the old international rule by law order lingered on in fundamental respects, informed by the structural Eurocentricity of the system it inherited from the League of Nations. Although the passage of the resolution was procedurally valid, its terms were substantively illegal under the UN Charter for being in violation of the prevailing law and practice on self-determination of peoples in class A mandated territories. Because that law required the General Assembly to defer to the freely expressed wishes of the people concerned and because the indigenous non-European majority was against partition, there were only two courses of action open to the UN in Palestine in 1947: (1) immediate independence; or (2) conversion of the country into a UN trusteeship.

In the event, territorial partition was the option recommended by a General Assembly then dominated by hegemonic European states and their settler-colonial offshoots. Many of these states saw in the question of Palestine an opportunity to rectify Europe's age-long Jewish question in the wake of the Holocaust. Accordingly, the majority of UNSCOP and the General Assembly chose to treat the acquired international legal rights of the Jewish people to a Jewish national home as equivalent to their right to a Jewish State at the Palestinians' expense. A close examination of the UNSCOP records reveals at least three factors that demonstrate a disregard for international law during the course of its work, and which influenced the General Assembly in attempting to facilitate the creation of this Jewish State through the passage of resolution 181(II). Between a Eurocentric bias in UNSCOP's composition and terms of reference, its unwillingness to sufficiently engage the AHC, and its evident contempt for the application of democratic governance to the non-European people of Palestine, the institutional roots of the rule by law nature of resolution 181(II) were laid bare. To make matters worse, the record indicates that UNSCOP's deliberations were tainted by what can be regarded as a cognitive dissonance as to the inevitability of violence befalling Palestine's indigenous population following partition.

Resolution 181(II) effectively legislated into UN law the contingency and disenfranchisement of the Palestinian Arabs, thereby reifying Palestine's legal subalternity inherited from the interwar period. But there was a deeper twist. With partition, the international legal goalposts had now indelibly shifted. By virtue of events shaped by and within the UN, no longer would the subaltern Palestinians be able to claim sovereignty over the whole of their historical patrimony. From now on, any right to self-determination they would be allowed to legitimately assert within the UN system, if at all, would be confined to

6 Conclusion

the truncated remnants of that patrimony. In today's context, where the Palestinian people continue to struggle for universal recognition of their sovereign right to self-determination in the OPT, the two-state paradigm that resolution 181(II) set on course within the UN system has ironically assumed great import for the subaltern class, both politically and legally. Viewed in the context of 1947, however, the rule by law character of the partition resolution was something that confirmed Palestine's subaltern status under international law and organization. It began a pattern within the UN system in which the promise of international law would be repeatedly proffered to the Palestinian people, but which would, in turn, continually be withheld in some fashion or another. As will be demonstrated in the following chapters, overcoming this dilemma has been marked by a cruel paradox for the Palestinian people as an embodiment of the global subaltern, for they have at once had to become inured to the injustice of their contingent and qualified membership in the international legal order in order to find the space within which they may establish full and equal membership in that very same order.

4

1948 and After: The UN and the Palestinian Refugees

1 INTRODUCTION

This chapter covers the United Nations' (UN) management of the most immediate and enduring consequence of the 1948 war: the Palestinian refugee problem. Immediate, because it resulted from events triggered by General Assembly resolution 181(II) of 29 November 1947. Enduring, because it remains the largest and most protracted refugee problem since World War II (WWII).[1] From the initial trauma of mass expulsion, dispossession, and property appropriation by European settlers who rapidly supplanted them, to the intergenerational anguish of remaining wards of the international community, the Palestinian refugees have come to embody, physically and metaphysically, the core issues at the heart of the question of Palestine. What and where is Palestine? Who and where are its people? Why were they uprooted? And, above all, why do they remain dispossessed and in forced exile? These are the existential questions that have characterized Palestinian diasporic existence since 1948.

During the Palestinian refugees' prolonged alienation from their land and property – now going on seventy-five years – the UN has been one of the principal sites where answers to these questions have been sought and furnished. This is not insignificant, given that within a short time after the 1948 Nakba, denial of the very existence of Palestine and the Palestinian people, as such, had become *de rigeur* in some quarters, particularly in the west.[2]

---

[1] Albanese, F. & Takkenberg, L. *Palestinian Refugees in International Law*, 2nd ed. (Oxford, 2020) at 68.

[2] Early Zionists fabricated the myth that Palestine was a 'land without a people for a people without a land'. By 1969, Israeli Prime Minister Golda Meir's view that the Palestinian people 'did not exist' had become part of the general Zietgeist in much of the 'civilized' west. *See* Said, E.W. *Orientalism* (Vintage, 1979) at 27; and Cattan, H. *The Palestine Question* (Saqi, 2000) at 219–220.

1 Introduction

In this context, for its provision of a global platform for representations of what actually happened to Palestine and its people in 1948 and as a source of stability and legitimacy for the humanitarian needs, rights, and claims of the Palestinian refugees, the UN has played a vital role over the decades. It is perhaps for this reason that the conventional wisdom has long held that the UN's management of the Palestinian refugee problem is demonstrative of the Organization's commitment to the international rule of law.

This chapter interrogates this view by critically examining the early evolution, object, purpose, and functioning of what has been called the 'distinctive institutional and normative regime' created by the UN for the Palestinian refugees in the immediate aftermath of the Nakba.[3] This regime, spearheaded by two subsidiary organs of the General Assembly – the United Nations Conciliation Commission for Palestine (UNCCP) and the United Nations Relief and Works Agency for Palestine Refugees in the Near East (UNRWA) – is distinctive because it stands apart from the international institutional and normative regime applicable to all other refugees in the world, as administered by a third subsidiary UN organ, the United Nations High Commissioner for Refugees (UNHCR). Contrary to the regime governing protection and assistance for refugees globally, this distinctive regime has resulted in what has been identified in the literature as a 'protection gap' for Palestinian refugees.[4] Building on this literature,[5] the main claim here is that the protection gap that affects Palestinian refugees originates in the same Eurocentric interests and failure to take Palestine and its people seriously that produced the plan of partition in 1947. This in turn resulted in an attempt, ultimately in vain, by the UN to legislate a principled means of managing the fallout in a manner ostensibly in line with international law. As will be demonstrated, the attending confusion and anomalous legal framework governing Palestinian refugee rights is reflective of a continued international rule by law. An examination of how this framework has operated in practice will show that it has helped perpetuate Palestinian legal subalternity in the international legal order.

---

[3] Albanese & Takkenberg, *supra* note 1 at 125.

[4] *See, e.g.,* Akram, S. & Al-Azza, N. *Closing Protection Gaps*, 2nd ed. (Badil, 2015); Albanese & Takkenberg, *supra* note 1.

[5] *See, e.g.,* Akram, S. 'Reinterpreting Palestinian Refugee Rights under International Law' in Aruri, N., ed., *Palestinian Refugees* (Pluto, 2001); Albanese & Takkenberg, *supra* note 1; Boling, G. *The 1948 Palestinian Refugees and the Individual Right of Return* (Badil, 2007); Kattan, V. 'The Nationality of Denationalized Palestinians' (2005) 74 *Nord. JIL* 67; Lynk, M. 'The Right to Restitution and Compensation in International Law and the Displaced Palestinians' (2003) 21(3) *Refuge* 2, 96; Quigley, J. 'Displaced Palestinians and a Right of Return' (1998) *Harv. ILJ* 171; Rempel, T. 'The Right to Return: Drafting Paragraph 11 of General Assembly Resolution 194(III), December 11, 1948' (2020) 21 *PYIL* 77.

112   *1948 and After: The UN and the Palestinian Refugees*

The remainder of this chapter offers a summary of the international rule of law relevant to refugee status, including protracted refugee situations. It then critically juxtaposes this general framework against the situation of the Palestinian refugees, including the distinctive institutional and normative regime established for them, with a specific focus on its initial object and purpose and its evolution and operation as gleaned from the UN record.

2 THE UN, REFUGEES, AND INTERNATIONAL LAW

2.1 UNHCR and the 1951 Convention Regime for Protection and Assistance, Including Durable Solutions

Modern international refugee law is codified in a number of instruments, the most important of which are the 1951 *Convention Relating to the Status of Refugees* and its 1967 *Protocol*.[6] These treaties originate in the interwar years, when the international community addressed mass-displacement problems through the promulgation of specifically tailored *ad hoc* arrangements, only some of which were binding.[7] Immediately following the unprecedented mass displacements occasioned during WWII, considerable advancements were made through the establishment of UNHCR and the conclusion of the 1951 Convention and its 1967 Protocol. This new regime provided an array of rights to which virtually every refugee in the hands of states parties would hitherto be entitled. This basket of rights – styled 'protection and assistance' in modern international refugee law and practice – includes the all-important duty to find durable solutions for refugee problems.[8] As demonstrated below, its content derives not only from international refugee law but also from other areas of public international law.

UNHCR was established by the General Assembly on 14 December 1950 and began operations on 1 January 1951.[9] Under its Statute, UNHCR is mandated to provide 'international protection' to refugees through, *inter alia*: '[p]romoting the conclusion and ratification of international refugee conventions for the protection of refugees'; '[p]romoting the admission of

---

[6] *Convention Relating to the Status of Refugees*, 28 July 1951, 189 UNTS 137 (entered into force 22 April 1954) ['1951 Convention']; *Protocol Relating to the Status of Refugees*, 31 January 1967, 606 UNTS 267 (entered into force 4 October 1967) ['1967 Protocol']. *See also Convention Relating to the Status of Stateless Persons*, 28 September 1954, 360 UNTS 117 (entered into force 6 June 1960).

[7] Zimmermann, A., ed. *The 1951 Convention Relating to the Status of Refugees and Its 1967 Protocol: A Commentary* (Oxford, 2011), 6–36.

[8] UNHCR, *Refugee Protection* (UNHCR, 2001) at 8.

[9] A/RES/428(V), 14 December 1950.

2 The UN, Refugees, and International Law   113

refugees ... to the territories of States'; and seeking 'permanent solutions'
for refugee problems.[10] Under the 1951 Convention, states parties undertake
to cooperate with UNHCR in facilitating its duty to supervise the application of the Convention.[11] From an original nineteen signatories, the 1951
Convention today boasts a total of 145 states parties.[12]

The gateway for access to protection and assistance under the 1951
Convention is the definition of the term 'refugee' contained in Article 1A(2).
It provides, in relevant part, that a refugee is anyone who,

> owing to well-founded fear of being persecuted for reasons of race, religion,
> nationality, membership of a particular social group or political opinion, is
> outside the country of his nationality and is unable or, owing to such fear,
> is unwilling to avail himself of the protection of that country; or who, not
> having a nationality and being outside the country of his former habitual
> residence as a result of such events, is unable or, owing to such fear, is unwill-
> ing to return to it.[13]

The 1951 Convention thereby operates through the prism of a single definition
of the term 'refugee', as opposed to earlier *ad hoc* instruments. Despite initially being temporally and geographically limited, since 1967, the definition
has been universal in scope.[14] The object and purpose of the Convention refugee definition is to provide surrogate protection of the convention to individuals where there is a risk of persecution on the basis of one or more of the five
listed grounds in their country of nationality or former habitual residence.[15]
Once the threshold of the Convention refugee definition is met, a wide array
of protection and assistance may be sought under the 1951 Convention, often
on an equal footing with nationals and/or aliens within the host state, including access to durable solutions.[16]

In practice, UNHCR's mandate over durable solutions envisions three specific durable solutions for refugee problems: voluntary repatriation, local integration into the country of first asylum, or resettlement in a third country.[17]
Given the socio-economic stresses refugee problems have increasingly placed

---

[10] *Statute of the Office of the United Nations High Commissioner for Refugees*, arts. 1 & 8,
attached as annex to A/RES/428(V), 14 December 1950 ['UNHCR Statute'].

[11] 1951 Convention, *supra* note 6, art. 35.

[12] *See* United Nations Treaty Collection, Status of Treaties, Convention Relating to the Status
of Refugees, 28 July 1951, at: https://treaties.un.org/Pages/ViewDetailsII.aspx?src=TREATY&mt
dsg_no=V-2&chapter=5&Temp=mtdsg2&clang=_en.

[13] 1951 Convention, *supra* note 6, art. 1(A)(2).

[14] *See id.*, art. 1(A)(2) & 1(B)1; *and* 1967 Protocol, *supra* note 6.

[15] Hathaway, J. & Foster, M. *The Law of Refugee Status*, 2nd ed. (Cambridge, 2014) at 362.

[16] 1951 Convention, *supra* note 6, arts. 12–31.

[17] UNHCR, *State of the World's Refugees* (Oxford, 2006) at 129.

114 *1948 and After: The UN and the Palestinian Refugees*

on countries of first asylum and the general hesitancy of third states to offer resettlement, voluntary repatriation is regarded as the preferable and most desirable, durable solution as a matter of state practice.[18] Thus, in 2020 UNHCR reported that whereas some 3.4 million displaced people returned to their areas or countries of origin, only 34,400 refugees were resettled.[19]

One challenge for international refugee law is how the protection of the 1951 Convention extends to protracted refugee crises.[20] When durable solutions remain elusive over successive generations, the continued protection of the 1951 Convention extends to the descendants of refugees on the basis of the principle of family unity.[21] This means that under international law, children born to refugees acquire the same status as their parents on a non-discriminatory basis unless the individual legal status of the child dictates otherwise.[22] In 2020, UNHCR estimated that approximately 15.7 million refugees – *not including* Palestinian refugees – were in protracted refugee situations, with at least 1 million children born as refugees in that year alone.[23]

2.2 *Other International Law Relevant to Refugee Protection and Assistance, Including Durable Solutions*

The 1951 Convention Regime must not be read in isolation from other bodies of international law. This includes the international law governing nationality, international human rights law (IHRL), international humanitarian law (IHL), international criminal law (ICL), and the law governing state responsibility. Each of these is briefly addressed below.

2.2.1 International Law of Nationality

International refugee law is predicated upon the notion that refugee protection is furnished or withheld by the state, *viz.* the country of nationality or, in

[18] *Id.*, at 129–130.

[19] UNHCR, Global Trends: Forced Displacement in 2020, at: www.unhcr.org/60b638e37/ unhcr-global-trends-2020, at 3 ['Global Trends 2020'].

[20] UNHCR defines a protracted refugee situation as 'one in which 25,000 or more refugees from the same nationality have been in exile for at least five consecutive years in a given host country' *Id.*, at 20.

[21] *Final Act of the United Nations Conference of Plenipotentiaries on the Status of Refugees and Stateless Persons*, 1951, A/CONF.2/108/Rev.1.

[22] Goddard, B. 'UNHCR and the International Protection of Palestinian Refugees' (2009) 28: 2&3 *Ref. Surv. Q.* 475, at 494.

[23] According to UNHCR, the largest protracted refugee situations, aside from the Palestinian refugees, in 2020 were from Afghanistan, Burundi, and South Sudan. Global Trends 2020, *supra* note 19 at 3, 20.

2 The UN, Refugees, and International Law 115

situations of statelessness, former habitual residence. When examining refugee questions, it is therefore important to understand what international law provides in matters governing nationality.

States are generally free to determine who their nationals are, and nationality is usually conferred through consequence of birth in the territory of the state (*jus soli*), birth to a national of the state (*jus sanguinis*), or by formal act of the state (nationalization).[24] But this freedom is not absolute. One limitation is the prohibition on the denationalization by a state of parts or all of its population, including where there has been a change in sovereignty over the territory in question.[25] The rule that nationality follows a change in sovereignty was well established in state practice through the series of 'minority treaties' signed by the allied and axis powers (e.g. US, France, Turkey, etc.) following World War I (WWI),[26] such that it had achieved customary status by that time. Writing in 1928, McNair affirmed that 'the inhabitants of ... conquered or ceded territory become the subjects of the State which annexes the territory, and their former nationality is extinguished by substitution of the new'.[27] To him, '[t]hese modes of acquisition of nationality are modes settled by the customary Law of Nations'.[28] As noted by Crawford, '[i]f a new state, relying on the absence of a municipal law, tried to deport a part of its permanent population (e.g. on grounds of ethnicity), it would be acting in clear breach of its obligations and would be internationally responsible'.[29] Importantly, no state can plead provisions of its internal law to evade its obligations under international law, especially when such internal law may be part of an internationally wrongful act that strips a person of the ability to avail themselves of the protection of their country of nationality.[30]

---

[24] Crawford, J. *Brownlie's Principles of Public International Law*, 9th ed. (Oxford, 2012) at 495–498.

[25] Akram, S. 'Palestinian Nationality and 'Jewish' Nationality: From the Lausanne Treaty to Today' in Farsakh, L. ed. *Rethinking Statehood in Palestine* (University of California Press, 2021) at 194.

[26] *See, e.g.*, Treaty of Neuilly (1919), Rumanian Minorities Treaty (1919), Treaty of Versailles (1919), Treaty of St. Germain (1919), Treaty of Trianon (1920), Treaty of Sèvres (1920), and Treaty of Lausanne (1923). Kattan, V. *From Coexistence to Conquest* (Pluto, 2009) at 221.

[27] Oppenheim, L. *International Law: Volume I – Peace*, McNair 4th ed, (Longmans, 1928) at 536. *See also Draft Articles on Nationality of Natural Persons in Relation to the Succession of States, with Commentaries*, Report of the International Law Commission on the Work of its Fifty-First Session (1999), Yearbook of the International Law Commission, 1999, II(2).

[28] Oppenheim, *id.*, at 534.

[29] Crawford, *supra* note 24 at 504.

[30] *Id.*, at 505.

2.2.2 International Human Rights Law

International refugee law is also heavily informed by IHRL.[31] Indeed, the role of IHRL as a primary interpretive tool for the 1951 Convention has been affirmed by municipal courts and writers alike,[32] including as being undergirded by 'core norms of non-discrimination law'.[33] Thus, citing the UN Charter and the 1948 Universal Declaration of Human Rights (UDHR),[34] the preamble of the 1951 Convention expressly affirms 'that human beings shall enjoy fundamental rights and freedoms without discrimination'.[35] Article 3 of the 1951 Convention prohibits discrimination in its application on the basis of 'race, religion or country of origin',[36] and according to UNHCR, this requirement extends to other forms of discrimination, including gender-based discrimination.[37]

IHRL also informs our understanding of durable solutions. Along with affirming the right of everyone to a nationality, Article 15 of the UDHR provides that '[n]o one shall be arbitrarily deprived of his nationality' and Article 17 affirms that '[n]o one shall be arbitrarily deprived of his property'.[38] This is a corollary of the law prohibiting denationalization of a population on change of sovereignty, where the effective link of a person to their country can be severed in both physical and material terms. In addition, Article 13(2) of the UDHR affirms that '[e]veryone has the right to leave any country, including his own, and to return to his country'.[39] This also finds expression in the International Covenant on Civil and Political Rights (ICCPR), Article 12(2) of which provides that '[e]veryone shall be free to leave any country, including his own' and Article 12(4) of which provides that '[n]o one shall be arbitrarily deprived of the right to enter his own country'.[40] The right to leave and to return to one's country is inexorably linked to the predicament of being a refugee, with the right to return assuming particular importance when it comes to durable solutions. Thus, the Human Rights Committee has affirmed that

---

[31] UNHCR, Convention and Protocol Relating to the Status of Refugees, Introductory Note at 3, at: www.unhcr.org/3b66c2aa10 ['UNHCR Introductory Note'].

[32] Hathaway and Foster, *supra* note 15 at 193.

[33] *Id.*, at 390–391.

[34] *Universal Declaration of Human Rights*, A/RES/217A(III), UNGAOR, 3rd Sess., Supp. No 13, A/810 (1948) 71 ['UDHR'].

[35] 1951 Convention, *supra* note 6, preamble.

[36] *Id*, art. 3.

[37] UNHCR Introductory Note, *supra* note 31 at 3.

[38] UDHR, *supra* note 34, arts. 15(2), 17(2).

[39] *Id.*, art. 13(2).

[40] *International Covenant on Civil and Political Rights*, 16 December 1966, 999 UNTS 171 (entered into force 23 March 1976), art. 12 ['ICCPR'].

2 The UN, Refugees, and International Law 117

'[t]he right to return is of the utmost importance for refugees seeking voluntary repatriation. It also implies prohibition of enforced population transfers or mass-expulsions to other countries'.[41] Other international and regional human rights treaties affirm the right to leave and to return to one's country[42] and several writers assert the right is established as a matter of custom going back to ancient times,[43] or at least since the middle ages with the promulgation of *Magna Carta* in 1215.[44]

2.2.3 International Humanitarian and Criminal Law

Because refugee crises are often produced through armed conflict, various principles of IHL and ICL prohibiting deportation and affirming the rights to leave and to return must also be considered because durable solutions for refugees and other displaced persons may be implicated. The 1945 Charter of the International Military Tribunal (IMT) proscribed deportation of a civilian population as both a 'war crime' and a 'crime against humanity'.[45] In 1946, the IMT held that the war crime of deportation was well established in customary international law by at least 1939.[46] These two core crimes, together with the rest of the so-called 'Nuremberg Principles', were unanimously affirmed by the General Assembly on 11 December 1946.[47] Rapid development of the law thereafter followed. The four Geneva Conventions of August 1949, with their Additional Protocols I and II of June 1977, codified a host of protections against deportation of civilians in both international and non-international armed conflict,[48] imposing obligations on high contracting parties to criminally

---

[41] CCPR General Comment No. 27: Article 12 (Freedom of Movement), 2 November 1999, CCPR/C/21/Rev.1/Add.9, para. 19 ['General Comment No. 27'].

[42] *International Convention on the Elimination of all forms of Racial Discrimination*, 7 March 1966, 660 UNTS 195 (entered into force 4 January 1969), art. 5(d)(ii); *African Charter on Human and Peoples' Rights*, 27 June 1981, 1520 UNTS 217, art. 12(2).

[43] Kattan, *supra* note 26 at 210.

[44] Mallison, T. & S. *The Palestine Problem in International Law and World Order* (Longman, 1986) at 174; Mazawi, M. *Palestine and the Law* (Ithaca, 1997) at 176.

[45] *Agreement for the Prosecution and Punishment of the Major War Criminals of the European Axis*, 8 August 1945, 82 UNTS 280, arts. 6(b) and (c). Although the 'Nuremberg' Charter was signed at London by France, United Kingdom, United States, and USSR, nineteen other states 'adhered' to the Agreement, seventeen before the Nuremberg trial began. Roberts, A. & Guelff, R. *Documents on the Laws of War*, 3rd ed. (Oxford, 2000) at 175.

[46] *Trial of the Major War Criminals before the International Military Tribunal*, Nuremberg, vol. XXII, IMT Secretariat, 1948, *as reprinted* in Roberts & Guelff, *id.*, at 178.

[47] A/RES/95(I), 11 December 1946.

[48] *See, e.g., Geneva Convention Relative to the Protection of Civilian Persons in Time of War*, 12 August 1949, 75 UNTS 287 (entered into force 21 October 1950), arts. 49 & 147 ['Fourth Geneva Convention']; *Protocol Additional to the Geneva Conventions of 12 August 1949, and Relating to*

118   *1948 and After: The UN and the Palestinian Refugees*

proscribe such acts and prosecute or extradite perpetrators,[49] and affirming the principle of repatriation for displaced victims.[50] On the basis of this conventional law and widespread state practice, the International Committee of the Red Cross (ICRC) has affirmed the customary status of the prohibition on the 'forced displacement of civilians for reasons related to an armed conflict, whether within or outside the bounds of national territory', thus covering refugees (i.e. people who have crossed an international border) and internally displaced persons.[51] It has likewise affirmed the customary nature of the rule that '[d]isplaced persons have a right to voluntary return in safety to their homes or places of habitual residence as soon as the reasons for their displacement cease to exist'[52] and the rule that '[t]he property rights of displaced persons must be respected'.[53] Finally, based on the Nuremberg principles and the practice of the *ad hoc* international criminal tribunals for the former Yugoslavia (ICTY) and Rwanda (ICTR) established by the Security Council in the 1990s, the 1998 Rome Statute of the International Criminal Court proscribes the 'unlawful deportation or transfer' of civilians as a war crime.[54] It further categorizes such acts as 'crime[s] against humanity' when committed as part of a widespread and systematic attack directed against any civilian population with knowledge of the attack.[55]

2.2.4 State Responsibility

Violation of any of the above principles engages the law of state responsibility.[56] The foundational principles of this law were well established in the interwar period.[57] Thus, in *Chorzow Factory* the Permanent Court of International

---

the Protection of Victims of International Armed Conflicts, 8 June 1977, 1125 UNTS 3 (entered into force 7 December 1979), art. 85 ['Additional Protocol I']; *Protocol Additional to the Geneva Conventions of 12 August 1949, and Relating to the Protection of Victims of Non-International Armed Conflicts*, 8 June 1977, 1125 UNTS 609 (entered into force 7 December 1978), art. 17.

[49] Fourth Geneva Convention, *id.*, arts. 146, 147.

[50] *Id.*, arts. 6, 36–38, 45, 48, 97, 127, 132–136, 139, 158. Additional Protocol I, *supra* note 48, arts. 3(b), 75, 85, 99.

[51] Henckaerts, J.M. & Doswald-Beck, L., eds. *ICRC Customary International Humanitarian Law*, Vol. 1 (Cambridge University Press, 2005) at 457 (Rule 129).

[52] *Id.*, at 462 (Rule 132).

[53] *Id.*, at 472 (Rule 133).

[54] *Rome Statute of the International Criminal Court*, July 17, 1998, U.N. Doc. 32/A/CONF. 183/9, 37 I.L.M. 999 (entered into force July 1, 2002), arts. 8(2)(a)(vii) & 8(2)(b)(viii) ['Rome Statute'].

[55] *Id.*, art. 7(1)(d).

[56] Where applicable, individual criminal responsibility is also engaged.

[57] For the principle that an internationally wrongful act engages the responsibility of the state so engaged in that act, *see Responsabilité internationale des Etats à raison des dommages causés sur leur territoire à la personne et aux biens des étrangers*, Institut de Droit International, Lausanne,

2 The UN, Refugees, and International Law

Justice (PCIJ) opined that '[i]t is a principle of international law that the breach of an engagement involves an obligation to make reparation in an adequate form'.[58] The Court later elaborated:

> The essential principle contained in the actual notion of an illegal act – a principle which seems to be established by international practice and in particular by the decisions of arbitral tribunals – is that reparation must, as far as possible, wipe out all the consequences of the illegal act and reestablish the situation which would, in all probability, have existed if that act had not been committed. Restitution in kind, or, if this is not possible, payment of a sum corresponding to the value which a restitution in kind would bear; the award, if need be, of damages for loss sustained which would not be covered by restitution in kind or payment in place of it – such are the principles which should serve to determine the amount of compensation due for an act contrary to international law.[59]

The modern law of state responsibility is restated in the International Law Commission's 2001 Draft Articles on Responsibility of States for Internationally Wrongful Acts (ARSIWA), widely considered a codification of custom.[60] Under the ARSIWA, an internationally wrongful act of a state occurs when conduct consisting of an action or omission is both attributable to the state under international law and constitutes a breach of an international obligation of that state.[61] Thus, mass denationalization by a state of its population, or *refoulement* by that state of one or more refugees, would qualify as internationally wrongful acts attributable to it. As international

---

September 1927, at: www.idi-iil.org/app/uploads/2017/06/1927_lau_05_fr.pdf. For the principle that an internationally wrongful act must be attributable to the state and be a breach of the state's obligations under international law *see Phosphates in Morocco (Preliminary Objections)*, 14 June 1938, PCIJ, Aer. A/B/, No. 74, at 28–29. For a discussion of state responsibility in relation to Palestinian refugees, *see* Kattan, *supra* note 5 and Scobbie, I. 'The Responsibility of Great Britain in Respect of the Creation of the Palestine Refugee Question' (2003–04) *YIMEL* 39 at 44.

[58] *Case Concerning the Factory at Chorzow (Claim for Indemnity) (Jurisdiction)*, 26 July 1927, PCIJ, Ser. A, No. 9, p. 21.

[59] *Case Concerning the Factory at Chorzow (Claim for Indemnity) (Merits)*, 13 September 1928, PCIJ, Ser. A, No. 17, p. 47. *See also* Scobbie, *supra* note 57 at 46.

[60] Draft Articles on Responsibility of States for Internationally Wrongful Acts, Report of the International Law Commission on the Work of its Fifty-Third Session (23 April – 1 June and 2 July-10 August 2001), Yearbook of the International Law Commission, 2001, II(2), A/CN.4/SER.A/2001/Add.1 (Part 2), at 26–30 ['ARSIWA']. For the customary nature of the ARSIWA, *see Application of the Convention on the Prevention and Punishment of the Crime of Genocide* (Bosnia and Herzegovina v. Serbia and Montenegro), 26 February 2007, ICJ Reports 2007, p. 43, para. 401. *See also* Crawford, J. *State Responsibility* (Cambridge, 2013) at 43.

[61] ARSIWA, *id.*, art. 2.

1948 and After: The UN and the Palestinian Refugees

obligations may be breached through a composite series of actions or omissions defined in the aggregate as wrongful, the law of state responsibility also contemplates continuing breaches as extending over the entire period, starting with the first of the actions or omissions of the series and lasting for as long as these actions or omissions are repeated and remain in violation of the international obligations of the state.[62] This has particular relevance for protracted refugee problems that arise from internationally wrongful acts of a state and which remain unremedied in line with the international legal obligations of that state (e.g. where a state refuses to repatriate refugees it has denationalized).

The legal consequences of an internationally wrongful act produce three general obligations for the wrongdoing state: First, if continuing, it must cease the act forthwith.[63] Second, it must offer appropriate assurances and guarantees of non-repetition if circumstances so dictate.[64] Third, it must make full reparation for the injury caused by the act, including any material or moral damage.[65] A core tenet of the law of state responsibility is that states may not negotiate the consequences of their actions if those actions are themselves illegal: *ex injuria jus non oritur*.[66]

---

[62] *Id.*, art. 15.

[63] *Id.*, art. 30(a). Although the text of the article does not reference any time limits within which cessation must occur, ICJ jurisprudence suggests cessation must occur forthwith. See *Legal Consequences of the Construction of a Wall in the Occupied Palestinian Territory*, Advisory Opinion, 9 July 2004, ICJ Reports 2004, paras. 151 & 163. See also *Legal Consequences of the Separation of the Chagos Archipelago from Mauritius in 1965*, Advisory Opinion, 25 February 2019, ICJ Reports 2019, p. 95, para. 183, where the Court indicated the wrongful conduct must cease 'as rapidly as possible'. This was subsequently interpreted by the General Assembly as requiring cessation within 'six months'. A/RES/73,295, 22 May 2019.

[64] ARSIWA, *supra* note 60, art. 30(b).

[65] *Id.*, art. 31.

[66] While art. 52(1) of ARSIWA imposes an obligation on an injured state to, *inter alia*, notify the responsible state of any decision to take countermeasures and to offer to negotiate with that State, such recourse to negotiation remains the sole prerogative of the injured state, and only then if it invokes countermeasures. Negotiation cannot be invoked by the responsible or any other state under the ARSIWA. In any event, even where invoked by an injured state, it is doubtful whether the ARSIWA contemplates recourse to negotiations if doing so would frustrate the overall obligation of the responsible state to abide by the underlying primary rule it has violated. Such an allowance would sabotage the object and purpose of the ARSIWA and the international rule of law itself. For a judicial opinion in which these principles are followed, *see Case Concerning Armed Activities on the Territory of the Congo* (Democratic Republic of the Congo v. Uganda), 19 December 2005, ICJ Reports 2005, p. 168, paras. 261 & 345, where, after determining that Uganda was internationally responsible for making reparations to DRC for illegal actions arising on the territory of the DRC, the ICJ deferred to the DRC's wish to resolve the issue by negotiation with Uganda, failing which the matter would be settled by the Court. In so doing, the Court made clear that while '[i]t is not for the Court to determine the final result of these negotiations ... the Parties should seek in good faith an agreed solution based on the findings of the present Judgment' (i.e. based on international law). For further application of this principle to the UN's management of the question of Palestine, see Chapter 5.

2.2.5 Conclusion

The law governing refugee status, including prolonged refugee problems, is in the first instance set out in the 1951 Convention regime. It is also buttressed by other relevant bodies of international law, including the law governing nationality, IHRL, IHL, ICL, and state responsibility. In the pages that follow, an assessment of the distinctive institutional and normative regime created by the UN for the Palestinian refugees will be undertaken against the principles outlined above. Throughout, it is imperative to keep the overall object and purpose of the law governing refugee status in mind: namely that all states have an obligation to refrain from generating refugee crises and statelessness, including through mass denationalization. Where they do, refugees are entitled to protection and assistance, including access to durable solutions, in line with international law and practice.

3 PALESTINIAN REFUGEES AND THE INTERNATIONAL RULE BY LAW

Writing in 2001, Benny Morris, the doyen of Israel's 'new historians' and author of a seminal text on the Palestinian refugee problem,[67] summarized the single most important truth about modern political Zionism. 'From the start', noted Morris, 'the Zionists wished to make the area of Palestine a Jewish State. Unfortunately, the country contained a native Arab population'.[68] As he put it, how was 'a round peg to fit into a square hole?'[69] The answer lay in the forced exile and dispossession of the majority of Palestine's native population in 1948.[70] According to Morris, but for those constitutive acts of ethnic cleansing, the State of Israel would not exist today, thus depriving Zionism of its raison d'être.[71] But it would be a mistake to regard the Zionist movement as the only protagonist for whom such an elemental truth was and remains

---

[67] Morris, B. *The Birth of the Palestinian Refugee Problem Revisited* (Cambridge, 2004).

[68] Morris, B. 'Revisiting the Palestinian Exodus of 1948' in Rogan, E. & Shlaim, A., eds. *The War for Palestine* (Cambridge, 2001) at 39.

[69] *Id.*

[70] Khalidi, R. *The Hundred Years' War on Palestine* (Picador, 2020) at 75–76; Pappe, I. *The Ethnic Cleansing of Palestine* (One World, 2006).

[71] In Morris's words: 'A Jewish state would not have come into being without the uprooting of 700,000 Palestinians. Therefore it was necessary to uproot them. There was no choice but to expel that population. [...] [I]f the desire to establish a Jewish state here is legitimate, there was no other choice'. *See* Shavit, A. 'Survival of the Fittest' (interview with Benny Morris), *Ha'aretz Magazine*, 8 January 2004, at: www.haaretz.com/1.5262454. *See also* Morris, 'Revisiting,' *supra* note 68 at 40.

relevant. At the UN, following the fateful work of the Special Committee on Palestine (UNSCOP) and the General Assembly in 1947, a similar circle would need to be squared, so to speak; only this time, with respect to the Palestinian refugees.

At bottom, the issue has revolved around the UN's need to make sense, in institutional and legal terms, of its moral responsibility for the Palestinian refugee problem, while simultaneously legitimating the existence of the settler-colonial entity materially responsible for that problem through the imposition of the two-state paradigm against the express wishes of the indigenous majority Palestinians. Ralph Wilde has usefully touched upon this by lamenting that 'the starting point for international law' on Palestine 'is to accept Israeli statehood as a given. In consequence, Palestinian freedom', including for Palestinian refugees, 'must fit around and/or be articulated in relation to Israel's needs', created as it was 'on the basis of the Nakba'.[72] Although the UN cannot be held directly culpable for the ethnic cleansing of Palestine in 1947–1949, it had a large hand in triggering events leading to that result (see Chapter 3). Related to this, and as will be demonstrated, the UN record on the Palestinian refugee problem reveals that the 'protection gap' at its root originates in the very same international rule by law that reified Palestinian legal subalternity in the UN system in 1947. Failure by the UN to take Palestinian refugee rights and claims seriously, while at the same time asserting the opposite to be the case, is a marked feature of this long and sordid story.

The rest of this chapter undertakes a broad assessment of three issues. First, it briefly surveys the origins of the UN's distinctive institutional and normative regime for Palestinian refugees. Why was this distinctive regime created in the first place and how has that rationale stood the test of time? Second, it examines the UN's early effort to find durable solutions for the Palestinian refugees through UNCCP. Was UNCCP's approach sufficiently centred around prevailing international law governing refugee protection and rights? Third, it examines the role of UNRWA in the provision of protection and assistance to Palestine refugees. What is UNRWA's mandate and relationship to UNHCR and the 1951 Convention regime, and how faithfully has it maintained its self-styled 'rights-based' approach to refugee protection and assistance? By examining these three issues, it is possible to better understand the limits of the distinctive institutional and normative regime applicable to Palestinian refugees, thereby enabling a fuller appreciation of what the rule by law inherent in that regime has wrought for them. To set the stage, it is

---

[72] Wilde, R. 'Using the Master's Tools to Dismantle the Master's House: International Law and Palestinian Liberation' (2019–20) 22 *PYIL* 3 at 71.

3 Palestinian Refugees and the International Rule by Law 123

useful to begin with an overview of the facts surrounding the creation of the Palestinian refugee problem and the response of the UN, as assessed against relevant international law.

3.1 The Palestinian Refugee Problem: Immediate Causes, Enduring Results

Recall that under the 1951 Convention, refugees are persons with a well-founded fear of persecution for specified socio-political reason(s) in relation to their country of nationality or former habitual residence which they have left, and are unable or, owing to that fear, unwilling to return to.[73] In contrast, the Palestinian refugee problem involves the forced exile of a native population from its own country in the context of state secession by another entity.[74] Although the exile of that native population is premised upon a well-founded fear of racial, religious, and national-based persecution, *it is their continued exile that forms the essence of their ongoing persecution.* The focus of inquiry when assessing the Palestinian refugee problem under international law must therefore begin by examining the lawfulness of the production of refugees *en masse* by a new state through the expulsion and arbitrary denationalization of its native population on secession from another entity, and the decision by that new state to bar return, restitution, and compensation for discriminatory reasons.

As covered in Chapter 3, the 1948 war was fought in two phases. The first phase (December 1947–14 May 1948) was non-international in character and occurred while the British were still formally responsible for law and order in the country. The protagonists were the well-organized, equipped, and trained Zionist armed groups – Haganah, Irgun, and Lehi – and loose bands of unorganized and ill-equipped Palestinian Arab irregular forces who were outnumbered five to one.[75] The second phase (15 May 1948–20 July 1949)[76]

---

[73] 1951 Convention, *supra* note 6, art. 1A(2).

[74] Kattan, *supra* note 26 at 209–210. *But see* Ronen, Y. 'Schrödinger's Occupation: Jerusalem, 1948–49' (2023) 58(3) *Texas ILJ* (forthcoming), where the author argues Israel occupied West Jerusalem in 1948. If true, the implication is that all territory taken by Israel beyond the partition resolution in 1948 was occupied by it and therefore taken by conquest.

[75] Khalidi, R. *The Iron Cage* (Beacon, 2007) at 131. Pappe, *supra* note 70 at 87, indicates that in 1948 half of Israel's 50,000-strong armed force was British-trained in WWII.

[76] *Egypt-Israel, General Armistice Agreement,* Rhodes (23 February 1949) S/1264/Corr.1; *Hashemite Jordan Kingdom-Israel,* General Armistice Agreement, Rhodes (3 April 1949) S/1302/Rev.1; *Lebanon-Israel General Armistice Agreement,* Ras Al-Nakoura (23 March 1949), S/1296; *Israel-Syria General Armistice Agreement,* Hill 232, 20 July 1949. The front from which Iraqi forces withdrew in March 1949 was covered by the Jordan-Israel armistice agreement.

was an international armed conflict between the regular forces of the new State of Israel (a consolidation of Haganah, Irgun, and Lehi) and small portions of regular armed forces of Egypt, Iraq, Lebanon, Syria, and Transjordan. By close of hostilities, the territory of Israel comprised some 78 per cent of mandate Palestine, well beyond the territory earmarked for the Jewish State under the partition plan.[77] This transformation of Palestine was partially consolidated by a seismic demographic shift in the country's population – what Chaim Weizmann, first Israeli President, cynically hailed as 'a miraculous clearing of the land'.[78]

The number of Palestinian refugees in 1948/49 has been debated from the outset,[79] fuelled in part by different figures recorded by international actors on the ground. Two 1949 UN reports, one from UNCCP and another from the UN Economic Survey Mission (ESM), gave figures of 711,000 and 774,000, respectively.[80] The United Nations Relief for Palestine Refugees (UNRPR), a predecessor of UNRWA, recorded some 960,000 refugees.[81] The secondary literature conservatively places the number at approximately 700,000 to 750,000,[82] with over 300,000 exiled prior to Britain's departure on 14 May 1948 and the remainder exiled thereafter.[83] This means that approximately 80 per cent of the Arab population of the territory that became the State of Israel was forcibly exiled.[84] This does not include a further 320,000–440,000 Palestinian refugees from the 1967 hostilities.[85] In keeping with the principle of family unity,[86] the present number of Palestinian refugees rests between approximately 5.7–12 million, the lower figure representing the number of *Palestine* refugees registered with UNRWA (see below).[87]

---

[77] Hadawi, S. *Palestinian Rights and Losses* (Saqi, 1988) at 81. On the secession aspect of the war, *see* Dugard, J. *The Secession of States and their Recognition in the Wake of Kosovo* (Hague Academy, 2013) at 182–187.

[78] Masalha, N. *Expulsion of the Palestinians*, 2nd ed. (IPS, 1993) at 175.

[79] In 1949, Arab officials cited numbers as high as 900,000–1,000,000, while Israeli officials cited numbers as low as 520,000. *See* Albanese & Takkenberg, *supra* note 1 at 35.

[80] The ESM figure included some 17,000 Jewish 'Palestine' refugees. *See id.*

[81] *Id.*

[82] Albanese & Takkenberg, *supra* note 1 at 37, give the figure of 750,000; Khalidi, *supra* note 70 at 58, gives approximately 720,000; Morris, *supra* note 68 at 37, gives 700,000.

[83] Smith, C.D. *Palestine and the Arab-Israeli Conflict* (St. Marten's, 1992) at 143, gives the 300,000 figure. The remainder is likely over 400,000, based on figures given by Albanese & Takkenberg, Khalidi and Morris, *id.*

[84] Khalidi, *supra* note 70 at 58.

[85] Albanese & Takkenberg, *supra* note 1 at 49–50.

[86] *See* text accompanying *supra* notes 21–22.

[87] For the 12 million figure, *see* Akram, *supra* note 25 at 194. For the 5.7 million figure, see *UNRWA in Figures*: www.unrwa.org/sites/default/files/content/resources/unrwa_in_figures_2021_eng.pdf.

3 Palestinian Refugees and the International Rule by Law 125

Early Zionist accounts denied the Nakba, including through fantastical claims that the Palestinian refugees fled voluntarily or on Arab orders.[88] The State of Israel maintains this denial,[89] with Israeli legislation passed in 2011 punishing commemoration of the Nakba,[90] and one former Deputy Foreign Minister branding the Nakba an 'Arab lie' in 2020.[91] Nevertheless, Palestinian accounts of the Nakba from the 1950s and 1960s,[92] to say nothing of a rich and uniform oral history,[93] have largely been corroborated by Israel's 'new historians'.[94] The only disagreement in the scholarship concerns whether the Nakba itself was planned by the Zionists prior to the 1948 armed conflict, with Morris arguing that it was born of war, not design, and critics arguing this position is belied by Morris's own evidence demonstrating 'that Palestine's Arabs were expelled systematically and with premeditation'.[95] This appears to be a distinction without a difference, however, because a general consensus exists between Morris and his detractors that: (1) almost all shades of Zionist opinion

---

[88] Morris, *supra* note 67 at 2; Said, E. & Hitchens, C. *Blaming the Victims* (Verso, 1989) at 73.

[89] Scheindlin, D. 'Israelis, Drop Your Denial and Recognize the Nakba,' 21 May 2020, +972 *Magazine*, at: www.972mag.com/nakba-refugees-israeli-denial/; Taba Non-Papers, Palestinian Position Paper on Palestinian Refugees and the Israeli Response, 21–22 January 2001, www.mideastweb.org/taba.htm.

[90] Kapshuk, Y. & Strömbom, L. 'Israeli Pre-Transitional Justice and the Nakba Law' (2021) 54:3 *Isr. LR* 305.

[91] Tzipi Hotovely served as Deputy Foreign Minister 2015–2020. She is now Israel's Ambassador to the United Kingdom. *See* 'New Israeli Ambassador in Britain Describes Nakba as "Arab lie",' 8 December 2020, *Middle East Monitor*, at: www.middleeastmonitor.com/20201208-new-israeli-ambassador-in-britain-describes-nakba-as-arab-lie/.

[92] Arif al-Arif, *The Nakba* (reprinted, IPS, 2013); Zurayq, C. *The Meaning of the Disaster*, R. Bayley Winder trans. (Khayat, 1956). Khalidi, W. *From Haven to Conquest* (1971). For later work by Walid Khalidi, *see All That Remains* (IPS, 1992), and 'Plan Dalet: Master Plan for the Conquest of Palestine' (1988) 18 *J. Pal. Stud.* 4.

[93] Sa'adi, A. & Abu-Lughod, L., *Nakba* (Columbia University Press, 2007).

[94] Pappe, *supra* note 70; Masalha, *supra* note 78; Masalha, N. *A Land Without a People* (Faber & Faber, 1997); Morris, *supra* note 67.

[95] Morris, *supra* note 67 at 588; Finkelstein, N., 'Myths, Old and New' (1991) 21:1 *J. Pal. Stud.* 66 at 67. *See also* Khalidi, *Plan Dalet, supra* note 92, Masalha, *supra* note 78 at 177, and Pappe, *id.*, at 86, who argue that the Nakba was long prepared by the Zionist leadership and carried out through operational plans, principally Plan D. The critique of Morris appears warranted. Despite his assertion that 'Plan D was not a political blueprint for the expulsion of Palestine's Arabs', he concedes that 'given the nature of the war and the admixture of the populations, securing the interior of the Jewish State and its borders in practice meant the depopulation and destruction of the villages that hosted the hostile militias and irregulars'. He notes that 'Plan D provided for the conquest and permanent occupation or levelling, of villages and towns [...] in the event of resistance, the armed forces in the village should be destroyed and the inhabitants expelled'. In his words, 'the plan gave each brigade discretion in its treatment of villages in its zone of operations. Each brigade was instructed: "in the conquest of villages in your area, you will determine – whether to cleanse or destroy them".' *See* Morris, *supra* note 67 at 164–165.

126   *1948 and After: The UN and the Palestinian Refugees*

and leadership during the Mandate period advocated, in one form or another, the displacement of the indigenous Arabs from Palestine;[96] and (2) this is in fact what happened in 1948 through the acts of Zionist/Israeli armed forces, under an operational plan issued by their high command in March of that year codenamed 'Tochnit Dalet', or Plan D.[97] In this context, it is important to recall UNSCOP's express recognition that the Jewish State could emerge 'only by the use of some considerable force', which the Zionists informed UNSCOP they in fact possessed and were willing to employ.[98] As covered in Chapter 3, the UN ignored its own findings and evidence of the impending disaster at hand.

The manner of Palestine's ethnic cleansing consisted of innumerable acts of widespread and systematic violence aimed at expelling or encouraging the mass flight of the indigenous population from the country. This included the wholesale and indiscriminate bombardment, siege, and expulsion of the Palestinian Arab population from cities, towns, and villages,[99] at least thirty-one confirmed massacres of civilians (including use of mass graves as means of concealment),[100] rape, and other forms of sexual and gender-based

---

[96] Masalha, *supra* note 78 at 1–2, notes that: 'It should not be imagined that the concept of trans-fer was held only by maximalists or extremists within the Zionist movement. On the contrary, it was embraced by almost all shades of opinion, from the Revisionist right to the Labour left. Virtually every member of the Zionist pantheon of founding fathers and important leaders supported it and advocated it in one form or another, from Chaim Weizmann and Vladimir Jabotinsky to David Ben-Gurion and Manahem Ussishkin'. *See also* Morris, *supra* note 67 at 39–64, 588.

[97] *See* Morris, *id.*, at 163–166; Khalidi, *Plan Dalet, supra* note 92; Masalha, *supra* note 78 at 177; Pappe, *supra* note 70 at 86–126.

[98] UNSCOP, Report to the General Assembly, 2nd Sess, Vol I, A/364, supplement 11, at 32, 3 September 1947 *See also* Chapter 3, Section 5.

[99] For example, in mid-July 1948, 50,000 Palestinian inhabitants of the cities of Lydda and Ramleh were expelled by the Hagana under command of Yigal Allon and Yitzhak Rabin, the latter of whom would become prime minister of Israel. *See* Pappe, *supra* note 70 at 166–169. Morris affirms that '[t]here was an almost universal one-to-one correspondence between Jewish attacks in specific localities and on specific towns and Arab flight from these localities and towns'. *See* Morris, B. *1948 and After* (Oxford, 1994) at 31.

[100] *See* Pappe, *id.*, at 258, where the author indicates an additional six massacres may have taken place. This is a conservative figure. Salman Abu Sitta has documented 141 'massacres and atrocities'. *See* Abu Sitta, S. *Atlas of Palestine, 1948* (PLS, 2004) at 65. Some of the more notorious massacres took place at Deir Yasin (9–10 April 1948; Tantura (22 May 1948); Safsaf (29 October 1948); and al-Dawayima (29 October 1948). *See* Pappe, *id.*, at 90–92, 133–137, 184, 195–198. Morris, *supra* note 67 at 470, reports the following eye-witness account of the al-Dawayima massacre given by an Israeli soldier who relayed that the village had been cap-tured by the 89th battalion without a fight: 'The first [wave] of conquerors killed about 80–100 [male] Arabs, women and children. The children they killed by breaking their heads with sticks. There was not a house without dead. [...] One commander ordered a sapper to put two old women in a certain house ... and blow it up.... The sapper refused.... The commander

3 *Palestinian Refugees and the International Rule by Law* 127

violence,[101] psychological terror campaigns broadcasting horrors to befall the population if it did not flee,[102] biological warfare,[103] and a host of scorched earth tactics, including the deliberate destruction of between 392 and 418 Palestinian villages, whence at least half of the refugees were expelled.[104]

As the ethnic cleansing was unfolding and well before the last armistice agreement was signed in 1949, the Israelis further consolidated their conquest by seizing, looting, and settling Palestinian refugee and state property.[105] On the eve of the Hagana offensives under Plan D in April 1948, David Ben Gurion, Israel's first Prime Minister, said that 'we shall enter the empty villages and settle in them.... In peace time we would not have been able to do this'.[106] Accordingly, Morris reports that '[a]bout 135 new [Jewish] settlements were established between the start of the hostilities in November 1947 and the end of August 1949' (i.e. *during* the war) and that '[m]ost were established on Arab-owned land and dozens were established on territory earmarked by the UN partition for the Palestine Arab State'.[107] Tens of thousands of new Jewish settlers were moved by Israel into Palestinian Arab refugee houses that remained intact.[108]

Although the magnitude of the dissolution of Palestine and its ethnic cleansing goes well beyond the pecuniary,[109] the monetary value of Palestinian losses

---

then ordered his men to put in the old women and the evil deed was done. One solider boasted that he had raped a woman and then shot her. One woman, with a newborn baby in her arms, was employed to clean the courtyard where the soldiers ate. She worked a day or two, in the end they shot her and her baby. [...] [C]ultured officers ... had turned into base murderers and this not in the heat of battle ... but out of a system of expulsion and destruction. *The less Arabs remained – the better. This principle is the political motor for the expulsions and the atrocities'* [emphasis added].

[101] Pappe, *id.*, at 208–211.

[102] *See, e.g.,* Morris, *supra* note 67 at xvi–xx, 230.

[103] Morris, B. & Kedar, B. 'Cast Thy Bread: Israeli Biological Warfare during the 1948 War' (2022) *MES*, https://doi.org/10.1080/00263206.2022.2122448.

[104] The figure of 392 is given in Morris, *supra* note 67 at xvi–xxii. The figure of 418 is offered in Khalidi, *All That Remains, supra* note 92 at 585.

[105] *Id.*, at xxxii. Writing of the Palestinian refugees, Khalidi notes at xxxii: 'Their immovable assets – commercial centers, residential quarters, schools, banks, hospitals, clinics, mosques, churches, and other public buildings, parks and utilities, all passed *en bloc* into the possession of the citizens of the nascent State of Israel. Also appropriated intact by Israelis were the personal movable assets: furniture, silver, pictures, carpets, libraries, and heirlooms'.

[106] Morris, *supra* note 67 at 370–371.

[107] *Id.*, at 369.

[108] Morris, *id.*, at 395, reports that by April 1949 at least '110,000 [new Jewish settlers] had been settled in abandoned Arab houses'. *See also* Khalidi, *All that Remains, supra* note 92 at xxxii.

[109] Hadawi, *supra* note 77 at 183. Having taken place merely four years after the Holocaust, the weight of the moral questions presented by the Nakba alone has given rise to important critical scholarship. *See* Bashir, B. & Goldberg, A., eds. *The Holocaust and the Nakba* (Columbia, 2018).

128   *1948 and After: The UN and the Palestinian Refugees*

suffered as a result has never been fully accounted for. Portions of it were thrice assessed by UNCCP – each time a refinement of the previous figure[110] – as amounting to approximately P£120 million in 1952,[111] P£205 million in 1961,[112] and US$1.378 billion in 1962.[113] Based on the framework of post-WWII Jewish mass claims against Germany, which accounted not merely for moveable and immovable property losses, but also for human capital losses (e.g. psychological injury, lost future opportunity, etc.), Atef Kubursi has assessed Palestinian losses at P£1.182 billion in 1948.[114]

Another means of consolidating Palestine's ethnic cleansing was an Israeli cabinet decision of 16 June 1948 to bar return of the Palestinian refugees to their homes and property.[115] This was followed by various administrative acts (e.g. the blocking of Palestinian refugee bank accounts) and passage of legislation aimed at giving the imprimatur of legality to it all. The first such legislation was the *Emergency Regulations (Absentees' Property)* of 2 December 1948.[116] Under this law, Israel seized the property of persons it declared 'absentee',[117] defined as any person who on or after 29 November 1947 (the date of the UN partition): was a citizen or subject of an Arab state; was in any Arab state for any length of time; was in any part of Palestine not under Jewish control; or

---

[110] For a critique of the UNCCP's methodologies and estimates, *see* Kubursi, A. 'An Economic Assessment of Total Palestinian Losses in 1948,' in Hadawi, *supra* note 77 at 123–127.

[111] UNCCP, *Historical Survey of Efforts of the United Nations Conciliation Commission for Palestine to Secure the Implementation of Paragraph 11 of General Assembly Resolution 194(III)*, Question of Compensation (working paper prepared by the Secretariat), 2 October 1961, A/AC.25/W.81/Rev.2, para. 97 ['UNCCP Historical Survey Compensation']. In 1948 1P£ = 1GB£.

[112] UNCCP, *Working Paper Prepared by the Commission's Land Expert on the Methods and Techniques of Identification and Valuation of Arab Refugee Immovable Property Holdings in Israel*, 28 April 1964, A/AC.25/W.84. *See also* Fischbach, M. *Records of Dispossession* (Columbia, 2003) at 272.

[113] This figure was never published. Its relatively larger value is likely because it was arrived at by including loss of livelihood, not merely property, by taking six factors into account: (1) value of immovable property; (2) value of moveable property; (3) monetary payment as an adjustment for loss of interest on property; (4) an adjustment to account for depreciation in currency; (5) compensation for loss of public property; and (6) a reintegration allowance for refugees. *See* Fischbach, *id.*, at 283–287.

[114] Kubursi *supra* note 110 at 183–189.

[115] Ben-Gurion told his cabinet: 'we must prevent at all costs their return'. Morris, *supra* note 67 at 318–319. The prohibition of return included Palestinians internally displaced within the new State of Israel. *See* Albanese & Takkenberg, *supra* note 1 at 37.

[116] Fischbach, *supra* note 112 at 21–24. This was later amended as the *Absentees' Property Law*, 1950, *infra* note 117.

[117] Under art. 30(a) of the *Absentees' Property Law, 1950*, the burden of proof of challenging such a declaration was imposed on the absentee. *See Absentees' Property Law, 1950*, 14 March 1950, *Laws of the State of Israel: Authorized Translation from the Hebrew*, Vol. 4. Government Printer, Jerusalem, (1948–1987), pp. 68–82.

3 Palestinian Refugees and the International Rule by Law 129

was in any place other than their habitual residence, even if such place as well as their habitual residence was within Israeli-occupied territory.[118] This broad definition enabled maximum acquisition by the Israeli Custodian of Absentee Property of Palestinian Arab property, including that of both the refugees and those who remained internally displaced in what became Israel.[119] Absentee property was then leased and sold by the Custodian back to the state, through the Israel Development Authority, and quasi-governmental bodies, such as the Jewish National Fund (JNF),[120] in order for the property to be exploited for exclusive Jewish use.[121] In terms of real property alone, the scope of Zionist plunder of Palestinian property through this mechanism was illustrative of the calamity that had befallen the Palestinian Arabs. According to the UN, in 1945 Jews owned only 5.6 per cent of the country;[122] by the end of the war, 93 per cent of what became Israel was in fact Palestinian private or publicly owned property summarily usurped by the new state.[123]

A second piece of Israeli legislation that helped transform Palestine was the *Law of Return* of 5 July 1950, providing that '[e]very Jew has the right to come to this country as an *oleh*' (i.e. an immigrant).[124] As a Basic Law, the *Law of Return* possesses quasi-constitutional status in Israel. It means that any Jew in the world, regardless of where or to whom they were born, may immigrate to Israel, automatically receive citizenship, and be entitled to settle in or on Palestinian refugee property as of right. The inequity of this is banally accepted among leading Israeli jurists. For instance, Menachem Elon, former Deputy President of the Supreme Court of Israel, has noted that the *Law of Return* must prioritize 'Jewish values' over 'democratic values' because of the *raison*

---

[118] Fischbach, *supra* note 112 at 21.

[119] These internally displaced persons are referred to as 'present absentees' under Israeli law. *Id.*, at 21–22, 26.

[120] The JNF was established in 1901 as the principal vehicle of the Zionist Organization, and then the Jewish Agency, for the acquisition of land for exclusive Jewish use in Palestine. *See* Masalha, *supra* note 78 at 24; Hadawi, *supra* note 77 at 67–67; Fischbach, *supra* note 112 at 59, 63–64.

[121] Fischbach, *supra* note 112 at 22–27. As noted by Hadawi, *id.*, land administered by the JNF is held 'as the inalienable property of the Jewish people' and cannot be leased or worked by any non-Jew.

[122] In 1945, of Palestine's 26,323,023 dunam landmass, the Jewish community owned only 1,491,699 dunams to the Arab community's 12,574,774 dunams, the remainder being publicly owned land. Ad Hoc Committee on the Palestinian Question, Summary Records of Meetings 25 September – 25 November 1947, UN GAOR, 2nd Sess, Annex 25, Report of Sub-Committee 2, A/AC.14/32 and Add.1 at 292–293 & Appendix VI.

[123] This figure includes 48 per cent private and 45 per cent public Palestinian Arab ownership. *See id.*, and Abu Sitta, *supra* note 100 at 33.

[124] *Law of Return*, 1950, 5 July 1950, art. 1, Sefer Ha-Chukkim, No. 51, p. 159.

130   *1948 and After: The UN and the Palestinian Refugees*

d'être of Israel as the Jewish State.[125] Therefore, as noted by Susan Akram, '[i]mmigration to Israel under the Law of Return is exclusively reserved for Jews' and under Israeli law 'all Jews around the world are automatically "Jewish nationals" and part of the Israeli state'.[126] As Palestinian refugees are not Jewish, and Israel only recognizes Jewish – rather than Israeli – nationality as the prime legal determinant for rights in the country,[127] this law operates with glaring discriminatory effect.

A third piece of legislation that helped crystalize Palestine's ethnic cleansing was the *Citizenship Law* of 1 April 1952.[128] Under this law, only four paths to acquisition of Israeli citizenship exist. The first is immigration to Israel in accordance with the *Law of Return*,[129] unavailable to Palestinian refugees because they are not Jewish.[130] The second is residence in Israel. This requires the claimant to have been registered as present in the country on 1 March 1952 *and* to have been 'in Israel, or in an area which became Israel territory after the establishment of the State, from the day of the establishment of the State [i.e. 14 May 1948] to the day of the coming into force of this law [i.e. 1 April 1952], or entered Israel legally during that period'.[131] Given the blanket bar on Palestinian refugee return, none of them would qualify for citizenship under this provision. The third is birth to an Israeli citizen,[132] equally impossible for Palestinian refugees to satisfy for the above-noted reasons. The fourth is naturalization,[133] also impossible for Palestinian refugees, as they are arbitrarily barred from being physically within Israel for a prescribed period of at least three years prior to the application for naturalization.

The *Citizenship Law* did not stop there. It also retroactively repealed the Palestine citizenship, *en bloc*, of the Palestinian refugees. Prior to the

---

[125] Elon, M. 'The Values of a Jewish and Democratic State: The Task of Reaching a Synthesis' in Kellermann, A., et al. *Israel Among the Nations* (Kluwer, 1998) at 192.

[126] Akram, *supra* note 25 at 200.

[127] *George Rafael Tamarin v. State of Israel*, (1970) 26 PD I 197 and *Ornan v. Ministry of the Interior*, (2013) CA 8573/08.

[128] *Citizenship Law*, 1 April 1952, Sefer Ha-Chukkim No. 95, p. 146. The *Citizenship Law* is often erroneously referred to in the literature as 'Nationality Law'. But in fact, as affirmed by the Supreme Court of Israel in *Tamarin* and *Ornan*, *id.*, there is no such thing as 'Israel nationality' under Israeli law, rather only 'Jewish nationality'. Akram, *supra* note 25 at 201. The Hebrew title of the law (Chok Ha-Azrachut) literally translates as 'Citizenship Law'. *See* https://fs.knesset.gov.il/2/law/2_lsr_211774.PDF.

[129] *Id.*, art. 2.

[130] *See supra* note 128. *See also, Basic Law – Israel as the Nation State of the Jewish People* (2018), Statute Book 2743, 26 July 2018, at 898.

[131] *Id.*, art. 3

[132] *Id.*, art. 4.

[133] *Id.*, art. 5.

3 Palestinian Refugees and the International Rule by Law 131

establishment of Israel in 1948, citizenship of Palestine was governed by two instruments, in succession. Under the first, the *Treaty of Lausanne* of 24 July 1923, Ottoman subjects habitually resident in the Empire *ipso facto* became nationals of territories that Turkey ceded control over to the allied powers at the end of WWI, including Palestine.[134] Under the second, the *Palestine Citizenship Order* of 24 August 1925, Palestinian citizenship included every person who was formerly an Ottoman citizen habitually resident in Palestine as well as every person thereafter born in Palestine.[135] The Israeli *Citizenship Law* expressly repealed the *Palestine Citizenship Order* of 1925,[136] indicating that 'any reference in any provision of law to Palestinian citizenship or Palestinian citizens shall henceforth be read as a reference to Israel citizenship or Israel citizens'.[137] Therefore, the *Citizenship Law* not only rendered it legally impossible for Palestinian refugees to acquire citizenship in Israel through residence, birth, or naturalization, but it also unilaterally purported to annul their prior citizenship, thereby rendering them denationalized stateless persons in one fell swoop.

3.2 The Palestinian Refugee Problem under International Law

Israel's ethnic cleansing of the Palestinian refugees – including the wholesale dispossession and usurpation of their property, mass denationalization, and denial of repatriation and restitution – constitute gross and systematic violations of the relevant international laws reviewed above. This conclusion is based on the application of prevailing law as it stood in 1947–1949 and, where appropriate, on the basis of relevant international law as it has developed since then in accordance with the 1928 *Island of Palmas* case, given that many of these violations are of a continuing character whose resolution must follow the conditions required by the evolution of the law.[138] Israel's legal position, exemplified for example by the work of Ruth Lapidoth and Yaffa Zilbershats,

---

[134] *Treaty of Peace with Turkey signed at Lausanne*, 24 July 1923, 28 LNTS 11, art. 30. Palestinian citizenship under international law took effect on 6 August 1924 when the Treaty of Lausanne was ratified. *See* Akram, *supra* note 25, 195–196.

[135] These orders were amended from time to time through 1945. Akram, *supra* note 25 at 196.

[136] *Citizenship Law, supra* note 128, art. 18(a) ('The Palestinian Citizenship Orders, 1925–1942 are repealed with effect from the day of the establishment of the State').

[137] *Citizenship Law, supra* note 128, art. 18. The English language translation of the law refers to 'Israel nationality' or 'Israel nationals'. This is a mistranslation of the original Hebrew, which refers to 'Israel citizenship' or 'Israel citizens'. *See supra* note 128.

[138] The principle of intertemporal law was restated by Judge Huber in *Island of Palmas*: 'a juridical fact must be appreciated in the light of the law contemporary with it, and not of the law in force at the time such dispute in regard to it arises or falls to be settled'. But he added: 'a distinction must be made between the creation of rights and the existence of rights. The same principle which subjects the act creative of a right to the law in force at the time the

1948 and After: The UN and the Palestinian Refugees

takes issue with these conclusions.[139] As demonstrated below, their arguments remain unconvincing for two reasons: (1) they deny the existence of key facts regarding the Nakba, including as confirmed by Israeli legislation and primary archival sources; and (2) they fail to apply, or are based on questionable interpretations of, relevant international law.

On war crimes, a case-by-case evaluation of each individual act committed in 1947–1949 is not possible here, nor is it easy given the passage of time and intervening events. Nevertheless, it is not difficult to conclude that, when taken together, the innumerable acts of well-documented widespread and systematic violence directed at the Palestinian Arab population at the time – including systematic expulsion, massacre, rape, destruction and usurpation of private property, and scorched earth tactics – evince a pattern of conduct that presumptively qualifies in the aggregate as, *inter alia*, deportation of a civilian population, recognized at Nuremberg as a war crime under then prevailing customary international law.[140] There is no statute of limitations on war crimes and no one has ever been held to account for these acts. Similarly, given the ongoing nature of the unlawful deportation and transfer of civilians and the requirement to repatriate displaced victims of armed conflict promulgated in the 1949 Fourth Geneva Convention, to which Israel is party, and affirmed in customary IHL, it can be argued that Israel remains in violation of these norms.[141] In arguing that Palestinian refugee victims of the Nakba do not have a right to return under international law, Zilbershats asserts, without any evidence, that 'the Palestinian refugee problem began in 1948, after the British left', i.e. *only after* 15 May 1948.[142] She does not acknowledge that the expulsions began months prior to May 1948, nor does she discuss the well-established details of Plan D. Likewise, Lapidoth posits that '[i]n the wake of the 1948–49 Arab-Israeli war' the Palestinian refugees 'fled to the neighbouring Arab countries … either of their own volition or due to pressure from the Arab States'.[143] This perpetuates the myth that the Palestinians fled of their

---

right arises, demands that the existence of the right, in other words its continued manifestation, shall follow the conditions required by the evolution of law'. *Island of Palmas Case (Netherlands, USA)*, 4 April 1928, Reports of International Arbitral Awards, Vol. II, 829–871, at 845 ['*Island of Palmas*'].

[139] Zilbershats, Y. 'International Law and the Palestinian Right of Return to the State of Israel' in Benvenisti, E., Gans, C. & Hanafi, S. *Israel and the Palestinian Refugees* (Springer, 2007); and Lapidoth, R. 'The Right of Return in International Law, with Special Reference to the Palestinian Refugees' (1986) 16 *IYHR* 103.

[140] *See* text accompanying *supra* notes 45–46.

[141] *See* text accompanying *supra* notes 48–53.

[142] Zilbershats, *supra* note 139 at 199.

[143] Lapidoth, *supra* note 139 at 111–112.

3 Palestinian Refugees and the International Rule by Law 133

own accord or on Arab orders and, inexplicably, *only after* the 1948 war. On these accounts, the issue of war crimes committed against the Palestinian refugees during the 1948 Nakba is either not addressed,[144] or not taken seriously, including through victim blaming.[145]

Likewise, on mass denationalization of a population, even if one takes the strained view that the acts of widespread and systematic violence directed at the Palestinian Arabs were not intended to result in their expulsion, there is no debate that Israel took deliberate administrative measures in 1948 to bar Palestinian refugee return and to usurp their property, followed by the passage of legislation after the war to cement this state of affairs, including through mass denationalization. This legislation remains in place and, together with the person of the refugees and their descendants who have never relinquished their claims, is unequivocal proof of Israel's ongoing violation of the general rule requiring that the nationality of the inhabitants of a territory follows a change in sovereignty over that territory.[146] In addition, these administrative and legislative measures stand in stark contrast to the terms of General Assembly resolution 181(II), which required each envisioned state to adopt democratic constitutions, establish government on the basis of universal suffrage, and guarantee to all persons equality before the law.[147] Although Israel did not abide by the territorial terms of resolution 181(II), its declaration of statehood of 14 May 1948 expressly relied on the resolution as a basis for its juridical right to exist.[148] Accordingly, on 15 May 1948, it communicated to the UN Secretary-General its intention to 'promote the development of the country for the benefit of all inhabitants' and to 'uphold full racial and political equality of all citizens without distinction of race, creed or sex'.[149] Instead of addressing how its administrative and legislative measures collectively operate to exclude Palestinian refugees in violation of this representation to the UN, Israeli arguments obfuscate the relevant law and facts. Thus, despite

[144] For example, Lapidoth, *id.*, fails to treat war crimes.

[145] For example, Zilbershats, *supra* note 139 at 212–215, acknowledges that 'deportations and forced expulsions are forbidden according to international criminal law', but she incredibly characterizes what happened to the Palestinian refugees in 1947–49 as a mutual population exchange between Israel and the Arab States. *See also* text accompanying *infra* notes 152–157.

[146] *See* text accompanying *supra* notes 25–30.

[147] A/RES/181(II), 29 November 1947, annex Plan of Partition with Economic Union, Part 1, Section B, para. 10.

[148] The Declaration stated that the 'recognition by the United Nations of the right of the Jewish people to establish their state' contained in resolution 181(II) 'is irrevocable', and that the state was established 'on the strength' of this resolution. *See Declaration of the Establishment of the State of Israel*, 14 May 1948, at: www.knesset.gov.il/docs/eng/megilat_eng.htm.

[149] Cablegram dated 15 May 1948 addressed to the Secretary-General by the Foreign Secretary of the Provisional Government of Israel, S/747, 15 May 1948.

134   *1948 and After: The UN and the Palestinian Refugees*

the express terms of Israel's *Citizenship Law*, Zilbershats curiously posits that 'Israel did not revoke the Palestinian refugees Palestine citizenship', rather '[t]his citizenship simply expired once the British terminated their Mandate over Palestine on 15 May 1948'.[150] Likewise, without addressing Israel's absentee property legislation, nor how the *Citizenship Law* impacts Palestinian refugees, Lapidoth blithely asserts that the *Law of Return* 'does not close the State's doors to anybody, but only creates a preference in favour of Jews'.[151] The *Law of Return*'s obvious adverse effects on the denationalized Palestinian refugees simply doesn't register. We are further remarkably told by both Zilbershats[152] and Lapidoth[153] that, rather than forcible expulsion and denationalization of the Palestinians, the Nakba was in fact an instance of mutual 'population transfer' between Israel and the Arab states. Neither of them account for the customary principle requiring nationality to follow a change of sovereignty, nor for the obvious fact that neither Palestine nor the Palestinian refugees had anything to do with the Jewish populations of other Arab states. Against this backdrop, these authors then assert that such transfer of populations was not inconsistent with prevailing international practice, as evinced by the 1923 post-war agreement between Greece and Turkey for reciprocal transfer of portions of their populations, the 1945 agreement between the Allied Powers at Potsdam to transfer 'in an orderly and humane manner' Germans in eastern Europe back to Germany, and the 1947 exchange of Hindus and Muslims between India and Pakistan.[154] The trouble with this line of argument, however, is that these cases were regulated by agreement, the first two concerning the population transfers themselves,[155] the latter concerning the property left behind by the refugees.[156] In contrast, as noted by Victor Kattan, 'there was no agreement between Israel and the Arab states over the expulsion of

---

[150] Zilbershats, *supra* note 139 at 204.

[151] Lapidoth, *supra* note 139 at 121–122.

[152] Zilbershats, *supra* note 139 at 213 ('It is important to note that the Arab population's flight from Israel occurred concurrent to the emigration of Jews from neighbouring Arab states. [...] Therefore, the actual result of the political changes in the Middle East and the war in 1948 was a transfer of populations').

[153] Lapidoth, *supra* note 139 at 111–112 ('In the wake of the 1948–49 Arab-Israeli war, many Palestinian Arabs (who never were nationals or permanent residents of Israel) fled to the neighbouring Arab countries, and simultaneously a large number of Jews fled from their homes in Arab countries to Israel.').

[154] *See also* Benvenisti, E. & Zamir, E. 'Private Claims to Property Rights in the Future Israeli-Palestinian Settlement' (1995) 89 *AJIL* 295.

[155] Kattan, *supra* note 26 at 211, 214.

[156] *See* Benvenisti & Zamir, *supra* note 154 at 323–324 & fn. 164, who note that India and Pakistan agreed in a joint declaration of 3 September 1947 that 'both governments will take steps to look after the property of refugees and restore it to its rightful owners'.

3 *Palestinian Refugees and the International Rule by Law*   135

the Palestinians'.[157] Indeed, as discussed below, despite UN attempts to garner *ex post facto* agreement of Israel and the Arab states to this end, no such agreement was ever concluded. The upshot is that the Palestinian refugees themselves never acquiesced in the consequences of their mass expulsion, denationalization, and pillage of their property. These were unilateral illegal acts of Israel and its pre-state militia that ran the course of the 1947–1949 hostilities, the consequences of which continue to this day.[158]

Regarding IHRL violations, it is not difficult to conclude that Israel's blanket bar on the return of Palestinian refugees to their homes and property violates the customary international law right of refugees to return.[159] Given the continuing nature of the forced exile and mass denationalization of the Palestinian refugees and their descendants, and on the basis of *Island of Palmas*,[160] Israel is also in violation of the UDHR's prohibition against the arbitrary deprivation of nationality and property, as well as its affirmation of the right of everyone to return to their country, even though that instrument was promulgated on 10 December 1948, at the same time the Nakba was unfolding.[161] The same holds true for Israel's violation of the ICCPR, to which it is party, in particular Article 12(2) providing that '[e]veryone shall be free to leave any country, including his own' and Article 12(4) that '[n]o one shall be arbitrarily deprived of the right to enter his own country'.[162] Some writers have stressed the qualified nature of the right to return as codified in the ICCPR, given reference in Article 12(4) to being 'arbitrarily deprived' and the apparently limiting effect of the words 'his own country'.[163] Thus, Lapidoth argues that the right to return does not exist for Palestinian refugees because 'they have never been nationals or permanent residents of Israel'.[164] This, however, is a *non sequitur* given that it rests on Israel having forcibly exiled and denationalized the Palestinians in the first place. For Zilbershats, Israel is permitted under Article 4(1) of the ICCPR to derogate from any obligation it may have to repatriate Palestinian refugees given it has been in an official state of emergency since its founding and doing so would

---

[157] Kattan, *supra* note 26 at 215.
[158] *Id.*, at 211.
[159] *See* text accompanying *supra* notes 43–44.
[160] *See supra* note 138.
[161] UDHR, *supra* note 34, arts. 13(2), 15(2), 17(2). Adopted by consensus of the General Assembly, by at least 1966 the UDHR had come to be regarded as a codification of custom.
[162] ICCPR, *supra* note 40, arts. 12(2), 12(4).
[163] Radley, K. 'The Palestinian Refugees: The Right to Return in International Law' (1978) 72:3 *AJIL* 586 at 612–614; Weiner, R. 'The Palestinian Refugees Right to Return and the Peace Process' (1997) 20:1 *Bost. Col. I&CLR* 1 at 37–41.
[164] Lapidoth, *supra* note 139 at 114.

136   *1948 and After: The UN and the Palestinian Refugees*

allegedly harm the Jewish character of Israel as the self-determination unit of the Jewish people.[165] This too is a *non sequitur*, as no such derogation is permitted under the ICCPR, given it would be rooted in discrimination based solely on the grounds of race or religion.[166] These Israeli arguments have been roundly rejected by the Human Rights Committee. It has noted that the arbitrariness qualification of Article 12(4) 'is intended to emphasize that it applies to all State action, legislative, administrative and judicial' and that any interference with the right to return should be consistent with the ICCPR and, in any case, be 'reasonable in the particular circumstances'.[167] In its opinion, 'there are few, if any, circumstances in which deprivation of the right to enter one's own country could be reasonable. A State party must not, *by stripping a person of nationality or by expelling an individual to a third country*, arbitrarily prevent this person from returning to his or her own country'.[168] As to the construct 'his own country', the Human Rights Committee has opined that Article 12(4) 'does not distinguish between nationals and aliens', as evidenced by its usage of the term 'no one'.[169] In its view:

> The scope of 'his own country' is broader than the concept 'country of his nationality'. It is not limited to nationality in a formal sense, that is, nationality acquired at birth or by conferral; it embraces, at the very least, an individual who, because of his or her special ties to or claims in relation to a given country, cannot be considered to be a mere alien. This would be the case, for example, *of nationals of a country who have there been stripped of their nationality in violation of international law, and of individuals whose country of nationality has been incorporated in or transferred to another national entity, whose nationality is being denied them.*[170]

It is apparent from this that Article 12(4) of the ICCPR is to be read broadly, consistent with principles of non-discrimination and equality and the general prohibition on denationalizing a population on change of sovereignty.

Finally, Israel bears state responsibility for the internationally wrongful acts set out above. On the basis of the law as it existed in 1947–1949, in particular as affirmed by the PCIJ in *Chorzow Factory*, three principles of reparation are relevant here.[171] First, Israel is bound to ensure reparation for the Palestinian refugees which, as far as possible, wipes out all the consequences of its illegal

---

[165] Zilbershats, *supra* note 139 at 204.
[166] ICCPR, *supra* note 40, art. 4(1).
[167] General Comment No. 27, *supra* note 41, para. 21.
[168] *Id* [emphasis added].
[169] *Id.* para. 20.
[170] *Id* [emphasis added].
[171] *See* text accompanying *supra* notes 58–59.

3 Palestinian Refugees and the International Rule by Law 137

acts against them with the aim of re-establishing the situation which would, in all probability, have existed if those acts had not been committed. Israel is therefore bound to facilitate the voluntary return and reinstatement of the Palestinian refugees to the homes, property, and nationality they would have enjoyed but for its illegal acts in 1947–1949 and after.[172] Second, Israel is also bound to make reparation through provision of restitution in kind or, if this is not possible, payment of a sum corresponding to the value which a restitution in kind would bear. This means that, in the event the property of the Palestinian refugees no longer exists (e.g. for having been destroyed), Israel is bound to provide them with property equivalent to that which otherwise would have remained in their possession but for Israel's illegal acts, or compensation in lieu. This principle would apply whether or not the refugees in question chose to return. Third, Israel is also obliged to pay damages for losses sustained by the Palestinian refugees that would not otherwise be covered by the restitution in kind or payment in lieu. This means that Israel is bound to pay compensation to Palestinian refugees for a host of human capital losses, such as psychological injury and lost future opportunity. Because of the ongoing nature of some of the internationally wrongful acts committed against the Palestinian refugees, including their descendants, relevant rules of the law of state responsibility that have been progressively developed and codified in ARSIWA must also be considered, the central tenets of which mirror those above.[173]

3.3 The Palestinian Refugee Problem and the UN: Failing to Square the Circle

The distinctive institutional and normative regime applicable to Palestinian refugees, and by extension the protection gap, is anchored in two related resolutions of the General Assembly: resolution 194(III) of 11 December 1948, governing durable solutions, and resolution 302(IV) of 8 December 1949, governing protection and assistance.

---

[172] Israeli scholars argue that Palestinian return is practically impossible either because their villages or property no longer exists, or because it has been taken over by Jewish Israelis, and because return would threaten the Jewish character of the state. See e.g., Miller, E. 'The Intractable Issue: Palestinian Refugees and the Israeli-Palestinian Peace Negotiations,' June 2012, ICSR, at: https://icsr.info/wp-content/uploads/2012/08/1346247918ICSRAtkinPaperSeries_ElhananMiller.pdf. But Palestinian scholar, Salman Abu Sitta, has painstakingly mapped Palestinian villages and lands against present day built up Israeli Jewish spaces and concentrations of population. He determines that return is both practicable and possible. See Abu Sitta, S. 'The Right of Return: Sacred, Legal and Possible' in Aruri, supra note 5 at 195.

[173] See also text accompanying supra notes 60–66.

138   *1948 and After: The UN and the Palestinian Refugees*

Under the terms of resolution 194(III), the General Assembly established UNCCP.[174] Consisting of three Member States – France, Turkey, and the United States – UNCCP was tasked with seeking a negotiated peace agreement between the Arab States and Israel, including the fate of the Palestinian refugees.[175] In this respect, paragraph 11 of resolution 194(III) is important, as it is often presented as indicative of the UN's commitment to international law on the Palestinian refugee issue. It affirms:

> that the refugees wishing to return to their homes and live at peace with their neighbours should be permitted to do so at the earliest practicable date, and that compensation should be paid for the property of those choosing not to return and for loss of or damage to property which, under principles of international law or in equity, should be made good by the Governments or authorities responsible.[176]

To this end, UNCCP was instructed 'to facilitate the repatriation, resettlement and economic and social rehabilitation of the refugees and the payment of compensation', and to maintain close relations with 'appropriate organs and agencies of the United Nations', including UNRPR.[177] Attempts by UNCCP to mediate a durable solution for the Palestinian refugees between Israel and the Arab states were to no avail, however. In short, UNCCP was powerless in the face of Israel's refusal to allow voluntary return of all Palestinian refugees and compensation, in line with its international legal obligations to do so. This was not helped by the General Assembly's failure to exert appropriate leverage over Israel to comply with these obligations.[178] Although UNCCP's conciliation efforts ended in 1952 and its documentation tasks were fully completed by 1963, its mandate was never terminated. It continues to report on an annual basis to the General Assembly that it regrets that the terms of resolution 194(III) have yet to be implemented and 'that it has nothing new to report'.[179] But this runs hollow, given that its attempt to seek a durable solution for the Palestinian refugees in effect lasted for only the first three of its seventy-five-year existence and that even this emaciated effort was misguided and half-hearted. As demonstrated below, the UN record shows that UNCCP suffered from many of

[174] A/RES/194(III), 11 December 1948.
[175] *Id.*, paras. 5, 6.
[176] *Id.*, para. 11.
[177] *Id.*
[178] See text accompanying *infra* notes 267–271.
[179] *See, e.g., Seventy-Fifth Report of the United Nations Conciliation Commission for Palestine,* A/76/282, 10 August 2021.

3 Palestinian Refugees and the International Rule by Law

the same failings that implicated UNSCOP before it, namely a failure to fully apply prevailing international law in its dealings with Israel, the party responsible for the ethnic cleansing of Palestine, and a failure to take seriously the situation of the Palestinian victims of these acts, including through meaningful engagement with their representatives.

Under the terms of resolution 302(IV), passed one year after the creation of UNCCP, the General Assembly recognized 'that, without prejudice to the provisions of paragraph 11 of General Assembly resolution 194(III) of 11 December 1948, continued assistance for the relief of the Palestine refugees is necessary to prevent conditions of starvation and distress among them and to further conditions of peace and stability'.[180] It accordingly established UNRWA, which took over from UNRPR, and mandated it to 'carry out in collaboration with local governments the direct relief and works programmes as recommended by the Economic Survey Mission' and 'to consult with the interested Near Eastern Governments concerning measures to be taken by them preparatory to the time when international assistance for relief and works projects is no longer available'.[181] So it was that UNRWA began its long history of humanitarian service to the Palestine refugees which, although meant to be temporary, continues to this day. At the time of writing, some 5.7 million persons are registered with the Agency as Palestine refugees, which renders them eligible for its core services – education, health, and relief and social services – in its geographical area of operations, namely Jordan, Lebanon, Syria, the West Bank (including East Jerusalem), and Gaza Strip.[182] Indispensable though this basic protection and assistance have been to the lives of generations of Palestine refugees, UNRWA is unfortunately not the vehicle for 'advancing their rights and wellbeing' that it claims to be.[183] A review of the UN record demonstrates that, despite resolution 302(IV)'s proviso that the Agency's work be done without prejudice to the rights of Palestine refugees to return to their homes and property in accordance with resolution 194(III), UNRWA was in fact initially designed by the UN to serve as a means to resettle the Palestine refugees in their places of refuge following the 1948 Nakba. As will be demonstrated, the record of the

---

[180] A/RES/302(IV), 8 December 1949, para 5.

[181] *Id.*, para. 7.

[182] *See*, the UNRWA website (www.unrwa.org) for a general restatement of the Agency's mandate. For statistics on numbers of Palestine refugees, see *UNRWA in Figures, supra* note 87.

[183] *See*, e.g., Remarks by UNRWA Commissioner-General Philippe Lazzarini, Ministerial Meeting Co-Hosted by Jordan and Sweden on the Margins of the General Assembly High-Level Segment, 22 September 2022, at: www.unrwa.org/newsroom/official-statements/remarks-unrwa-commissioner-general-philippe-lazzarini.

ESM demonstrates that this intention was animated by Eurocentric, orientalist, and paternalistic attitudes towards the refugees themselves, attitudes that would indirectly reverberate in the Agency's discriminatory refugee registration system, still in place today. By the time UNRWA's resettlement attempts failed in the 1950s, resulting in the operational entrenchment of the above-mentioned core humanitarian services, the protection gap afflicting the refugees had become reified in the international legal order. With UNRWA having never been expressly vested by the General Assembly with a mandate to seek durable solutions, and with UNCCP's durable solutions efforts effectively wound up by 1952, little would be done within the UN to realize a just and durable solution for the Palestinian refugees in line with their rights under international law, despite the almost rote lip service paid by the General Assembly in annual reaffirmations of those rights, including as outlined in resolution 194(III).[184]

Finally, the protection gap is further anchored in another important UN institutional and conventional regime, namely UNHCR and the 1951 Convention. At the heart of this aspect of the gap is Article 1D of the 1951 Convention, which excludes Palestinian refugees from the benefits of the convention under certain circumstances and includes them under others. But this 'separate and special status'[185] created by the General Assembly for Palestinian refugees in recognition of the UN's unique responsibility towards them has resulted in a great deal of confusion in practice, exacerbating the protection gap afflicting Palestinian refugees.[186] It has only been in recent years that UNHCR and UNRWA have cooperated to address these issues, many of which remain unresolved. As will be seen, despite the good intentions behind the separate and special status fashioned for the Palestinian refugees, and in the absence of an effective durable solutions mandate for them while the 1951 Convention regime has evolved into a universal one, the Palestinian refugees have remained subject to a contingent legal status on the international plane. Ironically, this situation represents a compounded contingency of the UN's own making: it only exists because of the UN's failed attempt to legislate a principled means to manage the fallout of its initial illegal action aimed at the partition of Palestine in 1947. To appreciate the extent to which the UN has failed to square the circle for the Palestinian refugees in this regard, we must take a deeper look into the UN record.

---

[184] *See, e.g.*, A/RES/75/95, 10 December 2020.

[185] Statement of Mr. Baroody (Saudi Arabia), UN GAOR, 5th Sess., 328th Mtg. at para. 55, 27 November 1950.

[186] Albanese & Takkenberg, *supra* note 1 at 68.

3 *Palestinian Refugees and the International Rule by Law* 141

3.3.1 A Spirit of Erasure: The Origins of the Distinctive Institutional and Normative Regime

The backdrop for the distinctive institutional and normative regime for Palestinian refugees was the UN's fateful action in 1947. With the refusal of UNSCOP and the General Assembly to take Palestinian and Arab claims seriously regarding the inherent contradictions, illegality and dangers of partition, a troubling pattern of erasure of Palestinian reality took hold within the Organization. And it started at the very top.

In his 1947–1948 annual report, Secretary-General Trygve Lie blamed only 'powerful Arab interests, both inside and outside Palestine' for 'defying' the partition resolution and engaging 'in a deliberate effort to alter by force the settlement envisioned therein'.[187] No mention was made of the Zionists' violation of the plan's basic tenets that produced the Palestinian refugee problem, namely the requirements for democratic government, protection of minorities, and equality before the law. This is puzzling, given UNSCOPs earlier public conclusion that the Zionist programme could only be realized through the use of 'some considerable force' and its awareness of Zionist intentions and capabilities to use such force if need be.[188] The Secretary-General could not plead ignorance, as he was appraised of developments on the ground during the war which, by that time, had resulted in the actual ethnic cleansing of at least 300,000 of the country's indigenous Arab population from the area envisioned for the Jewish State, well before any Arab army entered the fray.[189]

This pattern of obfuscation continued and was tainted by the Secretary-General's Eurocentric and orientalist bias. In his subsequent annual report, Lie displayed astonishing ignorance of Middle Eastern history while revealing a barely disguised colonial and imperial worldview that might well have been penned by Lord Balfour himself. He wrote that:

> The establishment of the State of Israel in Palestine without a major war is one of the epic events of history, coming, as it does, at the end not merely of thirty years, but of 2,000 years of accumulated sorrows, bitterness and conflict. For Christian, Jew and Moslem alike Palestine symbolizes historic

---

[187] Annual Report of the Secretary-General on the Work of the Organization, 1 July 1947–30 June 1948, UN GAOR, 3rd Sess., Supp. No. 1, A/565, 1948, at 3.

[188] *See* Chapter 3, section 5.

[189] Cablegram from Secretary-General of League of Arab States to the Secretary-General of the United Nations, 15 May 1948, S/745. The cablegram indicates that 250,000 Palestinian refugees had been produced by that date, but subsequent reports revealed this to have been an underestimation. *See supra* note 83.

142   *1948 and After: The UN and the Palestinian Refugees*

forces beside which the present ideological conflict appears to be a transitory phenomenon.[190]

Leaving aside his failure to maintain independence and impartiality as the chief administrative officer of the Organization,[191] what is to be made of the Secretary-General's proclamation that the forced expulsion of 80 *per cent* of the Palestinian population from what became the State of Israel was not the result of 'a major war', if not an attempt to downplay that catastrophe, even as it was unfolding before his very eyes? By reducing the situation in Palestine to merely an 'ideological conflict', 'transitory' in nature, the Secretary-General revealed a cold indifference about what was being perpetrated under his watch. What other conclusion can be drawn from his public celebration of Israel's establishment, with its affinity for the mythological Zionist national narrative? With a few strokes of his diplomatic pen, lost were the details of the disaster that befell the hundreds of thousands of Palestinian refugees who, through no fault of their own, had been marked for removal and replacement.[192]

This is not to say that the Secretary-General did not reference Palestinian refugees. He did. But he did so in a manner devoid of any consideration of their constituent political rights as part of the Palestinian Arab collective. Foreshadowing a pattern that would emerge in the UN system thereafter, the Palestinian refugees were treated largely as a humanitarian problem as such. Thus, in his review of UN operations for 1948–1949, Lie blandly recounted that 'nine hundred thousand Arabs are receiving assistance from the United Nations' and that 'many of them must be resettled or repatriated'.[193] He then summarized some of the proposals made by UNCCP in its mediation between the Arab States and Israel, concluding simply that none of the delegations 'have felt able to accept any of them'.[194] At no point was the animus behind the ethnic cleansing of Palestine referred to, nor even the Israeli decision to bar return and usurp their property. It was as though the refugees were the product of some natural disaster, wholly outside the control of those responsible for it, in violation of prevailing public international law of which the Organization was ostensibly the principal guardian.

---

[190] Annual Report of the Secretary-General on the Work of the Organization, 1 July 1948–30 June 1949, UN GAOR, 4th Sess, Supp. No. 1, A/930, 1949, at ix ['Secretary-General's Annual Report 1948–49'].

[191] *Charter of the United Nations*, 24 October 1945, TS 993, art. 100 ['UN Charter'].

[192] Biographical literature reveals that Lie supported the Zionist cause behind the scenes, including while at the UN. *See* Tveit, O.K *Deception*, trans. (Kagge Forlag, 2018).

[193] Secretary-General's Annual Report 1948–49, *supra* note 190, xv.

[194] *Id.*, p. 6.

3 Palestinian Refugees and the International Rule by Law 143

The Secretary-General was not alone in this attitude. These views were indicative of a general spirit that prevailed within the Organization at the time. This is evident in the work of Count Folke Bernadotte, the first United Nations Mediator for Palestine, whose reports led to the passage of resolution 194(III) and the establishment of UNCCP. As the former Vice President of the Swedish Red Cross during WWII, Bernadotte possessed first-hand experience in dealing with the consequences of war crimes and crimes against humanity.

On 14 May 1948, the General Assembly mandated Bernadotte to, *inter alia*, employ good offices to 'promote a peaceful adjustment of the future situation of Palestine'.[195] That his work suffered from a failure to take Palestinians seriously may be surprising because the literature on international law and the Palestinian refugees relies on important wartime observations made by Bernadotte.[196] The most famous of these, set out in his general Progress Report, stated that:

> [i]t is ... undeniable that no settlement can be just and complete if recognition is not accorded to the right of the Arab refugee to return to the home from which he has been dislodged by the hazards and strategy of the armed conflict between Arabs and Jews in Palestine. The majority of these refugees have come from territory which, under the Assembly resolution of 29 November, was to be included in the Jewish State. The exodus of Palestinian Arabs resulted from panic created by fighting in their communities, by rumours concerning real or alleged acts of terrorism, or expulsion. It would be an offence against the principles of elemental justice if these innocent victims of the conflict were denied the right to return to their homes while Jewish immigrants flow into Palestine, and, indeed, at least offer the threat of permanent replacement of the Arab refugees who have been rooted in the land for centuries.[197]

To this was added observations regarding refugee property and scorched earth tactics:

> There have been numerous reports from reliable sources of large-scale looting, pillaging and plundering, and of instances of destruction of villages

---

[195] A/RES/186(S-2), 14 May 1948, para. 1.

[196] *See, e.g.*, Albanese & Takkenberg, *supra* note 1 at 346–347, 348; Kattan, *supra* note 26 at 216, 219; Pappe, I. *A Modern History of Palestine* (Cambridge, 2004) at 144. But there is ample evidence of Bernadotte's lack of seriousness in considering the Palestinian Arabs. In June 1948, he confided in his personal diary that '[t]he Palestine Arabs have at present no will of their own. Neither have they ever developed any specifically Palestinian nationalism. The demand for a separate Arab State in Palestine is consequently relatively weak'. Bernadotte, F. *To Jerusalem* (Hodder and Stoughton, 1951) at 113.

[197] *Progress Report of the United Nations Mediator on Palestine*, A/648, 16 September 1948, at 14 ['Progress Report of UN Mediator'].

144   *1948 and After: The UN and the Palestinian Refugees*

without apparent military necessity. The liability of the Provisional Government of Israel to restore private property to its Arab owners and to indemnify those owners for property wantonly destroyed is clear, irrespective of any indemnities which the Provisional Government may claim from the Arab States.[198]

In setting out 'specific conclusions' which, in his view, provided 'a reasonable, equitable and workable basis for settlement', Bernadotte reported that:

> The right of the Arab refugees to return to their homes in Jewish-controlled territory at the earliest possible date should be affirmed by the United Nations, and their repatriation, resettlement and economic and social rehabilitation, and payment of adequate compensation for the property of those choosing not to return, should be supervised and assisted by the United Nations conciliation commission....[199]

For these and similar observations, Bernadotte paid the ultimate price. On 17 September 1948, merely one day after issuing his Progress Report, he was assassinated by Lehi.[200] Yet this does not mean Bernadotte took Palestinian rights and claims as seriously as he should have, nor that the broader UN had turned a corner in its treatment of Palestine. A close review of his general Progress Report reveals many of the same problems that plagued the work of UNSCOP and the General Assembly in 1947, impacting the eventual contours of the distinctive institutional and normative regime for Palestinian refugees.

First, as of the date of Bernadotte's report, 16 September 1948, the General Assembly had not placed Palestine on the agenda of its third session, set to commence merely one week later.[201] This is incredible, given that it was only ten months since the General Assembly passed its partition plan, setting Palestine alight. This suggests the General Assembly continued to maintain a cognitive dissonance respecting the fate of the country's indigenous population, then literally being ethnically cleansed in real time.

Second, Bernadotte appears to have harboured a similar contempt for democratic principles that affected UNSCOP's majority. This emerges from his urging the General Assembly to pass a fresh resolution outlining a peace settlement and his position that '[t]he Arab States, even if opposed to it in debate and in voting should, as good Members of the United Nations, recognize a moral obligation to accept the will of the majority according to

---

[198] *Id.*

[199] *Id.*, at 18.

[200] The Security Council denounced the assassination as 'a cowardly act which appears to have been committed by a criminal group of terrorists in Jerusalem'. *See* S/RES/57, 18 September 1948. *See also* the Preface to this book.

[201] Progress Report of UN Mediator, *supra* note 197 at 3.

3 Palestinian Refugees and the International Rule by Law 145

democratic practice'.[202] The irony was unmistakable. By what logic did the Mediator think he could urge the Arab States to abide by majority rule in the General Assembly, when it was that very General Assembly that undermined the principle of majority rule in resolution 181(II) giving rise to the fall of Palestine and the expulsion of the Palestinian refugees in the first place?[203] As provided in his Progress Report, Bernadotte might have responded that the plan of partition had been 'outrun and irrevocably revised by the actual facts of recent Palestine history',[204] thereby rendering resolution 181(II) nugatory. But what were these 'actual facts'? With even greater irony, they concerned only one thing: the *fait accompli* that was the establishment of the State of Israel through sheer force of arms, with the imprimatur of the UN no less. Bernadotte wrote:

> The most significant development in the Palestine scene since last November is the fact that the Jewish State is a living, solidly entrenched and vigorous reality. [...] The Jewish State, established under the cloak of United Nations authority, can be eliminated only by force. [...] The combination of Jewish strength and international intervention has decided the issue of the Jewish State. [...] The Arabs have consistently advocated a unitary Arab State in Palestine, with full rights and guarantees for the Jewish minority, as the acceptable solution of the Palestine problem. In the light of developments during recent months the Arab position is unrealistic.[205]

If ever there was a shift of the goalposts by the UN, this was it. Merely months before, UNSCOP's majority and the General Assembly treated the 'great numerical preponderance' of Palestinian Arabs in the country as negligible and regarded Arab calls for a unitary democratic state as an 'extreme' position.[206] Now the UN was telling the Palestinian Arabs that the establishment of Israel on their land through force of arms merely four months after the end of the Mandate was an 'entrenched and vigorous reality', and that continued Arab calls for democracy in the country were therefore 'unrealistic'. But why was not the preceding fact of indigenous Palestinian Arab existence and numerical preponderance going back millennia shown the same deference? Would not the 'actual fact' that these people were now in forced exile 'under

---

[202] *Id.*, at 4.
[203] *See* Chapter 3, section 3.2. This point was repeatedly made by Arab States and delegates in the General Assembly's discussion of the Mediator's progress report. *See, e.g.,* Statement of Mr. Shukarriu, UN GAOR, 3rd Sess., 1st Comm., 201th mtg., A/C.1/201 (1948), 16 November 1948, at 649–650.
[204] Progress Report of UN Mediator, *supra* note 197 at 5.
[205] *Id.*, at 5–6.
[206] *See* Chapter 3, Section 4.3.

146 1948 and After: The UN and the Palestinian Refugees

the cloak of United Nations authority' be enough to compel the UN to reassess how peace could be achieved consistent with international law?

As it happens, the UN Mediator did make settlement proposals, but these were not entirely consistent with prevailing international law regarding the Palestinian refugees.[207] Despite his pronouncements on repatriation, restitution, and compensation, he suggested that an alternative solution for the Palestinian refugees might be appropriate: population exchange. In Bernadotte's words, UNCCP should be established and 'lend its good offices ... to any efforts toward exchanges of populations with a view to eliminating troublesome minority problems'.[208] But given his WWII experience, he must have known that any such exchange would necessarily involve a rejection of the principle of customary international law requiring nationality of a population to follow a change of sovereignty. It might further result in releasing those who ordered and/or carried out war crimes during the Nakba of criminal responsibility for their acts. Tellingly, when the General Assembly subsequently discussed Bernadotte's Progress Report and the establishment of UNCCP, Israel consistently rejected the return of the Palestinian refugees absent peace with the Arab States, arguing that, in any event, the guiding principle should be 'that demographic homogeneity should be achieved in order to avoid a minority problem'.[209]

It may be regarded as unduly harsh to criticize the UN Mediator for only partially addressing the prevailing international law relevant to the mass expulsion, denationalization, and looting the property of the Palestinian refugees. After all, as Bernadotte himself put it, his role did not involve the 'handing down of decisions', as 'the task of the meditator is to ... encourage compromise rather than strict adherence to legal principles'.[210] But therein lies the problem. In the face of what all available evidence indicated was a mass refugee problem resulting from clear violations of the law governing nationality, IHL, IHRL, and ICL by one party to the conflict, why did the General Assembly think that appointing a mediator to facilitate a negotiated compromise between that party and the Arab States would be a suitable way to arrive at a durable solution? Why would the UN refuse to require peace based on 'strict adherence to legal principles', including the laws of state and

---

[207] Nor were his proposals consistent with the existence of an independent Palestinian Arab state per resolution 181(II), in that he suggested that the remainder of Arab Palestine merge with Transjordan and enter into a union with Israel. *See* Progress Report of UN Mediator, *supra* note 197 at 7–8.

[208] *Id.*, at 18.

[209] *See, e.g.*, Statement of Mr. Eban (Provisional Government of Israel), UN GAOR, 3rd Sess., 1st Comm., 226th mtg., A/C.1/226 (1948), 3 December 1948, at 907.

[210] Progress Report of UN Mediator, *supra* note 197 at 8.

3 Palestinian Refugees and the International Rule by Law

individual criminal responsibility? What of the fact that the Mediator's efforts excluded any engagement with the political representatives of the Palestinian refugees themselves who continued to reject this grievous injustice?[211]

This pattern of failing to take the Palestinian Arabs seriously continued when the General Assembly considered the Meditator's proposals ahead of its passage of resolution 194(III) and the establishment of UNCCP. Echoing UNSCOP's unwillingness to sufficiently encourage or facilitate engagement with the Arab Higher Committee (AHC) a year earlier,[212] some European and settler-colonial member States obstructed AHC participation in the General Assembly debate on the Mediator's proposals while granting the provisional government of Israel full and automatic access.[213] The ostensible problem, according to countries like Guatemala,[214] Poland,[215] Soviet Union,[216] and Ukraine,[217] was the AHC's representation of itself as the provisional government of 'All Palestine'.[218] This could not be accepted, according to these States, either because it ran counter to the terms of partition resolution 181(II), or because some Western states had already recognized the provisional government of Israel. Arab States, such as Egypt,[219] Iraq,[220] Lebanon,[221] and Syria,[222] pointed out the double-standard, in so far as adherence to the terms of resolution 181(II) was not cited by any member of the General Assembly as a condition for allowing Israeli participation,[223] even as hundreds of thousands of Palestinian Arabs were being ethnically

---

[211] The Mediator restricted his own engagement to the Arab States and Israel. This was the case even after receiving a communication dated 25 July 1948 from the Arab Higher Committee regarding Jerusalem, to which the Mediator does not appear to have directly responded. *See id.*, at 12.

[212] *See* Chapter 3, Section 4.2.

[213] UN GAOR, 3rd Sess., 1st Comm., A/776, 7 December 1948, at 524–525.

[214] Statement of Mr. Garcia Granados (Guatemala), UN GAOR, 3rd Sess., 1st Comm., 169th mtg., A/C.1/169 (1948), 23 October 1948, at 241.

[215] Statement of Mr. Lange (Poland), UN GAOR, 3rd Sess., 1st Comm., 200th mtg., A/C.1/200 (1948), 15 November 1948, 637–638.

[216] Statement of Mr. Bogomolov (USSR), UN GAOR, 3rd Sess., 1st Comm., 169th mtg., A/C.1/169 (1948), 23 October 1948, at 237. Statement of Mr. Tsarapkin (USSR), *id.*, at 637 & 638.

[217] Statement of Mr. Manuilsky (Ukraine), UN GAOR, 3rd Sess., 1st Comm., 169th mtg., A/C.1/169 (1948), 23 October 1948, at 239–240.

[218] UN GAOR, 3rd Sess., 1st Comm., UN Doc A/C.1/335, 18 October 1948.

[219] Statement of Andraos Bey (Egypt), UN GAOR, 3rd Sess., 1st Comm., 200th mtg., A/C.1/200 (1948), 15 November 1948, at 636–637.

[220] Statement of Mr. Jormerd (Iraq), UN GAOR, 3rd Sess., 1st Comm., 200th mtg., A/C.1/200 (1948), 15 November 1948, at 635.

[221] Statement of Mr. Ammoun (Lebanon), UN GAOR, 3rd Sess., 1st Comm., 169th mtg., A/C.1/169 (1948), 23 October 1948, at 237–238.

[222] Statement of Mr. El-Khouri (Syria), UN GAOR, 3rd Sess., 1st Comm., 169th mtg., A/C.1/169 (1948), 23 October 1948, at 240.

[223] The Israeli representative 'was happy that the admission of its representatives as representatives of the State of Israel had met with no opposition'. Statement of Mr. Shertok (Provisional

148   *1948 and After: The UN and the Palestinian Refugees*

cleansed in real time in violation of those very terms.[224] The General Assembly was also reminded that the provisional government of All Palestine was in fact recognized by a number of Arab and non-Arab states. After haggling over these arguments for a month, during which time greater numbers of Palestinian Arabs were displaced, the General Assembly finally agreed to allow the AHC access to the debates, albeit without recognizing the legitimacy of its claim to represent an 'All Palestine government'.[225]

When substantive debate on the Mediator's proposals finally began, the AHC representative pointed out the absurdity of the Zionist argument that 750,000 Palestinian refugees willingly abandoned their rooted lives and property *en masse* and that they should be resettled in other Arab countries.[226] To him, the expulsion of the Palestinian refugees was a challenge to the UN Charter,[227] just as the assumptions upon which the Mediator's proposals were based would continue to implicate the Organization:

> The Mediator had been greatly influenced, indeed blinded, by the de facto situation. He had seen that the Jews controlled a large area and that their Provisional Government had been recognized by a certain number of States. By refusing to look for the underlying causes, he had not allowed justice to play the full part in the solution which it was for him to put forward. [...] Did the fait accompli of the occupation of a territory by a minority which proclaimed itself as a government have to be accepted? Did the fact have to be ignored that that minority represented only a third of the population, was composed of foreigners, owned only 7 percent of the land, had by its violence caused the flight of 750,000 of the original inhabitants and had indulged in looting and massacre? How much was a government set up by terror and assassination worth? Recognition of the principle of the fait accompli in Palestine under the aegis of the United Nations would mean in the judgment of history, the repudiation of elementary principles of international law and justice as well as the sanctioning of any kind of crime.[228]

Rather than deal with the substance of this plea to fact, reason and law, the Israeli representative continued denying responsibility for Palestine's ethnic

Government of Israel), UN GAOR, 3rd Sess., 1st Comm., 200th mtg., A/C.1/200 (1948), 15 November 1948, at 647.

[224] For an indication that the General Assembly knew what was happening in real time, *see*, *e.g.*, statements of Mr. Davies (United Kingdom) and Mrs. Roosevelt (United States), UN GAOR, 3rd Sess., 3rd Comm., 117th mtg., A/C.3/117 (1948), 29 October 1948, at 277 & 281.

[225] UN GAOR, 3rd Sess., 1st Comm., A/776, 7 December 1948, at 525.

[226] Statement of Mr. Cattan, UN GAOR, 3rd Sess., 1st Comm., 207th mtg., A/C.1/207 (1948), 22 November 1948, at 697.

[227] *Id.*, at 701.

[228] *Id.*, at 703–704.

3 Palestinian Refugees and the International Rule by Law 149

cleansing. Although 'military operations inflicted sufferings on innocent people,' he said, the 'only valid criterion by which ultimate moral blame for acts committed in war could be assessed was that of initial responsibility for the war', which lay with the Arabs – a convenient rhetorical move aimed at shielding Israeli actions from scrutiny under IHL, IHRL, and ICL.[229] In line with the Mediator, the representative asserted the General Assembly had to now 'affirm the existence of the State of Israel' as 'worthy of membership in the United Nations which had arisen out of the Assembly's own action in the past'.[230] This urge to recognize the new *de facto* situation borne of mass atrocity, and to couch it as being in conformity with the terms of General Assembly resolution 181(II), was advanced by various European and settler-colonial states, including Australia,[231] Canada,[232] the Netherlands,[233] and Uruguay.[234] Although some of these states addressed the humanitarian needs of the Palestinian refugees, reversing the course of events that rendered them refugees in the first place was the last thing on their minds. This aroused the exasperated concern of the Pakistani representative for whom the writing was on the wall regarding the UN's transformation of the Palestine question from a political issue to a humanitarian one. Why, he wondered, was the 'conscience' of the United Nations 'less aroused over the displacement of Arabs than that of the Jews?' If the General Assembly's approach to the Palestinian refugee problem was going to be 'that of relief and financial assistance', then why was that not enough for the displaced European Jews?[235]

Thus, the immediate origins of the distinctive institutional and normative regime were informed essentially by the same erasure of Palestinian Arab experience that affected UNSCOP and the 1947 General Assembly before it. Between treating the new State of Israel as a *fait accompli* despite emerging through clear violations of the terms of resolution 181(II), the insistence of mediation as the means through which the ethnic cleansing of Palestine

---

[229] This is because of the fundamental distinction between the *jus ad bellum* and *jus in bello*. Statement of Mr. Eban (Provisional Government of Israel), UN GAOR, 3rd Sess., 1st Comm., 208th mtg., A/C.1/208 (1948), 23 November 1948, at 716.

[230] *Id.*

[231] Statement of Mr. Hood (Australia), UN GAOR, 3rd Sess., 1st Comm., 208th mtg., A/C.1/208 (1948), 23 November 1948, at 708.

[232] Statement of Mr. Pearson (Canada), UN GAOR, 3rd Sess., 1st Comm., 206th mtg., A/C.1/206 (1948), 22 November 1948, at 692.

[233] Statement of Mr. Spits (Netherlands), UN GAOR, 3rd Sess., 1st Comm., 209th mtg., A/C.1/209 (1948), 23 November 1948, at 730.

[234] Statement of Mr. Fabregat (Uruguay), UN GAOR, 3rd Sess., 1st Comm., 210th mtg., A/C.1/210 (1948), 24 November 1948, at 739.

[235] Statement of Sir Zafrullah Khan (Pakistan), UN GAOR, 3rd Sess., 1st Comm., 210th mtg., A/C.1/210 (1948), 24 November 1948, at 733 & 737.

150   1948 and After: The UN and the Palestinian Refugees

was to be 'resolved' without regard to 'strict adherence' to international law, and the emergence of humanitarianism as the frame of reference for the Palestinian refugees, the preservation of Palestinian international legal subalternity at the UN continued to take shape.

3.3.2 UNCCP and Durable Solutions for Palestinian Refugees

UNCCP was created on 11 December 1948 through General Assembly resolution 194(III). Among the hundreds of UN resolutions on record, none possesses as great a value for Palestine and its people than resolution 194(III).[236] This is because of its affirmation of the right to return and compensation and the responsibility of the UN for the Palestinian refugee problem implied in it.[237] Lost in the popular imagination, however, is the resolution's role in helping solidify Palestinian contingency on the international legal plane. This emerges through a critical engagement with two aspects of resolution 194(III) and its aftermath, namely: (1) the limiting language of the resolution; and (2) the way in which UNCCP's durable solutions mandate was discharged.

On the resolution's limiting language, paragraph 11 provided, in part, that 'the refugees wishing to return to their homes and live at peace with their neighbours should be permitted to do so at the earliest practicable date...'. This differed from the Mediator's progress report which asserted that 'the *right* of the Arab refugees to return to their homes in Jewish-controlled territory at the earliest *possible* date should be affirmed by the United Nations'.[238] Why the variance in language? What is the precise meaning of 'wishing to return', 'live at peace with their neighbours', and 'earliest practicable date'?[239] Would the mere wish to return connote the existence of a legal *right* to do so? Would the choice of return be contingent on some duty to 'live at peace' beyond ordinary civic obligations without fear of being denationalized or deported? What threshold event must occur for the timing of return to qualify as 'practicable'?

The lack of clarity in this language only made early efforts to resolve the refugee problem more difficult. During UNCCP's mediation, beginning at

---

[236] *See, e.g.,* Abu Sitta, S. 'The Right of Return: Sacred, Legal and Possible' in Aruri, *supra* note 5.

[237] *See* text accompanying *supra* note 176.

[238] Progress Report of UN Mediator, *supra* note 197, at 18 [emphasis added].

[239] Reference to 'Arab refugees' in the Mediator's report was also changed in resolution 194(III) to 'refugees' to account for non-Arab refugees in the war. While the overwhelming number of 1948 refugees were of Arab origin (750,000–900,000), UN records indicate that approximately 17,000 Jewish persons were also rendered refugees because of the war. *See* UNCCP, Final Report of the United Nations Economic Survey Mission for the Middle East, Part I Final Report and Appendices, A/AC.25/6, 28 December 1949, at 18 ['ESM Report'].

3 Palestinian Refugees and the International Rule by Law 151

Lausanne in 1949, Israel's position remained that the Palestinian refugees had no right, as such, to return to their homes and property.[240] For support, Israel could rely on the fact that although the draft of what became resolution 194(III) included reference to the Mediator's progress report, that reference was struck from the final text of the resolution by the General Assembly and with it any express mention of a 'right' to return as such.[241] Likewise, at Lausanne, Israel continued to argue that the principle of 'demographic homogeneity' aimed at avoiding a 'minority problem' in its territory should govern and that any return, if at all, should be subject to practical security arrangements and peace with the Arab States.[242] For support, Israel could rely on the United Kingdom's proposal, agreed to by the General Assembly, to replace the words 'earliest possible date' with 'earliest *practicable* date',[243] and Guatemala's view that 'if the Arabs are allowed to return to Jewish territory in Palestine while war was continuing, they would only contribute to the ill-will between the parties'.[244]

None of this is to suggest that these arguments were convincing from an international law standpoint. On the contrary, the Mediator's reference to a 'right' to return and compensation accurately reflected customary international law.[245] Furthermore, as noted by Syria, return of refugees meant return of unarmed civilians to their homes and property,[246] persons who, in any case, were entitled under international law to continued nationality in their country regardless of the existence of peace with the Arab states and changes in sovereignty over the territory from which they were expelled. What it is to say, however, is that the qualifying language of resolution 194(III) gave rise to enough questions between the parties to render it more difficult for UNCCP to mediate an agreement consistent with the principle of refugee choice and preference for voluntary repatriation in line with international law.

Recognizing the confusion wrought by this language, in May 1950 the UNCCP secretariat prepared a working paper confirming that the phrase

---

[240] UNCCP, Analysis of Paragraph 11 of the General Assembly's Resolution of 11 December 1948 (working paper prepared by the Secretariat), Restricted, A/AC.25/W/45, 15 May 1950 ['UNCCP Working Paper on Paragraph 11'].

[241] *Id.*, at 1. *See also* Rempel, *supra* note 5 at 176–177.

[242] Statement of Mr. Eban (Provisional Government of Israel), UN GAOR, 3rd Sess., 1st Comm., 226th mtg., A/C.1/226 (1948), 3 December 1948, at 906–907.

[243] Statement of Mr. Beeley (United Kingdom), UN GAOR, 3rd Sess., 1st Comm., 226th mtg., A/C.1/226 (1948), 3 December 1948, at 910 [emphasis added].

[244] Statement of Mr. Garcia Granados (Guatemala), UN GAOR, 3rd Sess., 1st Comm., 226th mtg., A/C.1/226 (1948), 3 December 1948, at 904.

[245] *See, e.g.*, Boling, *supra* note 5.

[246] *See, e.g.*, Statement of Mr. El-Khouri (Syria), UN GAOR, 3rd Sess., 1st Comm., 226th mtg., A/C.1/226 (1948), 3 December 1948, at 908–909.

'those wishing to return' was intended by the General Assembly 'to confer upon the refugees as individuals the *right* of exercising a free choice' between 'repatriation and compensation for damages suffered, on the one hand, or no return and compensation for all property left behind, on the other'.[247] It further confirmed that the meaning of the term 'at the earliest practicable date' did not 'make the repatriation of the refugees conditional upon the establishment of a formal peace'.[248] Finally, it clarified that the practicability requirement meant that the refugees should be able to return when conditions were 'stable', which in its view were established by the signing of the four armistice agreements of 1949.[249] Still, problems of interpretation lingered. Thus, despite suggesting that the proviso 'to live at peace with their neighbours' was not a 'limiting condition', UNCCP admitted that it signalled: (1) 'the General Assembly's intention' to prevent 'a potential fifth column in Israel'; (2) returnees 'would be obligated to give advance assurances' of their peaceful intentions; (3) Israel could reserve 'the right to exercise its veto on the return of any refugee whose past action, it considered, indicated that he was not peace loving'; and (4) 'the onus of proof of innocence might be placed on the refugee wishing to return'.[250] Leaving aside the curious notion that the refugees could be a 'fifth column' in their own homes, these limiting conditions were (and remain) alien to the international law governing reparations for mass displacement and denationalization of civilian populations. In fact, the UDHR's prohibition on arbitrary deprivation of nationality and property, and its affirmation of the right to return to one's country, does not include any of the limiting provisions delineated in resolution 194(III).[251] The importance of this is underscored by the fact that the UDHR and resolution 194(III) were promulgated by the same General Assembly – only *one* day apart – in December 1948. All this to say, despite efforts of UNCCP to clarify the limiting terms of paragraph 11 of resolution 194(III), questions remained open in the immediate aftermath of the Nakba. This allowed Israel to entrench its position during negotiations, a position that remains even more unyielding today.

This leads us to UNCCP's durable solutions mandate. The UN record reveals three overlapping issues that rendered the UNCCP's effort to mediate a negotiated resolution problematic from the standpoint of the Palestinian refugees: (1) the bias of UNCCP's membership; (2) the failure by the UNCCP to engage with official Palestinian political representatives;

[247] UNCCP Working Paper on Paragraph 11, *supra* note 240 at 2 [emphasis added].
[248] *Id.*, at 7.
[249] *Id.*
[250] *Id.*, at 4.
[251] UDHR, *supra* note 34, arts. 13(2), 15(2), 17(2).

3 Palestinian Refugees and the International Rule by Law 153

and (3) the fundamental impediment to finding an international law-based resolution to the Palestinian refugee issue inherent in UNCCP's conciliation function.

With a tripartite membership of France, Turkey, and the United States, the Palestinian refugees were faced with a similar cultural and political bias in UNCCP that marked the work of UNSCOP before it. According to the leading historian on UNCCP, Michael Fischbach, UNCCP was 'a body whose policies toward Israel largely had been shaped by the Americans to avoid angering the Israelis as much as possible'.[252] As such, '[t]he United States remained focused on refugee resettlement first and foremost'[253] and Washington 'established certain policy positions that became "red zones" beyond which it – and through its influence on the commission, the UNCCP – would not cross'.[254] The first of these was that the Palestinian refugees were to be placated with compensation, the purpose of which 'would be to finance the massive resettlement of most Palestinians into the surrounding Arab countries'.[255] The second of these was that 'the United States and the world community would end up paying most of the costs of compensation, not Israel itself.[256] As cryptically noted by the UNCCP itself in 1949, '[t]he Commission considered that in the long run the final solution of the problem would be found within the framework of the economic and social rehabilitation of all the countries of the Middle East' – a euphemism, as we shall see, for a solution based largely on resettlement in surrounding Arab countries.[257]

Unsurprisingly, another feature of UNCCP that mirrored UNSCOP was its failure to engage with the political representatives of the Palestinian refugees. From the beginning of its mandate in January 1949, the 'issue of who would represent the Palestinians themselves proved contentious'.[258] According to Fischbach, UNCCP refused to meet representatives of the AHC as official representatives, but rather invited them to attend hearings as only one of several non-governmental organizations. When the AHC predicably refused, UNCCP instead met with a handful of individual Palestinian refugee landowners from

---

[252] Fischbach, *supra* note 112 at 286.
[253] *Id.*, at 90.
[254] *Id.*, at 88.
[255] *Id.*
[256] *Id.*
[257] UNCCP, *Historical Survey of Efforts of the United Nations Conciliation Commission for Palestine to Secure the Implementation of Paragraph 11 of General Assembly Resolution 194(III), The Question of Reintegration by Repatriation or Resettlement* (working paper prepared by the Secretariat), 2 October 1961, A/AC.25/W.82/Rev.1, para. 10 ['UNCCP Historical Survey Reintegration'].
[258] Fischbach, *supra* note 112 at 85.

only one depopulated Palestinian city, Haifa.[259] This pattern of refusing to deal with the AHC on its own terms appears to have continued throughout the operational life of UNCCP. Thus, in 1961, and after appearing before the special political committee of the General Assembly, a delegation from the AHC attempted to meet UNCCP but were denied access. Joseph Johnson, the then American special representative of UNCCP on compensation, 'refused to see the delegation and dismissed their claim officially to have represented the Palestinians at the UN'.[260] A review of UNCCP's historical survey of its efforts to secure the implementation of paragraph 11 of General Assembly resolution 194(III) confirms that the only parties it engaged in its conciliation efforts were the states involved in the 1948 war, excluding the AHC.[261] Therefore, the loss of Palestine not only stripped the Palestinian refugees of their homes, property, and nationality, but also their very agency and standing to seek redress from the UN, a body that bore direct responsibility for their plight.

The biggest problem with UNCCP's durable solutions mandate was the fact that it was tasked with facilitating a *negotiated* resolution of the Palestinian refugee problem. Given that the problem resulted from clear violations of international law, including the law governing nationality, IHL, IHRL, and ICL, the General Assembly's preference for conciliation as the method of ensuring respect for the rights of the refugees – even as narrowly construed in resolution 194(III) – did not stand to reason. The fact that the rule that nationality follows a change in sovereignty was well established through the interwar 'minority treaty' practice of the very members of UNCCP itself only added insult to injury.[262] The Israeli side denied responsibility for the Palestinian refugee problem, but the Mediator's progress report and real-time evidence provided to the General Assembly demonstrated the opposite to be true. By conditioning the search for an international law-based durable solution on negotiation between a recalcitrant wrongful state and other states that did not formally represent the victims themselves, the mechanism was hamstrung from the start for being in violation of the rules on state responsibility.[263] As stated by the Iraqi representative in the General Assembly at the time: '[h]ow could Arab rights to their own homes, which they had inhabited in Palestine, be a matter of bargain and negotiation?'[264]

---

[259] *Id.*

[260] *Id.*, at 282.

[261] *See* UNCCP Historical Survey Compensation, *supra* note 111 *and* UNCCP Historical Survey Reintegration, *supra* note 257, neither of which make any reference to the AHC.

[262] *See* text accompanying *supra* note 26.

[263] *See* text accompanying *supra* notes 56–66.

[264] Statement of Mr. Jamali (Iraq), UN GAOR, 4th Sess., 223rd Plen. Mtg., A/PV.223, 22 September 1949, at 17.

3 Palestinian Refugees and the International Rule by Law 155

It did not take long for UNCCP to admit its conciliation effort had failed. In its first meeting with the parties in February 1949, the commission sought assurances from Israel, already given by the Arab states, that it merely accept 'the principle established by the General Assembly resolution [194(III)], permitting the return to their homes of those refugees who expressed the desire to do so'.[265] Israeli prime minister, David Ben Gurion, refused to reply to the question, affirming only the limiting language of resolution 194(III) requiring refugees to 'live at peace with their neighbours'. He held fast to Israel's position: no repatriation absent peace with the Arab states and, in any case, resettlement in those states would be the main solution.[266]

If UN-mediated conciliation was ever going to produce results in line with the rights of the refugees to voluntary repatriation and compensation, the Organization would have to leverage the only thing it possessed – power over membership of Israel in the UN.[267] This might explain why, amid Israel's application for UN membership in the spring of 1949, it softened its position on the refugee question. When UNCCP convened at Lausanne in April 1949, Israel offered to accept the population of the Gaza Strip, some 100,000 Palestinian refugees among them, in exchange for sovereignty there.[268] The gesture was short-lived, with Israel walking it back following its admission to UN membership on 11 May 1949.[269] On 5 August 1949, Israel informed UNCCP that its offer 'would be limited by considerations affecting the security and the economy of the State', reserving the right to resettle the 100,000 in areas of its choosing rather than in their original homes as per resolution 194(III).[270] By 30 October 1950, the offer as a whole was rescinded during a second round of meetings at Geneva. Israel informed UNCCP that 'it would be inadvisable to allow the refugees to continue to believe that some of them would be repatriated', as the 'retention of such a hope might prevent them from co-operating in schemes for resettlement'.[271] By the time a third peace

---

[265] UNCCP Historical Survey Reintegration, *supra* note 257, para. 7.

[266] *Id.*, para. 8.

[267] Statement of Mr. Rahim Bey (Egypt), UN GAOR, 4TH Sess., Ad Hoc Political Comm., 52nd Mtg., 30 November 1949, at 313.

[268] UNCCP Historical Survey Reintegration, *supra* note 257, para. 12.

[269] A/RES/273(III), 11 May 1949. The preamble of resolution 273 recalled both resolution 181(II) and 194(III), noting Israel's declaration that it 'unreservedly accepts the obligations of the United Nations Charter and undertakes to honour them from the day when it becomes a Member of the United Nations'. *See also* Chapter 6, section 4.5.

[270] UNCCP Historical Survey Reintegration, *supra* note 257, para. 22. The UNCCP did not then know that on 16 June 1948, the Israeli cabinet decided to bar return of the Palestinian refugees to their homes and property. *See* text accompanying *supra* note 115.

[271] UNCCP Historical Survey Reintegration, *supra* note 257, para. 47.

156   *1948 and After: The UN and the Palestinian Refugees*

conference was convened at Paris in 1952, UNCCP essentially admitted that conciliation had been a failure. The following excerpt from its historical survey is worth quoting at length:

> When in 1948 the General Assembly first had resolved that the refugees should be permitted to return to their homes, the land and houses which those people had abandoned in their flight were considered to be still, for the most part, intact and unoccupied. The operation involved in their return did not, therefore, present any very great difficulties; all that would have been necessary was for those refugees who wished to do so to undertake the journey to return and resume their interrupted lives, perhaps with a little financial assistance from the international community. It was this kind of movement and return that the Conciliation Commission had been instructed to facilitate. For reasons that were beyond the Commission's task of facilitation, this movement did not come to pass. The respective attitudes of the parties on this matter – attitudes which produced a complete deadlock as regards the refugee question – were well known. The Arab States insisted upon a prior solution of the refugee question, at least in principle, before agreeing to discuss other outstanding issues. In their opinion, a solution of the refugee problem could be reached only as a result of unconditional acceptance by Israel of the right of refugees to be repatriated. Israel, on the other hand, had maintained that no solution of the refugee question involving repatriation could be envisaged outside the framework of an over-all settlement. As regards the right of the refugees to return, Israel refused to accept a principle that might involve it in a repatriation operation of unknown extent. The Commission was unable to conciliate these two points of view.[272]

The Paris talks of 1952 were the last of UNCCP's conciliation efforts. In that year, the General Assembly reduced its budget,[273] prompting UNCCP to shift its work towards the identification and valuation of Palestinian Arab refugee property as well as the release of Palestinian Arab bank accounts and safety deposits in Israel.[274]

Curiously, the literature tends to treat UNCCP's failure to mediate as the sole result of the political intransigence of Israel and the Arab States.[275] But that ignores the collusion of the UN itself, in so far as the record demonstrates it paid insufficient attention in its early years to international law in both the creation and operationalization of UNCCP while also refusing to engage the representatives of the Palestinian refugees on their own terms. In line with

---

[272] *Id.*, paras. 63–65.
[273] Albanese & Takkenberg, *supra* note 1 at 84.
[274] UNCCP Historical Survey Reintegration, supra note 257, paras. 49–76.
[275] *See, e.g.*, Albanese & Takkenberg, *supra* note 1 at 83–84; *and* Goddard, *supra* note 22 at 480.

3 Palestinian Refugees and the International Rule by Law 157

Bernadotte's exhortation to 'encourage compromise rather than strict adherence to legal principles', it appears that the rights of the Palestinian refugees were rendered unattainable through UNCCP by design.

The pattern of refusing to ensure Israel repair its violation of Palestinian refugee rights in line with principles of refugee choice continued within the UN for many years thereafter, while the refugees themselves languished in forced exile generation after generation. One example of this is found in Security Council resolution 242. Adopted in response to the June 1967 war, the Security Council called for a 'just settlement of the refugee problem' without so much as identifying that it was the *Palestinian* refugee problem that was in issue.[276] From these nameless refugees re-emerged a new Palestinian national movement in the form of the Palestine Liberation Organization (PLO) in 1964. And when the PLO and Israel commenced the Oslo process in 1993, the UN created a new body – the Office of the UN Special Coordinator for the Middle East Peace Process (UNSCO) – to provide good offices to the parties. UNSCO was never specifically mandated 'to facilitate the repatriation, resettlement and economic and social rehabilitation of the refugees and the payment of compensation' as per resolution 194(III). Indeed, under almost exclusive US auspices, the Oslo accords never expressly referred to resolution 194(III), but were based on Security Council resolutions, including 242 (1967), 338 (1973), and 1515 (2003), the latter of which endorsed the 'performance-based roadmap to a permanent two-state solution to the Israeli-Palestinian conflict'. This further watered down the UN's position on durable solutions, as the 'roadmap' introduced even more limiting language through its call for 'an agreed, just, fair, and realistic solution to the refugee issue'.[277] On these terms, the special coordinator's focus has been to facilitate so-called 'final status' negotiations, including on the Palestinian refugees. Although these negotiations formally commenced in 1999, they last convened in 2001 without result.

Thus, from the General Assembly's creation of the UN Mediator in May 1948 to the present day, the UN has remained stuck on the fanciful notion that the only way to resolve the Palestinian refugee problem is through negotiation. This, despite the clear requirements of international law, including the law of state responsibility, and the knowledge that the only thing standing in the way is a recalcitrant wrongdoing state that continues to enjoy the benefits of its wrongful conduct. The upshot is that since at least 1963, and with the arguable exception of a few years between 1999 and 2001, the UN has

---

[276] S/RES/242 (1967), 22 November 1967.

[277] Letter dated 7 May 2003 from the Secretary-General addressed to the President of the Security Council, S/2003/529, 7 May 2003, annex.

158 *1948 and After: The UN and the Palestinian Refugees*

not mandated any of its organs to seek durable solutions for the Palestinian refugees as a group in line with international law, thereby consolidating the protection gap that continues to mark their collective experience.[278]

3.3.3 UNRWA, UNHCR, and Protection and Assistance for Palestine Refugees

UNRWA was established on 8 December 1949 through General Assembly resolution 302(IV) and mandated to provide the Palestine refugees with 'direct relief and works programmes', as recommended by the ESM. Although resolution 302(IV) stated this assistance was without prejudice to the rights of the refugees under paragraph 11 of resolution 194(III), this saving clause was effectively rendered a dead letter in UNRWA's early years by the ESM's recommendations aimed at resettling the refugees in the Arab states. A review of the ESM record and the General Assembly debates that followed indicate that UNRWA was intended to be a vehicle through which such resettlement was to take place, despite the countervailing efforts of various Arab states. This was compounded by an attitude of the ESM that was not only duplicitous in its claim to preserve the rights of the refugees, but openly paternalistic towards them and their legitimate grievances.

As a subsidiary of the UNCCP, the ESM harboured a bias against the Palestinian refugees like that exhibited by the UN on Palestine to that point. The ESM's composition was identical to UNCCP's, with an American chair and two deputy chairs from France and Turkey, in addition to a third from the United Kingdom.[279] Given the American prioritization of resettlement in the work of the UNCCP, this did not bode well. In its first interim report of 16 November 1949, the ESM obscured the facts about the mass denationalization and expulsion of the Palestinian refugees. Although the UN possessed intimate knowledge of how and why Palestine was depopulated,[280] the ESM absurdly asserted that 'the plight of the refugees is both a *symptom* and a cause of grave *economic* instability'.[281] It therefore recommended 'that steps be taken to establish a

---

[278] Akram, S. 'UNRWA and Palestine Refugees' in Costello, C., Foster, M. & McAdam, J. *The Oxford Handbook of International Refugee Law* (Oxford, 2021) at 651.

[279] *United Nations Conciliation Commission for Palestine, Fourth Progress Report*, 15 September 1949, A/992, para. 28.

[280] UNCCP acknowledged that '[a]s regards refugees from Palestine in particular, they were obliged to leave their homes because they were of Arab origin. This fact is not questioned'. *See* UNCCP, *Definition of a 'Refugee' Under Paragraph 11 of the General Assembly Resolution of 11 December 1948 – Note by the Principal Secretary*, A/AC.25/W/61, 9 April 1951.

[281] UNCCP, *First Interim Report of the United Nations Economic Survey Mission for the Middle East*, A/1106, 16 November 1949, at 14 [emphasis added] ['ESM First Interim Report'].

3 Palestinian Refugees and the International Rule by Law 159

programme of useful public works for the employment of able-bodied refugees as a first measure towards their rehabilitation'.[282] This invention, out of whole cloth, of an economic reason for the Nakba was but another manifestation of the UN's shifting of the goalposts on the Palestinians. Not even the Zionists suggested that the Palestinian refugee problem was a symptom of economic woes. This was yet further evidence of the UN's failure to take the Palestinians seriously, even as the ESM feigned concern for their wellbeing.[283] Thus, the ESM recognised that although the 'great majority' of the Palestinian refugees wanted to be repatriated and rejected resettlement,[284] a 'political stalemate in the relations between the Arab countries and Israel precludes any early solution of the refugee problem by means of repatriation or large-scale resettlement'.[285] But this didn't mean that resettlement on some scale was not on the cards. Indeed, according to Benjamin Schiff, the ESM's reference to 'rehabilitation' was but a euphemism for resettlement, which the proposed public works were designed to ensure.[286] We know this because elsewhere the ESM indicated that its relief and works programme was 'intended … *to reduce the refugee problem* to limits within which the Near Eastern Governments can reasonably be expected to assume any *remaining* responsibility'.[287] Accordingly, the ESM indicated that one of the main purposes of its programme would be to 'increase the *practical alternatives* available to refugees, and thereby *encourage a more realistic view of the kind of future they want and the kind they can achieve*'.[288] Given the ESM's knowledge that UNCCP-facilitated negotiations had produced a stalemate, it is hard not to conclude that it knew that its programme was logically aimed at resettlement in all but name. For the programme encouraged the refugees to establish economic roots in Arab host states, while searching for more 'realistic' and 'practical' solutions for their future.

With no small measure of paternalism, the ESM affirmed that another purpose of its programme would be to 'halt the demoralizing process of pauperization' among the Palestinian refugees, the 'outcome of a dole prolonged', as if their plight was the result of structural poverty.[289] This condescending,

---

[282] *Id.*

[283] It also appears to be the first in a long and failed history of peacebuilding through economic development in Palestine. *See, e.g.,* Odeh, R. 'Economic Peace and the Israeli-Palestinian Conflict' (2018) ICSR, at: https://icsr.info/wp-content/uploads/2018/12/KPMED-Paper_Economic-Peace-and-the-Israeli-Palestinian-Conflict.pdf.

[284] ESM First Interim Report, *supra* note 281 at 18.

[285] *Id.,* at 16.

[286] Schiff, B. *Refugees Unto the Third Generation* (Syracuse, 1995) at 20.

[287] ESM First Interim Report, *supra* note 281 at 15 [emphasis added].

[288] *Id.,* at 17 [emphasis added].

[289] *Id.*

160   *1948 and After: The UN and the Palestinian Refugees*

arguably racist attitude was a marked feature of the ESM's work. In its final report of 18 December 1949, it went so far as to envelop the plight of the refugees into an economic development model for the whole of the Middle East, this time with an orientalist bent. The ESM acknowledged that its report did:

> ... not deal directly with the problem of the refugees from Palestine. Yet the obstacles in the way of economic development in the Middle East are much the same as those hampering the rehabilitation of the Arab Refugees. [...] The contrast between poverty and plenty ... is a source of envy, a stimulant to unrest, a basis for fear and an incitement to wars [...] The highly developed nations of the world did not make their way by wishing. By work and risk they forced the earth, the soil, the forests and the rivers to yield them riches. [...] Such development is essential to stability. Such development can help assure and maintain peace.[290]

Thus, almost immediately following the ethnic cleansing of Palestine, the predicament of the Palestinian refugees had been fundamentally recast at the UN. From a matter involving the stripping from a national group of its collective and individual right to exist in its native land in violation of international law, the refugees had now been reduced to a socio-economic problem of Third World 'idleness' in need of a developmental/humanitarian solution and 'economic peace', lest 'envy', and 'fear' lead to further war.

The General Assembly debates in 1949 concerning the establishment of UNRWA confirmed this. These debates were highly polarized and, with limited exceptions,[291] continued to pit the Arab and Islamic bloc of states against the European, settler-colonial, and Western majority. Whereas the former urged the UN to uphold the international rule of law in its handling of the Palestinian refugee issue, the latter either argued for 'practical' solutions to the problem, in line with the ESM recommendations, or simply refused to address the matter. Thus,

---

[290] UNCCP, *Final Report of the United Nations Economic Survey Mission for the Middle East: An Approach to Economic Development in the Middle East*, A/AC.25/6, 18 December 1949, at vii-viii.

[291] *See, e.g.*, Statement of Mr. Luns (Netherlands), UN GAOR, 4th Sess., Ad Hoc Political Comm., 55th Mtg., 2 December 1949, at 329, who indicated that the Netherlands was 'disappointed to note that, since 11 December 1948, no steps had been taken to ensure, in an effective manner, the repatriation of the refugees. The State of Israel had, to a great extent, owed its creation and its membership in the United Nations to the indignation which had been aroused throughout the world by the Nazi persecution of the Jews. However, if the State of Israel evaded its moral duty with respect to the problem of Arab refugees, world opinion would turn against it and it would be the first to suffer the consequences. The Netherlands delegation, which had always felt the keenest and deepest sympathy for the sufferings of the Jews, recognized the fact that the complex problem of repatriation represented very serious difficulties. It nevertheless insisted that the resolution 194 (III) should be applied'. A similar intervention was made by the representative of Denmark in the same debate.

3 Palestinian Refugees and the International Rule by Law 161

after recalling the rights of the Palestinian refugees under paragraph 11 of resolution 194(III) and the need for the General Assembly to 'set up adequate machinery for their implementation', the Lebanese representative criticized the ESM programme as a means by which 'the basic political rights of the Arabs could be bought off by economic expedients'.[292] Likewise, the Egyptian representative asserted that the Palestinian 'refugees clamoured not for relief, but for repatriation; not for a dole, but for a return to normal living in their own communities and freedom to enjoy their homes and property'.[293] Similarly, the Saudi representative asserted that though relief and economic assistance for the Palestinian refugees was 'important, those measures alone could not provide a solution to the refugee problem. The authorities concerned must be urged to facilitate the implementation of paragraph 11 of resolution 194 (III) of the General Assembly which reaffirmed the right of the Arab refugees to return to their homes'.[294] The Lebanese delegate put it best when he impugned the UN's role in altering the frame of reference on the nature of the Palestinian refugee problem:

> [i]t was a matter of great surprise that although its resolution 194 (III) had not even begun to be implemented, the United Nations should now seem to turn from that basic question to deal exclusively with assistance to refugees. Had that attitude on the part of the United Nations been the result of Israel's refusal to carry out its resolution? If that were so, it would be tantamount to the United Nations sanctioning the insubordination of one of its Members, as well as a serious violation of the rights of the refugees, and it would mean that the Organization were powerless to enforce its will.[295]

These pleas to principle and the rule of law fell on deaf ears in the western-dominated General Assembly. With a demographically preponderant Jewish State now secured through the displacement of Palestine's indigenous population, these states would do nothing to reverse course, regardless of what international law required. Thus, the Dominican representative opened the General Assembly debate asserting 'that practical solutions would soon be found for the problem of the Palestine refugees'.[296] This was followed by the

---

[292] Statement of Mr. Malik (Lebanon), UN GAOR, 4th Sess., 228th Mtg., A/PV.228, 26 September 1949, at 69–71.

[293] Statement of Mr. Rahim Bey (Egypt), UN GAOR, 4th Sess., Ad Hoc Political Comm., 54th Mtg., 2 December 1949, at 316.

[294] Statement of Mr. Dejany (Saudi Arabia), UN GAOR, 4th Sess., Ad Hoc Political Comm., 54th Mtg., 2 December 1949, at 319.

[295] Statement of Mr. Azkoul (Lebanon), UN GAOR, UN GAOR, 4th Sess., Ad Hoc Political Comm., 55th Mtg., 2 December 1949, at 324.

[296] Statement of Mr. Henriquez Ureña (Dominican Republic), UN GAOR, 4th Sess., 229th Plen. Mtg., A/PV.229, 26 September 1949, at 90.

162   *1948 and After: The UN and the Palestinian Refugees*

British representative who indicated that although the ESM's programme 'might be criticized for failing to deal with repatriation and compensation', his delegation supported its 'constructive and realistic approach' towards the refugees 'pending a final political settlement'.[297] The US delegate supported this position.[298] Likewise, the Canadian representative stated that his 'delegation was in full agreement' with the ESM's 'realistic proposals'.[299]

If there was any doubt about where the General Assembly was headed regarding the operationalization of the ESM's resettlement programme, it was laid to rest by the president of the ICRC, then leading the humanitarian response in Palestine. In briefing the General Assembly on its operations in Palestine, the ICRC president noted that the ESM:

> opened up reassuring and encouraging prospects, because its proposals were likely to make it possible, in the very near future, *to settle in permanent homes and in an active and useful life some hundreds of thousands of refugees*, who would thus be freed from idleness which had been forced on them ... [...] The Red Cross, realizing that the difficult task was one for a strictly neutral and humanitarian agency, had shown itself ready to act to the fullest extent possible. [...] But owing to that same neutrality, the Red Cross was duty-bound to transfer the tasks entrusted to it to other authorities as soon as the situation became settled, and as soon as *the problem to be solved was one of reconstruction and resettlement.* [...] *[T]he programme for the settlement of refugees in permanent homes should be examined without delay by the Assembly*, because relief, even if prolonged was essentially provisional and intended to enable the authorities concerned to take the necessary steps to achieve *the only permanent solution, which was resettlement.* [...] Although it was not for the International Red Cross to express an opinion on the various proposals for *resettlement, it nevertheless sincerely hoped that the General Assembly would not adjourn without having taken formal and constructive decisions in that field.* The responsibility voluntarily assumed by the Red Cross ... should not be extended unduly.[300]

The message was clear. As an independent and neutral organization, the ICRC could not allow itself to be publicly implicated in the drive to resettle the Palestinian refugees against their will and in contravention of their

[297] Statement of Sir Alexander Cadogan (United Kingdom), UN GAOR, 4th Sess., Ad Hoc Political Comm., 51st Mtg., 30 November 1949, at 308.
[298] Statement of Mr. Ross (United States), UN GAOR, 4th Sess., Ad Hoc Political Comm., 51st Mtg., 30 November 1949, at 308.
[299] Statement of General McNauhton (Canada), UN GAOR, 4th Sess., Ad Hoc Political Comm., 55th Mtg., 2 December 1949, at 328.
[300] Statement of Mr. Ruegger (ICRC), UN GAOR, 4th Sess., Ad Hoc Political Comm., 44th Mtg., 25 November 1949, at 256 [emphasis added].

3 Palestinian Refugees and the International Rule by Law 163

international legal rights. Another organization had to be fashioned for that purpose. That organization was UNRWA.

In the General Assembly debates on the creation of UNRWA, the Arab states understood that most of the European-dominated membership could not be persuaded to prioritize principle over pragmatism. The only other thing to be done, therefore, was to introduce a saving clause into the terms of UNRWA's mandate. With lip service still being paid by some Western states for a durable solution that included a measure of repatriation, a door had been left ajar. Accordingly, Egypt successfully urged the General Assembly to include a provision in resolution 302(IV) indicating that UNRWA's mandate to provide relief and works programmes should be discharged without prejudice to the rights of the Palestinian refugees under paragraph 11 of resolution 194(III).[301]

Thus, from the start of its operations, UNRWA's mandate was beset with an inherent contradiction. On the one hand, it was designed to give effect to the ESM's resettlement scheme. On the other hand, it was to do this without prejudice to the rights of the refugees to return and compensation under paragraph 11 of resolution 194(III). This comes through in the terms of General Assembly resolution 393(V) of 2 December 1950, passed just eight months after UNRWA began its operations in May 1950. It provided that:

> without prejudice to the provisions of paragraph 11 of General Assembly resolution 194(III) of 11 December 1948, the reintegration of the refugees into the economic life of the Near East, either by repatriation or resettlement, is essential in preparation of the time when international assistance is no longer available, and for the realization of conditions of peace and stability in the area.

But how would reintegration into the economic life of the Near East, 'either by repatriation or resettlement', occur if Israel barred the return of the refugees and the UN was unable or unwilling to compel it to change its position in line with its obligations under international law? In such circumstances, it was clear that 'reintegration' in fact meant resettlement, notwithstanding the saving clause. This much was openly admitted by UNCCP when it noted that the general objective of UNRWA's 'reintegration' programmes for Palestinian refugees 'was to facilitate their permanent integration and settlement in the Middle East'.[302] Of course, the refugees well understood this and accordingly refused to participate in any substantial way in the scheme, an attitude shared

---

[301] Statement of Mr. Rahim Bey (Egypt), UN GAOR, 4th Sess., Ad Hoc Political Comm., 52nd Mtg., 30 November 1949, at 314.
[302] UNCCP Historical Survey Reintegration, *supra* note 257, para. 82.

164   *1948 and After: The UN and the Palestinian Refugees*

by the Arab host states. By 1956, UNRWA recognized the impossibility of the task, noting in its annual report to the General Assembly that year 'that the refugees' desire to return to their homeland continues unabated' and that '[s]o long ... as nothing is done to help requite this longing for their homeland, either by giving them the choice between repatriation and compensation provided for in paragraph 11 of General Assembly resolution 194 (III) of 11 December 1948, or through some other solution acceptable to all parties, the long-term task assigned to the Agency will prove unrealizable'.[303]

Since then, UNRWA has continued to provide what it now calls its core 'human development' services to the refugees – education, health, and relief and social services – and its mandate has repeatedly been renewed by the General Assembly pending 'a just and lasting solution' to their plight.[304] But because UNRWA is not expressly vested with a mandate to find durable solutions, and the UNCCP mandate to do so effectively wound up in 1952 with the collapse of negotiations between the Arab states and Israel, the protection gap for Palestinian refugees has become a fixed feature of the international legal landscape. Although UNHCR has had a mandate to seek durable solutions for refugees worldwide since 1950, limitations on its mandate render it unable to perform a similar function for the vast majority of Palestinian refugees residing in the Arab host states.

This takes us to the relationship between UNHCR and UNRWA. In broad terms, two factors undergird the ongoing protection gap faced by Palestinian refugees through these two institutions. The first factor relates to the different definitions used by each to determine who falls under their respective mandates. For UNHCR, a 'refugee' is defined with reference to Article 1A(2) of the 1951 Convention as anyone who, 'owing to well-founded fear of being persecuted for reasons of race, religion, nationality, membership of a particular social group or political opinion, is outside the country of his nationality and is unable or, owing to such fear, is unwilling to avail himself of the protection of that country'.[305] For UNRWA, a 'Palestine refugee' is defined as any person 'whose normal place of residence was Palestine during the period 1 June 1946

---

[303] Annual Report of the Director of the United Nations Relief and Works Agency for Palestine Refugees in the Near East, 1 July 1955–30 June 1956, A/3212, 30 June 1956, para. 7. Another factor that brought the Agency's reintegration programmes to a halt was the fact that although the General Assembly pledged $200 million in support, only $27.5 million was given. *See id.* Table 1.

[304] Statement of UNRWA Commissioner-General to the Advisory Commission Meeting on UNRWA, 14 November 2022, at: www.unrwa.org/newsroom/official-statements/statement-unrwa-commissioner-general-advisory-commission-meeting-unrwa.

[305] For stateless persons, the country of reference can also be the 'country of former habitual residence'. *See* text accompanying *supra* notes 13–15.

3 Palestinian Refugees and the International Rule by Law   165

and 15 May 1948, and who lost both home and means of livelihood as a result of the 1948 conflict'.[306] The differences between these definitions are readily apparent. The 1951 Convention definition is universal in scope, requires alienage from a country of nationality, and the existence of a well-founded fear of persecution based on specific socio-political grounds. Its purpose is to determine eligibility for the surrogate protection of the 1951 Convention, which includes access to durable solutions. The UNRWA definition is circumscribed by reference to a single country of origin, alienage from which is not required, is not fear-based, and is temporally limited to events emanating from the 1948 war.[307] Its purpose is to determine eligibility for registration and service provision from UNRWA and does not include durable solutions. Unfortunately, as noted by Francesca Albanese and Lex Takkenberg, '[t]he scope of UNRWA's definition suffers from a number of particularities and does not capture the entire group of Palestinian refugees whose situation remains unresolved'.[308] For instance, it does not cover descendants of refugees through the female line (see below), nor persons who lost only their homes or livelihoods in 1948, nor those who sought refuge outside of UNRWA's area of operations, nor the 1967 displaced persons.[309] This is, in part, why the category of *Palestinian* refugee is larger than that of *Palestine* refugee.[310]

The second factor relates to the interpretation to be given to Article 1D of the 1951 Convention. It provides that:

> This Convention shall not apply to persons who are at present receiving from organs or agencies of the United Nations other than the United Nations High Commissioner for Refugees protection or assistance.
>
> When such protection or assistance has ceased for any reason, without the position of such persons being definitively settled in accordance with the relevant resolutions adopted by the General Assembly of the United Nations, these persons shall *ipso facto* be entitled to the benefits of this Convention.[311]

Under its first paragraph, Article 1D excludes Palestinian refugees from the 1951 Convention, given they are understood to be receiving protection or assistance from UNRWA. Under its second paragraph, Palestinian refugees are automatically included within the ambit of the 1951 Convention when such

---

[306] UNRWA, *Consolidated Eligibility and Registration Instructions*, 14 October 2009, at: www.unrwa.org/resources/strategy-policy/consolidated-eligibility-and-registration-instructions ['CERI'].

[307] It is also circumscribed by gender discrimination. *See* text accompanying *infra* notes 325–334.

[308] Albanese & Takkenberg, *supra* note 1 at 91.

[309] *Id.*

[310] *See* text accompanying *supra* note 87.

[311] 1951 Convention, *supra* note 6, art. 1D.

166 *1948 and After: The UN and the Palestinian Refugees*

protection or assistance ceases for any reason in the absence of a durable solution as set out by the General Assembly (i.e. resolution 194(III)). Although it is not apparent on its face, Article 1D was drafted at the behest of the Arab states with the intention of accounting for the UN's responsibility for the Palestinian refugee problem.[312] But despite these good intentions, Article 1D has resulted in a great deal of confusion in practice over time and has often been interpreted by states so as to exclude Palestinian refugees from the rights codified in the 1951 Convention.[313] Indeed, it wasn't until 1991 – four decades after the promulgation of Article 1D – that a judicial opinion acknowledged the inclusionary nature of the second paragraph of Article 1D.[314] According to Akram, a survey of municipal jurisprudence of more than thirty states has revealed over a dozen different interpretations of Article 1D.[315] Questions abound: who does Article 1D cover and from what period of time? What effect, if any, does the cessation of UNCCP's durable solutions mandate have in determining whether claimants are considered to no longer be receiving protection or assistance? Are descendants of refugees covered?

Beginning in 2002, UNHCR issued a series of interpretive notes on Article 1D aimed at clarifying these and other questions, often in consultation with UNRWA.[316] Nevertheless, considerable obscurity remains. For instance, the first paragraph of Article 1D excludes from the benefits of the 1951 Convention persons who 'are *at present* receiving' protection or assistance from UN organs other than UNHCR. But according to UNHCR, it would be 'incorrect to read article 1D as applying only to those persons who were Palestinian refugees in

---

[312] The Lebanese delegate reminded the General Assembly that: 'The existence of the Palestine refugees, on the other hand, was the direct result of a decision taken by the United Nations itself, with full knowledge of the consequences. The Palestine refugees were therefore a direct responsibility on the part of the United Nations and could not be placed in the general category of refugees without betrayal of that responsibility'. Statement of Mr. Azkoul (Lebanon), UN GAOR, 5th Sess., 328th Mtg. at para. 47. *See also* Statement of Mr. Baroody (Saudi Arabia), UN GAOR, 5th Sess., 328th Mtg. at paras. 49, 52 & 55, 27 November 1950. *See also* Albanese & Takkenberg, *supra* note 1 at 80–81.

[313] Albanese & Takkenberg, *supra* note 1 at 85.

[314] *Id.*, at 108. *See Bundesverwaltungsgericht, Urteil vom 4.6.1991- Bverwg 1 C 42.88* [German Federal Administrative Court, 4 June 1991]. The historical practice of treating Article 1D as solely an exclusion clause might also be due to Article 7(c) of the UNHCR Statute, *supra* note 10, which provides that the competence of UNHCR 'shall not extend to a person who continues to receive from other organs or agencies of the United Nations protection or assistance'. The UNHCR Statute has no inclusion clause equivalent to that set out in Article 1D of the 1951 Convention. *See* Albanese & Takkenberg, *supra* note 1 at 124–125.

[315] Akram, *supra* note 278 at 650.

[316] For the latest note *see* UNHCR, *Guidelines on International Protection No. 13: Applicability of Article 1D of the 1951 Convention relating to the Status of Refugees to Palestinian Refugees,* December 2017 ['UNHCR Note Art. 1D'].

3 Palestinian Refugees and the International Rule by Law   167

1951', as has been done by the United Kingdom Court of Appeal.[317] For support, UNHCR relies on a rejection of this argument by the Court of Justice of the European Union.[318] But influential scholars, such as James Hathaway and Michelle Foster, continue to maintain the more restrictive UK position, on the strength, *inter alia*, of the ordinary meaning of the words 'at present' in Article 1D.[319] Similarly, UNHCR maintains that the only 'organ or agency of the UN' other than UNHCR that is presently contemplated under Article 1D is UNRWA.[320] Accordingly, where UNRWA's 'protection or assistance has ceased for any reason' without the position of Palestinian refugees being definitively settled in accordance with the relevant General Assembly resolutions, a Palestinian claimant shall *ipso facto* be entitled to the benefits of the 1951 Convention. But this fails to sufficiently account for UNCCP, whose durable solutions function effectively ceased in 1952.[321] As a body that was in the minds of the drafters of the 1951 Convention,[322] there is no compelling legal reason not to consider UNCCP as an 'organ or agency of the UN' other than UNHCR as per Article 1D, with the corollary effect that the inclusion clause must have been triggered when its protection functions ceased in 1952. This is ironically supported by UNHCR's own position that the construct 'protection or assistance' is to be read disjunctively, meaning that the cessation, for any reason, of either 'protection' or 'assistance' would be enough to trigger inclusion.[323] Finally, according to UNHCR, descendants of 'Palestine refugees' through both the male and female lines fall within the personal scope of Article 1D and are therefore excluded from the benefits of the 1951 Convention, given they are deemed to be receiving protection or assistance from UNRWA if physically present in UNRWA's area of operations.[324] The problem, however, is that UNRWA's definition of a 'Palestine refugee' excludes descendants through the female line, meaning such persons – female and male – are not eligible for registration as 'Palestine refugees' under the Agency's regulatory

---

[317] *Id.*, at 8. *See also Amer Mohammed El-Ali v. The Secretary of State for the Home Department and Daraz v. The Secretary of State for the Home Department,* United Kingdom Court of Appeal, 26 July 2002, [2002] EWCA Civ. 1103, para. 33.

[318] *Bolbol v. Bevándorlási és Állampolgársági Hivatal,* C-31/09, Court of Justice of the European Union, 17 June 2010, paras. 47–48.

[319] Hathaway and Foster, *supra* note 15 at 514–515.

[320] UNHCR Note Art. 1D, supra note 316 at 2.

[321] Sufficiently, because while UNHCR does acknowledge that beginning in 1951 UNCCP began reporting its failure to implement paragraph 11 of resolution 194(III), it fails to account for the legal consequences of same *vis á vis* the second paragraph of Article 1D. *See* UNHCR Note Art. 1D, *supra* note 316, at fn. 3.

[322] Albanese & Takkenberg, *supra* note 1 at 114.

[323] UNHCR Note Art. 1D, *supra* note 316 at 10. *But see* Goddard, *supra* note 22 at 508–509.

[324] UNHCR Note Art. 1D, *supra* note 316 at 6.

168   *1948 and After: The UN and the Palestinian Refugees*

framework.[325] Although UNRWA extended that framework in 2006 to render such persons eligible to receive Agency services, these services have in fact not been universally provided for lack of necessary resources.[326] In any case, registration – and therefore recognition – as a refugee, as such, remains off limits. The rule by law inherent in this issue warrants some discussion.

The exact number of Palestinian refugees negatively affected by UNRWA's on-going gender discrimination has never been publicized by the agency. However, it is safe to say that the figure is likely in the several hundreds of thousands or more.[327] The negative impact on the generations of Palestinian refugees affected cannot be underestimated. Aside from the protection gap regarding UNRWA's socio-economic humanitarian assistance noted above, the most serious concern relates to the civil and political rights of the refugees themselves. When a durable solution for their plight eventually falls to be resolved in accordance with international law, it will be necessary to determine who qualifies as a Palestinian refugee as such. Because the first resource in making that determination will doubtless be UNRWA, absence from its refugee rolls will not be a hurdle easily traversed for those affected.[328] None of this would be the case but for the gender discrimination codified in UNRWA's definition of a Palestine refugee. This framework violates the principle of non-discrimination that rests at the heart of international refugee and human rights law,[329] and ironically includes international legal standards generated by the UN itself.[330] But why does this gender discrimination exist and why it has persisted for so long?

Surprisingly, this issue has received scant attention in the literature.[331] According to Christine Cervenak, the gender discrimination in UNRWA's definition of a Palestine refugee is the result of an assumption adopted by early agency officials 'that Palestinian women would "follow their husbands" for cultural and legal reasons'.[332] Although these agency officials included members

---

[325] CERI, *supra* note 306, arts. 1 & 2.4.

[326] Lilly, D. 'Palestinian Refugees and the Global Compact on Refugees,' May 2021, Refugee Studies Centre, Oxford, at 14.

[327] Based on an internal UNRWA study written by the present author in 2004, the number of persons negatively impacted was estimated at approximately 350,000 individuals as of that year. This estimate was arrived at by multiplying the average family size of Palestine refugees from 1949–2004 by the number of MNRs known to the Agency.

[328] Cervenak, C. 'Promoting Inequality: Gender-Based Discrimination in UNRWA's Approach to Palestine Refugee Status' (1994) 16 *HRQ* 300, at 303.

[329] *See* text accompanying *supra* notes 33–37.

[330] Cervenak, *supra* note 328 at 302.

[331] *See id.*, and Albanese & Takkenberg, *supra* note 1, for the most serious consideration of the issue.

[332] Cervenak, *supra* note 328 at 347.

3 Palestinian Refugees and the International Rule by Law 169

of the local Palestinian community, then as now, nothing in UNRWA's regulatory framework could have been adopted without the direction, control, and approval of the agency's international staff, led by its then Director. Regardless, once the definition was tacitly approved by the General Assembly in its repeated renewals of the agency's mandate, the imprimatur of the UN had been indelibly stamped on its content.[333] In its most charitable reading, therefore, the record suggests that the gender discrimination in UNRWA's definition of a Palestine refugee exists because agency officials in the 1950s, and eventually the General Assembly itself, deferred to local customs and practices as perceived by them (including through yet another orientalist lens), despite the ostensibly universal human rights norms of non-discrimination promulgated by the Organization itself, including in the UN Charter and the UDHR. From a subaltern perspective, the rule by law here is unmistakable. Although a cultural relativist argument might posit UNRWA's definition as evidence of an attempt to take Palestinians on their 'own' terms, the opposite is in fact true because it continues the trend of the UN effectively insisting that Palestinians are not good enough to have the benefit of the full range of international law applied to them on account of some perceived worldview projected upon them from on high. In many ways, the UN approach here is reminiscent of Westlake's juridical division of the world between civilized subjects and uncivilized objects.[334] In this sense, selectivity in the application of international law by the Organization to Palestine, ostensibly done in the best interests of the Palestinian refugees themselves through the distinct institutional and normative regime fashioned for them, has only reaffirmed their contingency on the international plane.

For reasons of economy, it is impossible to address the many other complex and persistent questions regarding Article 1D in a manner that substantially adds to the existing literature.[335] Suffice to say, it is the very fact of the 'widely divergent and often inconsistent interpretations' of Article 1D in the practice of states and scholars that demonstrates the extent of the protection gap that continues to plague Palestinian refugees as a group, and which underpins the continued rule by law they are subjected to.[336]

---

[333] In 1959, Secretary-General Hammarskjold noted 'that UNRWA's working definition of a person eligible for its services ... is not contained in any resolution of the General Assembly but has been stated in Annual Reports of the Director and tacitly approved by the Assembly'. *See Proposals for the Continuation of United Nations Assistance to Palestine Refugees*, A/4121, 15 June 1959, at 9.

[334] *See* Chapter 2, section 3.1.

[335] *See, e.g.,* Akram *supra* note 278; Albanese & Takkenberg, *supra* note 1; *and* references at *supra* note 5.

[336] Akram, *supra* note 278 at 650.

170   *1948 and After: The UN and the Palestinian Refugees*

4 CONCLUSION

The rule by law that abides in the way the UN has managed the Palestinian refugee problem is found in the distinctive institutional and normative regime generated by the Organization in the immediate aftermath of the 1948 Nakba. In 1948–1949, the Western and European-dominated General Assembly found itself presented with a conundrum partly of its own making. On the one hand, it had to find a means through which to address the immediate humanitarian situation faced by the Palestinian refugees, whose ethnic cleansing had been forewarned by the Arab states and should reasonably have been foreseen by UNSCOP.[337] On the other hand, in the immediate aftermath of the attempted destruction of European Jewry in WWII, it was loathe to take any action that would undermine the newly formed Jewish State it helped beget, despite the untold human, material and political costs paid by the Palestinian Arabs in consequence. This was the overall context within which the distinctive institutional and normative regime for Palestinian refugees was created by the UN.

Through UNCCP and UNRWA, that regime began in a manner ostensibly in line with the bespoke *ad hoc* refugee protection regimes that grew out of the interwar arrangements and shaped the post-WWII framework of international refugee law. However, a review of the UN record concerning the early quest to find a durable solution through UNCCP reveals a clear drive to overlook Israel's international legal obligations towards the Palestinian refugees in favour of settling the larger Arab-Israeli inter-State dispute – a dispute that, by operation of the state-centric nature of the UN itself, excluded the now disintegrated Palestine and its political representatives. As the general international refugee protection and assistance regime evolved into a universal one under the auspices of UNHCR, the distinctive regime fashioned in 1948–1949 for the Palestinian refugees through UNCCP and UNRWA increasingly remained out of step.

The resulting protection gap for Palestinian refugees – whether in the lack of a UN-endorsed durable solutions mandate for them as a collective, the contingent and confused understanding of their legal rights in state practice, the use of UNRWA as a resettlement scheme, or the ongoing gender discrimination in its regulatory framework – is demonstrative of the various ways international law has, at once, been overlooked and/or selectively applied by the UN with negative results. The outcome has been to challenge the conventional

---

[337] UNSCOP, Report to the General Assembly, 2nd Sess, Vol I, A/364, supplement 11, at 32, 3 September 1947 *See also* Chapter 3, section 5.

4 Conclusion

wisdom that presents the Organization as the guardian of the international rule of law when it comes to Palestinian refugees. This is not to say that the UN's distinctive institutional and normative regime for Palestinian refugees has not been valuable in protecting some of their rights, primarily by keeping their unresolved plight on the international agenda. It is to say, however, that when examined closely the UN record demonstrates that this regime has, virtually from the start, helped preserve and further embed Palestinian legal subalternity on the international plane, whatever its authors may have intended.

5

1967 and After: The UN and the
Occupied Palestinian Territory

1 INTRODUCTION

This chapter addresses Palestine's international legal subalternity through the United Nations' (UN) treatment of the legal status of Israel's prolonged military occupation of the occupied Palestinian territory (OPT). The main claim is that the UN's failure to consistently and clearly take a principled position on the very legality of Israel's half-century 'temporary' occupation of the OPT exposes a fundamental chasm in its position on the occupation, demonstrative of the continuation of the international rule by law under a different guise.

Central to this chapter is the cross-cutting theme of the structural limitations of Third World quasi-sovereignty in the post-decolonization era and its impact on the maintenance of international legal subalternity in world order. In contrast to the classical law governing conquest of territory during the age of empire, modern international law posits that occupation of enemy territory is meant to be temporary and that occupying powers may not claim sovereignty over foreign territory they occupy. Despite this, and as will be demonstrated, since 1967, Israel has systematically altered the status of the OPT with the aim of annexing it, *de jure* or *de facto*. In the intervening fifty-six-year period, the Palestinian people's right to self-determination in the OPT has been recognized by the UN, whose position has been held out as forming the only normative basis for its realization. Central to this, the UN has undertaken considerable documentation of a range of individual violations of international humanitarian law (IHL) and human rights law (IHRL) by the occupying power in furtherance of its purported rule of law ordering framework, yet it has paid scant attention to the legality of the occupation regime as a whole and the concomitant requirement that it be brought to an end *unconditionally*, in line with UN

1 Introduction

practice and the law governing state responsibility. Instead, emphasis has been placed on encouraging the parties to end the occupation through continued, though highly unbalanced and widely discredited, bilateral negotiations.

One consequence of this has been for the UN to have provided a measure of legitimacy to Israel's occupation of the OPT at a time when the Third World membership of the Organization has been pivotal in developing a universally binding international legal proscription against all forms of alien domination, subjugation, and exploitation, itself one of the bases upon which the right of the Palestinian people to self-determination rests. By choosing a humanitarian/managerial approach to assessing the legality of Israeli actions in the OPT, the constitutional propriety of its occupation regime has been taken as a given by the UN and has therefore been regarded intrinsically, if impliedly, to be legal. This chapter argues that through the UN's failure to consistently and clearly identify Israel's prolonged occupation of the OPT as illegal owing to its structural violation of peremptory norms of international law, the UN's position on the OPT runs counter to the conventional wisdom which has presented the re-emergence and relative gains made by the subaltern Palestinians within the Organization during decolonization and after as emblematic of the UN's commitment to finally uphold the international rule of law in their case. As an embodiment of the quasi-sovereignty of the Third World in the post-decolonization era, UN recognition of Palestinian rights in this period has thereby remained contingent and nominal in essence.

This chapter is divided into three parts. First, it outlines the ostensible universalization of the post-1945 liberal international legal order within the UN following decolonization, with reference to the cross-cutting theme of the contingency of Third World sovereignty. Second, it examines Palestine's embodiment of this Third World contingency by showing how the UN's approach to the OPT post-1967 has helped maintain, rather than remedy, its legal subalternity by reducing the question of Palestine almost exclusively to the humanitarian management of the occupation of the OPT through the IHL/IHRL paradigm without definitively addressing the occupation's legality. Third, it examines why the occupation of the OPT is illegal under international law as supported by the UN record, including discussion of relevant legal consequences of same. It posits that the General Assembly and International Court of Justice (ICJ) should be looked to as potential sites where the illegality of the occupation can be definitively established within the UN, thereby helping to mitigate Palestine's legal subalternity in the Organization.

174   *1967 and After: The UN and the Occupied Palestinian Territory*

2 DECOLONIZATION, THIRD WORLD SOVEREIGNTY, AND THE UN

When the UN was founded in 1945, European colonialism was still a marked feature of international life, with approximately one third of the global population – 750 million people – subject to some form of alien subjugation, domination, and exploitation.[1] Although international law was beginning to acknowledge the interests of colonized peoples, as evinced by the incorporation into the UN Charter of the principles of self-determination and human rights, the legitimacy of the UN's law-making role remained dubious in the shadow of empire. Decolonization therefore presented a means of realizing the universal promise of the UN Charter, unleashing the counter-hegemonic potential of international law for the global south.

The over three-fold increase in UN membership occasioned by decolonization shifted the automatic majority in the General Assembly from Europe to the 'new' Afro-Asian states, which in turn shifted the agenda of the Organization to issues that were of primary interest to the Third World,[2] namely decolonization and 'development'.[3] This enabled the progressive development of international law under the auspices of the UN that would fundamentally alter the course of the discipline. Moving beyond Chapters XI and XII of the Charter,[4] Third World states formed new political blocs, such as the Group of 77 and the Non-Aligned Movement (NAM), which helped promulgate new normative frameworks aimed at bolstering Third World sovereignty. This included, *inter alia*, the 1960 Declaration on the Granting of Independence to Colonial Countries and Peoples;[5] the 1961 Special Committee on Decolonization (a.k.a. the Committee of 24),[6] the 1962 General Assembly resolution on Permanent Sovereignty over Natural Resources,[7] and the 1970 Declaration on Principles of International Law concerning Friendly Relations and Co-operation among States in accordance with the Charter of the United Nations.[8] Among other things, these instruments and mechanisms affirmed principles of direct relevance to Palestine: the need to bring colonialism, in all its forms, to a speedy

---

[1] United Nations and Decolonization, at: www.un.org/en/decolonization/history.shtml.
[2] Luard, E. *A History of the United Nations, Vol. 2* (Macmillan, 1989) at 517–518.
[3] Kay, D.A. 'The Politics of Decolonization: The New Nations and the United Nations Political Process' (1967) 21:4 *Int. Org.* 808–809.
[4] These concern the declaration regarding non-self-governing territories and the international trusteeship system, respectively.
[5] A/RES/1514(XV), 14 December 1960 ['1960 Declaration on Colonialism'].
[6] A/RES/1654(XVI), 27 November 1961.
[7] A/RES/1803(XVII), 14 December 1962.
[8] A/RES/2625(XXV), 24 October 1970 ['Friendly Relations Declaration'].

2 Decolonization, Third World Sovereignty, and the UN   175

and unconditional end, that all peoples have the right to self-determination by virtue of which they freely determine their political status and freely pursue their economic, social, and cultural development, and that the subjection of peoples to alien subjugation, domination, and exploitation constitutes a violation of the principle of self-determination, fundamental human rights, and the UN Charter.[9]

Yet, despite these gains, evidence suggests that the rule by law nature of the old international order survived decolonization. Despite the almost complete eradication of classic forms of colonialism between the 1960s and 1980s, several regions continue to be afflicted by what effectively amounts to neo-colonial rule, with seventeen non-self-governing territories presently 'administered' largely by Western powers and monitored by the UN Committee of 24,[10] and two territories suffering contemporary forms of colonial rule through prolonged occupation in Western Sahara and the OPT. More deeply, even accounting for the achievement of Third World territorial sovereignty, certain structural inequities between the former imperial powers and their relatively newly independent colonies have remained, such that the full realization of Third World political, cultural, and economic sovereignty seems to have been impaired from the start. One striking example is represented in the neo-liberal mechanisms of the Bretton Woods institutions. Replete with legal conditions that privilege market fundamentalism through the Washington Consensus, these institutions have resulted in a considerable loss of Third World control over its economic sphere. The result has been the evolution of Third World sovereignty as unequal relative to that of its Western progenitors and the political legitimation of this situation within the work of the UN.[11]

Given the highly diverse experiences of the global south, Third World quasi-sovereignty has manifested itself in a multiplicity of ways. In principle, this condition appears across a wide spectrum of areas – territorial, political, cultural, economic – and varies depending on respective levels of 'development' and independence achieved by the peoples in question. What seems clear, however, is that beyond this spectrum of potential fields of manifestation, a unifying theme running throughout appears to be the unfulfilled promise of international law and institutions upon which they are based. As will be demonstrated, the impact of the quasi-sovereignty of the Third World

---

[9] *See, e.g.,* 1960 Declaration on Colonialism, *supra* note 5, at preamble, arts. 1&2; *and* Friendly Relations Declaration, *id.*

[10] Except for Western Sahara, a former Spanish colony the majority of which has been militarily occupied by Morocco since 1975, the remaining sixteen non-self-governing territories have been administered by France, New Zealand, the United Kingdom, and the United States.

[11] *See, e.g.,* Jackson, R. *Quasi-States* (Cambridge, 2011).

176   *1967 and After: The UN and the Occupied Palestinian Territory*

on the maintenance of Palestine's legal subalternity in the post-1967 era has manifested itself in a different way than that described above. Nevertheless, it has still been underpinned by the unifying theme of the unfulfilled promise of international law and institutions as promoted by the UN itself.

3 PALESTINE AS AN EMBODIMENT OF THIRD WORLD QUASI-SOVEREIGNTY

An examination of the UN's treatment of the question of Palestine during the decolonization period and after brings the themes of the circumscribed nature of Third World sovereignty through the rule by law into sharp relief. Decolonization enabled a gradual if incomplete recognition and legitimation at the UN of Palestinian legal personality and rights that, in some respects, approximated the recognition of Third World territorial sovereignty in this period. At the same time, a close examination of the UN record reveals that the Organization has operationally reduced the question of Palestine to a humanitarian problem, according to which the UN's task has largely been confined to monitoring and reporting violations of IHL and IHRL within the OPT without paying sufficient attention to the illegality of the very regime generating this outcome. As a result, UN recognition of Palestinian rights has only been nominal in nature. This is underscored by the fact that a central element of this humanitarian/managerial approach has been the UN's insistence that the end of the occupation of the OPT must be contingent on negotiations with a bad faith and infinitely more powerful occupant, which in effect offers no way for the Palestinians to actualize their putative sovereignty, ostensibly recognized as a legal entitlement by the Organization. The result has been to maintain Palestine's legal subalternity in the UN during a period in which the received wisdom posits the Organization as *the* standard-bearer of the international rule of law. These claims are fleshed out in further depth below.

3.1 *Bringing International Law to Bear in Palestine? Decolonization and the Gradual Recognition of Palestinian Legal Subjectivity at the UN*

As part of the Third World's promotion of decolonization as a means of reshaping the international legal order through the UN, specific effort was made to highlight the plight and international legal rights of the Palestinian people. This took place against the context of the institutional erasure of the Palestinian people within the UN following the Organization's attempt at partition and their resulting dispossession and collapse of their country in 1948. As covered in Chapter 4, in the twenty years following the 1948 Nakba, the

3 Palestine as an Embodiment of Third World Quasi-Sovereignty

question of Palestine was treated merely as a 'refugee problem' by the UN. In the aftermath of the 1967 war, during which Israel captured the OPT (see Map VII), the Security Council passed resolution 242 in which it continued this trend by cryptically calling for 'a just settlement of the refugee problem', without reference to Palestine or the Palestinians.[12] This diplomatic erasure was curious given Palestine's political independence had been provisionally recognized by the League of Nations as far back as 1919 and the plight of the Palestinian Arabs was known to the UN through the events surrounding partition. Decolonization offered an opportunity to correct this through an attempt to bring the counter-hegemonic promise of the international rule of law to bear in the UN's work on Palestine. Much like the Third World's preoccupation with economic development through the promise of the Bretton Woods institutions, the Palestinian people became preoccupied with gaining recognition of their plight, national movement, and legal rights within the UN.

The process was slow and was set against the political backdrop of the emergence of the Palestine Liberation Organization (PLO) in 1964 and events of 1967. In 1969, the General Assembly recognized 'that the problem of the Palestine Arab refugees has arisen from the denial of their inalienable rights under the Charter of the United Nations and the Universal Declaration of Human Rights' and accordingly reaffirmed 'the inalienable rights of the people of Palestine'.[13] In 1970, the General Assembly gave content to these inalienable rights when it recognized 'that the people of Palestine are entitled to equal rights and self-determination'.[14] In 1973, the General Assembly condemned 'all governments which do not recognize the right to self-determination and independence of peoples, notably the peoples of Africa still under colonial domination and the Palestinian people'.[15] This was followed in 1974, when the General Assembly voted to include a separate item entitled the 'Question of Palestine' on its agenda for the first time since 1952, with the aim of underscoring UN accountability for its actions in 1947, affirming the denial of Palestinian rights as the main impediment to peace, and laying the groundwork for the representatives of the Palestinian people to be given a platform at the UN to shape their own future.[16] This unfolded in a series of resolutions adopted that year in which the PLO was invited to

---

[12] S/RES/242, 22 November 1967.
[13] A/RES/2535(XXIV)(B), 10 December 1969.
[14] A/RES/2672(XXV)(C), 8 December 1970.
[15] A/RES/3070(XXVIII), 30 November 1973.
[16] *See* General Committee, Summary Records of the 228th to 223rd Meetings 19 September – 19 November 1974, UN GAOR, 29th Sess, 219th Mtg., item 111, at 11–13 (19 September 1974), where, for example, the Algerian representative stated that '[i]t was at the United Nations that the case

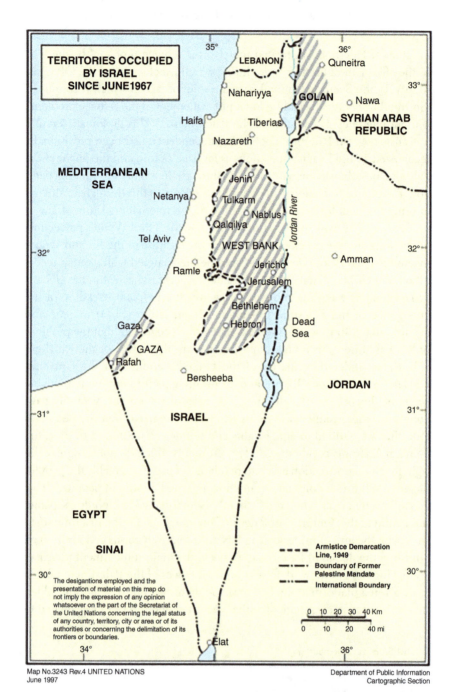

MAP VII *Territories occupied by Israel since June 1967, Map No. 3243 Rev.4, United Nations, June 1997.*
Author's note: Only the West Bank and Gaza Strip, including East Jerusalem, constitute the OPT.

3 Palestine as an Embodiment of Third World Quasi-Sovereignty 179

participate in the deliberations of the General Assembly on the question of Palestine in plenary meetings[17] and granted observer status in the sessions and work of the General Assembly, including international conferences convened under its auspices.[18] The high-water mark came with the passage of resolution 3236(XXIX) of 22 November 1974, in which the General Assembly reaffirmed the 'inalienable rights of the Palestinian people in Palestine, including: (a) the right to self-determination without interference; [and] (b) the right to national independence and sovereignty'.[19] In a landmark address before the General Assembly, Yasser Arafat, then Chairman of the Executive Committee of the PLO, highlighted that decolonization offered a unique opportunity for the UN to render its work and role more capable of implementing the principles of the Charter and human rights universally. In his view, the re-opening of the question of Palestine at the UN represented 'a victory for the world Organization as much as a victory for the cause of our people'.[20] Mirroring the Committee of 24 and other Third World initiated machinery designed to advance decolonization and development, in 1975 the General Assembly established the Committee on the Exercise of the Inalienable Rights of the Palestinian People (UNCEIRPP). Composed of twenty member states drawn from the Third World, the UNCEIRPP remains mandated to promote the realization of the inalienable rights of the Palestinian people. From that point, the General Assembly increased the number of its resolutions on Palestine, with the result that today there exists a large corpus of resolutions demonstrative of widespread state practice and *opinio juris* supportive of Palestinian legal subjectivity and rights. Thus, to the long record of General Assembly resolutions affirming the rights of Palestine refugees under resolution 194(III) of 11 December 1948,[21] has been added resolutions devoted to Palestine refugee property and

---

of Palestine should be reopened and the matter be treated not as a social problem caused by the Palestinian refugees but as a political problem. The time had come for the United Nations to rectify its mistake and focus its efforts on settling a crisis with which it had been encumbered almost since its creation'. Likewise, the Yugoslav representative deplored 'that the question of Palestine was regarded as a refugee problem rather than as a problem of the usurpation of a people's right to liberty and independence'. Finally, the Soviet representative indicated 'that a discussion by the General Assembly of the question of Palestine in all its aspects, with the participation of a representative of the Arab people of Palestine, would further the settlement of that question...'.

[17] A/RES/3210(XXIX), 14 October 1974.

[18] A/RES/3237(XXIX), 22 November 1974. This set a precedent for provision of UN observer status for the South-West Africa People's Organization, then struggling for independence of the Namibian people. *See* A/RES/31/152, 20 December 1976.

[19] A/RES/3236(XXIX), 22 November 1974.

[20] A/PV.2282 and Corr. 1, UN GAOR, 29th Sess, 2282nd Mtg., item 108, at 861–862, paras. 7–9, 19 (13 November 1974).

[21] *See, e.g.,* A/RES/194(III), 11 December 1948; *and* A/RES/70/83, 9 December 2015.

revenues,[22] the Palestinian people's right to self-determination,[23] the applicability to the OPT of the Geneva Convention Relative to the Protection of Civilian Persons in Time of War,[24] development assistance,[25] Jerusalem,[26] Israeli settlements in the OPT,[27] permanent sovereignty of the Palestinian people over its natural resources in the OPT,[28] international protection of the Palestinian people,[29] and the peaceful settlement of the question of Palestine,[30] among many others.[31]

Decolonization was thus responsible for giving greater substance to the UN's commitment to the universal application of international law in general, including its unique role in bringing it to bear on the Palestine issue. Evidence of the underlying promise to the Palestinian people inherent in this process is found in what the General Assembly has, since 1992, referred to as the UN's 'permanent responsibility' for the question of Palestine 'until the question is resolved in all its aspects in accordance with international law'.[32] The central importance of both international law and the unique role of the UN as guarantor of that law in helping forge a peaceful resolution to the question of Palestine has by now become a common article of faith within the international system. Nowhere has this faith been more reverent then among the Palestinians themselves.[33] Thus, notwithstanding the rule by law character of the UN's management of the question of Palestine between 1947 and 1969, the conventional view of the UN as guarantor of

---

[22] See, e.g., A/RES/70/86, 9 December 2015.

[23] See, e.g., A/RES/70/141, 17 December 2015.

[24] See, e.g., A/RES/70/88, 9 December 2015. Geneva Convention Relative to the Protection of Civilian Persons in Time of War, 12 Aug. 1949, 6 U.S.T. 3516, 75 U.N.T.S. 287 (entered into force 21 October 1950) ['Fourth Geneva Convention'].

[25] See, e.g., A/RES/70/108, 10 December 2015.

[26] See, e.g., A/RES/70/16, 24 November 2015.

[27] See, e.g., A/RES/70/89, 9 December 2015.

[28] See, e.g., A/RES/70/225, 22 December 2015.

[29] See, e.g., A/RES/70/90, 9 December 2015.

[30] See, e.g., A/RES/70/15, 24 November 2015.

[31] One notable resolution passed early in this period was A/RES/3379 of 10 November 1975 declaring Zionism to be 'a form of racism and racial discrimination'. In an unprecedented move, and following considerable American pressure, the resolution was revoked with the passage of A/RES/46/86 of 16 December 1991.

[32] See, e.g., A/RES/71/23, 30 November 2016.

[33] This was recently demonstrated in the 2017 address to the General Assembly of Mahmoud Abbas, successor to Arafat and current President of the State of Palestine, in which he stated that '[t]he path we have chosen as Palestinians and Arabs, and the path chosen by the world is that of international law'. Statement of His Excellency Mahmoud Abbas, President of the State of Palestine, Before the United Nations General Assembly, 72nd Session, New York, 20 September 2017, at: www.nad.ps/en/media-room/speeches/he-president-mahmoud-abbas-statement-un-general-assembly-72nd-session-2017.

3 Palestine as an Embodiment of Third World Quasi-Sovereignty   181

the universal international rule of law appears to have held. As will be seen, however, a critical examination of the evidence would not seem to justify this position.

3.2 The Maintenance of the International Rule by Law in Palestine: The Reduction of Palestine and the Limits of Palestinian Legal Subjectivity at the UN

A closer review of the UN's record in the decolonization period and after reveals that the rule by law character of the Organization's treatment of Palestine has continued through its unwillingness to bring the full normative regime of international law to bear on its treatment of the OPT in line with the international rule of law. Here, the stress is not so much on the illegality of a specific UN action. Rather, the problem is with the failure *by omission* of the UN to apply the full array of relevant international law to the issue at hand. And this while the Organization has held itself out as a protector of Palestinian legal subjectivity and rights while relying on Palestinian acquiescence in the legitimacy of prior illegal UN action (i.e. partition) as a condition of eventually gaining full membership in the Organization. More specifically, the problem rests in the UN's failure to clearly and consistently identify Israel's prolonged presence in the OPT as illegal as such, with all the consequences such illegality entails under international law.

To better understand this, it is helpful to examine the following three interrelated aspects of the UN's management of the question of Palestine in the post-1967 era: (1) the increased recognition of Palestinian legal subjectivity within the UN subject to the restriction of the territorial scope of Palestinian national claims to the OPT; (2) the proliferation of UN machinery focused on the humanitarian/managerial documentation of IHL and IHRL violations by the occupying power short of definitively characterizing Israel's continued presence in the OPT as illegal; and (3) the UN's conditioning of the end of Israel's occupation of the OPT on negotiations. Each of these will be taken in turn.

First, the 1988 recognition of Israel by the PLO signalled the latter's acceptance of the political legitimacy of the partition plan in resolution 181(II). Reminiscent of the Third World's acceptance of the principle of *uti possidetis*, this recognition was notable for the fact that its adherents had no part in fashioning its terms but were compelled to accept them as a *quid pro quo* for the achievement of a modicum of their national rights. This historic compromise resulted in greater levels of recognition of Palestine's international legal personality at the UN, albeit within the two-state framework. This included permission to use the designation 'Palestine' in the UN system,[34] a qualified right to participate in debate at the General Assembly,[35] and, following Palestine's unsuccessful 2011 application for UN membership, upgraded status as a non-member observer state in 2012,[36] thereby allowing it to accede to multilateral treaties, including the main IHL and IHRL instruments and the Rome Statute of the International Criminal Court (see Chapter 6).[37] This increased recognition of Palestinian legal subjectivity at the UN was accompanied by the usual affirmation of the Palestinian right to self-determination. Yet, it was only in 1988 that the General Assembly identified the territorial scope within which this self-determination should be affected when it affirmed 'the need to enable the Palestinian people to exercise their sovereignty over their territory occupied since 1967'.[38] The territorialization of Palestinian national rights in the post-decolonization era thus began with the PLO's compelled recognition of resolution 181(II) and the UN's recognition of the OPT – an area representing approximately half that proposed by the General Assembly in 1947 – as the self-determination unit of the Palestinian people. Since then, this position has been reaffirmed, expressly and impliedly, by each of the General Assembly,[39] the Security Council,[40] the ICJ,[41] the Economic and Social Council (ECOSOC),[42] and the Secretariat through the Secretary-General.[43] To the extent that the promise of the UN's extensive affirmation of Palestinian legal subjectivity has yet to materialize, the historical compromise that produced it has arguably assumed a Faustian bargain of sorts.

Second, since the decolonization era, there has emerged a proliferation of UN machinery devoted to a humanitarian/managerial approach through the documentation of discrete IHL and IHRL violations by the occupying power

---

[34] This change was done without prejudice to the observer status and functions of the PLO within the UN system. A/RES/43/177, 15 December 1988.

[35] A/RES/52/250, 13 July 1998.

[36] A/RES/67/19, 29 November 2012.

[37] Rome Statute of the International Criminal Court, July 17, 1998, U.N. Doc. 32/A/CONF. 183/9, 37 I.L.M. 999 (entered into force July 1, 2002) ['Rome Statute'].

[38] A/RES/43/177, 15 December 1988.

[39] See, e.g., A/RES/67/19, 29 November 2012.

[40] See, e.g., S/RES/2334, 23 December 2016 and S/RES/1515, 19 November 2003 where, in so far as the Security Council endorses a vision of two states, Israel and Palestine, living side by side in peace within secure and recognized borders on the basis of resolution 242, it is implied that the OPT is the self-determination unit of the Palestinian people.

[41] See Legal Consequences of the Construction of a Wall in the Occupied Palestinian Territory, Advisory Opinion, 9 July 2004, ICJ Reports 2004, paras. 115, 118, 122 ['Wall'].

[42] See, e.g., E/RES/2017/10, 7 June 2017.

[43] See, e.g., Peaceful Settlement of the Question of Palestine, Report of the Secretary General, S/2016/732, 24 August 2016, paras. 23, 40.

3 *Palestine as an Embodiment of Third World Quasi-Sovereignty* 183

in the OPT. This is the result of the prolonged nature of the conflict and an expression of the above-mentioned permanent responsibility of the UN for its resolution in line with international law. Among the bespoke machinery is the UN Special Committee to Investigate Israeli Practices Affecting the Human Rights of the Palestinian People and Other Arabs of the Occupied Territories,[44] the UN Special Rapporteur on the Situation of Human Rights in the Palestinian Territory Occupied Since 1967,[45] UNCERIPP and its secretariat in the Division for Palestinian Rights,[46] and the UN Register of Damage Caused by the Construction of the Wall in the OPT (UNROD).[47] More general machinery includes portions of the work of a host of subsidiary organs such as the United Nations Relief and Works Agency for Palestine Refugees in the Near East (UNRWA),[48] the Office of the UN High Commissioner for Human Rights,[49] the UN Human Rights Council (HRC),[50] the UN Educational Scientific and Cultural Organization (UNESCO),[51] the UN Office for the Coordination of Humanitarian Affairs (OCHA),[52] and the UN Conference on Trade and Development,[53] among others.[54] Important judicial, quasi-judicial, and/or investigative interventions have been carried out by the ICJ,[55] HRC mandated commissions of inquiry such as the Pillay,[56] Goldstone,[57] and

---

[44] The Special Committee was established by the General Assembly in 1968 under the style 'Special Committee to Investigate Israeli Practices Affecting the Human Rights of the Population of the Occupied Territories'. The contemporary name reflects the evolution of Palestinian legal subjectivity within the UN over time. *See* A/RES/2443(XXIII), 19 December 1968.

[45] The mandate of the Special Rapporteur was established by the Commission on Human Rights in resolution 1993/2A, 19 February 1993.

[46] *See* A/RES/71/21, 30 November 2016.

[47] A/RES/ES-10/17, 24 January 2007.

[48] A/RES/302(IV), 8 December 1949.

[49] *See, e.g., Implementation of Human Rights Council Resolutions S-9/1 and S-12/1, Report of the United Nations High Commissioner for Human Rights*, A/HRC/31/40, 20 January 2016.

[50] *See, e.g.,* A/HRC/34/28, 11 April 2017.

[51] *See, e.g., UNESCO Decisions Adopted by the Executive Board at Its 200th Session, Occupied Palestine*, Doc. No. 200 EX/Decisions, at 32, 18 November 2016.

[52] *See, e.g.,* UN OCHA, *Protection of Civilians Report*, 21 February 2023, at: www.ochaopt.org/poc/31-january-13-february-2023.

[53] *See, e.g., Economic Costs of the Israeli Occupation for the Palestinian People*, A/71/174, 21 July 2016.

[54] These include the International Labour Organization, UN Children's Fund, the UN Development Fund for Women, World Health Organization, World Food Program, the UN Human Settlements Program, and the UN Population Fund.

[55] *Wall, supra* note 41.

[56] Report of the United Nations Independent International Commission of Inquiry on the Occupied Palestinian Territory, including East Jerusalem, and in Israel, A/HRC/50/21, 9 May 2022 ['Pillay Report'].

[57] *Report of the United Nations Fact-Finding Mission on the Gaza Conflict*, A/HRC/12/48, 25 September 2009.

1967 and After: The UN and the Occupied Palestinian Territory

Davis[58] commissions, and a host of special procedures mandate holders.[59] Finally, the machinery includes scores of regular reports and resolutions issued by other principal organs of the UN, namely the General Assembly,[60] Security Council,[61] ECOSOC,[62] and the Secretariat through the Secretary-General.[63] Despite the broad scope of this comprehensive cataloguing of the occupying power's IHL and IHRL record in the OPT, it is notable for its conspicuous failure to comprehensively address the legality of Israel's very presence in the OPT.[64] Indeed, the hyper-legality of the UN's approach to the OPT through the relatively narrow confines of the IHL/IHRL paradigm has produced an absurdity. By focusing so much energy on documenting IHL/IHRL violations in the OPT over the decades, the UN has unduly raised expectations of what application of that humanitarian normative paradigm can reasonably achieve. This has led to a false, if misguided, hope among Palestinian officials and civil society that adherence to IHL/IHRL norms will eventually deliver the end of

---

[58] *Report of the Detailed Findings of the Independent Commission of Inquiry Established Pursuant to Human Rights Council Resolution S-21/1, A/HRC/29/CRP.4, 23 June 2015.*

[59] *See, e.g., Report of the Special Rapporteur on Violence Against Women, Its Causes and Consequences, on Her Mission to the Occupied Palestinian Territory/State of Palestine, A/HRC/35/30/Add.2, 8 June 2017; Report of the Special Rapporteur on Adequate Housing as a Component of the Right to an Adequate Standard of Living, and on the Right to Non-Discrimination in This Context, A/HRC/22/46/Add.1, 24 December 2012; and Report of the Special Rapporteur on the Promotion and Protection of the Right to Freedom of Opinion and Expression: Mission to Israel and the Occupied Palestinian Territory, A/HRC/20/17/Add.2, 11 June 2012.*

[60] The number of GA resolutions are copious. As an example, in 2022 alone the General Assembly passed 11 resolutions on Palestine, including: A/RES/77/247, 30 December 2022 (Israeli Practices Affecting the Human Rights of the Palestinian People in the Occupied Palestinian Territory, Including East Jerusalem); A/RES/77/126, 12 December 2022 (Israeli Settlements in the Occupied Palestinian Territory, Including East Jerusalem, and the Occupied Syrian Golan); A/RES/77/124, 12 December 2022 (Palestine Refugees' Properties and their Revenues); A/RES/77/208, 15 December 2022 (Right of the Palestinian People to Self-Determination); *and* A/RES/77/187, 14 December 2022 (Permanent Sovereignty of the Palestinian People in the Occupied Palestinian Territory, Including East Jerusalem, and of the Arab Population of the Occupied Syrian Golan Over Their Natural Resources).

[61] *See, e.g.,* S/RES/605, 22 December 1987; and S/RES/904, 18 March 1994.

[62] *See, e.g., Economic and Social Repercussions of the Israeli Occupation on the Living Conditions of the Palestinian People in the Occupied Palestinian Territory, including East Jerusalem, and the Arab Population of the Occupied Syrian Golan, E/RES/2014/26, 22 August 2014.*

[63] *See, e.g., Human Rights Situation in the Occupied Palestinian Territory, Including East Jerusalem: Report of the Secretary-General, A/HRC/31/44, 20 January 2016.*

[64] In recent years, only two of these special procedures have broached the subject of the lawfulness of Israel's occupation. At the request of Special Rapporteur Michael Lynk in 2017, *infra* note 71, and the Pillay Commission in 2022, *supra* note 56, the author advised these special procedures in the preparation of their reports while conducting this research. *See* text accompanying *infra* note 96.

3 Palestine as an Embodiment of Third World Quasi-Sovereignty   185

the occupation. This has been reinforced by the 'rights-based' humanitarian approaches presently driving all non-UN stakeholders in the OPT, including third states. Although occupation is meant to end under international law, nothing in the conventional IHL/IHRL paradigm expressly compels this result; rather, adherence to its norms merely operates to enhance the manner in which the occupation is administered pending its eventual end. Thus, by focusing on the IHL/IHRL framework instead of failing to definitively identify Israel's occupation as illegal as such, the UN has privileged a humanitarian/managerial approach to the OPT over a remedial/emancipatory one. This has ultimately lent Israel's presence in the OPT a legitimacy in which its legality has also been implied.

Third, and most important, has been the UN's position that the end of Israel's prolonged occupation of the OPT must be contingent on the conclusion of negotiations between it and the PLO. This is a universally held position among each of the relevant five principal organs and one that has been parroted throughout the UN system. Thus, the Security Council has since 1967 affirmed the need for Israel to withdraw from the OPT as part of a negotiated settlement under the land for peace formula.[65] Likewise, the General Assembly has on multiple occasions stressed 'the need for a resumption of negotiations' based on the principle of land for peace, 'with a view to achieving without delay an end to the Israeli occupation that began in 1967'.[66] For its part, ECOSOC has reiterated 'the importance of the revival and accelerated advancement of negotiations ... for the realization of the two-State solution ... based on the pre-1967 borders'.[67] To this has been added repeated calls by various Secretaries-General for a negotiated resolution of the end of the occupation, most recently Antonio Guterres who has gone so far as to assert that negotiation is 'the *only* way to achieve the inalienable rights of the Palestinian people'.[68] Finally, in 2004 the ICJ underscored the need 'to achieving as soon as possible, on the basis of international law, a negotiated solution to the outstanding problems and the establishment of a Palestinian State, existing side by side with Israel and its other neighbours'.[69] It is true

---

[65] S/RES/242, 22 November 1967, paras. 1, 3. S/RES/2334, 23 December 2016, preamble, and para. 9.

[66] A/RES/71/23, 30 November 2016, paras. 4, 16. *See also* A/RES/67/19, 29 November 2012, paras. 4, 5; *and* A/RES/66/17, 30 November 2011, para. 15.

[67] E/RES/2014/26, 16 July 2014, para. 17. *See also* E/RES/2017/10, 7 June 2017, para. 7.

[68] Guterres, A. 'Continuing Occupation Sends 'Unmistakable Message' that Both Palestinian, Israeli Hopes Remain Unattainable, Secretary-General Warns in Anniversary Statement,' Press Release SG/SM/18554, 5 June 2017 [emphasis added].

[69] *Wall, supra* note 41, para. 162.

that the UN's call for negotiation covers matters beyond the OPT as such. Indeed, one is hard pressed to imagine any resolution of these issues without some form of negotiation. But to the extent that this negotiations condition also qualifies the UN's position on ending the occupation itself, it is fraught with a telling paradox. Because the OPT has been determined by the UN to be the territorial unit within which the Palestinian people are entitled to exercise their right to self-determination under international law, the result has been for the UN to have frustrated, on its own terms, the very recognition it has bestowed upon the Palestinian people since decolonization. If realization of Palestinian self-determination in the OPT is a long-established right in the nature of a peremptory norm derogation from which is not permitted, how can the culmination of this right can be left to negotiation between an infinitely more powerful occupier and a beleaguered and vastly weaker occupied people? This is particularly so if the occupation itself is or has become illegal through the acts of a bad-faith occupant, as is the case with the OPT.

In so far as the above factors have been the basis of the UN's ostensibly rights-based approach to the question of Palestine through which the subaltern Palestinians have been encouraged to overcome their contingent status, the evidence suggests that they actually demonstrate the nature of Palestine's quasi-sovereignty inherent in the present international legal order. Palestinian acquiescence to the partition brought with it UN recognition of Palestinian national rights, if only in the OPT. Nevertheless, actual realization of those rights has been frustrated by the UN itself, owing to its failure to definitively characterize Israel's occupation as illegal, as such. Instead, the UN has dogmatically insisted on the chimera of negotiation as the only means through which the occupation's end is to be brought about. In this, we once again see a shifting of the goalposts for the subalterns who, having acquiesced to prior illegal acts of the UN (i.e. partition) cannot be allowed to rely in good faith that the gesture will be met with a commitment by the Organization to bring international law *fully* to bear in their case. In place of a position based upon the fulsome application of the international rule of law, the interests of the subaltern Palestinians are governed according to a rule by law dynamic, where rights are affirmed only to a point (e.g. IHL/IHRL), and implementation is left subject to the whims of a purportedly legitimate Israeli hegemon.

In the following section, we examine why Israel's continued occupation of the OPT is illegal, and what the consequences of this are in law. In addition, we examine how various organs of the UN can be resorted to in order to confirm this finding with a view to mitigating the effects of the rule by law nature of the Organization's handling of the question of Palestine post-1967.

4 THE ILLEGALITY OF ISRAEL'S CONTINUED PRESENCE IN THE OPT

4.1 Why Legality Matters: Negotiating the Illegal in Light of the Law of State Responsibility

Before delving into why Israel's continued presence in the OPT is illegal, a word about why its legality matters is in order. At the heart of the issue is the tension between the UN's position on the OPT with the relevant international law governing state responsibility. On the one hand, is the political consensus that the emergence of an independent Palestinian state in the OPT can only arise through a negotiated withdrawal of the occupying power and the conclusion of peace on the basis of the two-state formula. On the other hand, is the relevant international law concerning the responsibility of states for internationally wrongful conduct, an elemental foundation of which is the proposition that states may not negotiate the consequences of their illegal actions.[70] A review of the growing literature on the illegality of Israel's occupation of the OPT demonstrates a curious neglect of the international legal consequences of same in light of the law of state responsibility.[71] Nevertheless, in view of the above, it is submitted that understanding the international law governing state responsibility is a prerequisite to appreciating the continued rule by law character of the UN's handling of the OPT in the post-1967 era and how its effects might ultimately be mitigated.

---

[70] *See* Chapter 4, note 66.

[71] *See, e.g.,* Gross, A. *The Writing on the Wall* (Cambridge, 2017); *Report of the Special Rapporteur on the Situation of Human Rights in the Palestinian Territories Occupied Since 1967,* A/72/43106, 23 October 2017 ['Lynk Report']; Finkelstein, N. *Gaza* (UC Press, 2021), Appendix; and Wilde, R. 'Using the Master's Tools to Dismantle the Master's House: International Law and Palestinian Liberation' (2019–20) 22 *PYIL* 3, none of which engage with the law of state responsibility. *See also* Ben-Naftali, O., Gross, A. & Michaeli, K. 'Illegal Occupation: Framing the Occupied Palestinian Territory' (2005) 23:3 *Berkeley JIL* 551, where the authors merely restate in their conclusion, at 612, that a state 'whose conduct constitutes an internationally wrongful act having a continuing character is under an obligation to cease that conduct, without prejudice to the responsibility it has already incurred'. No other elements of the law of state responsibility are discussed, nor is the dilemma raised by the UN's conditioning of the end of the occupation on negotiation examined in this light. Similarly, the only article that raises the legal consequences of illegal occupation, *per se,* confines its discussion of negotiation as a means of ending such an occupation to one line. *See* Ronen, Y. 'Illegal Occupation and its Consequences' (2008) 41 *Isr. LR* 201 at 228. Although Ronen partially examines General Assembly and ICJ pronouncements on the legality of Israel's occupation of the OPT, her analysis does not examine the UN's position that the end of the occupation must be contingent on negotiation.

188   *1967 and After: The UN and the Occupied Palestinian Territory*

As noted in Chapter 4, the International Law Commission's 2001 Draft Articles on Responsibility of States for Internationally Wrongful Acts (ARSIWA) is widely considered to be a codification of customary international law governing state responsibility.[72] An internationally wrongful act of a state occurs when conduct consisting of an action or omission is both attributable to the state under international law and constitutes a breach of an international obligation of that state.[73] A state may breach an international obligation through a composite series of actions or omissions defined in aggregate as wrongful, in which case the breach extends over the entire period starting with the first of the actions or omissions of the series and lasts for as long as these actions or omissions are repeated and remain not in conformity with the international obligation of the state.[74] The state responsible for an internationally wrongful act is under three general obligations in respect of that act. First, if continuing, it must cease the act forthwith.[75] Second, it must offer appropriate assurances and guarantees of non-repetition if circumstances so dictate.[76] Third, it must make full reparation for the injury caused by the act, including any material or moral damage.[77] Finally, where a state's internationally wrongful conduct entails a serious – meaning gross or systematic – breach of an obligation arising under a peremptory norm of general international law, in addition to the above obligations of the wrongdoing state, all other states are under a twofold obligation to cooperate to bring the serious breach to an end through lawful means, and to refrain from recognizing as lawful the situation created by the serious breach nor render aid or assistance in maintaining that situation.[78]

---

[72] Draft Articles on Responsibility of States for Internationally Wrongful Acts, Report of the International Law Commission on the Work of its Fifty-Third Session (23 April – 1 June and 2 July-10 August 2001), Yearbook of the International Law Commission, 2001, II(2), A/CN.4/SER.A/2001/Add.1 (Part 2), at 26–30 ['ARSIWA']. For the customary nature of the ARSIWA, see *Application of the Convention on the Prevention and Punishment of the Crime of Genocide* (Bosnia and Herzegovina v. Serbia and Montenegro), 26 February 2007, ICJ Reports 2007, p. 43, para. 401. *See also* Crawford, J. *State Responsibility* (Cambridge, 2013) at 43.

[73] ARSIWA, *id.*, art. 2.

[74] *Id.*, art. 15.

[75] *Id.*, art. 30(a). Although the text of the article does not reference any time parameters within which cessation must occur, ICJ jurisprudence suggests cessation must occur forthwith. *See Wall*, *supra* note 41, paras. 151, 163. *See also Chagos*, *infra* note 196, para. 183, where the Court indicated the wrongful conduct must cease 'as rapidly as possible'. This was subsequently interpreted by the General Assembly as requiring cessation within 'six months'. A/RES/73,295, 22 May 2019.

[76] ARSIWA, *id.*, art. 30(b).

[77] *Id.*, art. 31.

[78] *Id.*, arts. 40, 41. *See, Wall*, *supra* note 41, para. 163.

4 The Illegality of Israel's Continued Presence in the OPT 189

The international law governing state responsibility is rooted in a desire to ensure the primacy of the international rule of law, in line with the ostensible organizing principle of the UN. In his commentary on the ARSIWA, James Crawford indicates that '[t]he responsible State's obligation of cessation thus protects both the interests of the injured State or States and the interests of the international community as a whole in the preservation of, and reliance on, the rule of law'.[79] Where a state responsible for an internationally wrongful act refuses to perform its obligations of cessation, non-repetition and reparation, as applicable, an injured state may take appropriate and proportional counter-measures to help induce such performance.[80] Where the obligation breached is owed to a group of states and is established for the protection of a collective interest of that group or is owed to the international community as a whole (i.e. obligations *erga omnes*), states other than the injured state are entitled to take lawful measures against the responsible state to ensure its observance.[81]

It therefore follows that where an internationally wrongful act has taken place and/or is continuing, international law neither mandates nor requires the responsible state to make adherence to its obligations of cessation, non-repetition, and reparation conditioned on negotiation.[82] To do so would be to legitimate that which is illegal. Rather, the law requires strict, unconditional, and timely performance of those obligations in keeping with its overall object and purpose, namely to ensure the international rule of law. This is particularly so where a state's internationally wrongful conduct entails a serious breach of an obligation arising under a peremptory norm of general international law. In such case, international law neither mandates nor requires third states (collectively or individually) to make adherence to their own obligations to bring such breaches to an end, to not recognize their legality nor to render aid or assistance in their maintenance, conditional on negotiation.

It is apparent, therefore, that the question of the legality of Israel's continued presence in the OPT, as such, is important because it animates the UN's supposed commitment to the international rule of law. If Israel's occupation is legal, for the Organization to contemplate its end through negotiation would amount to a mere invocation of Charter principles regulating the peaceful resolution of disputes. In such case, the legitimacy of the Organization's call for negotiations could not be impugned on the basis that it runs counter to international law, despite any disparity in negotiating power of the parties. If, on the other hand,

---

[79] Crawford, J. *The International Law Commission's Articles on State Responsibility* (Cambridge, 2005) at 197.

[80] ARSIWA, *supra* note 72, arts. 49–54.

[81] *Id.*, arts. 48, 54.

[82] *But see* Chapter 4, note 66.

190   *1967 and After: The UN and the Occupied Palestinian Territory*

Israel's presence is or has become illegal, for the Organization to condition its end on negotiation would run counter to the relevant international law governing state responsibility. In such a case, any disparity in negotiating power could be abused by the more powerful party to consolidate its illegal actions under a cloak of legitimacy provided by the UN. This would only operate to marginalize the weaker party, thereby prolonging injustice and conflict indefinitely.

This is presumably why, for instance, the UN has never suggested that the end of Israel's individual violations of IHL or IHRL in the OPT, including settlement and wall construction, be conditioned on negotiation.[83] It is also why the practice of the UN in respect of occupations in other contexts tends to demonstrate that where an occupation has been deemed illegal by the Organization, the end of that illegality has not been made contingent on negotiation. The cases of Russia's occupation of Ukraine,[84] South Africa's occupation of Namibia,[85] the Soviet Union's occupation of Afghanistan,[86] and Iraq's occupation of Kuwait[87] are the most prescient examples.

4.2 *The Need for Clarity in the UN's Practice on the OPT*

The UN's handling of Israel's prolonged occupation of the OPT stands out in so far as it has failed to *definitively* determine that presence to be illegal on the basis of its own UN record and has made its end subject to negotiation. The need for definitiveness derives from the fact that the Organization's treatment of the issue has suffered from inconsistency and contradiction. Although some UN organs began consideration of the matter with a principled approach, their positions have become diluted or legally confused over time. Still, other organs have remained silent altogether. The net result has

---

[83] *See, e.g.,* S/RES/2334, 23 December 2016. *See also* Bekker, P., 'The World Court's Ruling Regarding Israel's West Bank Barrier and the Primacy of International Law: An Insider's Perspective' (2005) 38:2 *Cornell ILJ* 553 at 560 ('Why should illegalities be subject to negotiations, which according to the ICJ are to proceed 'on the basis of international law'?').

[84] A/RES/ES-11/4, 13 October 2022. Although this resolution calls for 'de-escalation' of the general conflict through 'negotiation', it 'declares' Russia's 'temporary military control' of Ukraine has 'no validity under international law' and 'demands' that Russia 'immediately, completely and unconditionally withdraw all of its military forces from the territory of Ukraine'.

[85] A/RES/2248(S-V), 19 May 1967; A/RES/2325(XXII), 16 December 1967; A/RES/2372(XXII), 12 June 1968; A/RES/2403(XXIII), 16 December 1968; S/RES/246, 14 March 1968; S/RES/264, 20 March 1969, S/RES/276, 30 January 1970. *See also International Status of South-West Africa*, Advisory Opinion, (ICJ 11 July 1950), ICJ Reports 1950, p. 128 ['South-West Africa']; *Legal Consequences for States of the Continued Presence of South Africa in Namibia (South-West Africa) Notwithstanding Security Council Resolution 276 (1970)*, Advisory Opinion, 21 June 1971, ICJ Reports 1971, p. 16 ['Namibia'].

[86] A/RES/ES-6/2, 14 January 1980.

[87] S/RES/662, 9 August 1990; A/RES/45/170, 18 December 1990; A/RES/45/170, 18 December 1990.

4 The Illegality of Israel's Continued Presence in the OPT

been an undermining of the UN's stated commitment to the maintenance of the international rule of law in its policy on the question of Palestine and the unfulfilled promise of that policy for its people.

Thus, in 1975 and 1976 the General Assembly condemned the occupation as a 'violation of the Charter of the United Nations',[88] whereas from 1977 to 1981, it expressly qualified it as 'illegal'.[89] Between 1981 and 1991, the General Assembly dropped this reference and reverted to condemning the occupation as a 'violation of the Charter of the United Nations', albeit demanding Israel's 'immediate, unconditional and total withdrawal'.[90] Taken together, this practice suggests the General Assembly was of the view that at least by the eighth year of the occupation, Israel's presence in the OPT had become illegal for being in violation of the *jus ad bellum* provisions of the Charter and, accordingly, could not condition its end on negotiation in line with the law of state responsibility. The problem arises from the fact that from 1992 onward – just after the convening of the Madrid Peace Conference – all such references in General Assembly resolutions simply vanish. From that point on, the General Assembly has satisfied itself with an annual affirmation that 'the occupation itself' constitutes a 'grave', 'gross', or 'primary' violation only of 'human rights', while expressing the 'hope' that the parties are able to bring it to an end through negotiation.[91] The only other organ

[88] A/RES/3414(XXX), 5 December 1975; A/RES/31/61, 9 December 1976.

[89] *See* A/RES/32/20, 25 November 1977; A/RES/33/29, 7 December 1978; A/RES/34/70, 6 December 1979; A/RES/35/122E, 11 December 1980; A/RES/35/207, 16 December 1980; *and* A/RES/36/147E, 16 December 1981, the latter of which references 'illegal Israeli military occupation'.

[90] *See* A/RES/36/147E, 16 December 1981; A/RES/36/226A, 17 December 1981; A/RES/37/123F, 20 December 1982; A/RES/38/180D, 19 December 1983; A/RES/39/146A, 14 December 1984; A/RES/40/168A, 16 December 1985; A/RES/41/162A, 4 December 1986; A/RES/42/209B, 11 December 1987; A/RES/43/54A, 6 December 1988; A/RES/44/40A, 4 December 1989; A/RES/45/83A, 13 December 1990; *and* A/RES/46/82A, 16 December 1991.

[91] The reference to the occupation constituting a grave, gross or primary violation of human rights dates from 1981. *See* A/RES/36/147C, 16 December 1981; A/RES/37/88C, 10 December 1982; A/RES/38/79, 15 December 1983; A/RES/39/95, 14 December 1984; A/RES/40/161D, 16 December 1985; A/RES/41/63D, 3 December 1986; A/RES/42/160D, 8 December 1987; A/RES/43/58, 6 December 1988; A/RES/44/48, 8 December 1989; A/RES/45/74, 11 December 1990; A/RES/46/47, 9 December 1991; A/RES/47/70A, 14 December 1992; A/RES/49/36, 9 December 1994; A/RES/50/29, 6 December 1995; A/RES/51/131, 13 December 1996; A/RES/52/64, 10 December 1997; A/RES/53/53, 3 December 1998; A/RES/54/76, 6 December 1999; A/RES/55/130, 8 December 2000; A/RES/56/59, 10 December 2001; A/RES/57/124, 11 December 2002; A/RES/58/96, 9 December 2003; A/RES/59/121, 10 December 2004; A/RES/60/104, 8 December 2005; A/RES/61/116, 14 December 2006; A/RES/62/106, 17 December 2007; A/RES/63/95, 5 December 2008; A/RES/64/91, 10 December 2009; A/RES/65/102, 10 December 2010; A/RES/66/76, 9 December 2011; A/RES/67/118, 18 December 2012; A/RES/68/80, 11 December 2013; A/RES/69/90, 5 December 2014; A/RES/70/87, 9 December 2015; *and* A/RES/71/95, 6 December 2016.

of the UN that has qualified Israel's occupation as illegal as such has been ECOSOC. This has been done on an annual basis since 2010, while curiously also urging the international community to renew efforts aimed at the conclusion of a negotiated peace leading to the occupation's end, the requirements of the law of state responsibility notwithstanding.[92] For its part, the office of the Secretary-General has been more conservative. When Kofi Annan called upon Israel to 'end the illegal occupation' of the OPT in 2002, public criticism resulted in a quick reversal and clarification that his reference to illegality was meant to be understood in relation to the IHL and IHRL violations of the occupying power, not the nature of the occupation as such. Notably, this clarification included an affirmation of the standard UN position on the need for negotiations between the parties based on the land-for-peace formula.[93] In the *Wall* advisory opinion, the ICJ failed to opine on the legality of Israel's presence in the OPT, although in a separate opinion Judge Elaraby affirmed 'the illegality of the Israeli occupation regime itself'.[94] The silence of the majority on the legality of the occupation was made problematic by the fact of the Court's invocation of the need for negotiations as a means to resolve the conflict, as noted above. In addition, any value placed in Elaraby's illegality finding was undermined by his incorrect statement of law that occupation *per se* is always illegal.[95] The Security Council has never opined on the legality of Israel's presence in the OPT, an omission demonstrative of the lack of unanimity among member states on the legality of Israel's use of force in 1967. Finally, although both the former UN Special Rapporteur on Human Rights in the Palestinian Territories Occupied since 1967, Michael Lynk (2017), and the Pillay commission of inquiry (2022) have recently issued reports identifying Israel as an illegal occupant in the OPT, given their status as independent experts, their views cannot be taken as reflective of the official position of the UN.[96]

Therefore, given the incongruity and, at times, incoherence of the positions articulated by various organs of the UN, it is clear there is a need for the Organization to definitively confirm whether Israel's continued occupation of

---

[92] *See* E/RES/2010/6, 20 July 2010; E/RES/2011/18, 26 July 2011; E/RES/2012/25, 14 September 2012; E/RES/2013/17, 9 October 2013; E/RES/2014/1, 18 July 2014; E/RES/2015/13, 19 August 2015; E/RES/2016/4, 22 July 2016; *and* E/RES/2017/10, 4 August 2017.

[93] *See* UN GAOR, 57th Sess., 4488th Mtg. at 3, S/PV.4488 (12 March 2002); Fletcher, G.P. 'Annan's Careless Language,' *NYT*, 21 March 2002, A37; Eckhard, F. Letter to the Editor, 'A Delicate Word in the Mideast,' *NYT*, 23 March 2002, A16.

[94] *Wall, supra* note 41, Separate Opinion of Judge Elaraby at 124

[95] *See id.* where Elaraby opined: 'Occupation, as an *illegal* and temporary situation, is at the heart of the whole problem' [emphasis added].

[96] Lynk Report, *supra* note 71; Pillay Report, *supra* note 56. See Postscript.

4 The Illegality of Israel's Continued Presence in the OPT

the OPT is legal. This is perhaps why the literature on the legality of Israel's occupation has largely neglected to discuss the above-noted practice of the UN, instead taking it as a given that the international community treats Israel as the lawful occupant of the OPT.[97] By definitively addressing the illegality of Israel's occupation regime, the UN would be able to consummate its application of the international rule of law in the OPT, going beyond the usual humanitarian/managerial paradigm. This, in turn, would allow the Palestinian people to mitigate the effects of their quasi-sovereign and contingent status within the UN system.

4.3 The Illegality of Israel's Continued Presence in the OPT

Despite earlier academic affirmations of the illegality of Israel's occupation of the OPT, including by this author,[98] it was not until 2005 that scholarship emerged providing a more robust rationale for the assertion.[99] Building upon this and subsequent literature, this section explains why Israel's continued presence in the OPT is illegal, filling several gaps in the existing literature, particularly in relation to the UN's position on the matter.

Understanding why Israel's prolonged occupation of the OPT is illegal requires consideration of three branches of international law: the law governing the use of force (*jus ad bellum*), the law governing how force is used in armed conflict (*jus in bello* or IHL), and IHRL, including the law on self-determination. Because of the OPT's status as an occupied territory, the starting point must be the law of occupation.[100] As will be demonstrated, this *lex specialis* is underpinned by all three of these branches.

---

[97] Lynk Report, *supra* note 71, para. 18. *See also* Benvenisti, E. *The International Law of Occupation*, 2nd ed. (Oxford, 2012); Gross, *supra* note 71; Finkelstein, *supra* note 71; and Ben-Naftali, et al., *supra* note 71. The only exception to this is Ronen, *supra* note 71 at 216–221, who surveys the UN's position on the illegality of Israel's occupation based only on a sample of GA and ICJ practice, without going into that of other key organs of the Organization. The result is to give the false impression that the UN's position on the illegality of the occupation is more definitive than it actually is.

[98] Imseis 'Law, Reality and the Oslo 'Peace' Process' (2000) 20:3 *Oxford JLS* 469; Mazzawi *Palestine and the Law* (Garnet: 1997), 235.

[99] *Supra* note 71.

[100] The law of occupation is codified in the Fourth Geneva Convention, *supra* note 24, and the *Convention Respecting the Laws and Customs of War on Land*, 18 Oct. 1907, 36 Stat. 2277 ['1907 Hague Regulations']. Both treaties are regarded as codifications of customary international law. While Israel has not disputed the applicability of the 1907 Hague Regulations to the OPT, it argues the Fourth Geneva Convention, to which it is signatory, does not apply. The UN, including the ICJ, has rejected this. *See* S/RES/2334 (2016); A/RES/70/88, 2015; E/RES/2017/10; and *Wall*, *supra* note 41, para. 101. For discussion of the merits of the Israeli claim, *see* Imseis, 'On the Fourth Geneva Convention and the Occupied Palestinian Territory' (2003) 44:1 *Harvard ILJ* 65, 92–100.

As I have elsewhere written,[101] two fundamental principles underpin the law of occupation. First, occupation is a temporary condition during which the occupying power may act only as the *de facto* administrator of the territory for the benefit of the protected population. Under no circumstances may an occupying power permanently alter the status of the territory,[102] including through annexation, population transfer, or imposition of puppet regimes or regimes inimical to humanity as a whole (e.g. racial discrimination). The occupying power is accordingly bound to ensure the functioning of the prewar administration of the territory, including the obligation to respect the laws in force in the territory, amending them only to the extent required to enable the occupying power to meet its obligations under the law.[103] Second, under no circumstances does the fact of being in occupation of a territory entitle the occupant to sovereignty over it. Contemporary state practice, exemplified by the 2003 occupation of Iraq, affirms that the law of occupation defers to the principle of self-determination of peoples and its corollary that sovereignty lies in the people and not its ousted government. The right of peoples to self-determination has been recognized by the ICJ as a right *erga omnes*.[104] As such, occupying powers are obligated to respect that right and do nothing to permanently frustrate its exercise.[105]

These fundamental principles are rooted in the protection of at least three *jus cogens* norms of general international law: the prohibition on the acquisition of territory through the threat or use of force, the obligation of states to respect the right of peoples to self-determination, and the obligation of states to refrain from imposing regimes of alien subjugation, domination, and

---

[101] Imseis, *id.*, at 91–92.

[102] *Id.*, at 91. Although a principle of customary international law, this proposition finds expression in Article 4 of the Protocol Additional to the Geneva Conventions of 12 August 1949, and Relating to the Protection of Victims of International Armed Conflicts (Additional Protocol I), which provides that '[n]either the occupation of a territory nor the application of the Conventions and this Protocol shall effect the legal status of the territory in question'.

[103] These general propositions are given expression in a number of treaty provisions codifying both the Hague and Geneva law. Article 43 of the 1907 Hague Regulations, *supra* note 100, provides that the occupant 'shall take all the measures in his power to restore, and ensure, as far as possible, public order and safety, while respecting, unless absolutely prevented, the laws in force in the country'. Likewise, Article 64 of the Fourth Geneva Convention, *supra* note 24, provides that '[t]he penal laws of the occupied territory shall remain in force, with the exception that they may be repealed or suspended by the Occupying power in cases where they constitute a threat to its security or an obstacle to the application of the present Convention'.

[104] *Case Concerning East Timor* (Portugal v. Australia), 30 June 1995, ICJ Reports 1995, p. 90, para. 29; *Wall*, *supra* note 41, para. 88; and *Namibia*, *supra* note 85, para. 12.

[105] Benvenisti, *supra* note 97 at 198.

4 The Illegality of Israel's Continued Presence in the OPT 195

exploitation inimical to humankind, including racial discrimination.[106] As interdependent concepts, they inform virtually every aspect of the modern law of occupation as it exists in both treaty and custom.

Because the humanitarian imperative underpinning IHL contemplates the existence of a legal regime governing military occupation, it necessarily follows that occupation as such does not *ipso facto* represent an illegal state of affairs. That said, the fundamental distinction between the *jus ad bellum* and the *jus in bello* has rendered it generally accepted that occupations resulting from the impermissible use of force (i.e. aggression) are necessarily illegal,[107] whereas occupations resulting from a lawful use of force under the UN Charter are legal, *per se*, notwithstanding subsequent transgressions by the occupying power of the *jus in bello* during the occupation.[108] The legality of occupations has therefore traditionally only ever been conceived against these two separate paradigms; the *jus ad bellum* understood as providing the

---

[106] *Draft Conclusions on Identification and Legal Consequences of Peremptory Norms of General International Law (Jus Cogens)*, Report of the International Law Commission, Seventy-third session (18 April–3 June and 4 July–5 August 2022), A/77/10, pp. 86–88, Conclusion 23, paras. 7, 11, 14. *See also* Crawford, *supra* note 79 at 188, 246–247. Of note, neither the ILC nor Crawford's commentary on the ARSIWA expressly identify the inadmissibility of the acquisition of territory through the threat or use of force as a *jus cogens*, but rather only its parent principle, the general prohibition on the threat or use of force (i.e. aggression). Nevertheless, as Orakhelashvili has argued, 'once the exercise of sovereign authority entails, or is consequential upon, a breach of a peremptory norm, the acts performed become subject to the overriding effect of *jus cogens*. Not only are they illegal – which would be the case for every wrongful act – but they are also void', resulting in what he calls 'a jus cogens nullity'. *See* Orakhelashvilli, A. *Peremptory Norms in International Law* (Oxford, 2006) at 216, 218–223. But it is doubtful whether a *jus cogens* nullity should be understood as a separate sub-category of *jus cogens* norms, *per se*. The better view would be that there is little, if any, substantive legal difference or effect between the two, particularly because both are rooted in the identical purpose of safeguarding the most fundamental value of the international state system: respect for the territorial integrity and political independence of states. As a matter of state practice, this is presumably the rationale behind the virtually indistinguishable treatment these two precepts have been afforded on the international plane, particularly in resolutions of the Security Council and the General Assembly, including the Friendly Relations Declaration, *supra* note 8. In its 2004 written statement in the *Wall* advisory opinion, *supra* note 41, Palestine submitted that the prohibition on the acquisition of territory through force amounted to a *jus cogens* norm. It is of note that Crawford, later a judge on the ICJ, was then among counsel of record for Palestine. *See* Written Statement of Palestine. *Legal Consequences of the Construction of a Wall in the Occupied Palestinian Territory*, 30 January 2004, paras. 431, 468, 634, at: www.icj-cij.org/files/case-related/131/1555.pdf.

[107] Benvenisti, *supra* note 97 at 140. *See also* Friendly Relations Declaration, *supra* note 8, first principle, para. 10 ('[t]he territory of a State shall not be the object of military occupation resulting from the use of force in contravention of the provisions of the Charter').

[108] *But see* Dinstein, Y. *The International Law of Belligerent Occupation* (Cambridge, 2009) at 2, arguing that it is a 'myth surrounding the legal regime of belligerent occupation that it is, or becomes in time, inherently illegal under international law'.

normative framework for assessing the legitimacy of the original act giving rise to the occupation, the *jus in bello* perceived as providing a valuable normative framework within which to measure the behaviour of the occupant during an occupation, but inappropriate for, if incapable of, assessing the legality of the particular regime of occupation itself.[109] This traditional view was affirmed, in part, by Judge Koojimans in *Armed Activities (DRC v. Uganda)*, where he opined in *obiter* that: '[i]t goes without saying that the outcome of an unlawful act is tainted with illegality. The occupation resulting from an illegal use of force betrays its origin but the rules governing its regime do not characterize the origin of the result as lawful or unlawful'.[110] The problem with this traditional bifurcation is that it fails to consider a third possibility. Namely, where an initially lawful occupant engages in gross or systematic violations of international law involving breaches of obligations of a *jus cogens* and *erga omnes* character, by what rationale can it be said that the regime of force maintaining such a situation remains legal and therefore legitimate?

Despite the objections of at least one writer,[111] the present literature on Israel's prolonged occupation of the OPT suggests that occupation regimes not otherwise impugned by an initial violation of the *jus ad bellum* and which violate any one of these three peremptory norms must be regarded as illegal.[112] What is missing from this literature, however, is a thorough treatment of what the UN *as a whole* has said regarding the illegality of Israel's occupation of the OPT as well as an analysis of what the legal consequences of that illegality are, particularly as regards the Organization's negotiations condition.[113]

The legality of Israel's occupation of the OPT may be impugned on two grounds. First, it may be regarded as illegal *ab initio*, being the result of the impermissible use of force in 1967. Without discounting its merits, the problem with this argument for the purposes of this book is that the historical record as established in UN practice does not lend itself to a finding that Israel's invocation of force in 1967 was illegal, as such. Between the silence

---

[109] This is a view shared by Ben-Naftali et al., *supra* note 71 at 552, who ascribe the 'virtual immunity' enjoyed by Israel from any critical discussion of the legality of its occupation of the Occupied Palestinian Territory (OPT) to 'the perception of the occupation as a factual, rather than a normative, phenomenon. Thus posited, the fact of occupation generates normative results – the application of the international laws of occupation – but in itself does not seem to be a part of that, or any other, normative order'.

[110] *Case Concerning Armed Activities on the Territory of the Congo* (Democratic Republic of the Congo v. Uganda), 19 December 2005, ICJ Reports 2005, p. 168, para. 60 ['*Armed Activities (DRC v. Uganda)*'].

[111] *But see* Dinstein, *supra* note 108 at 2.

[112] *Supra* note 71. Not all of the authors cited rely on the three *jus cogens* norms referred to here. Yet the cumulative thrust of their arguments affirms all three are equally applicable.

[113] *But see* Ronen, *supra* note 71.

4 *The Illegality of Israel's Continued Presence in the OPT*   197

of the Security Council in 1967 and the subsequent confusion in General Assembly resolutions, it is difficult to point to any UN practice sufficient to ground this claim.[114] Second, even if the occupation was not illegal *ab inito*, it has been rendered illegal over time for being in violation of the aforementioned *jus cogens* norms. Relying primarily on the UN record, the remainder of this section briefly assesses various Israeli actions in the OPT against each of these *jus cogens* norms. In this respect, it is important to bear in mind that of all of its actions, Israel's policy of transferring its civilian population into the OPT in violation of the Fourth Geneva Convention,[115] the Rome Statute,[116] and customary international law[117] is the single most important factor animating its violations of these norms.

4.3.1 Prohibition on the Acquisition of Territory through the Threat or Use of Force

The question of whether occupied territory may be considered annexed is a factual one, not requiring formal declarations of annexation to be satisfied under international law.[118] Since 1967, Israel has effectively annexed a substantial portion of the OPT through a series of legislative, administrative, and other acts in contravention of the peremptory norm prohibiting the acquisition of territory through the use of force.

Following the 1967 war, Israel extended its municipal law and jurisdiction to occupied East Jerusalem, unilaterally expanding the city's 6.5 km² area to encompass 71 km² of expropriated Palestinian land in the surrounding areas of the West Bank.[119] In response, the General Assembly declared 'all measures taken by Israel to change the status of the city' to be 'invalid',[120] and the Security Council determined that 'all legislative and administrative actions taken by Israel, including expropriation of land and properties thereon, which tend to

---

[114] *See* S/RES/242, 22 November 1967. For GA resolutions, *see supra* notes 88–91. Leaving aside the position of the UN, as such, for an argument that Israeli actions were objectively illegal in 1967, *see* Quigley, J. *The Six Day War and Israeli Self-Defense* (Cambridge, 2013).

[115] Fourth Geneva Convention, *supra* note 24, art. 49.

[116] Rome Statute, *supra* note 37, art. 8(2)(b)(viii).

[117] Henckaerts, J.M. & Doswald-Beck, L., eds. *ICRC Customary International Humanitarian Law, Volume 1* (Cambridge, 2005), at 462 (Rule 130: 'States may not deport or transfer parts of their own civilian population into a territory they occupy').

[118] *See* Brownlie, I. *Principles of Public International Law*, 6th ed. (Oxford, 2003) at 140 ('there is no magic in the formal declaration of sovereignty by a government' over territories it intends to annex).

[119] Imseis, A. 'Facts on the Ground: An Examination of Israeli Municipal Policy in East Jerusalem' (2000) 15:5 *Am. U. ILR* 1039 at 1043–1047.

[120] A/RES/2253(ES-V), 4 July 1967.

198   *1967 and After: The UN and the Occupied Palestinian Territory*

change the legal status of Jerusalem, are invalid and cannot change that status'.[121] These resolutions affirmed the inadmissibility of the acquisition of territory by force. After the passage of Israel's 1980 Basic Law declaring Jerusalem to be its 'complete and united' capital, the Security Council reaffirmed this position, decided 'not to recognize the basic law, and such other actions by Israel that, as a result of this law, seek to alter the character and status of Jerusalem', and called upon 'all member states to accept this decision'.[122] Despite Israel's agreement in the Oslo accords to refrain from initiating 'any step that will change the status of the West Bank and Gaza Strip' during the interim phase of negotiations with the PLO,[123] since 1993 Israeli policies designed to alter the status of Jerusalem have been aggressively pursued, with thousands of Palestinians being evicted from the city while expanding the Israeli settler population exponentially. In response, the General Assembly and the Security Council have continued to denounce Israel's purported annexation of East Jerusalem as 'illegal', 'null and void', and having 'no validity whatsoever'.[124]

Beyond Jerusalem, Israeli actions elsewhere in the OPT have effectuated its annexation in all but name. This includes the unilateral expropriation of large segments of territory for Israeli settlements and related infrastructure (by-pass roads, electrical and sewage grids, tunnels, checkpoints, etc.), as well as the construction of the wall and its associated regime. As noted by a 2012 UN Fact-Finding Mission, each Israeli government since 1967 has 'openly lead and directly participated in the planning, construction, development, consolidation and/or encouragement of settlements' in the OPT through a variety of political, military, and economic means.[125] Whereas between 1967 and 1973, the number of Jewish settlers in the West Bank stood at just over 1,500,[126] by 1987 their number in the OPT, including East Jerusalem, had grown to 169,000.[127] Since 1993 – with the Oslo proviso that nothing be done

---

[121] S/RES/252, 21 May 1968. *See also* S/RES/267, 3 July 1969; S/RES/298, 25 September 1971.
[122] S/RES/478, 20 August 1980. *See also* S/RES/476, 30 June 1980.
[123] *See* Interim Agreement on the West Bank and Gaza Strip, Sept. 28, 1995, 36 I.L.M. 551, art. 31(7).
[124] *See, e.g.,* S/RES/2334, 23 December 2016; A/RES/71/25, 30 December 2016; A/RES/70/16, 24 November 2015; A/RES/69/24, 25 November 2014; A/RES/68/16, 26 November 2013.
[125] *Report of the Independent International Fact-Finding Mission to Investigate the Implications of the Israeli Settlements on the Civil, Political, Economic, Social and Cultural Rights of the Palestinian People Throughout the Occupied Palestinian Territory, Including East Jerusalem,* A/HRC/22/63, 7 February 2013, paras. 20–24 ['UN Fact-Finding Mission']. This report was endorsed by the UN Human Rights Council in its resolution 22/29, 15 April 2013.
[126] Shehadeh, R. *From Occupation to Interim Accords* (SOAS/Kluwer, 1997) at 3.
[127] United Nations Office for the Coordination of Humanitarian Affairs, 'The Humanitarian Impact on Palestinians of Israeli Settlements and Other Infrastructure in the West Bank,' July 2007, at 20.

4 The Illegality of Israel's Continued Presence in the OPT   199

by either party to prejudge the outcome of negotiations – the settler population has over quadrupled, with the Israeli Prime Minister himself putting the figure at 650,000 in 2011,[128] and the Israeli non-governmental organization Peace Now placing it at just under 700,000 in 2023.[129] Although the settler growth rate was nearly double that of Israeli citizens in 2019,[130] according to the UN Fact-Finding Mission, it was almost triple that of the yearly average in Israel in the period between 2002 and 2012.[131] OCHA reports that Israel has allocated over 43 per cent of the West Bank to local or regional 'settlement councils'.[132] These councils are located predominately within 'Area C' of the territory, which comprises over 60 per cent of the total area of the West Bank and within which Israel exercises exclusive control, including over planning and construction.[133] In January 2023, current Israeli prime minister, Benjamin Netanyahu, publicly affirmed that that his government will continue to 'promote and develop [Jewish] settlement' in the OPT.[134]

In 2004, the ICJ found Israel's wall and its associated regime in the OPT contrary to international law, as it 'gives expression *in loco* to the illegal measures taken by Israel with regard to Jerusalem and the settlements'.[135] The Court held that the wall risks 'further alterations to the demographic composition' of the territory 'in as much as it is contributing ... to the departure of Palestinian populations from certain areas'.[136] It further noted that the wall would incorporate, in the area between it and the 1949 armistice line, 'more than 16 per cent of the territory of the West Bank' and '[a]round 80 per cent of the settlers' in the OPT. The Court accordingly considered 'that the construction of the wall and its associated regime create a "fait accompli" on the ground that could well become permanent', in which case 'it would be tantamount to *de facto* annexation'.[137] Some twenty years on, Israel has expanded

---

[128] *Israeli Settlements in the Occupied Palestinian Territory, Including East Jerusalem, and the Occupied Syrian Golan*, Report of the Secretary-General, A/67/375, 18 September 2012, para. 7 ['Secretary-General's Settlements Report'].

[129] *Peace Now, Israeli Settlements 2023*, 5 January 2023, available at: https://peacenow.org.il/wp-content/uploads/2023/01/settlements_map_En_2023_.pdf.

[130] *Report of the Special Rapporteur on the Situation of Human Rights in the Palestinian Territories Occupied Since 1967*, A/HRC/47/57, 29 July 2021, para. 62.

[131] The mission cited the Israeli Central Bureau of Statistics for this figure. *See* UN Fact-Finding Mission, *supra* note 125, para. 28.

[132] As reported in *id.*, para. 37.

[133] Lynk Report, *supra* note 71, para.46.

[134] Ahmed, N. 'Jewish Supremacy is State Policy, says Netanyahu,' *Middle East Monitor*, 3 January 2023, at: www.middleeastmonitor.com/20230103-jewish-supremacy-is-state-policy-says-netanyahu/.

[135] *Wall, supra* note 41, para. 122.

[136] *Id.*

[137] *Id.*, para. 121.

4.3.2 The Right of Peoples to Self-determination

Israel's violation of the right of the Palestinian people to self-determination in the OPT has equally been driven by its settlement policy. According to Jean Pictet, the prohibition on civilian settlement by an occupying power was intended to prevent the imposition of demographic changes in occupied territory 'for political and racial reasons' and to frustrate attempts 'to colonize' such territory.[138] Yet, according to the UN record, that is precisely what has happened in the OPT since 1967. As noted by the UN Fact-Finding Mission, Israel has openly pursued a policy of 'demographic balance' in occupied East Jerusalem, most recently incorporated into the 'Jerusalem 2000' master plan, expressly envisioning a ratio of at least 60:40, Jew to Arab.[139] The Fact-Finding Mission further noted that Israel's settlement of the rest of the OPT has largely followed a series of 'master plans' drawn up by governmental or quasi-governmental bodies, including the Allon Plan (1967), the Drobles Plan (1978), the Sharon Plan (1981), and the Hundred Thousand Plan (1983),[140] envisioning civilian settlement as means to simultaneously colonize the OPT and forestall the emergence of an independent Palestinian state in it. Thus, in the words of the Drobles Plan:

> The best and most effective way of removing every shadow of doubt about our intention to hold on to Judea and Samaria [*viz.* the OPT] forever is by speeding up the settlement momentum in these territories. The purpose of settling the areas between and around the centers occupied by the minorities [*viz.* the Palestinian majority] is to reduce to the minimum the danger of an additional Arab state being established in these territories. Being cut off by Jewish settlements, the minority population will find it difficult to form a territorial and political continuity.[141]

In 2012, the Secretary-General reported that 'the current configuration and attribution of control over the land', dominated by Israel and its settlement

---

[138] Pictet, J., ed., *Commentary: IV Geneva Convention Relative to the Protection of Civilian Persons in Time of War* (ICRC, 1958) at 283.

[139] UN Fact-Finding Mission, *supra* note 125, para. 25. *See also*, Imseis, *supra* note 119 at 1054.

[140] UN Fact-Finding Mission, *supra* note 125, para. 23.

[141] Drobles, M. *Master Plan for the Development of Settlement in Judea and Samaria, as quoted in* Matar, I. 'Exploitation of Land and Water Resources for Jewish Colonies in the Occupied Territories' in Playfair, E., ed, *International Law and the Administration of Occupied Territories* (Oxford, 1992) at 446.

4 The Illegality of Israel's Continued Presence in the OPT

policy, 'severely impedes the possibility of the Palestinian people expressing their right to self-determination'. Confirming the success of the strategy outlined by Drobles, the Secretary-General noted that, 'because the settlements are scattered across the West Bank, including East Jerusalem, the territory of the Palestinian people is divided into enclaves with little or no territorial contiguity', with a resulting 'fragmentation' that 'undermines the possibility of the Palestinian people realizing their right to self-determination through the creation of a viable state'.[142] He further noted that given the 'settlements and the associated restrictions on access of Palestinians to large portions of the West Bank', the Palestinian people are impeded from exercising permanent control over their natural resources. Most vitally, this includes water, 'which Palestinians have virtually no control over' and 86 per cent of the Jordan Valley and Dead Sea area, which are 'under the *de facto* jurisdiction of the regional councils of the settlements and which prohibit Palestinian use'.[143] Similar views were articulated by the UN Fact-Finding Mission, which echoed the Secretary-General's concern over the threat the settlements pose to the 'demographic and territorial presence of the Palestinian people' in the OPT. It took issue with the fragmentation of the Palestinian territorial sphere, highlighting in particular the bisecting effect on the West Bank of the Ma'ale Adumim settlement, as well as the impediments posed by the settlements generally on Palestinian access to and control over their natural resources. It accordingly found that the right of the Palestinian people to self-determination 'is clearly being violated through the existence and ongoing expansion of the settlements'.[144]

These observations must be read in the context of the ICJ's 2004 finding that Israel is obligated to respect the right of the Palestinian people to self-determination in the OPT and that 'all states' are independently obligated 'to see to that any impediment, resulting from the construction of the wall, to the exercise' of that right 'is brought to an end'.[145] On the many occasions, the General Assembly and the Security Council have affirmed the right of the Palestinian people to self-determination, those resolutions have often been accompanied by statements stressing that the settlements constitute an 'obstacle' to the achievement of peace through a two-state solution,[146] thereby underscoring the nexus between the settlements and Israel's violation of

---

[142] Secretary-General's Settlements Report, *supra* note 128, para. 11.

[143] *Id.*, at paras. 11, 13.

[144] UN Fact-Finding Mission, *supra* note 125, paras. 33, 34, 36, 38.

[145] *Wall*, *supra* note 41, paras. 122, 149, 155, 159.

[146] *See, e.g.*, S/RES/2334, 23 December 2016; A/RES/70/89, 15 December 2015; A/RES/69/92, 5 December 2014; A/RES/68/82, 11 December 2014; and A/RES/67/120, 18 December 2012.

Palestinian self-determination. At any rate, both the Security Council and the General Assembly have passed resolutions recalling the ICJ's *Wall* advisory opinion, with the General Assembly demanding that Israel 'comply with its legal obligations' thereunder.[147]

Despite widespread belief, Israel has never formally agreed to the establishment of a Palestinian state in the OPT. In return for PLO recognition of Israel and its right 'to exist in peace and security', Israel has only recognized 'the PLO as the representative of the Palestinian people'.[148] Although recognition of a people perforce implies recognition of its right to self-determination, Israel has consistently adopted an emaciated view of the kind of 'sovereignty' it would allow the Palestinians, if at all. This Palestinian 'state' would be deprived of a military, control over its air space, territorial sea, borders, the Jordan valley, and territorial contiguity – akin to the Bantustans of Apartheid South Africa.[149] Doubtless, this would fall short of the attributes of statehood as universally accepted under international law.[150] Of note, the ruling Israeli Likud party continues to reject the establishment of a Palestinian state west of the Jordan river,[151] and Prime Minister Netanyahu has consistently promised to block the establishment of a Palestinian state in the OPT.[152] This was reflected in a series of 2017 public statements by Netanyahu that no settlement will be uprooted in the West Bank, that Israel will remain in the territory 'forever',[153] and that insofar as the notion of a Palestinian state is concerned, 'it's time we reassessed whether the modern model we have of sovereignty, and unfettered sovereignty, is applicable everywhere in the world'.[154] In line with the guiding principles of the current government of Israel, in January 2023

---

[147] *Id.*

[148] Watson, G. *The Oslo Accords* (Oxford, 2000) at 315–316.

[149] Le More, A. *International Assistance to the Palestinians After Oslo* (Routledge, 2008) at 170. *See also* Horowitz, D. 'Netanyahu Finally Speaks His Mind,' *The Times of Israel*, 13 July 2014, at: www.timesofisrael.com/netanyahu-finally-speaks-his-mind/, where the Israeli Prime Minister was quoted as saying 'I think the Israeli people understand now what I always say: that there cannot be a situation, under any agreement, in which we relinquish security control of the territory west of the River Jordan.'

[150] *Convention on the Rights and Duties of States*, Montevideo, 26 December 1933, 165 LNTS 19. The UN rejected the Bantustan model of 'statehood' resoundingly. *See* S/RES/402, 22 December 1976 *and* A/RES/31/6A, 26 October 1976. *See also* Chapter 6.

[151] Weiler, J. 'The Hateful Likud Charter Calls for Destruction of Any Palestinian State,' *Informed Comment*, 4 August 2014, at: www.juancole.com/2014/08/charter-destruction-palestinian.html.

[152] 'Netanyahu: No Palestinian State on My Watch,' *Times of Israel*, 16 March 2015, at: www .timesofisrael.com/netanyahu-no-palestinian-state-under-my-watch/.

[153] Berger, Y. 'Netanyahu Vows Never to Remove Israeli Settlements from West Bank: 'Were Here to Stay, Forever',' *Ha'aretz*, 29 August 2017, at: www.haaretz.com/israel-news/1.809444.

[154] Pfeffer, A. 'Netanyahu Suggests a Sovereign State Might Not Work for the Palestinians,' *Ha'aretz*, 3 November 2017, at: www.haaretz.com/israel-news/1.820891.

4 The Illegality of Israel's Continued Presence in the OPT   203

Netanyahu affirmed that 'the Jewish people have an exclusive and unquestionable right to all areas of the Land of Israel' – a Zionist euphemism that spans the whole of mandate Palestine, including the OPT.[155]

4.3.3 Prohibition on Racial Discrimination

Finally, Israel's settlement policy has introduced a system of government in the OPT that, according to the UN record, is systematically engaged in racial discrimination. The International Convention on the Elimination of All Forms of Racial Discrimination (ICERD), to which Israel is signatory without reservation, defines 'racial discrimination' as:

> any distinction, exclusion, restriction or preference based on race, colour, descent, or national or ethnic origin which has the purpose or effect of nullifying or impairing the recognition, enjoyment or exercise, on an equal footing, of human rights and fundamental freedoms in the political, economic, social, cultural or any other field of public life.[156]

Israel's view that international human rights law, including ICERD, does not apply to the OPT has been rejected by the UN, including the ICJ.[157] The racial discrimination underpinning the regime Israel has erected through the imposition of exclusively Jewish settlements in the OPT is systematic and widespread.

Among the transgressions of ICERD the settlements have engendered is the violation of the right to equal treatment before the law.[158] Israel's maintenance of separate legal systems in the OPT, the applicability of which is determined by the national or ethnic origin of the individuals concerned has effectively divided the population along racial lines. Thus, any person in the OPT who is Jewish, whether a citizen of Israel or not,[159] is governed by Israeli municipal law, extraterritorially applied to them *in personam* and to the occupied lands

---

[155] Ahmed, *supra* note 134. *See also* Yesh Din 'Policy Paper: What Israel's 37th Government's Guiding Principles and Coalition Agreements Mean for the West Bank,' January 2023, at: www.ofekcenter.org.il/wp-content/uploads/2023/01/what-Israels-37th-governments-guiding-principles-and-coalition-agreements-mean-for-the-West-Bank-Jan-2023.pdf.

[156] *International Convention on the Elimination of all forms of Racial Discrimination*, 7 March 1966, 660 UNTS 195, art. 1 ['ICERD'].

[157] *Wall, supra* note 41, para. 114.

[158] ICERD, *supra* note 156, art. 5.

[159] As noted in Chapter 4, Israeli law only recognizes Jewish, as opposed to Israeli, nationality. *See George Rafael Tamarin* v. *State of Israel*, 20 January 1972, *in Decisions of the Supreme Court of Israel* (Jerusalem: Supreme Court, 1972) Vol. 25, pt. 1, at 197 (in Hebrew) *as quoted in* Tilley, V. ed., *Beyond Occupation* (Pluto, 2012) at 119. On the application of Israeli municipal law to Jewish non-citizens of Israel in the OPT, *see* Tilley, *id.*, at 67.

upon which they illegally reside or travel. On the other hand, Palestinians in the OPT are governed by Israeli military law, which is draconian in both scope and effect, covering both civil and criminal matters.[160] Another violation is the right to security of the person and protection by the state against violence or bodily harm, whether inflicted by the government or individuals.[161] Since 1967, thousands of Palestinians have been killed or injured by Israel for protesting the occupation,[162] including through legally sanctioned extrajudicial execution[163] and torture,[164] none of which methods are routinely used against Israeli settlers. In addition, Israeli settlers – who, unlike Palestinians, are permitted and encouraged to own and bear arms – have regularly committed violence against the person and property of Palestinians with an impunity rooted in what the UN Fact-Finding Mission calls 'institutionalized discrimination' aimed at 'forcing Palestinians off their land'.[165] Yet another violation concerns the right to universal and equal suffrage.[166] Although Israeli settlers possess the right to vote, participate in, and stand for national Israeli elections, none of these rights are extended on an equal basis to the Palestinians in the OPT. This abject disenfranchisement stands out owing to the fact that, despite the existence of the Palestinian Authority – a body created through the Oslo process meant to temporarily exercise local and limited 'self-autonomy' in Palestinian enclaves in the OPT pending conclusion of peace – the Israeli government effectively exercises exclusive control over the territory in which these two populations reside and within which it remains the occupying power.[167] Another violation is the right to freedom of movement.[168] With Palestinian space fragmented into numerous discontiguous enclaves by Israeli settlements and related infrastructure, the only way they are able to move into and out of these enclaves, or into and out of occupied East Jerusalem, is with permits issued by the Israeli military. Only a very small minority of Palestinians obtain such permits, which are spatially and temporarily limited and are notoriously

---

[160] Tilley, *id.*, at 64–77.

[161] ICERD, *supra* note 156, art. 5.

[162] Tilley, *supra* note 159 at 131.

[163] *Id.*, at 132–133. *See also* Gross, *supra* note 71 at 243–244.

[164] Imseis, A. "Moderate' Torture on Trial: Critical Reflections on the Israeli Supreme Court Judgment Concerning the Legality of General Security Service Interrogation Methods' (2001) 19:2 *Berkeley JIL* 328. *See also* B'Tselem, *Absolute Prohibition: The Torture and Ill-treatment of Palestinian Detainees* (Jerusalem, May 2007) at: www.btselem.org/download/200705_utterly_forbidden_eng.pdf.

[165] UN Fact-Finding Mission, *supra* note 125, paras. 50–57, 107.

[166] ICERD, *supra* note 156, art. 5.

[167] The existence of the Palestinian Authority has not vitiated Israel's status as an occupying Power in the OPT. *Wall*, *supra* note 41, para. 78. S/RES/2334, 23 December 2016.

[168] ICERD, *supra* note 156, art. 5.

4 The Illegality of Israel's Continued Presence in the OPT

difficult and costly to obtain. No such administrative restrictions apply to settlers under the applicable law.[169] Finally, another violation is the right to leave and to return to one's country.[170] Leaving aside the Palestine refugees forcibly exiled as a result of the 1948 war (see Chapter 4), approximately 300,000 Palestinians either fled or were expelled from the OPT when Israel conquered it in 1967.[171] In addition, approximately 90,000 were abroad during the hostilities and therefore rendered refugees *sur place*.[172] Despite the Security Council having called upon Israel to facilitate the return of these people to the OPT, to this day Israel has refused.[173] In contrast, by operation of Israel's *Law of Return*, any person who is of Jewish heritage is automatically entitled to immigrate to Israel and take up residence in the OPT, irrespective of where they were born.[174] These are but a representative sample of the systematic violations of the ICERD that arise from the settler-colonial regime Israel has imposed on the OPT since 1967.[175]

In its concluding observations on Israel's 2012 periodic review under ICERD, the UN Committee on the Elimination of Racial Discrimination (CERD) observed that Israeli settlements in the OPT 'are an obstacle to the enjoyment of human rights by the whole population, without distinction as to national or ethnic origin'.[176] It expressed concern with Israel's refusal to apply ICERD in the OPT and the lack of equality guarantees under Israeli law, including a prohibition on racial discrimination.[177] It continued:

> The Committee is extremely concerned at the consequences of policies and practices which amount to *de facto* segregation, such as the implementation by the State party in the Occupied Palestinian Territory of two entirely separate legal systems and sets of institutions for Jewish communities grouped in illegal settlements on the one hand and Palestinian populations living in Palestinian towns and villages on the other hand. The Committee

---

[169] Tilley, *supra* note 159 at. 151–152.
[170] ICERD, *supra* note 156, art. 5.
[171] Report of the Commissioner-General of UNRWA, 1 July 1966–30 June 1967, A/6713, at 1.
[172] Tilley, *supra* note 159 at 163.
[173] S/RES/237, 14 June 1967.
[174] *Law of Return*, 1950, 5 July 1950, art. 1, Sefer Ha-Chukkim, No. 51, p. 159.
[175] Other violations of ICERD, *supra* note 156, include the rights to: nationality, property, freedom of thought, conscience and religion, peaceful assembly and association, work and the formation of trade unions, housing, public health, and education (art. 5). Of particular concern is the impact of the *Basic Law: Israel as the Nation-State of the Jewish People*, passed by the Knesset on 19 July 2018. For an English translation, *see*: https://main.knesset.gov.il/EN/activity/Documents/BasicLawsPDF/BasicLawNationState.pdf.
[176] *Concluding Observations of the Committee for the Elimination of Racial Discrimination, Israel*, CERD/ISR/CO/14-16, 3 April 2012, para. 4.
[177] *Id.*, para. 13.

is particularly appalled at the hermetic character of the separation of two groups, who live on the same territory but do not enjoy either equal use of roads and infrastructure or equal access to basic services and water resources. Such separation is concretized by the implementation of a complex combination of movement restrictions consisting of the Wall, roadblocks, the obligation to use separate roads and a permit regime that only impacts the Palestinian population (art. 3 of the Convention).[178]

These findings were echoed by the UN Fact-Finding Mission, which decried the '[t]he legal regime of segregation' operating in the OPT for having 'enabled the establishment and consolidation of the settlements through the creation of a privileged legal space for settlements and settlers'. In its view, this has resulted 'in daily violations of a multitude of the human rights of the Palestinians' in the OPT, 'including, incontrovertibly, violating their rights to non-discrimination, equality before the law and equal protection of the law'.[179]

The racial discrimination inherent in Israel's settlement regime in the OPT has given rise to concern that it is also engaged in the crime of apartheid, as proscribed in the International Convention on the Suppression and Punishment of the Crime of Apartheid.[180] Although Israel is not a signatory to the Apartheid Convention, the convention is declarative of customary international law and is therefore binding on all states. The Apartheid Convention defines the crime of apartheid as involving any number of 'inhumane acts' – including those proscribed by the ICERD above, as well as 'measures designed to divide the population along racial lines by the creation of separate reserves and ghettos for the members of a racial group or groups'[181] – when these acts are 'committed for the purpose of establishing and maintaining domination by one racial group of persons over another racial group of persons and systematically oppressing them'.[182] It is therefore the element of *mens rea* – in this case, the intention to racially dominate and systematically oppress – that renders the crime of apartheid distinct from the commission of what would otherwise be a series of discreet acts of racial discrimination. For reasons of economy, it is not possible to cover in sufficient detail the extent to which Israeli actions in the

---

[178] *Id.*, para. 24.

[179] UN Fact-Finding Mission, *supra* note 125, para. 49.

[180] *International Convention on the Suppression and Punishment of the Crime of Apartheid*, G.A. Res. 3068, U.N. GAOR, 28th Sess., Supp. No. 30, at 75, U.N. Doc. A/9030 (1973) ['Apartheid Convention'].

[181] Apartheid Convention, *id.*, art. II(d). *But see* ICERD, *supra* note 156, art. 5(v).

[182] Apartheid Convention, *id.*, art. II. *See also*, Rome Statute, *supra* note 37, art. 7(1)(j), which prohibits the crime of Apartheid as a crime against humanity.

4 The Illegality of Israel's Continued Presence in the OPT   207

OPT satisfy the constituent elements of the crime of apartheid here. Suffice to say, given the UN record establishes that Israel's prolonged occupation of the OPT is clearly characterized by systematic racial discrimination, an increasing number of opinions and studies have emerged advancing credible cases for the existence of Israeli apartheid against the Palestinian people.[183] This includes the views of the world's leading human rights organizations, Human Rights Watch,[184] and Amnesty International,[185] and the leading Israeli[186] and Palestinian[187] human rights organizations. It also includes the opinion of former UN Special Rapporteur Lynk, who concluded in his final report to the HRC that 'the political system of entrenched rule in the Occupied Palestinian Territory that endows one racial-national-ethnic group with substantial rights, benefits and privileges while intentionally subjecting another group to live behind walls and checkpoints and under a permanent military rule ... satisfies the prevailing evidentiary standard for the existence of apartheid'.[188] Of course, because none of these opinions and studies represent the official views of the UN, the Organization has yet to make a definitive pronouncement on the matter, despite the urging of at least one previous President of the General Assembly to do so in 2008.[189]

In sum, Israel's occupation of the OPT has become illegal through its systematic violation of at least three *jus cogens* norms as documented in the UN record: the prohibition on the acquisition of territory by force, the obligation

---

[183] Tilley, *supra* note 159 at 222–223; Dugard, J. & Reynolds, J. 'Apartheid, International Law and the Occupied Palestinian Territory' (2013) 24:3 *EJIL* 867 at 912; *and* UN ESCWA, *Israeli Practices Towards the Palestinian People and the Question of Apartheid*, Beirut, 2017, E/ESCWA/ECRI/2017/1, at: www.middleeastmonitor.com/wp-content/uploads/downloads/201703_UN_ESCWA-israeli-practices-palestinian-people-apartheid-occupation-english.pdf. *See also infra* notes 184–188.

[184] *A Threshold Crossed: Israeli Authorities and the Crimes of Apartheid and Persecution*, Human Rights Watch, 27 April 2021, at: www.hrw.org/report/2021/04/27/threshold-crossed/israeli-authorities-and-crimes-apartheid-and-persecution.

[185] *Israel's Apartheid Against Palestinians: Cruel System of Domination and Crime Against Humanity*, Amnesty International, 1 February 2022, at: www.amnesty.org/en/documents/mde15/5141/2022/en/.

[186] *A Regime of Jewish Supremacy from the Jordan River to the Mediterranean Sea: This is Apartheid*, B'Tselem, 12 January 2021, at: www.btselem.org/publications/fulltext/202101_this_is_apartheid; *The Occupation of the West Bank and the Crime of Apartheid: Legal Opinion*, Yesh Din, 9 July 2020, at: www.yesh-din.org/en/the-occupation-of-the-west-bank-and-the-crime-of-apartheid-legal-opinion/.

[187] Israeli Apartheid: Tool of Zionist Settler Colonialism, Al-Haq, 29 November 2022, at: www.alhaq.org/cached_uploads/download/2022/12/22/israeli-apartheid-web-final-1-pageview-1671712165.pdf.

[188] *Report of the Special Rapporteur on the Situation of Human Rights in the Palestinian Territories Occupied Since 1967*, A/HRC/49/87, 12 August 2022, para. 52.

[189] UN GAOR, 63 Sess., 57th plen. mtg. at 2, A/63/PV.57, 24 November 2008. *See also* Postscript.

to respect the right of peoples to self-determination, and the obligation to refrain from imposing regimes of alien subjugation, domination, and exploitation inimical to humankind, including racial discrimination. The systematic nature of Israel's violation of these norms is rooted in a series of discrete but interconnected violations of IHL and IHRL over an abnormally prolonged military occupation. In themselves, these discrete violations constitute internationally wrongful acts. What lends them their true normative bite, however, is that, when taken together, they constitute a composite series of actions defined in the aggregate as internationally wrongful. This situation gives rise to specific international legal consequences for both Israel and third states the substance of which clashes with the UN's long-standing position on the OPT. This position, focused merely on documenting a range of IHL and IHRL violations while at the same time affirming that the end of the regime giving rise to those violations be contingent on negotiation, has in turn been pivotal in maintaining Palestine's subaltern condition in the UN system. Below, we examine these legal consequences more closely, highlighting how they differ from the negotiations condition underpinning the UN's position on the OPT, and whether and to what extent they can assist in mitigating Palestine's continued contingency on the international plane.

4.4 Legal Consequences and the Mitigation of Palestinian International Legal Subalternity

Under the law of state responsibility, the legal consequences of Israel's illegal occupation of the OPT are threefold. First, it is obligated to end the occupation immediately, unconditionally, and totally. Second, it must offer appropriate guarantees of non-repetition. Third, it must make full reparation for injury caused, including any material and moral damage. Given the occupation involves gross and systematic breaches of *jus cogens* norms, the law of state responsibility imposes additional consequences on third states. These include the obligation to cooperate to bring Israel's occupation of the OPT to an end through lawful means and to refrain from rendering aid or assistance to Israel in maintaining its illegal occupation of the OPT.

The UN's conventional approach of conditioning the end of Israel's illegal occupation of the OPT on negotiation is problematic for three reasons. First, it runs counter to prevailing international law. Just as most municipal legal systems do not countenance common thieves negotiating the return of stolen property, international law does not contemplate states negotiating the terms of whether and to what extent their internationally wrongful conduct is brought to an end. This is particularly so where the conduct is the result of a composite

4 The Illegality of Israel's Continued Presence in the OPT

series of wrongful acts that violate peremptory norms, respect for which is non-derogable for being in the interest of, and owed to, the international community as a whole. In light of the 2012 upgrade in the status of Palestine at the UN to a non-member observer *state*, the implications of the UN's position on negotiations as a condition of ending the illegal occupation of Palestine are important. For they go beyond the mere rights that accrue to a protected population under IHL and IHRL, and touch upon the rights and duties of all states to refrain from the use of force against the territorial integrity and political independence of any other state, as codified in Article 2(4) of the UN Charter. It is not for nothing that this principle has been characterized as the 'cornerstone' and the 'heart' of the Charter system by both the ICJ[190] and publicists alike.[191] Without it, the international system would be vulnerable to a complete collapse under the spectre of a return to the age of total war and the legitimation of territorial aggrandizement through conquest. By conditioning the end of Israel's occupation of the OPT on negotiation, the UN is undermining its *raison d'être* as rooted in the international rule of law upon which the promise of the Organization is ostensibly built. In this sense, the upgrade in Palestine's status at the UN has elevated the urgency of the legal issues at play not only for the subaltern Palestinian people, but also for the Organization and its members as a whole. To the extent the UN continues to adopt a position at variance with the international rule of law, the legal rights and subjectivity of the Palestinian people purportedly recognized by it will remain contingent.

Second, the UN's insistence on negotiations as a condition of ending Israel's prolonged occupation of the OPT runs contrary to its own practice on foreign military occupations in other contexts. Where an occupation has been determined by the Organization to be illegal, the obligation to bring it to a speedy end has not been conditioned on negotiation, but has been unconditional in line with the law of state responsibility. The fact that the General Assembly and ECOSOC have, to varying degrees, affirmed the illegality of Israel's occupation of the OPT suggests that the Organization's negotiations condition is at odds with this practice. Nevertheless, because the UN has not been consistent in characterizing Israel's occupation as illegal, complications arise. The above assessment of the legality of Israel's occupation highlights a potential remedy for this in so far as it shows, on the basis of factual and legal determinations

---

[190] *Armed Activities (DRC v. Uganda), supra* note 110, para. 148.
[191] *See* Waldock, C. 'The Regulation of the Use of Force by Individual States in International Law' (1952) *Recueil des Cours*, Vol. II, at 492; *and* Henkin, L. 'The Reports of the Death of Article 2(4) are Greatly Exaggerated' (1971) *AJIL* 65 at 544.

established by the UN itself, that the occupation has indeed become illegal for its violation of a number of *jus cogens* norms of *erga omnes* character. The fact that the Organization has failed to adopt a position more in line with the requirements of international law on the issue is demonstrative of the continued rule by law at work on the question of Palestine.

Third, the UN's negotiations condition is problematic because it renders conflict resolution more difficult by providing a measure of political legitimacy to Israeli claims on the OPT without full regard for its track record of bad faith, again as established by the UN record itself. Given the disparity in negotiating power between occupier and occupied, it is hard to imagine how a negotiated resolution could be concluded at all, leave aside 'in conformity with the principles of justice and international law' as envisioned in the Charter, if the full weight of international law is not brought to bear on the situation. In the three decades since negotiations began at Oslo, Israel has consolidated its hold on the OPT under a public claim that it will never relinquish it, in complete contravention of the norms underpinning the law of occupation and its treaty obligations to refrain from prejudging the outcome of negotiations. How calling for continued negotiations in such a context can be regarded as an effective form of dispute resolution, instead of an effective endorsement of the internationally wrongful acts of the hegemonic party, beggars belief. It is against this context that the UN's conditioning of the end of the occupation of the OPT on negotiation falls well wide of the mark, representing a continuation of the rule by law character of the Organization's management of the question of Palestine in the post-1967 period.

The question arises whether the way is open for the UN to correct its position and, if so, whether this would vitiate Palestine's contingent status in the Organization? In line with the counter-hegemonic potential of international law, it is submitted that both the General Assembly and the ICJ should be looked to as potential sites where the illegality of the occupation of the OPT can be definitively established, with all of the legal consequences such a finding would entail. This would ultimately help Palestine mitigate the effects of its ongoing legal subalternity at the UN.

Because the General Assembly remains a venue where the State of Palestine enjoys continued widespread support, it holds an important place as an entry point on the issue. The temporal correlation between the onset of the Oslo process and the cessation of the General Assembly's characterization of Israel's occupation of the OPT as 'illegal' and/or in 'violation of the UN Charter' is notable. It can be reasonably assumed that this change in General Assembly practice was the result of the promise the Oslo process held out of the parties finally realizing a negotiated resolution based on the two-state formula.

4 The Illegality of Israel's Continued Presence in the OPT   211

Nevertheless, following thirty years of process, there has been little peace to show for it. On the contrary, the UN record demonstrates that Israel has used this time to consolidate its hold over the OPT through pursuance of patently illegal objectives, while paying lip service to 'peace'. Now that the peace process is all but dead,[192] the General Assembly could be engaged to revive its position on the illegality of the occupation. This would furnish the international community with greater leverage to call for the immediate, unconditional and total withdrawal of the occupation in line with the law of state responsibility.

Another possibility would be to seek an advisory opinion of the ICJ. The proposed question could ask:

> what are the legal consequences for all states and the United Nations arising from Israel's ongoing violation of the right of the Palestinian people to self-determination, including through its continued settlement, annexation and prolonged occupation of the State of Palestine, in particular whether the occupation is illegal and when and how it must come to an end, considering the rules and principles of international law, including the UN Charter, international humanitarian law, international human rights law, relevant Security Council and General Assembly resolutions, and this Court's advisory opinion of 9 July 2004?

Such a question would allow arguments to be advanced that go to the illegality of Israel's occupation based on the *jus cogens* norms identified above[193]. If, before the matter reaches the Court, previous General Assembly practice referring to the occupation of the OPT as 'illegal' and in 'violation of the Charter' can be reinvigorated, this will make it easier to advance such arguments before the Court.

Some have argued that seeking a second advisory opinion is 'not a good idea' and that other 'available tools must be revisited', including the 2004 *Wall* advisory opinion.[194] To be sure, aside from the establishment of UNROD, there has been little follow-up by the UN on the *Wall* advisory opinion, so the

---

[192] The death of the Oslo process has long been the subject of lamentation in the secondary literature. *See* Said, E. *The End of the Peace Process* (Vintage, 2001). The 6 December 2017 recognition by the United States of Jerusalem as Israel's capital, absent any peace deal between the Palestinians and Israelis, has been widely regarded as a confirmation of this. *See* Lazaroff, T. & Wilner, M. 'World Leaders Warn Peace Process Doomed after Trump Announcement,' 6 December 2017, *Jerusalem Post*, at: www.jpost.com/Arab-Israeli-Conflict/World-leaders-warn-peace-process-doomed-after-Trump-announcement-517234#/.

[193] *See* Postscript.

[194] United Nations, 'Experts Examine "De-Palestinization" of Jerusalem, Reality on Ground at United Nations Meeting on Israeli Settlements,' Brussels, 7 September 2015, Press Release, Department of Public Information, GA/PAL/1345.

point is well taken. Nevertheless, one of the problems with this view is its mistaken assumption that even a robust follow-up on the *Wall* advisory opinion would offer a break from the rule by law inherent in the UN's conventional humanitarian/managerial approach to the OPT. What good would follow-up bring, if the only result would be to enhance the manner in which Israel maintains its over half-century occupation and colonization of the OPT?

Although the *Wall* advisory opinion identified various Israeli violations of international law and called upon it and third states to bring those violations to an end, ending the occupation was not one of them. On the contrary, as noted above, after pronouncing on the illegality of the wall, the Court went to pains to call for 'a negotiated solution to the outstanding problems and the establishment of a Palestinian State, existing side by side with Israel', thereby upholding the conventional UN position.[195] A second advisory opinion would enable the ICJ to determine that Israel's very presence in occupied Palestine has become, in and of itself, illegal, and that its end cannot reasonably be pinned to continued negotiations between what the UN's own record shows is a bad-faith occupant and a besieged and captive people, but can only be fulfilled through immediate, unconditional, and total withdrawal in line with the law of state responsibility. In this respect, Palestine could look to the 2019 *Chagos* advisory opinion for useful precedent. In that case, the General Assembly requested the ICJ to determine the legal consequences of the United Kingdom's 'continued administration' of the Chagos Archipelago, having been separated from Mauritius when the UK granted the latter its independence in 1968.[196] In determining that the process of decolonization of Mauritius was not lawfully completed in 1968, the court opined that the UK was under an obligation to bring to an end its administration of the Chagos Archipelago 'as rapidly as possible'.[197] In a subsequent resolution welcoming the advisory opinion, the General Assembly demanded that the UK 'withdraw its colonial administration from the Chagos Archipelago unconditionally within a period of no more than six months'.[198]

Of course, neither the General Assembly nor the advisory jurisdiction of the ICJ are ordinarily endowed with authority to legally bind the international community. Therefore, neither a revival of General Assembly practice nor an advisory opinion of the ICJ would in themselves result in an end of the

---

[195] *Wall, supra* note 41, para. 162.

[196] *Legal Consequences of the Separation of the Chagos Archipelago from Mauritius in 1965,* Advisory Opinion, 25 February 2019, ICJ Reports 2019, p. 95 ['Chagos'].

[197] *Id.,* para. 183.

[198] A/RES/73/295, 22 May 2019.

4 The Illegality of Israel's Continued Presence in the OPT 213

occupation. They would, however, help the Palestinian people build further legal and political momentum in the UN in support of its rights in line with the international rule of law, thereby mitigating the effects of Palestine's contingent position within the Organization. In this regard, the role of third states would be vital, given the imbalance of power between the parties and the historical record since Oslo. In addition to requiring Israel to end its occupation forthwith and unconditionally, declaring Israel's continued presence in the OPT illegal would also enable the ICJ to require all states to cooperate to bring it to an end, to not recognize it as lawful, nor to render aid or assistance in maintaining it. Questions would arise concerning the scope of what measures third states would be required to take in order to bring Israel's illegal regime in the OPT to an end. But, as noted by Crawford, although such measures 'must be through lawful means, the choice of which [to pursue] will depend on the circumstances of the given situation'.[199] Set within the context of a finding that Israel's very presence in the State of Palestine, as opposed to a narrower set of practices undertaken within it, has become illegal, the way will thus be open to require third states to do much more, individually and collectively, than they have been required to do until now under the conventional UN approach given the higher order norms involved. This could include a host of targeted economic, political, and cultural measures, taken individually or collectively through the UN, as was done in support of other subaltern groups in other similar contexts.

For an instructive precedent, we can look to Namibia and the string of cases brought before the ICJ between 1950 and 1971 in respect of its occupation by South Africa.[200] It was in the last of these opinions that the ICJ ruled that the continued presence of South Africa in Namibia was illegal, that it was under an obligation to withdraw immediately, and that third states were required to recognize this illegality and to refrain from lending support or assistance to South Africa so long as it remained in Namibia.[201] But for prior political

---

[199] Crawford, *supra* note 79 at 249.

[200] *See South-West Africa, supra* note 85; *Voting Procedure on Questions Relating to Reports and Petitions Concerning the Territory of South-West Africa*, Advisory Opinion, 7 June 1955, ICJ Reports 1955, p. 67; *Admissibility of Hearings of Petitioners by the Committee on South-West Africa*, Advisory Opinion, 1 June 1956, ICJ Reports 1956, p. 23; and *Namibia, supra* note 85. Other authors have invoked the usefulness of the Namibia precedent to the question of Palestine. *See* Lynk Report, *supra* note 71; Dugard, J. 'A Tale of Two Sacred Trusts: Namibia and Palestine' in Maluwa, T., ed., *Law, Politics and Rights* (Martinus Nijhoff, 2014); Finkelstein, *supra* note 71; and Koury, S. 'Legal Strategies at the United Nations: A Comparative Look at Namibia, Western Sahara and Palestine' in Akram, S., Dumper, M., Lynk, M. & Scobbie, I. eds., *International Law and the Israeli-Palestinian Conflict* (Routledge, 2011).

[201] *Namibia, supra* note 85, para. 133.

and legal determinations made by various organs of the UN on the question, it is possible the Court may not have arrived at the principled conclusions it did. Key among these was the 1950 ruling by the Court affirming the General Assembly's supervisory role over Namibia, resolutions of the General Assembly terminating the mandate for South Africa's failure to abide by its obligations as mandatory, and resolutions of the Security Council affirming the illegality of South Africa's continued presence in Namibia. Although it wasn't until 1988 that South Africa ended its illegal occupation of Namibia, there is little doubt that this result was given vital legal momentum by the ICJ's 1971 advisory opinion and the merger of international legality with international legitimacy represented in the Organization's work through it. For the much less powerful Namibians, having the full force of international law upon which to rely made the legitimacy of their position and that of the UN that much stronger. As noted by Judge Weeramantry in the *Nuclear Weapons* advisory opinion:

> The Court's decision on the illegality of the *apartheid* regime [i.e. in Namibia] had little prospect of compliance by the offending Government, but helped to create the climate of opinion which dismantled the structure of *apartheid*. Had the Court thought in terms of the futility of its decree, the end of apartheid may well have been long delayed, if it could have been achieved at all. The clarification of the law is an end in itself, and not merely a means to an end. When the law is clear there is greater chance of compliance than when it is shrouded in obscurity.[202]

In a similar vein, Richard Falk has noted that the 'overall purpose of relying on international legal mechanisms in the absence of prospects for compliance is to alter the political climate in ways that make the realization of Palestinian rights, including the right of self-determination, more probable'.[203] It is submitted that an advisory opinion on the legal consequences of Israel's continued settlement and occupation of the OPT would offer a similar promise of clarity and alteration of the political climate, making change for the subaltern class affected more probable.

5 CONCLUSION

This chapter has examined the UN's handling of the legal status of Israel's fifty-six-year 'temporary' military occupation of the OPT. Its basic claim is that the UN's failure to consistently and clearly take a more principled position on

---

[202] *Legality of the Threat or Use of Nuclear Weapons*, Advisory Opinion, 8 July 1996, ICJ Reports 1996, p. 226, at 550.

[203] Falk, R. *Palestine's Horizon* (Pluto, 2017) at 92.

5 Conclusion

the very legality of Israel's occupation regime exposes a fundamental chasm in its position on the OPT and is ultimately demonstrative of the continuation of the rule by law in the Organization's handling of the question of Palestine post-1967.

Decolonization brought about a shift in the UN that changed the post-war late-imperial features of the Organization responsible for the 1947 plan of partition and the resulting reification of Palestinian legal subalternity in it. Through the ostensible enfranchisement of the Third World in the UN, this shift promised to help universalize the application of international law and the UN Charter in the work of the Organization. With most of the former Afro-Asian colonies now members of the system, the legal output of the UN became the product of a more representative community of nations than had hitherto been the case. This empowerment of the Third World gave rise to a gradual recognition by the UN of Palestinian legal subjectivity and rights, including the right to self-determination in the OPT as part of the two-state framework. The conventional wisdom presents these developments as emblematic of the UN's commitment to finally uphold the international rule of law in its management of the question of Palestine.

Yet, despite these important changes, the circumscribed nature of Third World quasi-sovereignty persisted following decolonization. For the Palestinian people, this has manifested itself in the maintenance of Palestine's legal subalternity in the system, as evidenced in the UN's adoption of a humanitarian/managerial approach to the occupation of the OPT. Under this approach, the Organization has satisfied itself merely with documenting a host of individual violations by the occupying power of IHL and IHRL without definitively addressing the legality of the very regime giving rise to those violations themselves, all while insisting on negotiations as the only means through which the occupation can be brought to an end. The curiosity of this position rests in the fact that there is more than enough in the UN record to demonstrate that Israel's occupation has become illegal over time for being in violation of three *jus cogens* norms of international law: being the prohibition on the acquisition of territory through the threat or use of force, the obligation to the respect the right of peoples to self-determination, and the obligation to refrain from imposing regimes of alien subjugation, domination, and exploitation inimical to humankind, including racial discrimination and apartheid. As an internationally wrongful act, prevailing international law of state responsibility does not allow for negotiation as a prerequisite for ending Israel's occupation, but rather requires that it be ended forthwith and unconditionally. This is affirmed by UN practice in other cases of illegal occupation. What is more, by making the end of the occupation contingent on the chimera of negotiation between what the UN record demonstrates is a bad faith and immensely more powerful occupant and an enfeebled population held captive by it, the UN has in effect undermined its own position. It has thereby made the realization of Palestinian rights under international law repeatedly affirmed by it impossible to achieve, while facilitating the consolidation of the illegal actions of the occupying power that operate to violate those rights under a cloak of legitimacy provided by the Organization.

Despite the conventional wisdom, it is apparent that the UN's recognition and affirmation of Palestinian legal subjectivity and rights in the OPT post-1967 can only be regarded as nominal in nature, contingent on the exercise of hegemonic forces virtually beyond reach. Once again, the promise of international law – this time in a far more truncated portion of Palestine as even envisioned in the partition plan – is repeatedly proffered by the UN, but ultimately withheld by operation of the Organization's own failure to bring the full application of prevailing international law to bear on the situation.

To be sure, the possibility for incremental positive change exists, in so far as recourse may be had to the General Assembly and ICJ to definitively establish the UN's position on the illegality of Israel's settler-colonial occupation regime. Although largely ignored in the literature, relevant practice exists in the General Assembly going back decades in which Israel's occupation of the OPT has been qualified as illegal in itself. Were this practice to be revived, including through a judicial affirmation of the ICJ, further strides could be made in the mitigation of Palestine's contingent position within the UN system.

6

2011 and After: Membership of Palestine in the UN

1 INTRODUCTION

This chapter addresses Palestine's international legal subalternity through its attempted admission to the United Nations (UN) in 2011. The main claim is that the UN's failure to admit Palestine to full membership under operation of a procedural power of the Security Council to recommend entities for admission is the latest manifestation of the perpetuation of Palestinian contingency in the UN system. Central to this chapter is the cross-cutting theme of the role of neo-imperial power in the maintenance of legal subalternity in international law and organization.

Following the Palestine Liberation Organization's (PLO) acceptance of resolution 181(II) in 1988 and the commencement of over two decades of state-building in the Occupied Palestinian Territory (OPT) resulting from the Madrid and Oslo processes, this truncated version of Palestine made considerable legal advances on the road to being universally recognized as a state, the *sine qua non* for UN membership. By 2011, this included recognition by over two-thirds of the General Assembly, membership in a number of international intergovernmental entities, and endorsements of Palestine's statehood by the Bretton Woods institutions, among other international actors. Set against this backdrop, this chapter critically examines Palestine's bid for membership of the UN of September–November 2011. In particular, it undertakes an international law assessment of the report of the Security Council's Committee on the Admission of New Members ('Committee'), which concluded that it could not unanimously recommend Palestine for membership in the UN in accordance with Article 4(1) of the UN Charter.[1]

---

[1] *Charter of the United Nations*, 59 Stat. 1031, TS 993, 3 Bevans 1153, 24 October 1945 ['UN Charter'].

217

218 *2011 and After: Membership of Palestine in the UN*

When measured against the prevailing international law and practice governing UN membership, the record demonstrates that Palestine's failure to gain admission in 2011 was the result of United States pressure to adopt an unduly narrow and erroneous application of Article 4(1). Thereafter, Palestine turned to the General Assembly, which upgraded its observer status to that of a non-member observer state in 2012. Although the legal consequences of this upgrade have been considerable, its juxtaposition against the refusal of the Committee to recommend membership to the Security Council as a result of US pressure is demonstrative, yet again, of the rule by law principle at work. Although the UN has allowed for a gradual and qualified recognition of some Palestinian legal subjectivity and rights over time, including through Palestine's upgrade to non-member observer state, it has failed to provide it with the legal and political foundation upon which those rights have a greater chance of being realized through full membership in the Organization, ultimately helping to perpetuate Palestine's international legal subalternity.

This chapter is divided into three parts. First, it sets out the international rule of law as embodied in the law and practice governing admission to UN membership. With few exceptions, this law and practice is marked by a liberal, flexible, and permissive interpretation of Article 4(1) of the Charter, ostensibly predicated on the principle of the universality of the Organization. Second, it contrasts this against Palestine's failed membership bid in 2011. Owing to the unduly narrow and erroneous interpretation of Article 4(1) taken by some members of the Committee under US pressure, it shows that Palestine has been unfairly kept from availing itself of the full protection of its rights under international law within the Organization, despite having considerably adjusted its own claims and national development to accommodate the two-state formula imposed upon it through prior UN action. Third, it examines the implications of Palestine's turn to the General Assembly and its upgrade to non-member observer state status in 2012. In keeping with the pattern of Palestine's treatment at the UN since the decolonization period, it posits that the move to the General Assembly represents a good example of both the promise and the limits of the counter-hegemonic use of international law by subaltern actors.

2 UN MEMBERSHIP AND THE PRINCIPLE OF UNIVERSALITY

2.1 *Universality of Membership as the General Principle*

The post-1945 emergence of the UN as the standard-bearer of the international rule of law is one of the Organization's defining features. A central

2 UN Membership and the Principle of Universality 219

aspect of this has been the Organization's universality of membership. Given the general purposes of the UN, not least the safeguarding of international peace and security, it is axiomatic that it remains 'an open organization with a universal vocation'.[2] Although a handful of states have chosen to remain outside the UN (e.g. Holy See, Switzerland until 2002), that is the exception to the rule of universal membership. Today, the Organization boasts a membership of 193 states.

UN membership is governed by Chapter II of the Charter. Under Article 3, 'original' members of the UN were those states that participated in the San Francisco conference, or associated with the allied powers, and who signed and ratified the Charter in June 1945.[3] Under Article 4, acquisition of membership subsequent to the Organization's founding is governed as follows:

> (1) Membership in the United Nations is open to all other peace-loving states which accept the obligations contained in the present Charter and, in the judgment of the Organization, are able and willing to carry out these obligations;
>
> (2) The admission of any such state to membership in the United Nations will be effected by a decision of the General Assembly upon the recommendation of the Security Council.[4]

Articles 3 and 4 are similar, in so far as they envision that only *states* may be members of the UN.[5] They differ in so far as the latter imposes substantive and procedural conditions that, with the exception of the condition of statehood, do not exist under the former. Appreciating the interdependence of these conditions – the substantive and procedural – is vital for a full understanding of Article 4 as the legal gateway to UN membership and the maintenance of the Organization's universal function.

Substantively, the Article 4(1) conditions have been determined by the ICJ as subjecting UN admission to a five-part test. The applicant must: (1) be a state; (2) be peace-loving; (3) accept the obligations of the Charter; (4) be able

---

[2] Ginther, K. 'Membership: Article 4' in Simma, B. ed. *The Charter of the United Nations*, 2nd ed., Vol. II (Oxford, 2002) at 178.

[3] This was with the exception of Poland, who did not sign until October 1945. *Id.* at 173–174.

[4] UN Charter, *supra* note 1, arts. 3 & 4.

[5] Because of the lack of political independence of some original members (e.g. Belorussia, India, Philippines, and Ukraine), Higgins argues inclusion of these entities in the Organization was *sui generis*. She cites various political reasons for the inclusion of these members. Yet, from an international legal standpoint, this does not square with the ordinary meaning of the term 'state' as used in Article 3. This is particularly so because (as Higgins herself notes) the Charter's drafters consciously chose to use the term 'state' over 'nation' when the latter had been proposed by the Philippine delegation. *See* Higgins, R. *The Development of International Law through the Political Organs of the United Nations* (Oxford, 1963) at 15–16.

220   2011 and After: Membership of Palestine in the UN

to carry out those obligations; and (5) be willing to do so.[6] Procedurally, the responsibility of determining whether an applicant meets these five criteria is jointly exercised by the Security Council and the General Assembly under Article 4(2). However, because a decision of the General Assembly requires a recommendation of the Security Council, admission of new members resides, in the first instance, with the Security Council whose permanent members may utilize their veto power.[7] The political implications are self-evident. With the great powers commanding permanent seats on the Security Council, the international law governing admission of new members to the UN is open to the exercise of hegemonic interest and abuse. For those applicants who find themselves negatively subjected to the exercise of such interest and abuse, the resulting disenfranchisement exposes the limits of the international rule of law.

2.2 History of Membership in the UN

In the UN's first decade, Cold War rivalry occasioned a deadlock on admission of new members resulting from narrow, at times overtly political, interpretations of the Article 4(1) criteria.[8] Accordingly, no consensus was reached on the normative content of the criteria during this period. Between 1945 and 1955, only nine of thirty-one applicant states were admitted to membership.[9] Only after the 1955 admission of sixteen members *en bloc* did a consensus of practice emerge. Since then, Article 4(1) has been interpreted in a very liberal, flexible, and permissive manner, giving it a normative content consistent with the principle of the universality of the UN's membership.[10] This liberal, flexible, and permissive approach is characterized by a clear rejection of formality and rigidity and is aimed at ensuring as broad a representation as possible of humanity, expressed through the membership of states within the UN. It is the openness and permissiveness of this normative content of Article 4(1) that underpins the international law governing UN membership.

Even at the height of the Cold War deadlock, the position of the Organization was unanimous on the importance of universality of membership and the

---

[6] *Conditions of Admission of a State to Membership in the United Nations (Article 4 of the UN Charter)*, Advisory Opinion, ICJ Reports 1948, p. 57, at 62 ['*Conditions of Admission*'].

[7] This was affirmed by the ICJ in *Competence of the General Assembly for the Admission of a State to the United Nations*, Advisory Opinion, ICJ Reports 1950, p. 4, 10.

[8] Ginther, *supra* note 2 at 179.

[9] *Id.*

[10] Higgins, *supra* note 5 at 14; Crawford, J. *The Creation of States Under International Law*, 2nd ed. (Oxford, 2006) at 179 & 182; and Quigley, J. *The Statehood of Palestine* (Cambridge, 2010) at 236.

2 UN Membership and the Principle of Universality

need for a liberal approach. In 1946, the Secretary-General noted that the 'founding Members of the United Nations and all of the great powers which form part of our Organization have agreed, on numerous occasions, that the United Nations must be as universal as possible'.[11] For its part, the US made clear that 'the Organization should move toward universality of membership' and urged the Security Council to 'take broad and far-sighted action to extend the membership of the United Nations now as far as is consistent with the provisions of Article 4 of the Charter'.[12] The principle of universal membership was subsequently endorsed in resolutions of the General Assembly[13] and continues to be reflected in the deliberations of both the General Assembly and the Security Council.[14]

For greater clarity, in 1948 the General Assembly requested an advisory opinion from the ICJ on, *inter alia*, whether a member of the UN, when called upon to consider an application for admission under Article 4 of the Charter, is 'juridically entitled to make its consent to the admission dependent on conditions not expressly provided by paragraph 1 of the said Article'.[15] In answering negatively, a majority of the Court opined that the 'natural meaning' of the text of Article 4(1) makes clear that the five conditions for membership thereunder are 'exhaustive' and that the 'provision would lose its significance and weight, if other conditions, unconnected with those laid down, could be demanded'.[16] The Court accordingly held that 'considerations extraneous to the conditions laid down in' Article 4(1) could not be employed to 'prevent the admission of a State which complies with them'.[17] In the Court's view, this includes 'new condition[s] ... concerning States other than the applicant State'.[18] It also includes 'political considerations', so long as such considerations cannot reasonably and in good faith be connected with the exhaustive conditions of admission under Article 4.[19] In a concurring separate opinion, Judge Alvarez opined that 'all States fulfilling the conditions required by Article 4 of the Charter have a *right* to membership in that Organization' and that the 'exercise of this right cannot be blocked by the imposition of other

---

[11] UN SCOR, 1st Yr., 54th Mtg., at 44, S/PV.54 (28 August 1946).

[12] *Id.*, at 41–42.

[13] *See, e.g.*, A/RES/197B(III), 8 December 1948; A/RES/506A(VI), 1 February 1952; *and* A/RES/718(VIII), 23 October 1953.

[14] *Repertory of Practice of United Nations Organs*, UN Charter, Article 4, Vol. 1 and Supplements 1–10 (1945–2009) ['Repertory of Practice'].

[15] *Conditions of Admission, supra* note 6 at 58.

[16] *Id.*, at 62.

[17] *Id.*, at 63.

[18] *Id.*, at 65.

[19] *Id.*, at 62–63.

222   *2011 and After: Membership of Palestine in the UN*

conditions not expressly provided for by the Charter', including 'grounds of a political nature'. In his view, for member states to do otherwise would be 'an abuse of right which the Court must condemn'.[20]

The ICJ's opinion affirming the exhaustive nature of the Article 4(1) criteria remains valid today. Whether Judge Alvarez was correct in his characterization of membership as a positive right where an applicant meets those criteria is arguable, given that Article 4(1) does not expressly speak of a 'right' to membership as such. Nevertheless, Article 4(1) does provide that membership 'is open' to applicant states that meet the criteria, implying such a right. As such, Alvarez's reading is more than plausible. Indeed, in his leading study of Article 4, Thomas Grant indicates that it is now a 'presumption that any State seeking admission will be granted admission'.[21]

The *Conditions of Admission* advisory opinion was critical in limiting the influence of political factors and the imposition of other extraneous conditions in UN admissions practice. This helped set the stage for the adoption of a permissive approach to the Article 4(1) criteria. Writing in 1963, Rosalyn Higgins noted that UN practice on Article 4(1) had, as early as that time, demonstrated a 'flexibility' in approach to the criteria that had become widely evident.[22] During decolonization, the admission of new states 'took place as a rule without even mentioning the [Article 4(1)] criteria'.[23] Since 1963, of the eighty-seven successful membership applications, all but five were approved without any objection.[24] This is not to suggest that all admissions decisions have been unproblematic or automatic.[25] But it is reasonable to say that the liberal, flexible, and permissive interpretation of the Article 4(1) criteria in the vast majority of cases has reduced that Charter provision to what Konrad Ginther calls 'a mere procedural formality'.[26] Grant concurs, noting that 'in time, the substantive criteria for admission came scarcely to be implemented at all'.[27] This has ultimately led to an 'unconditional universality' of membership within the Organization as the defining feature of the international law on UN membership.[28] The following brief survey of state practice bears this out.

---

[20] *Id.*, at 71.

[21] Grant, T. *Admission to the United Nations* (Martinus Nijhoff, 2009) at 244.

[22] Higgins, *supra* note 5 at 14.

[23] Ginther, *supra* note 2 at 180.

[24] Crawford, *supra* note 10 at 180, puts the figure at 85 successful applicants between 1963 and 2005. Since then, Montenegro and South Sudan have been admitted to membership without objection.

[25] *Id.*, at 180.

[26] Ginther, *supra* note 2 at 180. *See generally*, Grant, *supra* note 21.

[27] Grant, *supra* note 21 at 52.

[28] Ginther, *supra* note 2 at 180.

3 UN PRACTICE ON MEMBERSHIP CRITERIA

3.1 Statehood

Statehood is the first criterion for UN membership. International law proffers two theories on the existence of statehood.[29] Under the constitutive theory, a state exists only if it is recognized by other states, thus rendering it a product of political facts. In contrast, under the declarative theory an entity must possess the following four qualifications, codified in the 1933 Montevideo Convention on the Rights and Duties of States: (a) a permanent population; (b) a defined territory; (c) government; and (d) capacity to enter into relations with other states.[30] Although some have suggested additional factors under this theory, such as independence, sovereignty, and effectiveness,[31] the four Montevideo requirements are the standard followed in UN admissions practice. When any additional factors have been taken into account, they have only factored *as part* of the relevant Montevideo qualifications and treatment has not been uniform. In addition, there is a slight hybridity of the two theories in UN practice, in so far as recognition figures prominently in determining the fourth of the Montevideo qualifications. As noted by James Crawford, statehood is therefore a mixed question of law and fact.[32] All of this underscores the liberal, flexible, and permissive reading that the four qualifications are given in UN practice.

Thus, with respect to a permanent population, practice indicates that a state's population need not be homogenous. For example, Indonesia, Nigeria, and Yugoslavia are UN member states[33] whose populations consist of a multiplicity of ethnic, religious, and linguistic groups. Nor does a state's population have to be *in situ* for a prescribed period. Here, the member states of Australia, Canada, New Zealand, South Africa, and the United States stand out, with their mix of indigenous peoples, and descendants of latter arrivals. Finally, there is no lower or upper limit a state's population must reach. UN

---

[29] Crawford, *supra* note 10 at 19–28.

[30] *Convention on the Rights and Duties of States Adopted by the Seventh International Conference of American States*, Montevideo, 26 December 1933, art. 1, 165 LNTS 19 at 25 ['Montevideo Convention']. Although UN practice consistently refers to the Montevideo criteria when assessing an entity's statehood, some have questioned the validity of the criteria themselves. *See*, *e.g.*, Crawford, J. 'Israel (1948–1949) and Palestine (1998–1999): Two Studies in the Creation of States' in Goodwin-Gill, G. & Talmon, S. eds. *The Reality of International Law* (Oxford, 2012) at 113.

[31] Crawford, *supra* note 10 at 46, 62–89; Higgins, *supra* note 5 at 25.

[32] Crawford, *supra* note 30 at 95.

[33] A/RES/491(V), 28 September 1950; A/RES/1492(XV), 7 October 1960; Yugoslavia was an original member.

224   *2011 and After: Membership of Palestine in the UN*

membership includes microstates such as Tuvalu, Nauru, and Palau, whose populations number in the few thousands.[34] It is clear, therefore, that the population requirement has been applied permissively in UN admissions practice.

The defined territory criterion has been similarly construed. UN admissions practice applies no minimum size a territory must be.[35] Thus, microstates such as Liechtenstein, Monaco, and San Marino did not face objections to their membership despite their diminutive areas of 160, 2, and 61 km², respectively.[36] Likewise, great allowance has been made for the extent to which a territory must be demarcated by definite borders. As noted by the ICJ in *North Sea Continental Shelf*, '[t]here is … no rule that the land frontiers of a State must be fully delimited and defined, and often in various places and for long periods they are not'.[37] The best example is Israel, which gained UN membership despite not having settled borders with its neighbours.[38] Similarly, the defined territory qualification has sometimes been questioned on the basis of competing territorial claims of other states. Nevertheless, the existence of unsettled Iraqi claims to Kuwait and Moroccan claims to Mauritania did not frustrate either in gaining UN membership.[39] It is equally clear, therefore, that the defined territory requirement has enjoyed a liberal interpretation by the UN.

In practice, the government requirement has been bound up with notions of independence and effective control over territory and public administration.[40] Accordingly, government cannot be said to exist if it is not effective and/or independent. This requirement has also been construed broadly. Thus, neither an ongoing civil war, nor a *coup d'etat* dividing central government between two warring factions, nor even the continued presence of colonial Belgian forces, were dispositive for the Congo's UN admission in September 1960.[41] Likewise,

---

[34] Crawford, *supra* note 10 at 52. A/RES/55/1, 5 September 2000; A/RES/54/2, 14 September 1999; A/RES/49/63, 15 December 1994.

[35] Grant, *supra* note 21 at 240.

[36] A/RES/45/1, 18 September 1990; A/RES/47/231, 28 May 1993; A/RES/46/231, 2 March 1992. *But see* Grant, *id.*, at 240–244, who discusses the concern, in principle, of some member states as to the ability of microstates, in general, to assume their obligations as members.

[37] *North Sea Continental Shelf*, Judgment, ICJ Reports 1969, p. 3 at 32 ['North Sea Continental Shelf'].

[38] A/RES/273(III), 11 May 1949. *See* Higgins, *supra* note 5 at 17–18. *See also* text accompanying *infra* notes 126–132.

[39] Higgins, *id.*, at 18–19. A/RES/1872(S-IV), 14 May 1963; A/RES/1631(XVI), 27 October 1961.

[40] Higgins, *id.*, at 21.

[41] A/RES/1480 (XV), 20 September 1960. Crawford, *supra* note 10 at 56. The conflict made it impossible for the General Assembly to identify which warring faction should be allocated a seat at the UN. See UN GAOR, 15th Sess., 864th Mtg., at 6, A/PV.864 (20 September 1960). On Belgium's continued presence and the deployment of UN forces, *see* S/RES/143(1960). *See also* S/RES/145(1960); S/RES/146(1960).

3 UN Practice on Membership Criteria

neither the continued presence of colonial Belgian forces, nor a UN commission's finding negating their capacity for effective government, impeded Rwanda's and Burundi's UN admission in 1962.[42] Similarly, Guinea-Bissau's UN admission was not frustrated by its colonial power, Portugal, remaining in control of the country after independence.[43] Other emblematic cases concern original members. Thus, neither Belorussia nor Ukraine were independent when the UN was formed, but were rather constituent territories of the Soviet Union, which enjoyed 'broad legislative power' over these states.[44] Likewise, both the Philippines and India were still dependent territories of the US and Great Britain, respectively, when they helped found the UN in 1945.[45] Thus, practice indicates that the degree and extent to which the criterion of government must be independent and effective has been given a very wide and flexible interpretation by the UN.

The requirement of foreign relations capacity has also been construed flexibly and permissively in UN admissions practice. Staying with Belorussia and Ukraine, the Soviet Union maintained authority over their foreign trade and external defence, and neither were authorized by Moscow to independently conclude international treaties.[46] Likewise, Monaco was admitted to UN membership in 1993, despite ceding all authority over its defence to France, agreeing to govern itself in 'complete conformity with the political, military, naval and economic interests of France' and agreeing not to conduct its international relations without prior consultation with France.[47] Similarly, Micronesia and the Marshall Islands both gained UN admission in 1991, despite ceding 'full authority and responsibility for security and defense matters' to the US, as well as agreeing to coordinate foreign policy with Washington.[48] It is apparent from these and other cases[49] that the foreign relations capacity requirement has also been furnished with a very permissive interpretation by the UN.

---

[42] *See* A/RES/1746(XVI), 27 June 1962; A/RES/1748(XVII), 18 September 1962 *and* A/RES/1749(XVII), 18 September 1962. Higgins, *supra* note 5 at 23.

[43] A/RES/3205(XXIX), 17 September 1974. *See* Quigley, *supra* note 10 at 239.

[44] Quigley, *supra* note 10 at 236–237.

[45] *Id.*, at 239.

[46] *Id.*, at 236–237.

[47] A/RES/47/231, 28 May 1993. *Treaty Establishing the Relations of France with the Principality of Monaco*, arts. 1 & 2, 17 July 1918, 981 UNTS 359, at 364. Quigley, *supra* note 10 at 239–240.

[48] A/RES/46/2, 17 September 1991; A/RES/46/3, 17 September 1991. *Compact of Free Association, United States-Federated States of Micronesia-Marshall Islands*, U.S. Congress, §311(a), 99 Stat. 1770, 1822. Quigley, *supra* note 10 at 240–242.

[49] *See generally* Grant *supra* note 21.

3.2 Peace-Loving

Being 'peace-loving' is the second criterion for UN membership. It derives from the desire of the Charter's framers to disqualify the Axis powers from immediate membership in 1945.[50] The framers also agreed that an applicant's peace-loving credentials could not be judged by reference to its domestic political institutions.[51] During decolonization, when the vast majority of UN member states were admitted, the requirement of being peace-loving was relaxed to the point of being 'of no practical importance at all'.[52] When the criterion has figured into admission determinations, it has sometimes been assessed through whether the applicant has shown sufficient respect for UN Charter principles, including non-intervention and peaceful dispute resolution.[53] Even then, the threshold has remained low. The best evidence of this is the admission of states to UN membership despite being in situations of active and/or formal war. Thus, Israel was admitted in May 1949 while still formally at war with Egypt, Jordan, Lebanon, and Syria, having only concluded armistice agreements with the former three.[54] Likewise, the Congo was admitted while embroiled in a civil war in which UN peacekeepers were deployed.[55] Finally, Bosnia and Herzegovina were admitted in 1992 while in the middle of a multi-party war that would last for three more years.[56] It is evident, therefore, that the peace-loving criteria has been interpreted very permissively in UN admissions decisions.

3.3 Acceptance, Ability, and Willingness to Carry Out Charter Obligations

Acceptance of the obligations contained in the Charter is the third criterion for UN membership. This has historically been satisfied through the submission of an instrument affixed to the membership application in which the applicant

---

[50] Ginther, *supra* note 2 at 182.

[51] *Id.*

[52] *Id.*

[53] *Id.*

[54] In the debates on Israel's application for admission in May 1949, these factors did not preclude a finding that Israel was peace-loving for the purposes of Article 4(1). *See* UN GAOR, 3rd Sess., 207th Plen. Mtg., 11 May 1949 at 306–336. *See also* text accompanying *infra* notes 175–177. *See generally, Egypt-Israel, General Armistice Agreement*, Rhodes, 23 February 1949, S/1264/Corr.1; Lebanon-Israel, General Armistice Agreement, Ras Naqura, 23 March 1949, S/1296; *Hashemite Jordan Kingdom – Israel, General Armistice Agreement*, Rhodes, 3 April 1949, S/1302/Rev.1; *Israel-Syria, General Armistice Agreement*, Hill 232, 20 July 1949, S/1353.

[55] *See supra* note 41.

[56] A/RES/46/237, 22 May 1992.

3 UN Practice on Membership Criteria

solemnly accepts the obligations of the Charter, usually 'without any reservation'.[57] As a *pro forma* act, this requirement has not given rise to difficulties in practice.

Ability and willingness to carry out Charter obligations are the fourth and fifth criteria for UN membership. These have also been given a broad and liberal application in practice. Ability was originally intended to bar from membership states that lacked sufficient material and human resources to meet their Charter obligations. Yet, the admission of states with little to no military or financial capacity (e.g. Austria, Japan, the microstates, etc.) has rendered this criterion 'practically irrelevant'.[58] As to the willingness criterion, despite an early resolution of the General Assembly suggesting that it be assessed against factors capable of objective verification, this was never formally endorsed by member states in practice.[59] This may be due to the fact that there is a considerable overlap between the willingness and peace-loving criteria.[60] It is noteworthy that according to the *Repertory of Practice of the United Nations Organs* – which as at time of writing is available for the years 1945–2009 – 'although there have been statements of position [by member states] in respect of specific interpretations of the terms 'peace-loving state' and 'able and willing' to carry out the obligations of the Charter, 'there has never been any attempt, in proposals submitted to the Council or the Assembly, to define their meaning in any general sense'.[61] This too is indicative of a desire of the UN to maintain as open and permissive an application of these criteria as possible.

3.4 General Observations

The current law on admission to membership of the UN is relatively clear. As the ICJ affirmed in 1948, the Article 4(1) criteria of the Charter are exhaustive. No condition extraneous to them may factor into an admissions assessment. This includes conditions of a political nature, so long as such conditions cannot reasonably and in good faith be connected to the criteria themselves. Once those criteria are met, a presumption, and arguably a positive right, exists for UN membership. With the exception of the UN's first decade, the Organization's admissions practice has consistently applied the Article 4(1) criteria in a liberal, flexible, and permissive manner. In many cases, and in line with the principle of the universality of UN membership, substantive application of the criteria has been dispensed with altogether.

---

[57] Provisional Rules of Procedure of the Security Council, S/96/Rev.7, Rule 58. Rules of Procedure of the General Assembly, A/520/Rev.17, Rule 134. Repertory of Practice, *supra* note 14.
[58] Ginther, *supra* note 2 at 183.
[59] A/RES/506A(VI), 1 February 1952. Grant, *supra* note 21 at 59–60.
[60] Ginther, *supra* note 2 at 184.
[61] Repertory of Practice, *supra* note 14.

228   *2011 and After: Membership of Palestine in the UN*

From the standpoint of the maintenance and development of the international rule of law, the principle of universal membership of the UN is vital.[62] Although not all member states are equally endowed with material resources and capabilities, they juridically enjoy the same standing. Because sovereign equality of states remains a pillar of the Charter-based international legal order, access to that order is best secured through UN membership. Given the Security Council's role as the effective gatekeeper of UN membership, it is therefore not hard to see how and why admission to the UN remains a site where great power interest can give rise to the replacement of the international rule of law with an international rule by law.

As noted by Simon Chesterman, Ian Johnstone, and David Malone, cases of admission to the UN 'are interesting from a policy point of view because they illustrate how restrictions on participation can be used as a kind of sanction, registering disapproval of a regime or its policies'.[63] For those on the receiving end of such sanction or disapproval, it is the contingency of their own international legal status that such decisions affirm that this book is concerned with. In underscoring the international legal subalternity of the peoples and states left out of the system, the cross-cutting theme of neo-imperial interest reminds us of the power of law as a tool for the suppression of the weak. Although substantive parameters have been set by judicial opinion and state practice on the interpretation of the Article 4(1) criteria, the procedural power vested in the UN's principal political organs to apply those criteria under Article 4(2) in good faith holds within it a most significant and, in the end, controlling authority. It is to the application of that authority in the consideration of Palestine's application for UN membership that we now turn.

4 UN MEMBERSHIP OF PALESTINE AND THE INTERNATIONAL RULE BY LAW

4.1 The 2011 Application

Palestine's application for UN membership was submitted on 23 September 2011.[64] Unsurprisingly, it was rooted in prevailing international law, not only as reflected in the long-established UN position on the question of Palestine but

---

[62] Grant, *supra* note 21 at 79.

[63] Chesterman, S., Johnstone, I. & Malone, D. *Law and Practice of the United Nations*, 2nd ed. (Oxford, 2016) at 196.

[64] Application of Palestine for Admission to Membership in the United Nations, A/66/371-S/2011/592, 23 September 2011 ['Application for Membership'].

4 UN Membership of Palestine and the International Rule by Law 229

also as regards the law governing UN membership. The application accordingly based itself, *inter alia*, on General Assembly partition resolution 181(II) of 29 November 1947 and the Declaration of Independence of the State of Palestine of 15 November 1988. Reference was made to 'the successful culmination' of Palestine's 'State-building program', endorsed by the Quartet of the Middle East Peace Process (UN, US, Russia, European Union), and to the Palestinian people's right to self-determination, as affirmed by the Security Council,[65] General Assembly,[66] and ICJ.[67] The application recalled that 'the vast majority of the international community' has accorded 'bilateral recognition to the State of Palestine on the basis of the 4 June 1967 borders, with East Jerusalem as its capital' (i.e. the occupied Palestinian territory (OPT)), and indicated that it was consistent with Palestinian refugee rights under international law. Finally, the application reaffirmed Palestine's commitment to resume negotiations with Israel on all final status issues aimed at a just, lasting, and comprehensive resolution of the Israeli-Palestinian conflict, as endorsed by the Security Council and General Assembly.[68]

Following consideration of the application, the Committee – whose membership is identical to the Security Council – issued its report indicating that it 'was unable to make a unanimous recommendation' on Palestine's admission.[69] Since then, no action has been taken on Palestine's application for membership, further consideration of which effectively remains adjourned *sine die*. In effect, Palestine's application for admission was rejected. Notwithstanding the international legal basis of Palestine's application, a critical assessment of its appraisal by the UN reveals why its effective failure can be better understood as resulting from the exercise of the international rule by law.

In assessing the report of the Committee, two general and related points are salient. First, contrary to the liberal, flexible, and permissive application of the Article 4(1) criteria that characterizes UN admissions practice, the report reveals that some members of the Committee preferred an unduly narrow

---

[65] *See, e.g.*, S/RES/2334(2016) and S/RES/1515(2003) where, insofar as the Council endorses a two-state solution as per S/RES/242(1967), it is implied that the Palestinian people has a right to self-determination in an independent State of Palestine and that the OPT is the self-determination unit within which such right is to be exercised.

[66] *See, e.g.*, A/RES/2672(XXV)(C), 8 December 1970; A/RES/3236(XXIX), 22 November 1974; A/RES/70/141, 17 December 2015.

[67] Legal Consequences of the Construction of a Wall in the Occupied Palestinian Territory, Advisory Opinion, 9 July 2004, ICJ Reports 2004, at para. 118 ['*Wall*'].

[68] Application for Membership, *supra* note 64.

[69] Report of the Committee on the Admission of New Members Concerning the Application of Palestine for Admission to Membership in the United Nations, S/2011/705, 11 November 2011 ['Report of the Committee on Admission'].

230   *2011 and After: Membership of Palestine in the UN*

and strict approach. This made the usual method of *pro forma* consensus recommendations for membership impossible to reach, thereby frustrating Palestine's admission.[70] Second, because the report of the Committee was anonymous as to the particular views of given Security Council members, it is difficult to determine from that document alone the positions of individual members. For that, we must examine other contemporaneous UN records, in particular the verbatim record of the Security Council debate for 24 October 2011. Based on that record, it was the spectre of a certain US veto that made it impossible for Palestine's application to succeed.[71] Those Security Council members that indicated they might join the US, or were otherwise unclear as to their intentions, were Bosnia and Herzegovina,[72] Colombia,[73] Gabon,[74] Germany,[75] France,[76] Nigeria,[77] Portugal,[78] and the United Kingdom.[79] This lack of clarity introduced challenges for Palestine, not least because three of these states (Bosnia and Herzegovina, Gabon, and Nigeria) already enjoy full diplomatic relations with Palestine but were generally non-committal on the issue of its UN membership owing to US pressure being brought to bear on them and other members of the Security Council.[80] However, assuming positive votes from those three states, when combined with those Security Council members that did indicate they

---

[70] Some suggest consensus is required. *See, e.g.*, Moussa, J. 'Atrocities, Accountability and the Politics of Palestinian Statehood' (2016) XIX *PYIL* 42 at 60. But practice suggests otherwise. When the Committee recommended the Republic of Nauru's admission of membership, China indicated it was unable to associate itself with that recommendation. *See* Report of the Committee on the Admission of New Members Concerning the Application of the Republic of Nauru for Admission to Membership in the United Nations, S/1999/716, 25 June 1999. *See also* Chesterman et. al, *supra* note 63 at 205.

[71] Statement of Ms. Rice (USA), UN SCOR, 66th Sess., 6636th Mtg. at 12, S/PV.6636, 24 October 2011.

[72] Statement of Mr. Barbalić (Bosnia and Herzegovina), UN SCOR, 66th Sess., 6636th Mtg. at 24, S/PV.6636, 24 October 2011.

[73] Statement of Mr. Osorio (Colombia), UN SCOR, 66th Sess., 6636th Mtg. at 28, S/PV.6636, 24 October 2011.

[74] Statement of Mr. Messone (Gabon), UN SCOR, 66th Sess., 6636th Mtg. at 22, S/PV.6636, 24 October 2011.

[75] Statement of Mr. Berger (Germany), UN SCOR, 66th Sess., 6636th Mtg. at 15, S/PV.6636, 24 October 2011.

[76] Statement of Mr. Arnaud (France), UN SCOR, 66th Sess., 6636th Mtg. at 20–21, S/PV.6636, 24 October 2011.

[77] Statement of Mrs. Ogwu (Nigeria), UN SCOR, 66th Sess., 6636th Mtg. at 28–29, S/PV.6636, 24 October 2011.

[78] Statement of Mr. Moraes (Portugal), UN SCOR, 66th Sess., 6636th Mtg. at 27, S/PV.6636, 24 October 2011.

[79] Statement of Mr. Lyall Grant (United Kingdom), UN SCOR, 66th Sess., 6636th Mtg. at 18–20, S/PV.6636, 24 October 2011.

[80] Bosnia and Herzegovina (1992); Gabon (1988); and Nigeria (1988).

4 *UN Membership of Palestine and the International Rule by Law* 231

would vote positively – Brazil,[81] China,[82] India,[83] Lebanon,[84] the Russian Federation,[85] and South Africa[86] – it was clear that Palestine might achieve a 9 to 15 majority in favour, but would never be able to overcome a US veto.

The pivotal US role in the Security Council, therefore, highlights the specific hegemonic and neo-imperial power brought to bear in the Committee's consideration of Palestine's application. The exercise of the Security Council's powers to recommend membership of an applicant under Article 4(2) is the site where the rule by law was maintained in this case. In the assessment of the Committee's report below, special consideration will thus be given not only to comparing the Committee's approach with UN admissions practice in general, but also with the ostensible long-standing support of the US for the principle of the universality of UN membership,[87] and the manifestations of that support in the admission of one other member state with a special relevance to the case at hand, namely Israel in 1949.[88] The record shows that the double standard evident in the strict approach to the Article 4(1) criteria taken by the Security Council on Palestine's application, when compared with the liberal, flexible, and permissive approach normally adopted in UN admissions practice, including in respect of Israel, is demonstrative of the international rule by law.

4.2 *Conditions Extraneous to Article 4(1) Criteria*

Some members of the Committee sought to impose conditions extraneous to the Article 4(1) criteria in their evaluation of Palestine's application. Unsurprisingly, these were rooted in the UN's long-established position conditioning the end of Israel's occupation of the OPT on negotiation, covered in Chapter 5. Thus, a view was twice expressed in the committee's report that it

---

[81] Statement of Ms. Viotti (Brazil), UN SCOR, 66th Sess., 6636th Mtg. at 16, S/PV.6636, 24 October 2011.

[82] Statement of Mr. Li Baodong (China), UN SCOR, 66th Sess., 6636th Mtg. at 16, S/PV.6636, 24 October 2011.

[83] Statement of Mr. Ahamed (India), UN SCOR, 66th Sess., 6636th Mtg. at 13, S/PV.6636, 24 October 2011.

[84] Statement of Mr. Salam (Lebanon), UN SCOR, 66th Sess., 6636th Mtg. at 25, S/PV.6636, 24 October 2011.

[85] Statement of Mr. Churkin (Russian Federation), UN SCOR, 66th Sess., 6636th Mtg. at 18, S/PV.6636, 24 October 2011.

[86] Statement of Mr. Gumbi (South Africa), UN SCOR, 66th Sess., 6636th Mtg. at 23, S/PV.6636, 24 October 2011.

[87] *See* text accompanying *supra* notes 11–12.

[88] An application by Israel in December 1948 failed, but a reapplication in May 1949. See A/RES/273(III), 11 May 1949.

2011 and After: Membership of Palestine in the UN

should take the 'broader political context' into account in its assessment.[89] It was also noted that 'a two-State solution via a negotiated settlement remained the only option for a long-term sustainable peace and that final status issues had to be resolved through negotiations'.[90] Similarly, it was stated that 'the Committee's work should not harm the prospects of the resumption of peace talks' and 'that the Palestinian application would not bring the parities closer to peace'.[91] This reflects the views of the US, whose representative stated in the October 2011 Security Council debate that 'we believe that Palestinian efforts to seek Member State status at the United Nations will not advance the peace process, but rather will complicate, delay and perhaps derail prospects for a negotiated settlement. Therefore, we have consistently opposed such unilateral initiatives'.[92] Joining the US in that debate, specifically in referencing negotiations as the only means to Palestinian statehood (and, perforce, UN membership), were Colombia,[93] Germany,[94] and Portugal.[95]

To begin with, the notion 'broader political context' is so imprecise as to admit of no relevance to the Article 4(1) analysis. Furthermore, although a willingness to engage in peaceful resolution of disputes is relevant to the Article 4(1) 'peace-loving' criterion (below), UN admissions practice does not condition membership on successfully *concluding* negotiated peace with belligerent states. Indeed, underscoring the hypocritical nature of the US position on Palestine's application, Israel itself was admitted to membership in May 1949 with US support, yet had not concluded peace agreements with its neighbours, a fact readily acknowledged by the US at the time.[96] Likewise, the existence of statehood depends upon the fulfilment of the four Montevideo requirements, not the conclusion of peace agreements. Both the 'broader political context' and 'successful negotiations' conditions run afoul of the exhaustive

---

[89] Report of the Committee on Admission, *supra* note 69, paras. 4 & 6.

[90] *Id.*, para. 6.

[91] *Id.*, para. 7.

[92] Statement of Ms. Rice (USA), UN SCOR, 66th Sess., 6636th Mtg. at 12, S/PV.6636, 24 October 2011.

[93] Statement of Mr. Osorio (Colombia), UN SCOR, 66th Sess., 6636th Mtg. at 28, S/PV.6636, 24 October 2011 ('We understand and support the aspiration of the Palestinian people to have a State...', but 'negotiation is the only possible and robust path to achieve that objective').

[94] Statement of Mr. Berger (Germany), UN SCOR, 66th Sess., 6636th Mtg. at 15, S/PV.6636, 24 October 2011 ('As a matter of course', a Palestinian 'State will become a Member of the United Nations. But ... [t]here is no viable alternative to the resumption of negotiations. The two-State solution can be achieved only through a peace agreement').

[95] Statement of Mr. Moraes (Portugal), UN SCOR, 66th Sess., 6636th Mtg. at 27, S/PV.6636, 24 October 2011 ('[A]n independent and sovereign [Palestinian] State ... can be achieved only with direct and meaningful negotiations with their Israeli neighbours').

[96] *See* UN GAOR, 3rd Sess., 207th Plen. Mtg., 11 May 1949 at 306–336. *See also* text accompanying *infra* notes 197–198.

4 UN Membership of Palestine and the International Rule by Law   233

character of the Article 4(1) criteria as affirmed by the ICJ.[97] Neither can they be regarded reasonably and in good faith as permissive political considerations of relevance to any of those criteria in light of UN admissions practice.[98] In effect, these requirements constitute, in the words of the ICJ, 'new' and 'extraneous' conditions, improperly invoked to 'prevent the admission of a State'.[99]

Some members of the Committee rejected this approach. The *Conditions of Admission* Advisory Opinion was cited as affirming the exhaustive character of the Article 4(1) criteria.[100] At any rate, it was stated, 'Palestine's application was neither detrimental to the political process nor an alternative to negotiations'.[101] Were it otherwise, it was argued, 'Palestinian statehood would be made dependent on the approval of Israel, which would grant the occupying Power a right of veto over the right of self-determination of the Palestinian people'.[102] Of note, none of the final status issues to be negotiated between Israel and Palestine include the Palestinian right to statehood.[103] Indeed, Palestine informed the Security Council that it did not see any contradiction between negotiations with Israel over the final status issues and Palestine's application for membership. Rather, the two were 'mutually reinforcing'.[104]

Nevertheless, the imposition of factors extraneous to the Article 4(1) conditions by the US and others helped frustrate Palestine's admission. Interestingly, when Israel applied for membership, the US also cited extraneous factors, but only to argue the case *for* admission. Thus, on 2 December 1948, Philip Jessup, then US Ambassador-at-Large, informed the Security Council that 'something more' than the Article 4(1) criteria was 'being dealt with' in Israel's case; the Security Council was 'dealing here with the desire of a people who laboriously constructed a community, an authority and, finally a Government

---

[97] *Conditions of Admission, supra* note 6 at 62.

[98] *Id.,* at 62–63.

[99] *Conditions of Admission, supra* note 6 at 63 & 65.

[100] Report of the Committee on Admission, *supra* note 69, para. 5.

[101] *Id.,* para 7.

[102] *Id.* This was the position taken by Lebanon, who's ambassador articulated it publicly in the Security Council debate of 24 October 2011. *See* statement of Mr. Salam (Lebanon), UN SCOR, 66th Sess., 6636th Mtg. at 25, S/PV.6636, 24 October 2011.

[103] These are: Jerusalem, refugees, settlements, security and borders. *See* Declaration of Principles on Interim Self-Governing Arrangements, Israel-Palestine Liberation Organization, Art. V, 13 September 1993, 32 I.L.M. 1525, at 1529 ['Oslo I']. The issue of water would later be added. *See* statement of Mr. Mansour (Palestine), UN SCOR, 66th Sess., 6636th Mtg. at 8, S/PV.6636, 24 October 2011.

[104] *Id.,* at 6. The representative of Palestine also stated, *id.,* at 8, that: 'While committed to the peace process, we must reiterate clearly that the right of the Palestinian people to self-determination, freedom and independence is not up for negotiation, nor will it be the product of negotiations. It is an inalienable right and the sole domain of the Palestinian people. It has never been an issue for negotiations with Israel, nor will it ever be.'

234   *2011 and After: Membership of Palestine in the UN*

operating in an independent State, to see the State which they have thus arduously built take its place among the Members of the United Nations'.[105] Notably, Jessup conveniently overlooked the fact that the community being 'laboriously constructed' was, in real time, being forged through the mass expulsion of Palestine's indigenous population and the expansion of the putative new state's borders beyond those delimited by the General Assembly only months earlier.[106]

4.3 Statehood

UN practice on the first of the Article 4(1) criteria – that the applicant be a 'state' – has been very liberal.[107] It is unsurprising, therefore, to find that the US view regarding Israel's membership application was equally liberal. In the December 1948 Security Council debate on Israel's membership, Jessup opined that the term 'State' as used in Article 4(1) 'may not be wholly identical with the term "State" as it is used and defined in classic textbooks of international law'.[108] Although in that case, the US would nevertheless apply a close approximation of the Montevideo definition, its disposition was clearly to do so less vigorously than required.[109]

In the Committee's report concerning Palestine, there was no disagreement on the first of the four Montevideo requirements for statehood, namely a permanent population.[110] The OPT has a population of 4.5 million people,[111] thereby satisfying this requirement. Perhaps because of the indigeneity of this population and its historical tenure going back millennia, there was no need

---

[105] UN SCOR, 3rd Yr., 383rd Mtg., 2 December 1948, at 13–14. Jessup was given wide latitude by Washington to frame his government's arguments on Israel's admission. *See* Jessup, P. *The Birth of Nations* (Columbia, 1974) at 294.

[106] By that time the majority of the 750,000–900,000 Palestinian refugees were forcibly expelled by Zionist regular and irregular forces. *See* Morris, B. *The Birth of the Palestinian Refugee Problem Revisited* (Cambridge, 2004). This was a matter that would have been well known to Jessup, as the issue was actively being discussed in the General Assembly which, only nine days after he delivered his remarks to the Security Council, passed its own resolution affirming, *inter alia*, the right of the refugees to return to their homes. *See* A/RES/194(III), 11 December 1948. *See also* the statement of the representative of Syria, UN SCOR, 3rd Yr., 384th Mtg., 15 December 1948, at 25.

[107] *See* text accompanying *supra* notes 29–49.

[108] UN SCOR, 3rd Yr., 383rd Mtg., 2 December 1948, at 10.

[109] Wählisch, M. 'Beyond a Seat in the United Nations: Palestine's UN Membership and International Law' (June 2012) 53 *Harvard ILJ Online* 226 at 241.

[110] Report of the Committee on Admission, *supra* note 69, para. 10.

[111] *Estimated Population of the Palestinian Territory Mid-year by Governorate 1997–2016*, Palestinian Central Bureau of Statistics, at: www.pcbs.gov.ps/Portals/_Rainbow/Documents/gover_e.htm.

4 UN Membership of Palestine and the International Rule by Law   235

for the Committee to employ the usual wide appreciation given to this criterion in practice.[112] The same cannot be said of the flexibility with which the US argued for Israel's admission in 1948–1949.[113]

At that time, in recounting 'the traditional definition of a State in international law' before the Security Council, Jessup curiously asserted that the existence of 'a people' was the relevant qualification.[114] But as an expression of prevailing treaty and customary law in 1948, Montevideo referred to 'a permanent population', not a 'people'.[115] This was possibly done because the Jewish Agency's case for the existence of the State of Israel was based, in part, on its claim to be the state of the Jewish *people* as a whole, rather than of the whole of Palestine's population whose majority was indigenous Arab. This may explain Jessup's other curious assertion – uttered when the expulsion of the Palestinian Arabs hit its peak – that '[n]obody questions the fact that the State of Israel has a people. It is an extremely homogenous people, a people full of loyalty and enthusiastic devotion to the State of Israel'.[116] It is telling that in his discussion of the requirements of statehood in his own 1949 international law treatise, Jessup himself referred to 'a population' rather than a 'people', in deference to the Montevideo standard.[117] Be that as it may, these American interventions before the Security Council contributed to a very liberal understanding of this branch of Montevideo qualifications in favour of Israel, highlighting the malleability of the Article 4(1) requirements and emphasizing the incongruity of the American position on Palestine in 2011.

The Committee's assessment of Palestine's fulfilment of the second requirement of a defined territory was a matter of disagreement. Those in favour of admission correctly 'stressed that the lack of precisely settled borders was not an obstacle to statehood'.[118] Nevertheless, some members of the Security Council disputed Palestine's satisfaction of this qualification by questioning

---

[112] *See* text accompanying *supra* notes 33–34.

[113] *See supra* note 106 along with accompanying text.

[114] UN SCOR, 3rd Yr., 383rd Mtg., 2 December 1948, at 10.

[115] Montevideo Convention, supra note 30, art. 1.

[116] UN SCOR, 3rd Yr., 383rd Mtg., 2 December 1948, at 11. Jessup's position did not go unchallenged. In response to the US position that Israel had a permanent population, the Syrian representative pressed him: '[W]here are the people? Half the people of the territory which they [i.e. the Zionists] occupy have been expelled and dispersed throughout the country. They are now homeless, starving and dying. These are the people of the territory which they are occupying ... How can he [i.e. Jessup] say that [t]his people [i.e. those of Israel] are peace-loving and are complying with the requirements of Article 4 of the Charter?' *See* UN SCOR, 3rd Yr., 383rd Mtg., 2 December 1948, at 19.

[117] Jessup, P. A *Modern Law of Nations* (Macmillan, 1949) at 46.

[118] Report of the Committee on Admission, *supra* note 69, para. 10. *See* text accompanying *supra* notes 37–39.

its *control* over its territory. In support of this contention, both the *de facto* control of the Gaza Strip by Hamas and the Israeli occupation of the OPT were raised.[119] Although these factors might have some connection to the third Montevideo qualification of government (below), they have no relevance to the ground of a defined territory. This line of argument confuses two branches of the test for statehood.

The borders of what is today the OPT were set by UN-mediated armistice negotiations in 1949[120] and, since the PLO's 1988 recognition of Israel, have been accepted as delimiting the territorial unit within which the Palestinian people is entitled to exercise its right to self-determination.[121] Although these borders still need to be finalized through some form of agreement, the fact that they are unsettled does not render them insufficiently clear under the Montevideo test. That there has been a quarrel between Palestine's two main political parties (Fatah and Hamas) manifesting in a partially separate administration of the Gaza Strip from the West Bank has no logical impact on the existence of the OPT as a defined territory, as such. Nor does Israel's military occupation of the OPT detract from the sufficiently defined nature of Palestine's territorial sphere. As covered in Chapter 5, Israel is legally debarred from asserting its sovereignty over the OPT in any form given its status as an occupying Power.[122] Likewise, the only other state that has ever laid claim (and only then to a portion) of the OPT, namely Jordan, has since 1988 relinquished such claim in favour of the Palestinian people.[123] Nor does the fact that the territory of Palestine is physically discontiguous (i.e. between the West Bank, including East Jerusalem, and the Gaza Strip) frustrate this branch of Montevideo.[124] There are many UN member states that share that characteristic,[125] most prominently the US.

To appreciate the incongruity applied in Palestine's case, it is useful to examine the Security Council's treatment of the defined territory criterion in Israel's membership application, paying note of the US position at the time. The application was submitted during the 1948 war, when the territory originally allotted to the putative Jewish State in General Assembly resolution 181(II) was being considerably expanded through Zionist military and paramilitary operations.

---

[119] Report of the Committee on Admission, *supra* note 69, para. 11.
[120] See Egypt-Israel *and* Jordan-Israel armistice agreements, *supra* note 54.
[121] A/RES/43/177, 15 December 1988.
[122] This view was also affirmed by some members of the Committee. Report of the Committee on Admission, *supra* note 69, para. 11.
[123] Address to the Nation, King Hussein, Amman, 31 July 1988, at: www.un.org/unispal/test-page-date/.
[124] Quigley, *supra* note 10 at 210.
[125] E.g., Anglola, Azerbaijan, Brunei Darusasalam, East Timor, Oman, United Arab Emirates, and the US.

4 *UN Membership of Palestine and the International Rule by Law* 237

Syria objected that Israel 'has no boundaries' and therefore could not satisfy the defined territory branch of Montevideo.[126] In response, Jessup reminded the Security Council that '[o]ne does not find in the general classic treatment of this subject any insistence that the territory of a State must be exactly fixed by definite frontiers'.[127] He noted that 'many States have begun their existence with their frontiers unsettled', citing the expansion of the 'indeterminate' US frontier into 'land [that] had not even been explored'.[128] He concluded that 'the concept of territory does not necessarily include precise delimitation of the boundaries of that territory'.[129] This position influenced other members of the Security Council,[130] paving the way for Israel's admission. According to Higgins, 'Israel's admission is the best example of the statehood criterion of "defined territory"' because it reveals that 'this criterion has never been interpreted very strictly'.[131] In her view, 'given its customary liberal interpretation' in UN admissions practice, it was 'properly applied' in Israel's case.[132] Considering the permissive state of the law, it is hard to argue that Palestine's territory would not objectively meet this threshold. Yet that was the effect of the position taken by some members of the Committee under US pressure.

On the third Montevideo requirement, members of the Committee differed as to whether Palestine possessed an effective and independent government. Those arguing for admission cited reports of the World Bank, the International Monetary Fund and the Ad Hoc Liaison Committee for the Coordination of the International Assistance to Palestinians, all of which 'concluded that Palestine's governmental functions were now sufficient for the functioning of a State'.[133] The Quartet endorsed, largely EU-funded, state-building effort that evolved during the Oslo period built upon governmental institutions and legal structures inherited from the Ottoman, British, and Jordanian periods of control.[134] Despite being under military occupation, Palestine formally boasts

---

[126] UN SCOR, 3rd Yr., 383rd Mtg., 2 December 1948, at 19.

[127] *Id.*, at 11.

[128] *Id.* This is telling, in so far as Jessup failed to consider the claims of Native Americans in his assessment.

[129] *Id.*

[130] For example, even though the Zionists were expanding their control over a greater portion of Palestine than had been allotted the Jewish State under the partition resolution, the Soviet Union took the view that Israel's territory had been sufficiently defined through A/RES/181(II). *Id.*, at 22–23.

[131] Higgins, *supra* note 5 at 20.

[132] *Id.*

[133] Report of the Committee on Admission, *supra* note 69, para. 13.

[134] As noted by Quigley, *supra* note 10 at 214, 'a decree issued May 20, 1994, recites that "the laws, regulations and orders in force before June 5, 1967 in the West Bank and the Gaza Strip shall remain in force until unified"'.

238   *2011 and After: Membership of Palestine in the UN*

a constitutional parliamentary system, with executive, legislative, and judicial branches of government.[135] Its ministries serve across areas A and B of the OPT, covering *inter alia* education, finance, foreign affairs, health, interior, justice, labour, planning, and social affairs.[136] Its civil service now numbers in the tens of thousands and includes security and police services.[137]

Some Committee members nevertheless argued that Palestine failed the effective and independent governmental control test because since the 2007 split between Fatah and Hamas, the latter has been 'in control of 40 per cent of the population of Palestine' (i.e. Gaza). As such, it was argued that Palestine 'could not be considered to have effective government control over the claimed territory'.[138] In addition, the Israeli occupation was cited as 'a factor in preventing the Palestinian government from exercising full control over its territory'.[139] When measured against the broad and permissive UN admissions practice, these claims are revealed as both unduly narrow and, at times, confused.

A split in government – even by civil war – does not negate the existence of the effective government under Montevideo.[140] In Palestine's case, with the exception of a five-day period of armed street clashes in Gaza in 2007, the division between Fatah and Hamas has never descended to anything approximating civil war, remaining largely a matter of internal domestic legitimacy and function. As noted by Quigley, 'the fact that the administrative authority became split created practical difficulties', such as payment of civil service salaries in Gaza, but such difficulties are 'not relevant to the governance criterion for statehood'.[141] Although the split raises 'questions about the legitimacy of the governing institutions under domestic Palestine law', legitimacy of government has no bearing on the existence of statehood.[142] To be sure, the PLO (led by the West Bank-based Fatah party) continues to represent Palestine

---

[135] *Id.* at 215. Higgins, *supra* note 5 at 21, notes that in early practice some states exhibited a tendency to interpret the government qualification as needing to be democratic. Subsequent practice indicates that the lower standard of effectiveness has been preferred. *See* Grant, *supra* note 21 at 157, who says that democracy's connection, if any, to the criteria for admission under Article 4(1) is 'obscure' and tenuous at best.

[136] Permanent Observer Mission of the State of Palestine to the United Nations, New York, 'Government of the State of Palestine,' at: http://palestineun.org/about-palestine/government-of-the-state-of-palestine/.

[137] Quigley, *supra* note 10 at 214.

[138] Report of the Committee on Admission, *supra* note 69, para. 12.

[139] *Id.*, paras. 11–12.

[140] *See* text accompanying *supra* note 41. *See also* Higgins, *supra* note 5 at 21–22.

[141] Quigley, *supra* note 10 at 216.

[142] *Id.*, at 217.

4 UN Membership of Palestine and the International Rule by Law   239

internationally, including at the UN, and Hamas has effectively regarded itself as falling under it for that purpose.[143]

The assertion that the Fatah-Hamas split deprives Palestine of effective and independent government in the OPT suffers from another defect. It confuses the distinct issues of recognition of states with recognition of governments under international law.[144] As noted by Jasmine Moussa, '[i]t is not uncommon for a State to lack control over a particular part of its territory. This does not mean that its statehood can be denied' on the basis that the governing authorities are not internationally recognized.[145] This confusion arose in the Security Council debates concerning Israel's admission in 1949. Only in that case, the US made sure the Security Council did not let it get in the way of admission. Syria attempted to invalidate US recognition of Israel in May 1948 by arguing that that recognition was limited to Israel's provisional government as a *de facto* authority, rather than Israel as a *de jure* state.[146] In response, Jessup clarified that the Syrian objection suffered from 'some confusion … between recognition of the state of Israel and recognition of the provisional government of Israel'.[147] The two were distinct. Jessup affirmed that in entertaining Israel's application for membership, it was the former that the Security Council was concerned with, and it was to that end that the US's act of recognition of the State of Israel was to be understood.[148]

As to the claim that the occupation of Palestine negates its possession of effective and independent government, it is well to recall the many cases of states who were admitted to, or formed the original membership of, the UN while lacking independent government.[149] What renders Palestine's case even more clear-cut is the fact that the impediment to the full exercise of independence is a prolonged illegal occupation regime that, under international law, cannot override the sovereign right of the people to exercise self-determination in the territory in question. As opposed to temporarily administering the territory in the best interests of this people in accordance with its obligations under international law, the occupying power has systematically sought to permanently frustrate that people's right to self-determination through, *inter alia*, the unlawful annexation of the territory and the transfer of its own civilian

---

[143] *Id.*
[144] Moussa, *supra* note 70 at 58.
[145] *Id.*
[146] UN SCOR, 3rd Yr., 384th Mtg., 15 December 1948, at 25.
[147] UN SCOR, 3rd Yr., 385th Mtg., 17 December 1948, at 12.
[148] *Id.*
[149] This includes Belorussia, Burundi, Congo, Guinea-Bissau, India, Philippines, Rwanda, and Ukraine. *See* text accompanying *supra* notes 40–49.

240   *2011 and After: Membership of Palestine in the UN*

population into it.[150] It is therefore absurd to frustrate Palestine's admission by suggesting that it has not attained a sufficient level of independent and effective governmental control over its own territory owing to the illegal acts of the occupying power. As noted by the Lebanese delegate to the Security Council, to do so would be to furnish the occupying power with the authority to deny the realization of Palestine statehood *ad infinitum*, including the right of its people to self-determination.[151] In addition, as demonstrated by the cases of Denmark, France, and Kuwait, the mere fact of occupation does not negate the existence of the occupied state. This was the US view when it supported occupied Austria's membership application in 1947.[152] Although Crawford has argued that such cases are distinct from Palestine because they involve states that 'were once incontestably established as such',[153] Quigley rightly points out that because no other state can legitimately lay claim to the OPT, 'there is no reason in principle why a [Palestine] state cannot be brought into being under such circumstances'.[154]

Finally, regarding the fourth Montevideo requirement, the Committee differed on whether Palestine possessed foreign relations capacity. Some members questioned the capacity of the Palestinian Authority (PA) to engage in relations with other States, 'since under the Oslo Accords the Palestinian Authority could not engage in foreign relations'.[155] The trouble with this view is that it runs contrary to the liberal, flexible, and permissive interpretation given to this branch of Montevideo in UN admissions practice[156] and is only partially

---

[150] *See, e.g., Report of the Special Rapporteur on the Situation of Human Rights in the Palestinian Territories Occupied Since 1967*, A/72/43106, 23 October 2017

[151] *See* text accompanying *supra* note 102. Writing in 1999, prior to the achievements of the Palestinian state-building effort established by 2011, Crawford took the view that Palestine could not be a state owing to the fact that Israel's occupation deprives it of independent government. Yet, he qualified this by saying that '[t]here may come a point where international law (like English equity) is justified in regarding as done that which ought to have been done, if the reason it has not been done is the serious default of one party, and if the consequence of its not being done is serious prejudice to another, innocent, party. The principle that a state cannot rely on its own wrongful conduct to avoid the consequences of its international obligations is capable of novel applications, and circumstances can be imagined where the international community would be entitled to treat a new state as existing on a given territory, notwithstanding the facts.' *See* Crawford, *supra* note 30 at 24.

[152] *See* statement of Mr. Johhson (USA), UN SCOR, 2nd Yr., 119th Mtg., 21 August 1947, at 2128–2129 ('We all know that, in the case of Austria, there is military occupation. But I submit that this does not impair Austria's sovereignty in the field of international relations, which is the important point to consider in deciding whether Austria is eligible to become a Member of the United Nations at this time').

[153] Crawford, *supra* note 30 at 115.

[154] Quigley, *supra* note 10 at 221.

[155] Report of the Committee on Admission, *supra* note 69, para. 14.

[156] *See* text accompanying *supra* notes 46–49.

4 UN Membership of Palestine and the International Rule by Law   241

accurate on fact. Unlike some states, Palestine has never ceded its foreign relations capacity to another state. That capacity has always been performed by the PLO on behalf of the Palestinian people, as affirmed by decades of UN practice going back to 1974.[157] Indeed, it was the act of the PLO entering into the Oslo accords with Israel under US auspices that created the PA in the first place.[158] Although it is true that Oslo deprived the PA of 'powers and responsibilities in the sphere of foreign relations', it also expressly provided that those powers would be conducted by the PLO on the PA's behalf – a fact not mentioned in the Committee's report.[159] Moreover, since 1988, the designation 'Palestine' has been used in place of 'PLO' at the UN. Palestine has thus demonstrated a capacity to enter into foreign relations through the PLO, which has resulted in a robust diplomatic and treaty practice at the UN and with Israel itself.

The issue of foreign relations capacity returns us to the hybridity of the declaratory and constitutive theories of statehood, the nexus of which is the act of recognition. As noted by Higgins, UN practice 'undeniably reveals that most member states have considered the issue of recognition as relevant' in the Montevideo analysis, as 'it is evidence of the international status of an applicant' for membership.[160] Thus, those members of the Committee that favoured Palestine's application pointed to Palestine's membership in the Non-Aligned Movement, the Organization of Islamic Cooperation, the Economic and Social Commission for Western Asia, the Group of 77, and the United Nations Educational, Scientific and Cultural Organization as evidence of its foreign relations capacity. Most significantly, they noted that 'over 130 States had recognized Palestine as an independent sovereign State'.[161] As noted by Quigley, this level of recognition has given rise to Palestine's rich treaty and diplomatic/consular relations practice, the latter of which allow it to 'perform the tasks that are typical of diplomatic missions, maintaining political contact with host states'.[162] Based on the wide ambit afforded the foreign relations capacity branch of Montevideo in UN admissions practice, it is hard to suggest that Palestine does not meet the required threshold.

---

[157] See e.g., A/RES/3210(XXIX), 14 October 1974; A/RES/3237(XXIX), 22 November 1974; A/RES/43/177, 15 December 1988.

[158] See. e.g., Oslo I, supra note 103.

[159] Interim Agreement on the West Bank and Gaza Strip, Israel-Palestine Liberation Organization, Art. IX(5), 28 September 1995, 36 I.L.M. 551 at 561.

[160] Higgins, supra note 5 at 42.

[161] Report of the Committee on Admission, supra note 69, para. 14. As at the time of writing this figure has increased to 139 states. See Permanent Observer Mission of the State of Palestine to the United Nations, 'Diplomatic Relations,' at: http://palestineun.org/about-palestine/diplomatic-relations/.

[162] Quigley, supra note 10 at 211–213.

242   *2011 and After: Membership of Palestine in the UN*

The Committee's unduly narrow approach in assessing this requirement in Palestine's application is once again underscored by the different position of the US concerning Israel's application in 1948–1949. In urging the Security Council to take a liberal approach then, Jessup noted that 'we already have, among the Members of the United Nations, some political entities which do not possess full sovereign freedom to form their own international policy'.[163] He noted 'that neither at San Francisco nor subsequently has the United Nations considered that complete freedom to frame and manage one's own foreign policy was an essential requisite of United Nations membership'.[164] In view of the US position then, and its subsequent reflection in wider UN practice, the fact that Palestine's case failed to garner the full support of the Committee on this ground is striking.

4.4 *Peace-Loving*

Some members of the Committee questioned Palestine's satisfaction of the second Article 4(1) criteria, namely its peace-loving character. They cited Hamas's refusal 'to renounce terrorism and violence'.[165] Although it is true that Hamas has engaged in low-intensity armed operations against the occupying power, it is also true that the movement has often transgressed the laws of war while doing so in ways typical of the modus operandi of non-state actors engaged in asymmetrical conflict.[166] This has not stopped Israel from negotiating agreements with it (e.g. truce, prisoner exchange, etc.).[167] Based on relevant international law and practice, none of these facts seem to be reason enough to disqualify Palestine's character as a peace-loving state.

The flexibility applied on this condition has been very wide in practice.[168] Palestine has demonstrated a commitment to pacifically resolving its dispute with Israel. Rooted in the PLO's recognition of Israel and the two-state formula in 1988, this commitment is manifest in almost three decades of engagement in negotiations to that end. It was unequivocally reiterated in both Palestine's application for membership as well as in the October 2011 Security

---

[163] UN SCOR, 3rd Yr., 383rd Mtg., 2 December 1948, at 10.

[164] *Id.*

[165] Report of the Committee on Admission, *supra* note 69, para. 16.

[166] See *Report of the United Nations Fact-Finding Mission on the Gaza Conflict*, A/HRC/12/48, 25 September 2009.

[167] At the time of Palestine's application for membership, Israel had just negotiated an exchange of prisoners with Hamas. *See* statement of Mr. Ahamed (India), UN SCOR, 66th Sess., 6636th Mtg at 14, S/PV.6636, 24 October 2011.

[168] *See* text accompanying *supra* notes 50–56.

4 UN Membership of Palestine and the International Rule by Law   243

Council debate.[169] It was additionally demonstrated through Palestine's extensive resort to multilateralism, including diplomatic and legal mechanisms of dispute resolution at the UN, as evident in its active support and reliance on the ICJ in 2004.[170] Thus, those members of the Committee in favour of Palestine's membership noted that Palestine was peace-loving 'in view of its commitment to the achievement of a just, lasting and comprehensive resolution of the Israeli-Palestinian conflict'.[171] For them, 'Palestine's fulfilment of this criterion was also evident in its commitment to resuming negotiations on all final status issues on the basis of the internationally endorsed terms of reference, relevant United Nations resolutions, the Madrid principles, the Arab Peace Initiative and the Quartet road map'.[172] The representative of Brazil put it best when she said that '[t]he ultimate demonstration that Palestine is a peace-loving State is precisely the decision to turn to international law and to the United Nations to realize its legitimate right to self-determination'.[173] In her view, '[i]nternational recognition of the Palestinian State and its admission in the United Nations as a full Member can help reduce the asymmetry that at present characterizes relations between the parties'.[174]

Merely being committed to peace negotiations has been deemed enough to satisfy the peace-loving criterion in UN admissions practice.[175] Thus, when Austria was considered for membership while under quadripartite Allied occupation in 1947, the US took the position that the absence of a peace treaty with the occupying powers did not disqualify it from membership.[176] Furthermore, when Israel's admission was approved in 1949, the US took the view that the mere promise of peace, as offered by Israel, was enough for it to pass the threshold. In arguing that Israeli admission should be approved, the US representative proclaimed that '[a] solid foundation for peace and stability in Palestine had been laid by the armistice agreements concluded between

---

[169] See Application for Membership, supra note 64; and statement of Mr. Mansour (Palestine), UN SCOR, 66th Sess., 6636th Mtg. at 7, S/PV.6636, 24 October 2011.

[170] Wall, supra note 67.

[171] Report of the Committee on Admission, supra note 69, para. 15.

[172] Id.

[173] Statement of Ms. Viotti (Brazil), UN SCOR, 66th Sess., 6636th Mtg. at 17, S/PV.6636, 24 October 2011.

[174] Id.

[175] See text accompanying supra notes 53–54.

[176] Statement of Mr. Johnson (USA), UN SCOR, 2nd Yr., 119th Mtg., 21 August 1947, at 2129 ('… the projected Austrian treaty is not a peace treaty essential to the restoration of good relations between former belligerents. […] … its conclusion is not in any way necessary to the establishment of normal relations between Austria and Members of the United Nations, [n]or … is [it] a prerequisite to the admission of Austria to the United Nations'). Austria was admitted to membership in 1955. See A/RES/995(X), 14 December 1955.

244   *2011 and After: Membership of Palestine in the UN*

Israel and *most* of the Arab States [i.e. Egypt, Jordan, and Lebanon]', that an armistice agreement with Syria was 'still in the process of negotiation' and that it was enough to 'hope' that an agreement would be concluded in the near future.[177] It bears recalling that at the time of Israel's application, Zionist and then Israeli forces were engaged in the systematic expulsion of the indigenous population from the country.[178] As discussed in greater depth below, these matters were well understood by UN member states, yet none of this was enough to taint Israel's peace-loving character.

Given the pivotal role played by the US in frustrating Palestine's 2011 membership application, the relevance of the above is not insignificant. Far from being a passive observer of the thirty-year Israeli–Palestinian peace process, the US has been its principal sponsor. The US is thus aware of Palestine's commitment to pacifically resolve the conflict based on relevant international law as outlined in UN resolutions and decisions. The fact that a final peace has yet to be concluded should not, as a matter of law and practice, detract from a determination that Palestine is sufficiently peace-loving under Article 4(1).

Both the Indian and South African representatives to the Security Council rejected conditioning Palestine's membership upon the conclusion of a peace agreement with Israel, the former rightly indicating that to do so would be 'legally untenable'.[179] Nevertheless, because of the unduly narrow position adopted by some members of the Security Council, including the hypocritical one adopted by the US, Palestine's peace-loving character was sufficiently impugned to block membership.

4.5 Acceptance, Ability, and Willingness to Carry Out Charter Obligations

Notwithstanding the very wide latitude given to the third, fourth, and fifth criteria in practice[180] – acceptance of Charter obligations and ability and willingness to carry them out – some members of the Committee concluded that Palestine did not satisfy these conditions. In particular, it was argued that 'the Charter required more than a verbal commitment' to this effect and that 'an

---

[177] Statement of Mr. Austin (USA), UN GAOR, 3rd Sess., 207th Plen. Mtg., 11 May 1949, at 313–314. Notably, the requirement of reaching peace with the Palestinian people did not figure in the US view. Wählisch, *supra* note 109 at 240–241.

[178] *See* Chapter 4, section 3.

[179] *See* statement of Mr. Ahamed (India), UN SCOR, 66th Sess., 6636th Mtg. at 14, S/PV.6636, 24 October 2011; and Statement of Mr. Gumbi (South Africa), UN SCOR, 66th Sess., 6636th Mtg. at 23, S/PV.6636, 24 October 2011.

[180] *See* text accompanying *supra* notes 57–61.

4 UN Membership of Palestine and the International Rule by Law   245

applicant had to show a commitment to the peaceful settlement of disputes and to refrain from the threat or the use of force'.[181] In this respect, 'it was stressed that Hamas had not accepted these obligations'.[182] In its membership application, Palestine offered the standard *pro forma* declaration affirming, *inter alia*, that it accepts the obligations contained in the Charter and solemnly undertakes to fulfil them.[183] It also affirmed its decades-long commitment to peacefully resolve its dispute with Israel through negotiation in line with UN resolutions and international law. That Hamas had engaged in low-intensity armed resistance to Israel's occupation was not disputed. Yet, by comparison, its low-intensity military actions could not approach the armed conflict accompanying the successful applications of other states, including Israel. It was because of these factors that other members of the Committee were satisfied that Palestine fulfilled these criteria.[184] In this regard, they rightly pointed out that when the UN considered Israel's application in 1948–1949, it was 'argued that Israel's solemn pledge to carry out its obligations under the Charter was sufficient to meet this criterion'.[185]

To appreciate the extent of the double standard applied to Palestine, it is worth recalling the context in which the UN's acceptance of Israel's solemn pledge was accepted as sufficient by the Organization. Israel's application for membership was submitted in the fall of 1948, after the civil war phase of the conflict and during the first Arab–Israeli war which commenced on 15 May 1948. By the time the application came before the Security Council and General Assembly in December 1948 and May 1949, the vast majority of the roughly 750,000–900,000 Palestinian refugees had been forcibly exiled as a result of the actions of the Haganah and Zionist dissident groups Lehi and Irgun, amounting to roughly 75–90 per cent of the Arab inhabitants of the country.[186] Additionally, the head of the UN Conciliation Commission for Palestine (UNCCP), Count Folke Bernadotte, had been assassinated by Lehi. Finally, Israel expanded its territory to control some 78 per cent of mandate Palestine, well beyond the terms of the partition resolution, including in violation of the *corpus separatum* (see Map IV).[187] In response, the General Assembly passed resolution 194(III) on 11 December 1948, calling on Israel to repatriate

---

[181] Report of the Committee on Admission, *supra* note 69, para. 18.
[182] *Id.*
[183] Application for Membership, *supra* note 64.
[184] Report of the Committee on Admission, *supra* note 69, para. 17.
[185] *Id.*
[186] *See generally*, Morris, *supra* note 106 and text of that note.
[187] Hadawi, S. *Palestinian Rights and Losses* (Saqi, 1988) at 81.

246   2011 and After: Membership of Palestine in the UN

the refugees 'at the earliest practicable date' and affirming that Jerusalem 'should be placed under effective United Nations control'.[188]

As a result, questions were raised during the May 1949 General Assembly debates on Israel's admission as to whether it accepted its commitments under the Charter and was able and willing to abide by them. Israeli representative, Aubrey Eban, was asked to clarify whether Israel would abide by the terms of General Assembly resolutions 181(II), respecting partition, and 194(III), respecting refugee repatriation and UN control over Jerusalem.[189] Eban relayed that Israel was only prepared to negotiate a handover of Jerusalem's holy sites to UN oversight with 'integration' of the city 'into the life of the State of Israel'.[190] Likewise, refugee repatriation was rejected in favour of resettlement outside Israel.[191] Finally, efforts to apprehend Bernadotte's assassins were said to be unsuccessful because 'the organization of the internal security in the State of Israel had been still in its initial stages' and the 'police force had not yet achieved the necessary degree of internal stability and efficiency which would have enabled it to cope swiftly and effectively' with the matter.[192] Oddly, this admission failed to give rise to questions not only of whether Israel was able to abide by its obligations under the Charter, but also whether it possessed effective governmental control over its claimed territory.

Despite the objections of the Arab states, the Israeli position found support among its Western allies, led by the US. Thus, in the December 1948 Security Council debate, Jessup recalled that 'in the terms of its application for membership,' Israel had indicated its acceptance of the obligations contained in the Charter and that there was 'no reason' to 'question the solemn assurance of Israel', as per standard practice.[193] He asserted that the 'willingness of Israel to carry out these obligations is made clear in its letter of application for membership' and that the US government was 'satisfied with the ability of the State of Israel' to do so.[194] Following Eban's May 1949 testimony to the General

[188] A/RES/194(III), 11 December 1948.

[189] See Ad Hoc Political Committee, UN GAOR, 3rd Sess., 45th Mtg., 5 May 1949; Ad Hoc Political Committee, UN GAOR, 3rd Sess, 46th Mtg., 6th May 1949; Ad Hoc Political Committee, UN GAOR, 3rd Sess., 47th Mtg., 6 May 1949; Ad Hoc Political Committee, UN GAOR, 3rd Sess., 48th Mtg., 7 May 1949; Ad Hoc Political Committee, UN GAOR, 3rd Sess., 49th Mtg., 7 May 1949; Ad Hoc Political Committee, UN GAOR, 3rd Sess., 50th Mtg., 9 May 1949; Ad Hoc Political Committee, UN GAOR, 3rd Sess., 51st Mtg., 9 May 1949.

[190] Ad Hoc Political Committee, UN GAOR, 3rd Sess., 45th Mtg., 5 May 1949, at 236.

[191] Id., at 239–240.

[192] Id., at 243. The head of the Lehi group, Yitzhak Yezernitzsky (a.k.a. Shamir) was never brought to justice for the Bernadotte assassination. He would eventually become Israel's seventh Prime Minister (1983–84; 1986–1992). See also the Preface to this book.

[193] UN SCOR, 3rd Yr., 383rd Mtg., 2 December 1948, at 12.

[194] Id.

4 UN Membership of Palestine and the International Rule by Law   247

Assembly regarding Israel's acceptance of General Assembly resolutions 181(II) and 194(III), the US maintained this position, asserting that those issues could not properly factor into assessing Israel's application under Article 4(1). According to the US representative, Warren Austin, the General Assembly could not be understood as being 'directly concerned with [the] definitive settlement of the questions of Jerusalem or of the Arab refugees', despite the fact that these issues flowed directly from its own resolutions.[195] Rather, those issues were a matter for the UNCCP to manage as part of its mediation effort. 'The point at issue', according to him, was simply 'whether the State of Israel was eligible for membership under Article 4 of the Charter'.[196] On the basis of Israeli promises to engage in peace negotiations, he concluded Israel fully met the criteria.[197] This permissive position was adopted by a number of states from the Western, European, and settler-colonial block in the General Assembly debate.[198]

None of this is to suggest that Israel's application received special treatment on the acceptance, ability, and willingness criteria in 1948–1949. On the contrary, its treatment was in line with the liberal, flexible, and permissive approach that would come to characterize UN admission practice after 1955. That Israel was deemed to satisfy these criteria in the context of an armed conflict in which the indigenous population of Palestine had largely been expelled and the contours of its putative state considerably expanded

---

[195] UN GAOR, 3rd Sess., 207th Plen. Mtg., at 313, 11 May 1949.

[196] *Id.*

[197] *Id.*

[198] *See for instance*, statement of Mr. Ignatieff (Canada), *id.*, at 317 (Canada 'based its position in respect of the admission of Israel on Article 4 of the Charter ... It trusted that Israel would recognize the responsibilities and obligations of Member States under the Charter to live in peace with other nations and settle disputes by pacific means.'); statement of Mr. Garcia Bauer (Guatemala), *id.*, at 320 (Jerusalem, Arab refugees, accountability for the Bernadotte assassination, and delimitation of final borders 'were not directly relevant to the decision on the admission of Israel'.); statement of Mr. Berendsen (New Zealand), *id.*, at 322 (New Zealand would 'expect from the Government of Israel the same respect for the decisions of the Organization as that which devolved upon all Member States'.); statement of Mr. Fabregat (Uruguay), *id.*, at 324–325 ('the requirements for the admission of the State of Israel to the United Nations had been completely satisfied'; General Assembly resolutions 181(II) and 194(III) were the province of the UNCCP and 'beyond the scope of Article 4 of the Charter.'); statement of Dr. Zaydin (Cuba), *id.*, at 327–328 ('The question of the admission of Israel to membership was completely divorced from other resolutions referring to such matters as the internationalization of Jerusalem and the surrounding areas, the problem of Arab refugees and the problem of boundaries, for the settlement of which a Conciliation Commission had been established by General Assembly resolution 194 (III) of 11 December 1948.... The sole question on the agenda was the application of Israel for membership. It was therefore inappropriate to consider other aspects of the problem.').

248   *2011 and After: Membership of Palestine in the UN*

to undefined frontiers, all while being saddled by the high-profile political violence of its own dissident groups, renders it as good a case as any to demonstrate the level of permissiveness these criteria have been given in practice.[199] For Palestine, the lesson in this has been all too familiar. Although the UN record shows that its leadership has been committed to peacefully resolve its dispute with Israel under US auspices for decades and certain dissident elements have not committed anywhere near the transgressions against peace as accompanied Israel's admission to membership, this was not enough to pass the threshold.

4.6 General Observations

An assessment of Palestine's failed 2011 application for UN membership reveals a double standard in the application of the principle of the universality of membership of the Organization under international law. This double standard highlights how international law can be used to entrench and propagate hegemonic interest, this time thorough the exercise of the neo-imperial power of the US. Based on UN practice, Palestine should have had little trouble qualifying for membership. It possesses the requisite elements for statehood under Montevideo and it can demonstrate that it is peace-loving, accepting of its Charter obligations, and able and willing to carry them out. Although it may not have been perfect, based on the liberal, flexible, and permissive standard set by UN admissions practice under Article 4(1), Palestine's candidacy met all of these criteria to a qualitatively equal or greater degree than many other UN member states, including Israel.

The UN record demonstrates that Palestine's membership was frustrated by the imposition of conditions extraneous to the Article 4(1) criteria, along with the unduly narrow application of those criteria by certain members of the Committee. The particular role played by the US was pivotal. Because the Security Council has the authority to recommend new members under Article 4(2) of the Charter and because the US made it clear that it would utilize its veto power to block Palestinian membership, the fate of the effort appears to have been doomed from the start. Some writers have suggested that Palestine's case was therefore wholly political and did not turn on whether the Article 4(1) criteria were actually met.[200] But this only captures half of the picture. The

---

[199] It is not insignificant that in June 1948, one month after Israel's admission to the UN, the repatriation of the Palestinian refugees was barred by a war-time decision of the Israeli cabinet. *See* Morris, *supra* note 106 at 318–319. See also Chapter 4, section 3.3.2.

[200] Chesterman et. al, *supra* note 63 at 195.

fact remains that the Article 4(1) criteria, or some semblance thereof, formed the basis of the Committee's consideration of Palestine's application.

The implications of this are clear. Palestine's application was not assessed in accordance with the universal legal standard governing UN membership under the international rule of law. Rather, its application was denied through a patently incongruous and at times confused interpretation of the relevant legal criteria, thereby allowing it to ironically take place behind a veil of legitimacy furnished by the terms of the Charter itself. The consequence has been to uphold the international rule by law in the UN system.

Viewed in the larger historical context, Palestine's 2011 application for UN membership can be understood as one of its more recent attempts to break free of its assigned and contingent status on the international plane. Following decades of state-building, itself constructed upon the PLO's acceptance of the inequities of prior UN action, one would have expected that Palestine would be deemed to have satisfied enough of the requirements under international law as affirmed by the Organization to have finally been released from the cruel ordeal of its subaltern legal position in the system. Yet, just as those prior inequities were the product of a systematic failure to take the Palestinian people and their rights seriously, so too has been the inequity of its failed attempt to gain membership in the UN. This is nowhere more evident than in the stark comparison of the treatment of its application with that of Israel's over six decades before it. The wholly inconsistent views taken by the US in respect of those two organically related cases underscore the cross-cutting theme of the neo-imperial power at the root of international legal subalternity in the contemporary period, leaving aside the systematic and structural hurdles the Palestinians will somehow have to surmount if liberation and freedom are to finally be realized. It is to their attempt to circumvent the inequities prevailing in the Security Council that we now turn, as represented in the upgrade of Palestine to non-member observer state status by the General Assembly in 2012.

5 NON-MEMBER OBSERVER STATE STATUS FOR PALESTINE

Having had its application for UN membership blocked at the Security Council, Palestine's status was upgraded to non-member observer state through General Assembly resolution 67/19 of 29 November 2012.[201] Based on the UN record, this option was pushed by certain members of the Security Council, in particular France. While remaining silent on the Article 4(1) criteria, it noted that full membership 'cannot be attained at once' owing to 'the

---

[201] A/RES/67/19, 29 November 2012.

250   *2011 and After: Membership of Palestine in the UN*

lack of trust between the main parties' and the surety of a US veto.[202] It therefore suggested the 'intermediate stage' of non-member observer state status building on prior gains of the PLO in the Organization.[203]

The upgrade had the effect of helping mitigate Palestine's contingent position in the international legal order. Whereas Palestine's juridical status as a state was widely debated prior to the upgrade,[204] thereafter much of that debate has become moot. This is because the upgrade enabled Palestine to engage in activity reserved only for states under international law. Thus, the Secretary-General confirmed that Palestine 'may participate fully and on an equal basis with other States in conferences that are open to members of specialized agencies or that are open to all states'.[205] Likewise, in accordance with his practice as depositary of multilateral treaties, the Secretary-General further confirmed Palestine's ability to enter into multilateral treaties open only to states and members of specialized agencies.[206] Accordingly, since the upgrade, Palestine has acceded to over forty multilateral treaties, including the major international human rights,[207] humanitarian law,[208] and criminal law conventions,[209] as well as treaties of more general purpose.[210] Likewise,

---

[202] Statement of Mr. Sarkozy (France), UN GAOR, 66th Sess., 11th Plen. Mtg. at 23, A/66/PV.11, 21 September 2011.

[203] *Id.* For sources of these gains, *see supra* note 157 and Chapter 5, section 3.1.

[204] *See, e.g.,* Quigley, *supra* note 10 and Crawford, *supra* note 30.

[205] *The Status of Palestine in the United Nations*, Report of the Secretary General, 8 March 2013, at 3, A/67/738 [hereinafter 'The Status of Palestine'].

[206] This includes treaties operating according to both the 'Vienna' and 'all states' formulas. *See* Summary of Practice of the Secretary-General as Depositary of Multilateral Treaties, 1999, at para. 79, ST/LEG/7/Rev.1

[207] *For example,* International Covenant on Civil and Political Rights, 16 December 1966, 999 UNTS 171; International Covenant on Economic, Social and Cultural Rights, 16 December 1966, 993 UNTS 3; Convention Against Torture and Other Cruel, Inhumane or Degrading Treatment or Punishment, 10 December 1984, UNTS 112; Convention on the Elimination of All Forms of Discrimination Against Women, 18 December 1979, 1249 UNTS 13; Convention on the Rights of the Child, 20 November 1989, 1577 UNTS 3; International Convention on the Elimination of All Forms of Racial Discrimination, 7 March 1966, 660 UNTS 195.

[208] *For example,* Geneva Convention for the Amelioration of the Condition of the Wounded and Sick in Armed Forces in the Field, 12 August 1949, 75 UNTS 31; Geneva Convention for the Amelioration of the Condition of the Wounded, Sick and Shipwrecked Members of Armed Forces at Sea, 12 August 1949, 75 UNTS 85; Geneva Convention Relative to the Treatment of Prisoners of War, 12 August 1949, 75 UNTS 135; Geneva Convention Relative to the Protection of Civilian Persons in Time of War, 12 August 1949, 75 UNTS. 287.

[209] *For example,* Convention on the Prevention and Punishment of the Crime of Genocide, 9 December 1948, 78 UNTS 277; International Convention on the Suppression and Punishment of the Crime of Apartheid, 30 November 1973, 1015 UNTS 243; Rome Statute of the International Criminal Court, 17 July 1998, 2187 UNTS 3.

[210] *For example,* Vienna Convention on the Law of Treaties, 23 May 1969, 1155 UNTS 331.

5 Non-member Observer State Status for Palestine 251

Palestine has become a member of a number of international organizations, including INTERPOL and the International Criminal Court.[211] As a result of the upgrade, therefore, there is little doubt that the *de jure* state of Palestine exists, and that among the many benefits it enjoys is the ability to make claims as a state under international law, and to contribute to its progressive development.[212] That Palestine is currently under occupation does not vitiate this legal reality; nor does the fact that some states have yet to recognize it, given universal recognition has never been a condition precedent for the existence of statehood, as evinced by the case of Israel.[213]

At the same time, symptomatic of the contingency of its position in the international order, Palestine's non-member observer state status does not provide it with the full range of rights and duties that accompany UN membership. For instance, Palestine's ability to engage in the General Assembly is still substantively and procedurally limited to matters relating to 'Palestinian and Middle East issues'.[214] Most importantly, as noted by the Secretary-General, with one minor exception, Palestine 'does not enjoy the right to vote' within the UN, 'including in elections'.[215] Nor may it 'submit its own candidacy for any election or appointment or submit the names of candidates for any election or appointment'.[216] It is this sweeping disenfranchisement that underscores the rule by law operating within the UN to the detriment of lesser actors like Palestine. Despite the gradual provision to Palestine of a series of privileges within the Organization, the fact that it remains unable

---

[211] Palestine's accession to the Rome Statue is a good example of the catalytic role played by A/RES/67/19. On 22 January 2009, Palestine sought to confer jurisdiction on the ICC by lodging an article 12(3) declaration with the Registrar of the Court. In determining whether the preconditions to the exercise of jurisdiction under Article 12 were met, the then Prosecutor, Luis Moreno Ocampo, affirmed that only states can confer such jurisdiction and, in his view, it was then unclear as to whether Palestine was a state for those purposes. Nevertheless, Ocampo noted that because states parties to the Rome Statute would have to deposit an instrument of accession with the Secretary-General, the latter's role was vital. Where an applicant's statehood is unclear, Ocampo noted that it is the practice of the Secretary-General to follow or seek the GA's directives on the matter. Accordingly, following the passage of A/RES/67/19 in November 2012, the State of Palestine acceded to the Rome Statute on 2 January 2015, and the Secretary-General accepted its instrument of accession on 6 January 2015.

[212] Moussa, *supra* note 70 at 95.

[213] *Id.*, at 59.

[214] A/RES/52/250, 7 July 1998.

[215] The exception relates to the International Residual Mechanism for Criminal Tribunals, the Statute of which provides that non-member states maintaining permanent observer missions at UN headquarters have the right to submit nominations for and to vote in the elections for the permanent and *ad litem* judges of the Residual Mechanism. *See The Status of Palestine, supra* note 205 at 2.

[216] *Id.*

to exercise the franchise as a member state owing to the exercise of great power prerogative demonstrates the central importance of such prerogative in the operation of the system. As such, the upgrade thus illustrates both the promise and the limits of international law for subaltern peoples. For while the existence of the *de jure* State of Palestine gives rise to a presumption that it satisfies the statehood criterion of the Article 4(1) conditions, getting over the Security Council's current narrow and strict construction of the test for membership in the Organization cannot be assured given the hegemonic position of the US. This is despite Grant's view that prevailing law and practice has created a presumption of UN admission if requested by a state.[217] Palestine therefore remains caught in a seemingly permanent condition of contingency. No matter the gains made through its stubborn belief in international law and the world's preeminent international institution, the operation of that very law and institution may be utilized to perpetually keep Palestine out.

6 CONCLUSION

The international vocation of the UN and its unique role as the guardian of international peace and security in the post-1945 era rest upon the principle of the universality of its membership. With the exception of its first decade, UN admissions practice has accordingly been marked by a liberal, flexible, and permissive interpretation of the admission criteria delineated in Article 4(1) of the Charter. So open has the practice been that the Article 4(1) criteria have been reduced to a mere procedural formality, leading to an unconditional universality of membership within the Organization as the defining feature of the international rule of law on UN membership.[218]

In contrast, an assessment of the Committee's consideration of Palestine's 2011 application for UN membership reveals that it was subjected to an unduly narrow, strict, and erroneous application of the Article 4(1) criteria at odds with long-standing UN admissions practice. The fact that the Committee was able to undertake this substantively anomalous position under cover of a procedural authority expressly granted it by Article 4(2) lends the result of its deliberation problematic. Far from an example of the objective application of the international rule of law governing UN membership, the Committee's refusal to recommend Palestine's application can better be understood as an instance of the international rule by law.

---

[217] Grant, *supra* note 21 at 244.
[218] Ginther, *supra* note 2 at 180.

6 Conclusion

Based on the UN record, the role of the US was vital in this regard and is a good demonstration of the third theme informing international legal subalternity, namely its dependence in the contemporary period on the exercise of neo-imperial power. This is demonstrated through a comparison of the profoundly inconsistent American approach concerning admission of other states, including Israel, with Palestine's application for admission. It is the juxtaposition of a broad and forgiving interpretation of the Article 4(1) criteria in these other cases, with a strict, narrow, and erroneous application of same in Palestine's, that highlights the essence of the problem. In this case, but for the 'abuse' – to quote Judge Alvarez – of the Security Council's legal authority under Article 4(2) of the Charter, Palestine may have been able to gain some ground in breaking free of its contingent status in the international system.

Aside from the immediate goal of UN membership, it is possible to understand Palestine's application for admission and, upon failing that, non-member observer state status, as being rooted in the counter-hegemonic potential of international law and institutions. In many ways, this effort represented a culmination of a prolonged struggle, dating from the decolonization era, to rely on these phenomena to realize Palestinian rights and territorial sovereignty. As yet complete, this struggle is itself founded upon a poignant acceptance of past inequities wrought through international law and institutions (e.g. League of Nations mandate, UN partition, etc.), accompanied by an evidently indelible belief in the centrality of those very laws and institutions in bringing overdue, if partial, justice. Given Palestine's international legal standing has suffered at the hands of the UN, one might think the Organization would be the last place its people would turn for deliverance. Yet, that is precisely what has transpired, in large part because there is nowhere else to turn. There is nothing in the Palestinian position, as articulated both in its application for membership and non-member observer state status, that is inconsistent with prevailing international law as affirmed by the UN. This counter-intuitive reliance on international law and institutions by the subaltern class has been pivotal in assisting that class in resisting its disenfranchisement and ultimately cultivating a greater measure of international legal personality of its own. In this way, it has given rise to an additional, but related, paradox. Rather than regarding international law and institutions as forms of restraint on state sovereignty, Palestine has used these phenomena as the primary means through which such sovereignty may be asserted and attained.[219] In this way, Palestine's navigation of its international legal subalternity serves as a useful model for subaltern groups everywhere.

---

[219] Moussa, supra note 70 at 43. *See also* Yoffie, A. 'The Palestine Problem: The Search for Statehood and the Benefits of International Law' (2011) 36 *Yale JIL* 497 at 501.

254   2011 and After: Membership of Palestine in the UN

Along with the emancipatory goals of this course of action, there is a certain magnanimity too, which is of no small consequence. Given the continued lip service paid by the international community towards a two-state solution to the question of Palestine, and the occupying power's over half-century course of forceful conduct which by its own admission is intended to frustrate this result,[220] Palestine's application for admission to UN membership represents an attempt (perhaps the last available) to preserve the ostensible two-state vision that the UN itself set in motion in 1947.

---

[220] *See* Chapter 5.

7

Conclusion

Howard Zinn once astutely observed that '[w]hat one sees in the present may be attributable to a passing phenomenon'; but 'if the same situation appears at various points in history, it becomes not a transitory event, but a long-range condition, not an aberration, but a structural deformity requiring serious attention'.[1] From an examination of key legal texts and moments in the historical record, this book has attempted to demonstrate that Palestine and its people have suffered the effects of such a long-range condition through the management of their lingering question at the United Nations (UN). I have identified this condition as international legal subalternity, the principal attribute of which is that those disenfranchised by it are continually presented with the promise of a more just and equitable future through the application of international law, bolstered by the unrivalled political legitimacy of the purveyor of that promise, the organized international community of states. Despite the lengths to which such groups go in reliance on this promise, its realization is perpetually kept out of reach in one form or another through the actions of the very same international community of states, which all too often either do not pay sufficient heed to the full array of international law's precepts or completely overlook them in practice.

Building on the work of the TWAIL network of scholars, I have argued that international legal subalternity is the result of the creation and use of international law as a tool by hegemonic power, the manifestation of which is the production and reproduction of subaltern underclasses who have little or no say in the substantive formation or application of the law that purports to govern them. Although hegemony in this context originally took a distinctly European imperial form between the seventeenth and early twentieth centuries, since the end of World War II (WWII), it has taken on a multilateral

[1] Zinn, H. *The Politics of History* (Beacon, 1970) at 44.

255

256 *Conclusion*

guise in the form of the UN under the all-important influence of a handful of neo-imperial states, foremost the United States (US). At the same time, the subaltern underclasses have almost exclusively come from the non-European world, initially in the form of colonized, non-self-governing peoples, then shifting to the quasi-independent 'post-colonial' Third World and a variety of non-state actors who remain on the margins of the international system (e.g. UN trusteeships, indigenous peoples, refugees, etc.). It is the contingent and abridged nature of the rights and membership of these subaltern classes that defines their collective experience in the international legal order, notwithstanding claims regarding the purported universality and fairness of that order and the access to justice it is ostensibly meant to provide.

Animating this collective experience is the evident clash one is able to trace over time between the international rule *of* law with what I have called the international rule *by* law. At bottom, this is a clash between two ordering principles of international relations in the post-WWII era. On the one hand, the international rule of law is ostensibly based on the universal application of international law to all. Received wisdom holds it out as the governing legal principle regulating international affairs. On the other hand, the international rule by law is rooted in a cynical use, abuse, or selective application of international legal norms by hegemonic actors under a claim of democratic rights-based liberalism, but with the effect of perpetuating inequity between them and their subaltern opposites. By juxtaposing the international rule of law against the international rule by law, one is able to better understand the nature of international legal subalternity as a fixed feature of the international order, despite the varied configurations it may assume.

Tracing these configurations across time reveals at least three related and overlapping themes that animate international legal subaltern condition. First, it originates in the European imperial encounter with the non-European world during the age of empire and the resultant structural Eurocentricity of the modern international legal order. Marked by the so-called standard of civilization, international law in this period was understood by post-Westphalian states and jurists to be the sole preserve of its European and/or Christian participants with non-European Others relegated to passive objects, giving international law its early rule by law character. Second, it has continued despite the ostensible creation of a liberal rights-based order in the post-WWII era founded upon the international rule of law as embodied in the UN and its Charter. Notwithstanding gains registered through the purported universalism of this new order, embodied primarily through the realization of Third World independence and membership in the UN, elements of the old rule by law order remained as evidenced in the qualitatively inferior legal rights and

Conclusion

standing these 'underdeveloped' quasi-sovereigns actually came to possess. Third, it has been allowed to persist in the post-decolonization era through the diktat of neo-imperial power masked as liberal, democratic, and rights-based. Notwithstanding the ostensible end to classic forms of European empire with the founding and growth of the UN, hegemonic states have served as the primary executors of this iniquitous order in their self-appointed role as its guardians. Although the permanent five members of the UN Security Council have been key among such actors, the unparalleled leader among them remains the US.

To complicate matters, the hegemonic/subaltern binary in the international legal order is not a one-way, linear relationship. On the contrary, its great paradox rests in the fact that there remains what TWAIL theorists have identified as a counter-hegemonic potential in modern international law and institutions, through which subaltern actors can challenge those very structures on their own terms. This typically involves subaltern criticism of prevailing law based upon a tactical application of that law against evolving social mores and sensibilities, which in turn produces fresh claims of fairness and results in some form of progressive development of the law. Yet, despite the possibility of pushback, TWAIL theory appears to suffer from a blind spot in so far as it suggests that this countermove can be utilized to irrevocably dislodge the qualified and contingent position of legal subalterns *per sé*. Through the case of Palestine, this book has attempted to demonstrate that international legal subalternity is a structural component of the international legal order, and that it cannot be eradicated as such, but rather only mitigated. As international law and institutions are challenged by subaltern groups and new law is made, the interests served by that law produce either partially assuaged or wholly new subaltern classes who are eventually compelled to continue the cycle. As a result, the legal subaltern condition may morph in respect of one or more subaltern group, or otherwise shift from one group to another, but it cannot structurally be undone.

International legal subalternity finds sustained expression in the UN's prolonged management of the question of Palestine. Contrary to the conventional wisdom that presents the UN as offering the only normative basis of a just and lasting peace in Palestine, there has been a continuing, though vacillating, gulf between the requirements of international law and UN action that has frustrated, rather than facilitated, that lofty end. Given that one core purpose of the UN is to maintain international peace and security in conformity with the principles of justice and international law,[2] understanding why and

---

[2] *Charter of the United Nations*, 59 Stat. 1031, TS 993, 3 Bevans 1153, 24 October 1945, art. 1(1).

258   *Conclusion*

how the UN has maintained Palestine's legal subalternity provides insight not only into why the conventional view is mistaken, but also how the UN might better perform its functions in line with its Charter.

The origins of Palestine's legal subalternity are not found within the UN itself but are rather located in the interwar period and the institutionalization of the international rule by law through the League of Nations. More specifically, the problem is rooted in British imperial secret treaty-making and diplomacy between 1915 and 1947, which legally privileged the Zionist movement's Jewish national home project over the previously assured political rights of the Palestinian Arab majority. As demonstrated through a brief survey of relevant documents culminating in the Mandate for Palestine, this resulted in the international legal disenfranchisement of the indigenous Palestinians in favour of a European settler-colonial movement. Unsurprisingly, the cross-cutting theme of the international legal order's structural Eurocentricity was most pronounced during this period. Without it, Palestine's legal subalternity would not have been so successfully codified into the mandate system. In a real sense, therefore, the international rule by law of this period was both a description of what was happening to the Palestinian Arabs as well as a prognostication of what was to come.

Despite the promise of a new liberal global order based on the international rule of law in 1945, the UN has remained true to the international rule by law ordering framework it had inherited. This was demonstrated through a legal analysis of the General Assembly's plan of partition for Palestine of November 1947 and the resulting reification of Palestine's legal subalternity in the UN system. Although the Assembly possessed the procedural power under international law to issue the resolution, it lacked the substantive power to recommend partition in violation of the prevailing law and practice on self-determination of peoples in class A mandates. The sacred trust principles folded into the UN Charter via the League of Nations Covenant, coupled with the British satisfaction of its obligations *vis à vis* the Jewish national home, meant that only two courses of action were legally open to the Assembly at the time: immediate independence of the whole of Palestine in line with the wishes of its inhabitants or UN trusteeship. An examination of the UN record, in the form of the UN Special Committee on Palestine (UNSCOP) public and private meetings and report as well as the Assembly debates that followed, demonstrates that partition was not based on these international legal considerations but was rather driven by hegemonic European states and their settler-colonial affiliates. Their goal was to rectify Europe's centuries-old Jewish question in the wake of the Holocaust. The failure to take seriously the rights and interests of Palestine's indigenous population was palpable, as

Conclusion 259

the cross-cutting theme of the structural Eurocentricity of international law and institutions once again reared its head. A close reading of the UNSCOP records underscores this and reveals at least three factors that led the Assembly to disregard the liberal international legal order then said to govern in favour of overriding European interests: a bias in UNSCOP's composition and terms of reference, its failure to sufficiently engage the Arab Higher Committee, and its contempt for principles of democratic governance. The cognitive dissonance displayed by UNSCOP as to the inevitability of violence befalling Palestine's indigenous people following partition only exacerbated the practical consequences of these fateful actions. In reifying Palestine's legal subalternity, the UN plan of partition imposed, in both normative and discursive legal terms, the two-state paradigm that has underpined the Organization's position on the question of Palestine to this very day. In so doing, it permanently circumscribed the territorial extent to which the Palestinian people could thereafter legitimately claim any sovereign rights in their own land, having had most of it wrested from them by a European settler-colonial movement with the imprimatur of the UN. But for the structural Eurocentricity of the international legal and institutional order inherited by the UN, it is questionable as to whether any of this would have unfolded the way it did.

This dynamic continued in the immediate aftermath of the 1948 Nakba through the UN's management of the Palestinian refugee problem. Being the foreseeable result of UN action in 1947, the Western and European-dominated General Assembly was obliged to address the fate of the Palestinian refugees in accordance with international law. Yet the UN record indicates that it did so in a manner that ensured nothing would impugn its own policy goal of ensuring that Israel – the entity it helped create and which was most directly responsible for the problem – remained essentially unaccountable to the Palestinian refugees under international law. Made up of two subsidiary organs of the General Assembly – the United Nations Conciliation Commission for Palestine (UNCCP) and the United Nations Relief and Works Agency for Palestine Refugees in the Near East (UNRWA) – this institutional and normative regime for Palestinian refugees is distinct from that applicable for all other refugees in the world as administered by a third subsidiary, the United Nations High Commissioner for Refugees (UNHCR). Although this distinct institutional and normative regime commenced in a manner consistent with the *ad hoc* refugee protection regimes of its day, the UN record indicates that as time has progressed, it has remained increasingly out of touch with the requirements of international law and practice relative to the protection and assistance of refugees under international law. The protection gap that has emerged has manifested itself in, *inter alia*: a failure of the UN to provide Palestinian refugees with collective access to durable solutions, including voluntary repatriation and restitution to their homes and property; an inconsistent and incongruent application of their legal rights in state practice in a manner consistent with the intended requirements of the 1951 Convention Relating to the Status of Refugees; the use of UNRWA as a resettlement scheme-cum-'temporary' humanitarian aid organization now in its eighth decade; and the normalization of UN-endorsed gender discrimination affecting generations of Palestinian women, men, and children. Contrary to the conventional wisdom that presents the UN as the custodian of the international rule of law regarding the Palestinian refugees, the distinct institutional and normative regime fashioned by the Organization for them in 1948–1949 has in fact demonstrated more of an international rule by law which, in turn, has helped preserve Palestinian contingency in the international legal order.

With the decolonization era, there was hope that the Eurocentricity of the UN would be upended by the rise of the Third World in the Organization and, for Palestine, in a manner that would mitigate the unjust events of 1947–1949. To this end, a partial recognition of Palestinian legal subjectivity and rights in the UN occurred at this time, most importantly the right to self-determination in the occupied Palestinian territory (OPT) as part of the two-state paradigm. This bolstered the conventional wisdom regarding the UN as the standard-bearer of the international rule of law. Yet a closer look at the humanitarian/managerial approach of the UN's position on the OPT post-1967 reveals how the second of the cross-cutting themes underpinning international legal subalternity, *viz.* the structural limitations of Third World quasi-sovereignty, ultimately allowed for the maintenance of Palestine's contingent position in the so-called post-colonial era. Under this approach, the new-look UN has satisfied itself merely with documenting myriad discrete violations by Israel, the occupying power, of international humanitarian and human rights law in the OPT without definitively addressing the legality of the very regime giving rise to those violations themselves. Instead, the UN has insisted on negotiations as the only means to end the occupation, despite the plethora of evidence in its own record to demonstrate that prevailing international law requires a more robust and simpler response. Based on the UN record, Israel's occupation has become illegal for its violation of several *jus cogens* norms, derogation from which is not permitted: the inadmissibility of territorial conquest; the obligation to respect self-determination of peoples; and the prohibition against regimes of alien subjugation, domination, and exploitation, including racial discrimination and apartheid. As such, Israel's occupation of the OPT has become an internationally wrongful act which, according to the law on state responsibility,

Conclusion 261

cannot be terminated except through unilateral, unconditional, and immediate withdrawal. By making withdrawal contingent on negotiation between what the UN record demonstrates is a bad-faith 56-year occupying power and the occupied population held captive by it, the Organization is not only ignoring prevailing international law on state responsibility, but it is also undermining its own stated goal of establishing peace between two sovereign states in the former Palestine mandate. It has thereby made the realization of Palestinian rights repeatedly reaffirmed by it impossible to achieve. Although it is possible for Palestine to have further recourse to the ICJ for an advisory opinion on the illegality of Israel's continued presence in the OPT, such a move would at most only help mitigate its subaltern condition. The UN's recognition and affirmation of Palestinian legal subjectivity and rights in the OPT in the post-1967 period can only be regarded as nominal in nature, continually dictated by the whims of hegemonic forces beyond Palestine's control.

The extent to which post-Cold War hegemonic action continues to shape Palestine's legal subalternity was addressed through an examination of the State of Palestine's 2011 application for UN membership. As the guardian of international peace and security, the principle of the universality of UN membership is the foundation upon which the Organization's success logically rests. Accordingly, the international rule of law governing UN admission has long been marked by a liberal, flexible, and permissive interpretation of the test for membership contained in Article 4(1) of the UN Charter. In contrast, a legal assessment of the UN Committee on Admission's consideration of Palestine's membership application demonstrates that it was subjected to an unduly narrow, strict, and resultantly flawed interpretation of the Article 4(1) criteria. An examination of the contemporaneous debates of the Council demonstrates that the main driver of this was the US, which used its legal authority as a permanent member of the Security Council to block membership for political reasons thinly veiled as sound legal ones. With no small measure of irony, this was highlighted through the juxtaposition of the broad and forgiving interpretation of the Article 4(1) criteria adopted by the US in respect of Israel's admission in 1949 – itself a reflection of the approach that would eventually become the international standard – with its unduly strict and narrow application of the criteria in Palestine's case in 2011. The resulting frustration of Palestine's UN membership demonstrates the third cross-cutting theme informing international legal subalternity: namely, its dependence in the contemporary period on the exercise of neo-imperial power masked as liberal, democratic, and rights-based. In this case, any pretention that Palestine's lack of success resulted from an objective application of the international law governing UN membership is undermined on two fronts. First, by the fact that it was plainly contrary to the prevailing law and practice on UN admissions. Second, that despite this anomaly, it was done under cover of a procedural authority expressly granted the Security Council under Article 4(2) of the Charter. This ultimately revealed the whole episode as yet another example of the international rule by law. Although resort to the General Assembly in 2012 offered a counter-hegemonic course to Palestine that produced a variety of gains in the way of affirming its status as a state under international law, the fact that full membership in the UN remains elusive reveals the limitations inherent in such an approach.

At the heart of the UN's failure to help bring about a peaceful resolution of the question of Palestine in line with the international rule of law is its complicity in the reification, maintenance, and perpetuation of Palestine's legal subalternity over time through the international rule by law. It is a common refrain of policymakers, pundits, and academics alike to bemoan the seemingly endless cycle of violence and failed diplomatic initiatives that have characterized the UN's prolonged management of the problem as resulting from a simple lack of political will or a crisis of impunity.[3] To be sure, there is no doubt that these and other problems exist. Nevertheless, on their own, they do not provide sufficient explanation for the situation as it continues to fester at the UN, now for the better part of a century. For that, this book has argued that the UN's failure to resolve the question of Palestine is a product of a long-range structural condition that inheres in the international legal and institutional order itself. The operation of this order pits hegemonic and counterhegemonic uses of law against one another, with international legal subalternity manifesting itself in various guises, always with the same disenfranchising result for those who suffer under it.

For Palestine, this has meant having to run an endless gauntlet of shifting goalposts from one legal moment to the next to merely maintain the most basic claims of its people under international law. Between the League of Nations mandate system and UN partition, international law and institutions were initially utilized to undermine and reify their international legal standing and position. Despite accepting the inequitable result of these fateful events, subsequent attempts to rely on international law and organization to mitigate their impact have yet to fundamentally produce the promise of justice and equality they portend. And yet the struggle continues in line with a stubborn belief in the liberal rights-based global order. This was well demonstrated in a 17 May 2018 statement to an open meeting of the Security Council, where

---

[3] See, e.g., Statement of Mr. Bamya (Palestine), UN SCOR, 73rd Sess., 8262nd Mtg. at 95–96, S/PV.8262, 17 May 2018.

Conclusion 263

the State of Palestine affirmed that '[d]espite being the victims of double standards' at the UN 'the Palestinian people have continued to place their faith in international law and have reaffirmed time and again their commitment to international law and to peaceful, legal and diplomatic means for achieving their inalienable rights'.[4]

It is unclear as to whether Palestine's counter-hegemonic resort to international law through the UN will enable it to break free from its long-range subaltern condition. To be sure, the number of areas in which that condition has manifested itself at the UN are not limited to those covered by this book which, for reasons of economy, could not be treated here. With the very limited material resources available to Palestine to address its existential situation, it is likely that its leadership will continue to resort to the use of international law and institutions as a tactical means to resist. Suffice to say, it is clear that Palestine's experience is one with wider relevance both for other subaltern groups and for the UN as a whole. For the former, examining how Palestine has negotiated the hegemonic forces pitted against it across varying paradigmatic changes in the global order offers a useful model to better understand, at a macro level, the politics, scope, and limits of contemporary international law and organization. For the latter, appreciating the extent to which the UN Organization continues to be implicated in a paradoxical role of serving as venue, facilitator, and/or progenitor of international legal subalternity is vital. Given the inordinately long duration of the question of Palestine at the UN, and the Organization's self-declared permanent responsibility for it until it is resolved in all of its aspects in accordance with international law, it is difficult to deny that Palestine remains *the* litmus test for the credibility of international law and the international system as a whole.[5]

[4] *Id.*, at 95.
[5] *Id.*, at 96.

Postscript

On 30 December 2022, as this book was entering production, the United Nations General Assembly adopted resolution 77/247, requesting the International Court of Justice (ICJ) to render an advisory opinion on the following questions:

(a) What are the legal consequences arising from the ongoing violation by Israel of the right of the Palestinian people to self-determination, from its prolonged occupation, settlement, and annexation of the Palestinian territory occupied since 1967, including measures aimed at altering the demographic composition, character, and status of the Holy City of Jerusalem, and from its adoption of related discriminatory legislation and measures?
(b) How do the policies and practices of Israel referred to … above affect the legal status of the occupation, and what are the legal consequences that arise for all States and the United Nations from this status?[1]

Based on the Court's general list, it will not give the requested opinion until after this book is published. Readers will recognize the questions put to the Court as directly relevant to the issues covered in Chapter 5, including the recommendation that resort be had to the ICJ for a definitive determination of the lawfulness of Israel's fifty-six-year presence in the occupied Palestinian territory (OPT). There is therefore much to look forward to in this development, not least the opportunity for the General Assembly to obtain judicial confirmation of its previous assertions of the occupation's illegality, beginning as far back as 1977 when the occupation was only in its tenth year.[2] If the analysis presented in these pages is correct, a finding of illegality may provide Palestine with the opportunity to

---

[1] A/RES/77/247, 30 December 2022.
[2] A/RES/32/20, 25 November 1977. *See also* Chapter 5, Section 4.2.

264

Postscript 265

break free from the negotiations condition that has long impeded efforts to end the occupation and tainted the UN's ostensible support for the realization of Palestinian rights that are of a peremptory nature, foremost its people's right to self-determination. From the manner in which the question has been framed, it is also possible that the Court may address issues broader than the occupation's legal status, including whether Israel has imposed a regime of racial discrimination and/or apartheid against the Palestinian people in part or in whole.

Aside from the immediate legal clarity the ICJ can bring to the UN's work on the question of Palestine, the manner in which it has been responded to by key states offers a window into the broader themes covered in this book. If any further evidence of the structural, long-range condition of Palestine's international legal subalternity was needed, it can be found in the level of hostility this development has garnered from certain hegemonic actors, the rationale used to undercut it, and the broader impact of that rationale for UN operations itself.

In the Fourth Committee debate on what became resolution 77/247, Israel's permanent representative denounced the General Assembly's engagement of the ICJ as a 'poisonous measure', and 'a weapon of mass destruction' in a 'jihad war of Israel demonization'.[3] In his view, '[b]y involving the ICJ, any hopes for reconciliation [between Israelis and Palestinians] are being driven off a cliff' and member states who support the move are little more than Palestine's 'marionettes', backing 'libelous resolutions' and 'endorsing incitement and terror'.[4]

It is neither surprising nor unique that a state engaged in wrongful conduct would not wish its actions to be held up to international legal scrutiny. But that we have arrived at a point in the UN's engagement with the question of Palestine where it can be seriously suggested in its hallowed halls that to have recourse to its principle judicial organ is tantamount to terror, treachery, and the like, demonstrates just how malignant the unresolved issue has become for the Organization.

Some posit that this malady exists due to a purported 'obsession' of the UN with Israel,[5] that it is unfairly singled out for opprobrium, and that this might even have to do with a 'lingering antisemitism' in the international community.[6] For evidence, adherents of this argument point to the batch of

---

[3] Statement of Mr. Erdan (Israel), UN GAOR, 77th Sess., 4th Comm., A/C.4/77/SR.25, 10 November 2022. Video of meeting *at*: https://media.un.org/en/asset/k1p/k1p3p1b46n.

[4] *Id.*

[5] Nebehay, S. 'US Seeks End to UN Rights Council's 'Obsession' with Israel,' *Reuters*, 1 March 2017, at: www.reuters.com/article/us-un-rights-usa-idUSKBN1683V7.

[6] Dershowitz, A. 'Israel: The Jew among Nations' in Kellermann, A., et al., eds. *Israel among the Nations* (Kluwer, 1998) at 129.

Postscript

annual General Assembly and Human Rights Council (HRC) resolutions and various reports of HRC mandated special procedures concerning Palestine. In recent years, this view has been partially adopted by some in the Western, European, and settler-colonial bloc of states with resultant changes in voting patterns and participation at the UN.[7] Of the twenty-six votes against resolution 77/247, all but five were from this bloc (or small pacific island states dependent on the US).[8] Between 2018 and 2021, the US withdrew from the HRC, citing purported anti-Israel bias.[9] Likewise, the US withdrew hundreds of millions of dollars in funding from the United Nations Relief and Works Agency for Palestine Refugees in the Near East in 2018[10] and from the UN Educational, Scientific and Cultural Organization following Palestine's admission to membership in that body in 2011,[11] thereby threatening the financial and operational health of the Organization. The argument appears to be that, despite the wretched facts on the ground, *too much* human rights attention is being paid to Palestine at the UN, rendering conflict resolution a more distant prospect. Thus, following its vote against resolution 77/247, the US permanent representative decried that '[t]he lopsided focus on Israel at the United Nations, including the … the recent request for an advisory opinion at the International Court of Justice, has brought Israelis and Palestinians no closer to peace'.[12]

---

[7] *See, e.g.,* Ahren, R. 'In Surprise Change, 13 Countries Vote against Pro-palestine UN Resolution,' *Times of Israel*, 4 December 2019, at: www.timesofisrael.com/in-surprise-change-13-countries-vote-against-pro-palestine-un-resolution/; Baroud, R. "Palestine is Still the Issue': UN Vote Exposes, Isolates Canada,' *MEMO*, 14 August 2020, at: www.middleeastmonitor.com/20200814-palestine-is-still-the-issue-un-vote-exposes-isolates-canada/.

[8] Democratic Republic of Congo, Kenya, Liberia, Togo.

[9] Roth, R. & Vazquez, M. 'US Official Rejoins Controversial UN Human Rights Council,' *CNN*, 14 October 2021, at: www.cnn.com/2021/10/14/politics/us-united-nations-human-rights-council/index.html.

[10] Beaumont, P. & Holmes, O. 'US Confirms End to Funding for Palestinian Refugees,' *Guardian*, 31 August 2018, at: www.theguardian.com/world/2018/aug/31/trump-to-cut-all-us-funding-for-uns-main-palestinian-refugee-programme.

[11] The US eventually withdrew from the organization in 2017. Rosenberg, E. & Morello, C., 'US Withdraws from UNESCO, the UN's Cultural Organization, Citing anti-Israel Bias,' *Washington Post*, 12 October 2017, at: www.washingtonpost.com/news/post-nation/wp/2017/10/12/u-s-withdraws-from-unesco-the-u-n-s-cultural-organization-citing-anti-israel-bias/. In July 2023, the US decided to return to UNESCO reportedly because of concerns that China had filled a 'leadership gap' in its absence. Lee, M., 'US Formally Rejoins UNESCO after Five-Year Absence,' *Associated Press*, 11 July 2023, at: https://apnews.com/article/us-unesco-6380e9bfc62c02e6669d227590d44341.

[12] Statement of Mrs. Thomas-Greenfield (United States), UN SCOR, 77th Sess., 9203rd Mtg. at 4, S/PV.9203, 28 November 2022.

Postscript 267

There is something amiss in all of this. The common thread that belies this line of thinking is that it does not even bother to address the substantive content of the mountain of UN resolutions and reports detailing Israel's violations of Palestinian rights under international law. The result is to blame the messenger, with the aim of deflecting attention away from that which requires immediate remedial action in the face of sweeping and prolonged impunity. But for the fact that Israel continues to benefit from the ethnic cleansing of Palestine, the usurpation of Palestinian refugee property and the colonization of the OPT, among myriad other illegal acts, this level of attention by the General Assembly and HRC would not be necessary. This, of course, says nothing of the fact that, in contrast to these bodies, Israel remains relatively protected in the Security Council by a US veto, shielding it from any real accountability.[13]

There is no denying that the UN record on Palestine, especially at the General Assembly and HRC, is voluminous. But there is a sound reason for this. Lost in the furore is the simple truth that the UN's 'permanent responsibility' for the question of Palestine until it 'is resolved in all its aspects in accordance with international law'[14] is the direct result of its unique role in the creation of the Palestine problem in the first place. The ghosts of 1947 loom large, and to pretend otherwise is folly. The above-noted response to the General Assembly's recent request of the ICJ is proof positive of this. At a time when the international rule of law is continually held out as the organizing principle of world order, there should be nothing wrong with the General Assembly having recourse to the ICJ for a legal opinion on matters touching upon the longest running issue on the UN's agenda. This latest episode is yet another reminder that, for some, such a universal international law remains more of an aspiration than a reality, and that there is still much work to be done.

---

[13] Lynk, M. 'What Does the US Get Out of Shielding Israel from Accountability at the UN?,' *DAWN*, 24 February 2023, at: https://dawnmena.org/what-does-the-u-s-get-out-of-shielding-israel-from-accountability-at-the-u-n/ ('Since 1973, the United States has cast 81 vetoes at the U.N. Security Council, far more than any other permanent member. [...] More than half of these American vetoes, 42, have been used to scuttle resolutions critical of Israel').

[14] A/RES/70/15, 24 November 2015.

Index

1948 war, 107, 123–124
  expansion of Israeli borders beyond
    partition, 102, 124
  international armed conflict phase, 101, 124
  Israeli decision to bar refugee return, 102,
    128, 133
  non-international armed conflict phase,
    101, 106, 123–124
1967 war, 157, 177, 197

Abdur Rahman, Sir, 87, 94
Abi-Saab, Georges, 11
Ad Hoc Liaison Committee for the
  Coordination of the International
  Assistance to Palestinians, 237
Aggression, 7, 195
AHC. *See* Arab Higher Committee
Akram, Susan, 130, 166
Albanese, Francesca, 165
Alvarez, Alejandro, 221, 222, 253
Anand, R.P., 11
Anghie, Antony, 5–6, 8, 43
Annan, Kofi, 192
Anti-Semitism, 31, 33
Arab Higher Committee, 83–88, 98, 101, 108,
  147–148, 153–154, 259
Arab League, 3
Arab Peace Initiative, 243
Arafat, Yassir, 179
ARSIWA. *See* state responsibility
Austin, Warren, 247
Australia, 77, 78, 149, 223
Austria, 240, 243

Balfour, Arthur, 35, 47
Balfour Declaration, 30, 41–42, 92
  incorporated into mandate for Palestine, 45
  Jewish question, aimed at resolving, 41
Bedjaoui, Mohammed, 11
Belgium, 224

Belorussia, 225, 226
Ben Dror, Elad, 104
Ben Gurion, David, 79, 90, 104, 127, 155
Bernadotte, Count Folke, xv–xvi, 143–146,
  245–246
  assassination of, xv–xvi, 144
  compromise preferred over law, 146, 150, 157
  democratic prinicples, contempt for, 144–146
  First Progress Report, xv, 145, 146
  mediation, inappropriateness of, 146–147
  Palestinian Arabs, refusal to engage with, 147
  Palestinians, bias against, fn. 196, 143
  population exchange, proposal of, 146
  Right of return of Arab refugees,
    affirmation of, 143–144
Bolsheviks, 40
Bosnia and Herzegovina, 226, 230
Brazil, 79, 231, 243
Bretton Woods, 94, 175, 177, 217
Brilej, Jose, 86
British House of Lords, 47
Burgis, Michelle, 17
Burundi, 225

Canada, 77, 97, 106, 149, 162, 223
*Case Concerning Armed Activities on the
  Territory of the Congo* (Democratic
  Republic of the Congo v. Uganda),
  120, 196, 209
*Case Concerning the Factory at Chorzow
  (Claim for Indemnity) (Jurisdiction)*,
  119, 136
*Case Concerning the Factory at Chorzow
  (Claim for Indemnity) (Merits)*, 119, 136
Cervenak, Christine, 168
Chesterman, Simon, 228
Chile, 78, 97
Chimni, Bhupinder, 11–12
China, 231
Churchill, Winston, 37

269

Index

Citizenship Law, 130–131, 134
  repeal of Palestine citizenship, 130
Cold War, 8
Colombia, 71, 230, 232
Colonialism, 2, 32, 88, 174–175
Committee of 24, 174–175, 179
Conditions of Admission of a State to
  Membership in the United Nations
  (Article 4 of the UN Charter), 220, 221, 233
Congo, 224, 226
Congress of Vienna, 10
Consent of the governed, 42–43, 45, 57, 59,
  68, 70, 72, 91, 94, 97, 99
Crawford, James, 66, 73, 115, 189, 213, 223, 240
Cuba, 71, 98–100
Curzon, Lord, 35, 47
Custodian of Absentee Property, 129
Czechoslovakia, 77, 88, 105

Davis, Mary McGowan, 184
Declaration on the Granting of Independence
  to Colonial Countries and Peoples, 174
Decolonization, 7, 10, 11, 23, 55, 56, 75,
  172–176, 179, 181, 182, 186, 212, 215, 218,
  222, 226, 253, 257, 260
Denmark, 81, 240
Dominican Republic, 79, 97, 161

Eban, Aubrey, 246
Economic and Social Council, 18, 182, 184,
  185, 192
Economic migrants, 15
Economic peace, 160
Economic Survey Mission, 124, 139, 158
  composition, 158
  Eurocentric, paternalistic & orientalist, 140,
    158–160
  Palestinian refugees, fabricated as symptom
    of economic woes, 158–159
  resettlement scheme, 162, 163
ECOSOC. See Economic and Social
  Council
Egypt, 70, 80, 101, 124, 147, 161, 163, 226, 244
Elaraby, Nabil, 192
Elias, Taslim, 11
Elon, Menachem, 129
Emergency Regulations (Absentees' Property), 128
Erakat, Noura, 16
ESM. See Economic Survey Mission
Etzel, 104
European Union, 229

Fabregat, Enrique Rodriguez, 87
Falk, Richard, 12, 214
Fatah, 236, 238, 239
Fidler, David, 12
Fischbach, Michael, 153

Foster, Michelle, 167
France, 34, 35, 38, 115, 138, 153, 158, 226, 230,
  240, 249
Friendly Relations Declaration, 174

Gabon, 230
Galili, Yisrael, 104
Garcia-Amador, Francisco, 11
Gathii, James, 11, 13
General Assembly, 18, 182, 184, 185, 210
  Eurocentric membership in 1947, 77, 170
  Mediator for Palestine, consideration of
    Progress Report of, 147–150
  partition of Palestine, debate of, 95–100
  recommendations, power to make, 67–70
  resolution 67/19, 249
  resolution 77/246, 264–266
  resolution 181(II), 22–24, 51–53, 57, 59–76,
    82, 83, 89, 100, 101, 106–109, 110, 133, 145,
    147, 149, 181, 182, 229
  resolution 194(III), xvi, 102, 138–140, 143,
    147, 150–152, 154–155, 157, 158, 161, 163,
    166, 179, 245
  resolution 302(IV), 137, 139, 158, 163
  resolution 3236(XXIX), 179
  resolutions as evidence of state practice, 73
  UNRWA, debate on establishment of,
    160–163
George, Lloyd, 47
Germany, 27, 76, 81, 128, 134, 230, 232
Ginther, Konrad, 222
Global south. See Third World
Goldstone, Richard, 183
Gramsci, Antonio, 3
Granados, Jorge Garcia, 88, 95, 96
Grant, Thomas, 222, 252
Great Arab revolt, 50
Great Britain. See United Kingdom
Greece, 134
Group of 77, 174, 241
Guatemala, 77–79, 88, 95
Guinea-Bissau, 225
Gurney, Sir Henry, 105
Guterres, Antonio, 1, 185

Haganah, 101, 103, 104, 123, 127, 245
Hamas, 236, 238, 239, 242, 245
Hathaway, James, 167
Hegemony, 5, 13, 16, 25, 82, 255
Heiskanen, Veijo, 19
Herzl, Theodor, 31, 32, 50
Higgins, Rosalyn, 73, 222, 237, 241
Holocaust, 50, 59, 81, 108, 258
Human Rights Council, 183, 207, 266
Hussein, ibn Ali (Sherif of Mecca), 34
Hussein-McMahon correspondence,
  30, 33–40

Index

ICCPR. *See* International Covenant on Civil and Political Rights
ICJ. *See* International Court of Justice
ICRC. *See* International Committee of the Red Cross
ICTR. *See* international criminal tribunals for Rwanda
ICTY. *See* international criminal tribunals for the former yugoslavia
IDPs. *See* internally displaced persons
India, 49, 77, 87, 94, 95, 134, 225, 231, 244
Indigenous peoples, 10, 15, 256. *See also* UNDRIP
Indonesia, 223
Internally displaced persons, 15, 16
International Committee of the Red Cross, 118, 162
International Court of Justice, 18, 43, 69, 183
  Article 2(4) UN Charter, on, 209
  Bernadotte, Count Folke, assassination of, xvi
  customary international law, and, 72
  General Assembly resolutions, on normative force of, 73, 75
  jurisdiction, bases of, 54
  Palestine's reliance on, 243
  partition plan, failed attempt to restort to, 70–71
  sacred trust of civilization, and the, 56, 58
  self-determination, right *erga omnes*, 194
International Covenant on Civil and Political Rights, 116, 135–136
International Criminal Court, 251
International criminal law
  deportation of civilians, 117, 118, 132
  refugees, 117–118
International criminal tribunals for Rwanda, 118
International criminal tribunals for the former yugoslavia, 118
International human rights law
  refugees, 116–117
  right to return, 116, 135–136
International humanitarian law
  1949 Fourth Geneva Convention, 132, 180, 197
  belligerent occupation, law of, 23, 172, 194–195
  deportation of civilians, 117, 132
  refugees, 117–118
  right to return, 117–118, 132
  transfer of civilians into occupied territory, 197, 200
International law
  classical positivism, and, 5, 30
  colonial Other, and its, 6
  counter-hegemonic potential of, 8–9, 11–12, 16, 174, 177, 210, 218, 253, 257, 262, 263

duality of, 9
Eurocentricity of, 7, 21, 26, 51, 90–91, 107, 256, 259
European imperialism, and, 5–6, 29, 30, 32, 55, 255
hegemonic/subaltern binary of, 6, 8, 13, 20, 96, 100, 257
history of, 5–8, 32
nature of, 5
non-intervention doctrine, and, 11, 15, 226
paradox of, 8
secret treaty-making, and, 21
self-executing, as not, 16
standard of civilization, and, 7, 15, 28–30, 33, 45, 85, 92, 95, 256
International Law Commission, 54, 119, 188
International legal subalternity, 13, 14, 26, 29, 76, 107, 172, 217, 255, 256
  cross-cutting themes of, 7–8
  defining feature of, 2
  long-range condition, as a, 11–13, 25, 255, 257, 262, 263, 265
  Palestine as embodiment of, 5, 8, 22, 23, 30, 32, 33, 45, 47, 52, 55, 59–60, 65, 72, 74–75, 84, 100–101, 108, 111, 122, 150, 171–173, 176, 210, 257
  Palestine's, origins of, 26–51, 258
International Military Tribunal, 117
International Monetary Fund, 237
International nationality law
  denationalization, prohibition of, 115–116
  nationality follows change of sovereignty, 134
  refugees, 114–116
International refugee law
  1951 refugee convention, 112–114, 116, 121–123, 140, 164–167, 260
  Article 1A(2), 113, 164
  Article 1D, 140, 165–167, 169
  definition of convention refugee, 113, 164
  denationalization, prohibition on, 121
  durable solutions, 113, 116. *See* United Nations High Commissioner for Refugees
  historical development of, 112–113
  other international law relevant to, 114–121
  protracted refugee crises, and, 114
  refoulement, 119
  right to return, 116
International Status of South-West Africa, Advisory Opinion, 69–70
Interpol, 251
Iran, 77
Iraq, 34, 38, 43, 45, 56, 70, 71, 80, 101, 123, 124, 147, 154, 190, 194, 224
Irgun, 101, 103, 123, 245
Island of Palmas, 131, 135

Index

Israel
  Declaration of Establishment of, 65, 73, 102, 133
  Nakba commemoration outlawed, 125
  settler colony, as, 5
  United Nations, membership of, 155, 224, 226, 231–237, 239, 242–248, 261
Israel Development Authority, 129

Jerusalem, xv, 76, 180, 198, 200, 247, 264
  1980 Basic Law, 198
  corpus separatum, 60, 245
  East, 139, 197–201, 204, 229, 236
  sanjak of, 37
Jessup, Philip, 233–235, 237, 239, 242, 246
Jewish Agency, 46, 49, 63, 68, 77, 79–81, 85–87, 89, 90, 96, 104, 235
  colonizing body, as, 49
  Lauterpacht, H., opinion to, 68
Jewish National Fund, 129
Jewish national home, 42, 46, 48–51, 57, 59, 63, 68, 72, 77, 90–92, 94, 96, 97, 108, 258
  Jewish State, as equivalent to, 90, 92, 96, 108
  use of force, as means to establish, 104–105, 126, 141
Jewish question, 31, 41, 59, 77, 82, 94, 108, 258
  partition of Palestine, and, 81–83
Jewish settlement
  1948 war, during, 127
  Drobles Plan, 200
  mandate Palestine, of, 49
  occupied Palestinian territory, of, 180, 197–208
  related infrastructure in OPT, 198
JNF. *See* Jewish National Fund
Johnson, Joseph, 154
Johnstone, Ian, 228
Jordan, 34, 38, 45, 56, 102, 124, 139, 201, 202, 226, 236, 237, 244
Judenstaat, Der, 31
Jus gentium, 10

Kattan, Victor, 69, 134
Khalidi, Rashid, 47
King-Crane Commission, 44–45, 103
  Zionism, views on, 44
Kipling, Rudyard, 29, 50
Koojimans, Peter, 196
Koskenniemi, Martti, 9
Kubursi, Atif, 128
Kuwait, 190, 224, 240

Lapidoth, Ruth, 131, 132, 134, 135
Late-empire, 2, 22, 26, 27, 40, 44, 48, 51, 95, 100, 215
Lauterpacht, Hersch, 58, 68–70
Law of Return, 129–130, 134, 205

League of Nations, 7, 17, 21, 26, 28–30, 33, 42, 43, 45, 47–51, 53–54, 56–59, 68, 70, 79, 84, 91, 101, 108, 177, 253, 258. *See also* League of Nations Covenant
  class A mandates, 55–57, 70, 71, 89, 99
  Council of, 45–46, 48
  final resolution of, 58
  imperial Europe, college of, 27
  institutionalization of international legal order, through, 27
  mandate system, 7, 27, 28, 43–45, 50
League of Nations Covenant, 27, 29, 30, 42, 43, 45, 47, 48, 53–55, 57–59, 68, 70, 79, 80, 91, 258. *See also* League of Nations
  Article 22, 28, 29, 43–44, 47, 48, 57
  class A mandates, 28, 43, 70, 71
  class B mandates, 43
  class C mandates, 43
  United Nations Charter, and, 53–54
Lebanon, 34, 35, 38, 43, 45, 56, 78–80, 98, 99, 101, 124, 139, 147, 161, 226, 231, 240, 244
Legal Consequences for States of the Continued Presence of South Africa in Namibia (South-West Africa) Notwithstanding Security Council Resolution 276 (1970), 43, 58, 213–214
Legal Consequences of the Construction of a Wall in the Occupied Palestinian Territory, 120, 182, 192, 195, 199–201, 203, 211, 212, 229
Legal Consequences of the Separation of the Chagos Archipelago from Mauritius in 1965, 212
Legality of the Threat or Use of Nuclear Weapons, 73, 75, 214
Lehi, 101, 103, 104, 123, 144, 245
  Bernadotte, assassination of, 144, 245
Lie, Trygve, 85, 141, 142
  orientalist bias of, 141–142
Liechtenstein, 224
Lisicky, Karel, 88
Lynk, Michael, 192, 199, 207

Madrid Peace Conference, 74, 191, 217, 243
Magna Carta, 117
Majority rule, 43–45, 47, 56, 57, 72, 89, 145
Malone, David, 228
Marshall Islands, 226
Marxism, 12
Matua, Makau, 11
Mauritania, 224
McDonnell, Sir Michael, 38
McMahon, Sir Henry, 34, 35
McNair, Arnold, 43
Membership of the United Nations, 24, 218. *See also* Palestine; United Nations
  acceptance, ability and willingness, 226–227, 244–248

Index

Article 4(1), 24, 217–223, 227–229, 234, 235, 242, 244, 247, 248, 252, 261
Article 4(2), 220, 228, 231, 248, 252, 253, 262
Cold War, 220
conditions extraneous to Article 4(1), 221, 227, 231–234
peace-loving, 226, 242–244
right, as a, 221, 227
Security Council as gatekeeper, 228
sovereign equality of states, 228
statehood and, 223–226, 234–242
universality, principle of, 53, 218–220, 222, 227, 252
Micronesia, 226
Military and Paramilitary Activities in and against Nicaragua (Nicaragua v. US) (Merits), 72
Monaco, 224, 226
Montevideo Convention on the Rights and Duties of States, 232, 234–238, 240, 248
Statehood, criteria for, 223
Morocco, 224
Morris, Benny, 121, 125, 127
Moussa, Jasmine, 239

Nakba, 103, 110, 111, 122, 125, 132, 134, 135, 139, 146, 152, 159, 170, 176, 259
commemoration outlawed in Israel, 125
ethnic cleansing, 103, 121, 122, 126–128, 130, 131, 139, 141, 142, 149, 160, 170
forseeability of, 103–105
general, 123–131
Israeli legislative scaffolding of, 128–131, 133
Plan D, 126, 127, 132
Zionist denial of, 125
NAM. *See* Non-Aligned Movement
Napoleon III, 35
Nauru, 224
Neo-imperialism, 7, 24, 217, 228, 231, 248, 249, 253, 256, 257, 261
Netherlands, 77, 82, 149
New historians, 107, 121, 125
New Zealand, 106, 223
Nigeria, 223, 230
Non-Aligned Movement, 174, 241
North Sea Continental Shelf, 224
Norway, 82
Nuremberg Principles, 117

Occupied Palestinian Territory, 8, 17, 23, 74, 217, 229, 236, 239, 260. *See also* Jewish settlement
annexation of, 172, 197–200
fragmentation of, 201
humanitarian/managerial approach of UN toward, 173, 176, 181–185, 193, 215, 260

ICJ advisory opinion, proposal for, 211–214, 216, 261, 264–267
legal status of, 23–24, 181, 186, 193–208, 210–215, 239, 260, 264
negotiations condition, and the, 23, 176, 181, 185–186, 190, 192, 196, 208–210, 215, 260, 265
OCHA. *See* United Nations Office for the Coordination of Humanitarian Affairs
Office of the UN Special Coordinator for the Middle East Peace Process, 157
Okafor, Obiora, 11
OPT. *See* Occupied Palestinian Territory
Organization of Islamic Cooperation, 241
Oslo accords, 157, 198, 210, 213, 217, 237, 240, 241
Otto, Dianne, 9, 11
Ottoman Empire, 27, 28, 34, 35, 38, 43, 237

PA. *See* Palestinian Authority
Pakistan, 99, 134, 149
Palacios, Leopoldo, 48
Palau, 224
Palestine
contingent, as, 22, 193, 209, 210, 216, 217, 249, 251
declaration of independence, 229
example to other subalterns, as, 253, 263
international legal history of, 30
international legal subalternity, long-range condition of, 255, 262, 263
international organizations, membership of, 251
legal subjectivity, 24, 30, 176–182, 216, 218, 260
mandate for, 17, 28, 30, 42, 45–50, 57, 58, 68, 91, 92, 258
membership of UN, and, 24, 181, 182, 217, 228–249
multilateral treaties, and, 250
non-member observer state status at UN, 24, 209, 218, 249–252
statehood of, 24, 217, 234–242
taking it seriously, 4–5, 8, 79, 90, 97, 111, 122, 141, 144, 147, 258
Third World contingency, embodiment of, 173, 176
United Nations obligations towards in 1947, 57–60, 78
Palestine Citizenship Order, 131
Palestine Liberation Organization, 24, 65, 74, 157, 177, 185, 198, 238, 241, 249, 250
resolution 181(II), recognition of, 74, 181–182, 217, 236, 242
Palestine refugees, 102. *See also* Palestinian refugees
definition of, 165
gender discrimination and, 140, 165, 167–170, 260

274 Index

Palestine Yearbook of International Law, 16
Palestinian Arab nationalism, 31
Palestinian Authority, 240
Palestinian citizenship, 46
Palestinian people
　denial of existence of, 110
Palestinian refugees, 22, 165. *See also* Nakba;
　　Palestine refugees
　1967 hostilities, 124
　bank accounts, 128
　barred from return, 102, 128, 133
　denationalization of, 130, 131
　distinctive institutional and normative
　　regime for, 111, 121, 122, 137, 141–150,
　　170–172, 259
　durable solutions for, 157, 158, 164, 168,
　　170, 260
　exile as persecution of, 123
　humanitarian problem, treated as, 142, 150,
　　160, 177
　immediate causes, 123–131
　international law, and, 131–137
　Israeli legislative scaffolding and, 128–131, 133
　Jewish nationality and, 130
　losses suffered 1948, value of, 128
　numbers, 101–102, 124–125, 139
　protection gap, 23, 111, 122, 137, 140, 158, 164,
　　168–170, 259
　right to return, xv–xvi, 131, 135–136, 150–152
　state responsibility of Israel for, 136–137
　United Nations moral responsibility for, 122
　United Nations support for, vital role of, 111
Partition plan. *See also* General Assembly,
　　resolution 181(II); United Nations
　　Special Committee on Palestine
　Arab State, viability in doubt from start, 93
　democratic government, contempt for,
　　89–100
　general, 52–53, 107, 111
　General Assembly debate of, 95–100
　International Court of Justice, attempt to
　　submit to, 70–71
　Jewish question, as means to resolve, 83, 108
　legality of, 65–72, 108, 140
　rule by law, as embodiment of, 72–76,
　　258–259
　self-determination, violation of prinicple
　　of, 98–100
　terms, 60–65
Pedersen, Susan, 28
Permanent Mandates Commission, 48.
　　See also League of Nations
Peru, 77
Philippines, 225
*Phosphates in Morocco (Preliminary
　　Objections)*, 119
Pictet, Jean, 200

Pillay, Navi, 183, 192
Pinsker, Leo, 31, 32
PLO. *See* Palestine Liberation Organization
PMC. *See* Permanent Mandates Commission
Poland, 82, 97, 147
Political Zionism. *See* Zionism
Portugal, 225, 230, 232
Provisional government of All Palestine, 148

Quartet, 229, 237, 243
Question of Palestine
　Jewish question, and the, 94
　longest-running dispute at UN, as, 2
　origin of the term, 79–81
　permanent responsibility of UN for, 23, 180,
　　183, 263, 267
　referred to UN by United Kingdom,
　　77–78
　refugee problem, treated as, 177
Quigley, John, 77, 89, 238, 240, 241

Rajagopal, Balakrishnan, 9, 11
*Reparation for Injuries Suffered in the Service
　　of the United Nations*, xvi–xvii
Ribeiro, Laura, 17
Rodríguez-Garavito, César, 14
Rome Statute of the International Criminal
　　Court, 118, 182, 197
Rule by law, 7, 13, 26, 48, 256, 262
　decolonization, and, 175
　definition of, 6–7
　international institutionalization of, 26–29,
　　50–51
　League of Nations, and the, 27, 29
　Lloyd George, 47
　mandate for Palestine, and the, 42, 50
　occupied Palestinian Territory, and the,
　　172, 181, 186, 187, 210, 212
　overview, 21–24
　Palestine, UN membership and, 231, 249,
　　251, 252
　Palestine in decolonization era, and,
　　176, 180
　Palestinian refugees and, 111, 122, 168, 169
　partition plan, and, 98, 100
　resolution 181(II), as embodiment of, 52, 53,
　　57, 65, 72–76, 83, 89, 107–109
　rule of law, as constrasted with, 7
　secret treaty-making, 33
　Sykes-Picot agreement, and, 40
　United Kingdom, and, 38, 48
　United Nations as site of, 53, 54
　UNSCOP, and, 76, 89, 91, 97, 100, 101, 108
Rule of law, 8, 13, 256, 262
　decolonization, and, 7, 174
　definition of, 6–7
　League of Nations, and the, 27, 28

Index

occupied Palestinian territory, and the, 172, 181, 186, 189, 191, 193, 209
oppressed, as tool of the, 12
overview, 21–25
Palestine, UN membership and the, 229, 248, 249
Palestine in decolonization era, and, 173, 177
Palestinian refugees and, 111, 160, 161
primacy, of, 1
refugees, 112
resolution 181(II), and the, 57, 59, 65, 70, 71
rule by law, as constrasted with, 7
sacred trust of civilization, and the, 59
state responsibility, and the, 189
UN membership, and, 218, 222, 228, 252
United Nations, and the, xvii, 2, 21, 51, 54, 108, 171, 176, 181, 228
UNSCOP, and, 77, 91, 94, 96, 100
Russia, 38, 229, 231
Rwanda, 225

Sacred trust of civilization, 28, 29, 43–44, 48, 55, 56, 58, 59, 68–70, 91, 258
Said, Edward, 4
San Marino, 224
Sandstrom, Emil, 86, 88, 104, 105
Saudi Arabia, 161
Schiff, Benjamin, 159
Secretariat, 18, 20, 182, 184
Secretary-General, 1, 20, 85, 141, 182, 184, 185, 192
Security Council, 18, 182, 184, 185
membership of UN, as gatekeeper of, 228
permanent members, 55
resolution 242, 157, 177
resolution 338, 157
resolution 1515, 157
Segev, Tom, 49
Self-determination, 7, 66, 75, 193, 194, 202, 208, 260
British violation of Palestinian right to, 47
class A mandates, in, 55–57, 59, 68, 70, 72, 94, 108, 258
colonialism and, 175
erga omnes character, 194
indigenous people, and, 10, 15
interwar period, in the, 27, 29, 42, 43, 48, 55
Israel's violation of Palestinian right to, 200, 239
law of occupation and, 194
Palestinian right to, 23, 65, 90, 91, 108, 172, 173, 177–180, 182, 186, 201, 214, 215, 229, 233, 236, 243, 260, 264
partition of Palestine, and, 22, 90–91, 98–100
resolution 181(II), GA debates and, 96–100
sacred trust of civilization, and, 44, 55, 56, 59, 91

UN Charter and, 43, 55, 101, 174
UNSCOP and, 89
Zionist desire to delay application in 1947, 90, 92
Settler colonialism, 5, 50, 77, 78, 79, 81, 82, 95, 97, 105, 108, 122, 147, 149, 160, 205, 216, 247, 258–259, 266
Slavery, 10, 15
Smuts, Jan Cristiaan, 28
Sokolow, Nahum, 41
Sousa Santos, Boaventura de, 14
South Africa, 78, 223, 231, 244
South-West Africa, 43. *See also Namibia*
Sovereign equality of states, 7, 11, 54, 228
Soviet Union, 27, 81, 82, 97, 106, 147, 190, 225, 226
Special Committee on Decolonization. *See* Committee of 24
Standard of civilization, 7, 15, 28–30, 45, 85, 92, 95, 256
State responsibility
2001 Draft Articles, 119, 137, 188, 189
foundational principles, 118–120
legal status of the OPT, and, 187–190, 208, 215
refugees and, 118–120, 136–137
Subaltern, 3, 25. *See also* international legal subalternity
duality of law, and the, 11
European Jews as, 31, 46
examples of the, 4, 15
origins and definition of the term, 3
state-centric international order and the, 9
TWAIL, and the, 13, 14
Subaltern cosmopolitan legality, 14
Supreme Council of the Principal Allied Powers, 45
Sweden, 77, 86, 106, 143
Sykes–Picot agreement, 30, 38–40
Syria, 34–35, 38, 39, 43–45, 47, 56, 70, 78, 80, 85, 99, 101, 124, 139, 147, 151, 226, 237, 239, 244

Takkenberg, Lex, 165
Tamanaha, Brian, 6
Third World, 3, 23
European colonialism, and, 12
jurists, 11
quasi-sovereignty of, 7, 172, 173, 175–176, 215, 256
soveriengty, circumscribed nature of, 260
use of UN and international law by, 11
Transjordan. *See* Jordan
Treaty of Lausanne, 131
Trusteeship, 57, 59, 68, 70, 72, 78, 90, 108, 256, 258

Index

Turkey, 27, 115, 131, 134, 138, 153, 158
Tuvalu, 224
TWAIL, 3, 5, 8, 9, 11–14, 16–17, 255, 257
    blind spot of, 11–16, 257

UDHR. *See* Universal Declaration of Human
    Rights
Ukraine, 225, 226
UN. *See* United Nations
UNCCP. *See* United Nations Conciliation
    Commission for Palestine
UNCEIRPP. *See* United Nations Committee
    on the Exercise of the Inalienable Rights
    of the Palestinian People
UNDRIP. *See* United Nations Declaration on
    the Rights of Indigenous Peoples
UNESCO. *See* United Nations Educational
    Scientific and Cultural Organization
UNHCR. *See* United Nations High
    Commissioner for Refugees
United Kingdom, 4, 21, 33, 34, 67, 73, 77, 78,
    80, 151, 158, 162, 167, 212, 225, 230, 237
    future government of Palestine, and, 69,
        77–78
    mandatory Power for Palestine,
        appointed as, 45
    secret treaty-making, and, 21, 29, 33, 38,
        40, 50
    withdrawal from Palestine, 105, 106
    Zionism, support for, 48–50
United Nations
    guarantor of international rule of law, as,
        xvii, 1, 53–55, 142, 171, 176, 180
    international legal personality of, xvi
    legitimacy of, 1–2
    membership, present number, 219
    membership of, 174
    nature of, 18–20
    permanent responsibility for question of
        Palestine, 23, 180, 183, 263, 267
    realpolitik, and, 1
    rule of law organizing principle, and the, 21
    universality, principle of, 73, 218, 252
United Nations Charter, 7, 9, 20, 24, 54–55,
        57, 58, 66, 69, 71, 79, 98, 108, 116, 148,
        169, 174, 175, 195, 210, 226
    Article 2(4), 209
    Article 4(1), 24, 217–223, 227–229, 234, 235,
        242, 244, 247, 248, 252, 261
    Article 4(2), 220, 228, 231, 248, 252, 253, 262
    Article 10, 67, 69, 70, 78
    League of Nations Covenant, and, 53–54,
        57–59
    self-determination, and, 43
United Nations Committee on the Admission
    of New Members, 24, 217, 261
    Security Council, members identical to, 229

United Nations Committee on the Exercise of
    the Inalienable Rights of the Palestinian
    People, 179
    Division for Palestinian Rights, 183
United Nations Conciliation Commission for
    Palestine, xvi, 22, 111, 122, 124, 128, 140,
        142, 143, 146, 147, 150, 152–155, 158, 159,
        163, 170, 245, 247, 259
    conciliation failed, 155–156
    identification and valuation of refugee
        property, 156
    international law, failure to apply, 139, 156
    mandate, 138
    membership, 138
    Palestinian Arabs, engagement with, 139
    Palestinian refugees, durable solutions,
        152–156, 164, 166, 167
    resolution 194(III), working paper on para.
        11 of, 151
United Nations Conference on Trade and
    Development, 183
United Nations Declaration on the Rights of
    Indigenous Peoples, 10, 15
United Nations Economic and Social
    Commission for Western Asia, 241
United Nations Educational Scientific and
    Cultural Organization, 183, 241, 266
United Nations High Commissioner for
    Refugees, 22, 111–114, 116, 122, 140, 164,
        166, 167, 170, 259
    durable solutions, 113, 164
    establishment, 112
    mandate, 112–113
    UNRWA, relationship with, 164–170
United Nations Human Rights Committee,
    116, 136
United Nations Mediator for Palestine.
    See Bernadotte, Count Folke
    General Assembly, consideration of
        Progress Report of, 147–150
    mediation, inappropriateness of, 146–147
United Nations Office for the Coordination
    of Humanitarian Affairs, 183
United Nations Office of the High
    Commissioner for Human Rights, 183
United Nations Palestine Commission, 73, 106
United Nations Register of Damage, 183, 211
United Nations Relief and Works Agency
    for Palestine Refugees in the Near East,
        22, 102, 111, 122, 124, 139, 140, 158, 160,
        164–170, 183, 259, 266
    core services, 164
    durable solutions, 164, 165
    establishment, 139, 158, 160–163
    gender discrimination and, 140, 165,
        167–170
    mandate, 139, 140, 163

Index

resettlement vehicle, designed as, 139, 163, 170, 260

resolution 194(III), and, 139, 163

UNHCR, relationship with, 164–170

United Nations Relief for Palestine Refugees, 124, 138, 139

United Nations Special Committee on Palestine, 22, 56, 122, 258

composition and terms of reference, bias of, 77–83, 108, 259

creation of, 76

democratic government, contempt for, 89–100, 108, 145, 259

Jewish Agency, and, 86–87

majority plan, 60–63, 76, 92–95, 100

minority plan, 76, 94–95

mission, summary of, 76, 86

Nakba, forseeability of, 103–105

Palestinian Arabs, engagement with, 83–89, 108, 259

racism, and, 88–90, 95–97

self-determination, violation of, 90–91, 98–100

violence befalling Palestine, knowledge of inevitability of, 100–108, 259

United Nations Special Committee to Investigate Israeli Practices, 183

United Nations Special Rapporteur on the Situation of Human Rights in the Palestinian Territory Occupied Since 1967, 183

United Nations Trusteeship Council, 18, 60. *See also* Trusteeship

United States, 5, 8, 10, 27, 41, 44, 106, 115, 128, 157, 158, 162, 223, 225, 226, 229, 230, 232, 257, 266

Palestine membership of UN, blocking of, 230–249, 252, 261

Security Council veto, and, 24, 218, 230, 248, 250, 267

slavery, and, 15

universality of UN, and, 221, 231

Universal Declaration of Human Rights, 116, 135, 152, 169

UNPC. *See* United Nations Palestine Commission

UNROD. *See* United Nations Register of Damage

UNRPR. *See* United Nations Relief for Palestine Refugees

UNRWA. *See* United Nations Relief and Works Agency for Palestine Refugees in the Near East

UNSCO. *See* Office of the UN Special Coordinator for the Middle East Peace Process

UNSCOP. *See* United Nations Special Committee on Palestine

Urquhart, Brian, xv

Uruguay, 77, 78, 82, 87

US. *See* United States

Use of force, 54

Uti possidetis, 10, 181

Weizmann, Chaim, 40, 41, 49, 124

West Bank, including East Jerusalem, and Gaza Strip. *See* occupied Palestinian Territory

Western Sahara, 175

Westlake, John, 33, 169

Wheaton, Henry, 32, 84

Whiteman's burden, 29

Wilde, Ralph, 122

Wilson, Woodrow, 26–28, 43, 44, 48–50, 55

World Bank, 237

World War I, 22, 27, 31, 33, 38, 44

World War II, 6, 7, 22, 26, 50, 77, 103, 108, 110, 143, 146, 255, 256

WWI. *See* World War I

WWII. *See* World War II

Yemen, 83, 98, 99

Yugoslavia, 77, 86, 87, 223

Zilbershats, Yaffa, 131, 132, 134, 135

Zinn, Howard, 255

Zionism, 5, 44

British committment to, 47

colonial and imperial nature of, 31–33, 50

emancipatory movement, as, 33

European imperialism, and, 32

historical development of, 31–33

mandate for Palestine, privileged in, 48

movement, 30, 57

Palestinian demography, as impeded by, 121

Zionist Congress, first, 33

Zionist Organization, 33, 45, 46

Zionist underground militias, 103. *See also* Etzel, Irgun, Lehi and Stern Gang

For EU product safety concerns, contact us at Calle de José Abascal, 56–1°, 28003 Madrid, Spain or eugpsr@cambridge.org.

www.ingramcontent.com/pod-product-compliance
Lightning Source LLC
LaVergne TN
LVHW020348030825
817679LV00035B/959